From Sapper to Spitfire Spy

'The military organisation with the best aerial reconnaissance will win the next war.'

General Werner Von Fritsch of the German High Command 1938

From Sapper to Spitfire Spy

The WWII Biography of David Greville-Heygate DFC

S.A. Greville-Heygate

Pen & Sword
AVIATION

First published in Great Britain in 2015 by
Pen & Sword Aviation
an imprint of
Pen & Sword Books Ltd
47 Church Street
Barnsley
South Yorkshire
S70 2AS

ISBN 978 1 47384 388 2

A CIP catalogue record for this book is available from the British Library

Typeset in Ehrhardt by
Mac Style Ltd, Bridlington, East Yorkshire
Printed and bound in the UK by CPI Group (UK) Ltd,
Croydon, CRO 4YY

Pen & Sword Books Ltd incorporates the imprints of Pen & Sword
Archaeology, Atlas, Aviation, Battleground, Discovery, Family History,
History, Maritime, Military, Naval, Politics, Railways, Select, Transport,
True Crime, and Fiction, Frontline Books, Leo Cooper, Praetorian Press,
Seaforth Publishing and Wharncliffe.

For a complete list of Pen & Sword titles please contact
PEN & SWORD BOOKS LIMITED
47 Church Street, Barnsley, South Yorkshire, S70 2AS, England
E-mail: enquiries@pen-and-sword.co.uk
Website: www.pen-and-sword.co.uk

Contents

Acknowledgements

With special thanks to my editor Neil Barber, Jeremy Greville-Heygate, Jimmy Taylor, Donna Thynne, Tim Hutton, Rosie Hickton, James Dunford Wood, Thomas Thorne, Anthony Hornidge, Steve Brooking, Denis Critchley-Salmonson, Michael Adler, Carol Felton, Charles Shepherd, Lucie Johnson, Charles Craig Harvey, Alan Clark, Francesca Stern, Hans Onderwater, Colin Ford, Ross McNeill, Stephen Fryer, John and Mark Wendelken, Keith Janes, Bob Hunt, Henry Crun and Henk Welting.

All the contributors of RAF Commands Forum Website including Andrew Fletcher, Col Bruggy, Steve Brew, Dennis Burke, Buz, Alex Crawford, Russ G. Carlos Guerreiro, Allan Hillman, Mark Hux, Norman Hood, Bertrand H, Andy Ingham, Jonny John E, Joss leclercq, Paul McMillan, Errol Martyn, Pierre, Renier and Alex Smart.

Note: Sometimes there were discrepancies between David's diary, Logbook, Squadron's Records and notes, but I kept dates, names and places as accurate a record as possible.

Every effort has been made to contact copyright holders of quotes and illustrations. the author will be glad to make good in future editions, any error or omission brought to her attention.

The publication of quotes or illustrations on which clearance has not been given is unintentional.

Glossary

BEF	British Expeditionary Force
'C' patrol	Shipping patrol in designated area 'C'
Circus	Fighter escorting bombing raid over enemy territory
CFI	Chief Flying Instructor.
C/O	Commanding Officer
Crammed	Intensively trained over a short period
Dicey	Dangerous/dicing with death
Doodlebug	Fieseler Fi 103 pulse-jet flying bomb. V-1
DFC	Distinguished Flying Cross
EFTS	Elementary Flying Training School
Enigma	German code.
Flak	German anti-aircraft fire. (Flugzeug Abwehr Kanone)
Flight	Subdivision of a squadron
Glycol	Ethylene Glycol, an engine coolant
GSU	Group Service Unit
Hedge Hop	Flying low to ground so the aircraft seems to hop over hedges
Hit the Deck	Crash into the ground
ITW	Initial Training Wing
LAC	Leading Aircraftman
Lagoon	Anti -shipping patrol off enemy coast
Luftwaffe	German air force
Me109	Messerschmitt Bf109 German fighter. Wartime reports used both BF109 and Me109.
MT	Mechanized Transport
NCO	Non-commissioned Officer
Op/Ops	Operational flying
OTC	Officer Training Corps
OTU	Operational Training Unit
Popular	Low altitude photography over enemy territory.
Proctor	Cambridge appointed staff to supervise students
RAFVR	Royal Air Force Volunteer Reserve
Revs (rpm)	Rotational speed, in revolutions per minute
Rhubarb	Daylight low level attacks on enemy aircraft, roads, trains or trucks using machine guns
R/T	Radio Telephone – Voice communication
Section	Subdivision of a flight
SFTS	Service Flying Training School

Sortie	Individual aircraft's Operational flight
Sprog	Novice pilot
Strike	Low-level attack
Sweep	Offensive formation to draw enemy aircraft
TA	Territorial Army
Tac/R	Tactical Reconnaissance
TAF	Tactical Air Force
WAAF	Women's Auxiliary Air Force
W/O	Wireless Operator

Introduction

This is the story of my father, David Greville-Heygate, one of the few men who served in both the Army and the RAF during the course of the Second World War. Called up by the Army at the start of the war, he manned an AA searchlight located just south of Wittering Airfield. Finding this work dreary and monotonous, and envying his older brother Charles's training in the RAFVR, David applied for Army Officer Training at Sandhurst. After gaining a commission as a Second Lieutenant in the Loyals and posted to Portsmouth, he had 'A bit of a row with the Brigadier,' and was finally able to transfer to the RAF. After gaining his Wings he was posted to Weston Zoyland as a Reconnaissance pilot. He flew a variety of aircraft based in England, the Netherlands and finally Germany.

After the war, David returned to civilian life. He began to write about his war years, but with failing health, his book never materialized.

David's 'voice' in this book has been recreated using edited material from diaries, notes, letters, family and friends' conversations and interviews, along with his flight Log Books and Squadron Records.

Sally-Anne Greville-Heygate
September 2014

Part I

Pre-War

Looking Back

September 1984. Looking back on what must to many seem a short and exceedingly troubled era, one might well ask, 'Why remember?' But it is a fact that as one gets older, the past grows not dim but clearer, and occupies a larger and wider place in one's quieter moments. The fortunate have the joyful days of their youth to recall in happy hours, with little worry or anxiety as to what the future may have in store. Others may remember their youthful days with less pleasure and with mixed feelings.

Tuesday, 30 September 1941. We set off to Childs Ercall to fly the single-seater Hurricane for the first time. Neville was due to fly first. While waiting for my turn, Foster asked me if I wanted to go up in the Master to do some low flying. Returning forty-five minutes later I saw Peter looking very pale. He said, 'Neville's in the deck.'

Neville's engine had cut at about a hundred feet. The Hurricane did a quarter spin straight into the ground and caught fire. Neville was thrown clear, but broke his neck and died instantly.

I took one up, feeling sure that this was my last time on terra firma. Take-off was difficult, but when actually flying, it felt a beautiful aircraft to control, however approaching the airfield at Tern Hill it seemed to have no desire to slow down for landing. I overshot the runway and began to wonder if I was ever going to get down.

Chapter One

The Munich Crisis and Life as a Cambridge Undergraduate: Spring 1938 to July 1939

'Only the Warmongers think there will be a war. I think there will be a long period of peace.'

Hitler's speech, *Western Daily Press*, 31 January 1939

Just eleven months after the First World War ended, David Greville-Heygate was born in the shire village of Great Bowden. His father, Realf Greville-Heygate was a Land Agent, but also owned a small farm with several horses, two dogs, a pony trap, a car and a dairy cow. The epitome of an Edwardian family, they were looked after by a few well loved servants, Mim the cook, Flude the handyman gardener and Dawson the groom. David had two brothers, Charles and Ronald, and a sister Marjorie. All were considerably older and although dearly loved by his oldest brother Charles, he was often teased by Ronald.

For the first few years of his life David was under the care of a strict Governess, but in 1926, upon reaching the age of seven, he was put on a train to Rosslyn House,

Dawson, the groom outside David's family home in Great Bowden. *(Family Collection)*

A flying boat near the Marine Aircraft Experimental Establishment, Felixstowe. *(Family Collection)*

a boarding school in Felixstowe. Collected by the Matron in a horse-cab, he joined thirty boys in his new world. After a first fitful night's sleep, David was shaken awake by the roar of a seaplane flying overhead:

> All night the local lightship's warning horn echoed through my head, and in the morning an ear-splitting noise took over. This exciting sound was followed by the wonderful sight of a sleek aircraft racing past. The Schneider Trophy

David on an outing from Rosslyn House School with his parents Realf and Annie. *(Family Collection)*

practise runs had started and my school was near to the flying boat base. So deafening were these aircraft that lessons were often abandoned and it was here, with such delicate grace of design, coupled with the magnificence of the great flying boats, my interest in aircraft began.[1]

After a happy time spent at Rosslyn House, David was sent to Marlborough College where he enjoyed his free hours on the cricket pitch or in the rackets court, but he complained bitterly about the compulsory Officer Training Corps which was run by Regimental Sergeant Major Lawrence.[2]

> Yet another hateful Wednesday. Surely parade must be one of the greatest curses of school life. There is always some stupid trivial little detail to deal with. Puttees for all parades is one. What's the good of puttees without the rest of the uniform? Robert Rolt, Henry Butcher[3] and I were chosen to take a squad of boys to be crammed for the Band and Signallers. After much monotonous arms drill, during which my fingers nearly fell off with cold and caused me to drop my rifle, we were dismissed.

With Hitler's rise to power, events in Europe began to look threatening. On 12 March, while David was being driven out for lunch in Andrew Craig Harvey's family

Stuart

THE MARLBOROUGH XI. OF 1938

So far this season Marlborough have drawn with Harrow and Winchester, beaten Cheltenham (G. E. Fletcher, 110), and lost to the Authentics, so they are not doing too bad. Picture taken on the Winchester match day

The names in the group are: (l. to r.; standing) J. A. Owen, A. P. D. Ballance, D. Comyn, M. Jewell, J. B. H. Knight, T. R. Juckes, and G. Heygate; (sitting) J. R. Sale, M. S. Mallinson, G. E. Fletcher (captain), D. G. Lacy-Scott, and G. F. Redfearn

(©*Tatler*)

David bitterly complained about the compulsory Wednesday afternoon OTC. He is standing fourth from right. *(Family Collection)*

Bentley, the 8th Army of the German Wehrmacht raced over the Austrian border to be greeted by cheering Austrians with Hitler salutes and Nazi flags. When Austria was proclaimed a State of the German Reich, France and England did no more than protest mildly, convincing Hitler that these were only made as concessions to popular feeling. This heightened state of tension in Europe meant that cadet training was stepped up.

> *23 March 1938.* Field Day. We were point platoon of the advancing attack and lots of fireworks were being thrown around. Although it was very sweaty work we had great fun and our platoon was highly praised by the War Office official observer. We then laid out message M, hung between two posts on strings, for the Lysander to come down and pick up, which it did on its third attempt.

At the end of June, David changed into his uniform for the last time, ready for the General's Inspection. The squad marched up to the fields with the band and fixed bayonets.

> During the inspection the General asked Robert Branford[4] what he was going to do when he left school. Robert calmly replied, 'Going into the church Sir,' much to our consternation, as he was actually hoping to go into the Indian Civil Service. Then we had a lot of squad drill, fooling around before going to Congregation in the Memorial Hall where the General gave a rotten speech.

Towards the end of term David and school friends Patrick Mahon, George Redfearn and Peter Jarrett went into town for a farewell tea. It would be the last time that they would meet. Redfearn, who went to work in Singapore, was captured by Japanese troops and died while working on the Bangkok-Moulmein railway in 1943. Jarrett went to Oxford University, then joined the RAF as an observer and was killed in air operations over Germany in October 1940. (Out of the thirty-six boys who started at Marlborough with David in May 1933, two were killed in accidents before the war, one in a motorbike accident in August 1939, six were killed on active service during the war and two taken PoW).[5]

David left school with a place to study Agriculture and Estate Management at Queens' College, however he became increasingly worried that Hitler's European ambitions may put pay to his plans. Hitler was by now demanding control of the Sudetenland in Czechoslovakia, and in September 1938, these demands led to the 'Munich Crisis'.

As the situation in Europe deteriorated, David and Andrew went up to visit Anson Howard.

> After lunch Anson's father who is the Provost of Coventry Cathedral took us up the tower and we had a wonderful view of Coventry. When I arrived home, I found Uncle Harry gloomily cleaning and storing tins of bully beef, tinned fruit and all sorts of other supplies. He is expecting to be called up at any moment by the War Office, to be put in charge of ammunition factories.

> *Sunday, 11 September.* I could not help wondering whether this would be the last occasion I should hear the bells peal in peace time, since I fear tomorrow's speech by Hitler seems to be a very decisive turning point in European history and yet I am optimistic that war is not yet imminent.

> *12 September.* I heard parts of Hitler's speech. He has not altered the situation much, but as to making it no better he has made it no worse as far as I can see.

In a desperate effort to avert war, representatives from Britain, France and Italy flew to Germany to negotiate with Hitler for a peaceful settlement, even if it meant sacrificing Czechoslovakia. The next few days were a time of anxious waiting.

> *26 September.* I hear that Market Harborough and Bowden only had 300 gas masks, though all the villages around us already have them. I listened to bits of Hitler's speech and the roars of applause, then heard a translation in the news, it is a definite ultimatum for October 1. Hitler has for the moment dropped the demands of the other minorities. He is a clever man and states that this will be his last territorial claim in Europe. I am not so sure.

Setting out his foreign policy in a speech in Berlin, Hitler assured Chamberlain that the German people desired nothing but peace, and the Czechs issued a hopeful statement of concessions. However, plans for evacuations from London were hastily prepared and David received a letter from his University telling him to bring his gas mask with him.

> After breakfast, Mr Knight the village school master, came in to ask Father about digging a bombproof shelter in Mr Hater's garden. Father suggested the village green and that is decided upon. We called in at the office and found Catells there who says 3,000 slum children are to be billeted on Kettering tomorrow and Mr

Allen has boarded up the windows in an anti-gas room.

On the brink of war, Army, Navy and RAF reserves were called-up, and at tea time there was news that there was to be a meeting between Mussolini, Hitler, Chamberlain and Daladier.

Thursday, 29 September. I applied for my gas mask at Mr Allen's but he had a telegram to withhold fitting and distribution. Then Jack and I went to Berkswell where there was much digging of AA trenches in parks and gardens, sandbags were being piled into position and ARP wardens were painting road curbs black and white for night-dimmed driving. Queens' College wrote to say that students were now not to go into residence until further notice owing to the situation, this is a great blow.

GOING UP TO CAMBRIDGE

STUDENTS TO AWAIT INSTRUCTIONS

FROM OUR CORRESPONDENT

CAMBRIDGE, Sept. 28

The Vice-Chancellor of Cambridge University, Professor H. R. Dean, M.D., Master of Trinity Hall, has issued the following statement:—

An informal meeting of tutors of colleges has considered measures which colleges might desire to take in the event of war. The postponement of the date of full term is a matter for the consideration of the University, but in view of the uncertainty of the outlook it was agreed that tutors of individual colleges might inform their undergraduate members that they should not come into residence until further instructions have been issued. The examinations which are usually held in September and October will take place as usual, and candidates entered for these examinations will be allowed to come into residence for the period of the examination. Although it is probable that many colleges may decide to postpone the return of the majority of the undergraduates, the case of any men who have special reason to return to Cambridge will receive consideration.

The Munich crisis lead to the Cambridge Vice Chancellor postponing the students return to university.

Finally, on September 30 an agreement was signed. Everybody was hopeful for peace, but anxiety rose as there was no reply from the Czechs. Eventually an hour late, they also signed as the only course open to them. Returning from Germany, Prime Minister Chamberlain drove through cheering crowds to Downing Street where he made a short speech stating, 'For the second time in our history, a British Prime Minister has returned from Germany bringing peace with honour. I believe it is peace for our time.'[6]

There was colossal cheering and bell-ringing for an armistice without war. Ronald, home for the purpose of a day or two's quiet before the fighting, was amazingly quite polite now that he can go back to work. Mother and Father are overjoyed and relieved that their three boys don't have to go to war and are full of gratitude to Mr Chamberlain for everything he has done for us.

With the Crisis over, David packed his bags and set off for Queens' College and he quickly immersed himself with all that life as an undergraduate could offer. As well as attending lectures, he became involved in a variety of activities including rackets, hockey and tennis. Along with friends Andrew Craig Harvey, Neville Arland Ussher and Anson Howard, over seventy Old Marlburions were studying at Cambridge. He also made friends with Peter Conant, Peter Storie-Pugh and Richard Osborn, whose family had recently returned from Australia.

David wrote from his new lodgings in Newham Road Cambridge:

October 10. My tutor, Mr McCullagh, says he thinks I am very lucky having these rooms which though small, are clean and nearby and says a nice landlady like Mrs Mott is worth a lot. After a good breakfast Andrew called in, he's decided that his Bentley, doing only 21 miles to the gallon, will be too heavy on petrol so he has bought a Flying Standard 14. He drove me round to his rooms where he lives in great luxury. Later I dropped in on 'steam fiend' Alex Moulton[7] who lives two doors away and is at King's College studying Mechanical Science.

News came from home that Charles had an interview with the RAF Volunteer Reserve and David somewhat reluctantly decided it was time to sign up for the University's Officer Training Corps, but was unsure which branch to join. Peter Conant was with the Artillery Unit, Anson Howard was learning to drive with the Gunners and Richard Osborn was flying with the University Air Squadron. However, with a passion for riding, David decided to try to join Peter Storie-Pugh and Andrew Craig Harvey in the Cavalry, two troops of which were still unmechanized.

While waiting for news, David met the secretary of the Cambridge University Socialist Club, one of the largest student political societies, which had taken the pacifist cause extremely seriously. The members arranged for several speakers to come and give lectures during the term. Although flattered by the attention of a third year student, David was not impressed by the meeting.

Margaret, a pretty third-year girl from Girton more or less bribed me to attend a short Socialist meeting saying that coffee and cigarettes were being provided. She gave a talk which was quite amusing but pretty rot. I then called in to see Desmond Lang – he is an awfully nice fellow – son of the Bishop of Woolwich and relative of Archbishop Cosmo Lang,[8] though one might not imagine it, judging from his character.

Later, Mr Potts, one of David's tutors, spoke to the undergraduates in the Old Chapel on matters of discipline and warned them to be careful on Guy Fawkes Night.

Mr Potts has a red moustache and beard but is a surprisingly docile-looking man even under such animalistic growths. He said that the police work up quite a grudge against all undergraduates and are 'likely to arrest quite innocent lambs wandering in the streets, since they may be wolves in sheep's clothing.'

At the weekend, school friend Donald Macdonald dropped into David's digs. He had just returned from the continent where he had been arrested several times.

Once while taking a picture of the Maginot Line a sentry popped out from nowhere and stuck a bayonet in his back and marched him off. Then while staying in a hotel in Vienna, the manager woke him up at 1 am to fill in a form, which Macdonald grudgingly did. An hour later the manager returned demanding his passport number which he had forgotten to fill in. Annoyed at being disturbed again Macdonald kicked him out, locked the door and went back to sleep. At dawn his door was kicked in by several Nazi police who arrested him for 'Assault and Battery and for not having his papers in order.'

Donald Macdonald's life was cut short early in the war while flying with No.603 Squadron. On 28 August, having flown less than twenty-five hours in Spitfires,

Macdonald was shot down. His older brother Harold flew with the same squadron and exactly a month later, he was also killed.[9]

David was excited to hear that he had been accepted by the mounted cavalry:

Parade was at 06.45 and I was given a keen little pony that jumped beautifully. First of all we did troop drill, then jumping in lanes and in lines in formation without reins or stirrups. I rode back with Andrew and Monckton.

We had the absurd matriculation ceremony in the Senate House. One pays £5 for it and the only privilege it brings is that one can be officially arrested by the Proctors. It is absolutely compulsory, for until one has attended it, no term's residence can be recognized.

Later Richard came over and told me that a friend had dived from the Queens' Bridge into the river for a 10/- bet and was now in hospital with a suspected broken skull.

While Charles took his first flight in a DH82 Tiger Moth at No.6 Elementary and Reserve Flying Training School at Sywell Aerodrome, David visited another undergraduate, John Earp, who was also hospitalized, having been kicked in the eye while playing rugby. Then he met up with Peter Wand-Tetley who dragged him somewhat reluctantly to the pub.

Peter used to fence and shoot for Marlborough and I do have to be rather careful when I meet him for he is one of those people who think a place is not worth going to if it has Proctorial Permission. Peter who visited South Africa as a journalist after he left school last year suddenly decided that he should like to go back. Finding a job as a purser on a small cargo steamer, they set sail during the Crisis and on the worst day they were by the Canaries, (very pro-Franco) and probably a German submarine base. They had all the lifeboats over the edge, ready to be dropped at a moment's notice, for their ship was carrying a great quantity of cargo. After a weekend in South Africa they sailed home.

David was right in believing Peter Wand-Tetley was a man prepared to take risks. When war broke out he was sent to the Middle East with No. 3 Special Service Battalion as part of the Layforce Commandos, took part in an amphibious landing at Bardia North Africa, fought in Crete, then posted to the SOE, he was parachuted into Greece in 1943 to train the partisans.[10]

I biked up to Coopers at 6.15 and rode to the Range fields. We had troop drill, jumping stirrupless and then dummy thrusting. It was all great fun. Gilbert Monckton[11] is kind and helpful and I rode home with an Etonian who knows Tim and Tel Vigors.

Several days later a talk was given to the CUSC at the Corn Exchange by Clement Attlee, the leader of the Labour Party who had opposed rearmament, but with the rising threat from Nazi Germany, now opposed Neville Chamberlain's policy of appeasement. Unfortunately, this talk clashed with a visit by Oswald Mosley, the leader of the British Union of Fascists. Not taking any chances, the Cambridge police decided to keep Mosley's supporters under strict surveillance.

This evening we had great fun as Mr Attlee came down to speak to the Socialist Club. His visit coincided with that of Sir Oswald Mosley, so we had swarms of policemen for the evening. The Fascists were not allowed to demonstrate and each person had to pay 4/6 for an after-dinner speech by Sir Oswald. The last time he came, a scheme was set afoot to auction his nether garments on Market Hill. The Socialists having no

David on his favourite horse, Brunette. *(Family Collection)*

such restrictions hired the Corn Exchange, rigged up terrifically loud speakers and proceeded to parade through the streets with torches shouting for 'Attlee and Freedom,' naturally attracting all the opposing supporters to go and cause a disturbance. Long before they reached the Corn Exchange their torches were extinguished and their banners had been torn to bits. For ten minutes Mr Attlee found he couldn't say a word for a terrific chorus of, 'We want Attlee's pants.' At last he spoke, and continued to do so for two hours, but little was heard owing to the scuffling at the back and the firework displays which were met with great disapproval by the Proctors. One offender was chased and eventually caught hiding out in Silver Street, another was hauled out of a disused barrel under a counter in the Market Place. Desmond Lang was fined £1 for a firework which hit the Proctors, it exploded many times, enveloping them in smoke and sparks. He denied being the guilty one but had to pay anyway.

Heeding Mr Potts' advice to keep a low profile on Guy Fawkes Night, David tentatively crept out to watch the fireworks. He scouted around with great caution, and from the badly battered undergraduates he saw being carted off, he considered himself very wise. The Market Square was full of undergraduates and townspeople, everybody lighting and throwing fireworks. Undergraduates, not worrying about the barbed wire round the lamps, climbed up and extinguished the lights. As soon as they could not hold on any longer they climbed down, whereupon police beat them on the head till they were unconscious, and dumped them into ambulances to be taken to hospital. If they escaped the police, they were caught by plain clothed men.

One bright youth, knowing the fate awaiting him when he descended, leapt over the circle of police – on the way snatching a helmet. He then lay flat on the ground motionless, the police seeing him lying still didn't know whether to hit him on the head or not and waited to see what happened. As the crowd surged forward, he leapt up under their legs and escaped unharmed with the helmet. A friend of Peter C was knocked silly and taken to a nursing home in an ambulance and at 4:30 escaped from it through a window. Fate unknown!

Cambridge Armistice Day was held on November 11 and was another day of great festivity as well as remembrance for the students, and they generally raised over £2,500 for the Earl Haig Fund set up to assist ex-servicemen.

> The undergraduates are awfully good about it and get up to all sorts of things, they dress up to collect money, barricade bridges for tolls and throw dirty water over cars stopped in the traffic and then charge 6d to wash them. All is done in such good humour that nobody grudges it. Finally there is an inter-college Donkey Derby and great Ball in the evening at the Dorothy Restaurant. The townspeople say it is the one day of the year they can forgive the undergrads for letting off steam. I watched a terrific fight after the Ball. Walter Newman gave the police a splendid battle until he was pushed into a Black Mariah and driven off. He slipped his bail and made off for America.

Later in the month, David witnessed two cavalry riding accidents. The first occurred when a rider in the No. 2 Troop Horse drew his sword for dummy thrusting and his horse bolted. The horse came down on the road and was badly cut about by the sword. The unfortunate trooper hit his head and was badly concussed. The second more serious incident occurred on 23 November. David saddled and mounted his favourite horse, Glory, galloped round the rifle range and then was joined by Gilbert Monckton. Being rather slippery, Monckton took his horse round the small lane and said it was fine, but when John Willett Reid[12] rode his horse round the corner it came down in a puddle and thinking it was rolling, Reid was about to hit it.

> Gilbert realized it wasn't and went to sit on its head; he received a terrific electrical shock and saw that the horse's mouth had become entangled in some electric wires and that it was being electrocuted. Kenneth Wood tried to pull the wire from its mouth, but without success. No wire-cutters were at hand but eventually John found an axe and cut the wires, but by this time the horse had died. The electrical wires were from a high-tension cable from the wireless experimental station some distance away.

Towards the end of November, David went down to Grange Road where it was confirmed that the Army was to pension off the last of the cavalry's horses and replace them with light tanks. They were given a lecture by Sergeant Jordon on the 'Principles of the Internal Combustion Engine' and having no desire to drive tanks, David decided that he would resign and try to transfer to the University Air Squadron.

On December 4, with his first term at University completed, he went home for the holidays. Just before Christmas, deep snow fell and a cold snap froze up the local lakes and canals. David went to dinner with cricketing friend, Mark Lee.

> Mark's sister Vivienne is a sweet thing. Fancy living 19 years and 3 miles away and not knowing her! After an excellent supper we played games, Up Jenkins etc but I couldn't concentrate very well and our side lost six before we suddenly bucked up and they lost six. The roads were awful for the drive back. The next day we all went to skate on the local canal, there was snow on the ice but otherwise it was very good. We had great fun, even though Charles fell through a weak patch in the ice and had to be pulled out.

During the holidays, David had a talk with Charles, who persuaded him not to resign from the Cavalry until he had a firm offer from the CUAS. Charles stressed the need to retain links with the armed forces, so David held fire on his planned resignation. At the end of January 1939, David went back to Queens'. The news from Europe was gloomy and there was an air of depression and pessimism in Cambridge about what would happen in the next few months.

> Although I was nearly bitten by it earlier in the week I have now become even more optimistic than before, just to contradict them! Even Anson is despondent and Gussy Jones, the fellow Charles and I met at Jimmy Barton's tennis party, has given up work for a fortnight, since he thinks there will be no May Exams.

In February, with the last of the horses retired, instead of jumping, David was manoeuvring a six cylinder, 25hp light tank Mark II. Gone was the excitement of the riding school. Tent-pegging was replaced by lectures on 'Track Tension and Adjustment' and bareback jumping by practical demonstrations of 'The Steering Clutches and Braking Mechanisms.' However, the earlier pessimistic gloom seemed to have lightened.

> *February 20.* I have been driving around in one of His Majesty's tanks this afternoon. It was quite fun but very jerky when one went over a bump. It has pre-selective gears and it is easy to drive. The engine is by your side but doesn't make very much noise except when you turn. This is a queer feeling, for one is going along and then to turn you must pull back one of the levers and thereby stop one caterpillar. The tank, instead of turning gradually like a car, turns directly round without moving forward at all.

During the next few weeks, David went to a large party at 'Mathews', held by Anthony Nutting,[13] had several strenuous games of rackets and attended several point-to-points in which both Andrew Craig Harvey and Anthony Nutting rode with moderate success and the odd fall. But all this excitement could not quite drown out the worrying news coming from Nazi Germany, and having got nowhere with his attempt to join the University Air Squadron, when asked to attend an interview for the 44th Leicestershire Regiment, David somewhat reluctantly agreed to go.

The train times were hopeless so I decided to make a day of it and I hired a car for 15/-, went out hunting in the morning,

"South Africa"
1900-1

Cambridge University Officers Training Corps

MECHANIZED CAVALRY

TRAINING PROGRAMME.   LENT TERM, 1939

COURSE I. From Friday, Jan. 20th–Tuesday, Feb. 14th

COURSE II. From Friday, Feb. 17th–Tuesday, March 14th

DATE FOR COURSE I	COURSE II	PLACE	TIME	SUBJECT
Friday 20-1-39	Friday 17-2-39	Headquarters	8.30 p.m.	Introduction to V.M.G.
Sunday 22-1-39	Sunday 19-2-39	Grange Road	2.15 p.m.	Tank Driving Track Maintenance. V.M.G.
Tuesday 24-1-39	Tuesday 21-2-39	Headquarters	8.30 p.m.	V.M.G. Load, Fire and Unload
Friday 27-1-39	Friday 24-2-39	Headquarters	8.30 p.m.	Lecture Tank Steering Mechanism
Sunday 29-1-39	Sunday 26-2-39	Grange Road	2.15 p.m.	Tank Driving Adjust : Steering Clutches. V.M.G.
Tuesday 31-1-39	Tuesday 28-2-39	Headquarters	8.30 p.m.	V.M.G. Mechanism. Tank Steering & Clutch & braking
Friday 3-2-39	Friday 3-3-39	Headquarters	8.30 p.m.	Lecture Tank Braking Mechanism
Sunday 5-2-39	Sunday 5-3-39	Grange Road	2.15 p.m.	Tank Driving Tank Brake Adjustments. V.M.G.
Tuesday 7-2-39	Tuesday 7-3-39	Headquarters	8.30 p.m.	V.M.G. Mechanism
Friday 10-2-39	Friday 10-3-39	Headquarters	8.30 p.m.	V.M.G. Mechanism Revise
Sunday 12-2-39	Sunday 12-3-39	Grange Road	2.15 p.m.	Tank Driving Lubrication Details Exam. Filters. Pressure Relief Valve
Tuesday 14-2-39	Tuesday 14-3-39	Headquarters	8.30 p.m.	General Revision Exam

Personnel for Courses remaining as for last Term.

Cambridge OTC tank training programme. *(Cambridge OTC)*

had tea with the family in the afternoon and set off for Northampton in the evening. The Colonel struck me as a charming man, 6 ft 6 ins and late of the Scots Greys. The pay is good and I am sure I will enjoy it if I get in.

However, the Colonel did not seem to be as enthusiastic about David joining up whilst still at Cambridge. He was not accepted as an Officer and by the beginning of May, David began to realize that he was now facing a period of compulsory conscription.

There is to be no Cavalry camp or Ball this year now. Everything I have done connected with the Army seems to have gone wrong. I should have joined the Territorial's but I put it off for the O.T.C. camp. Now Camp has been cancelled and I shall be in for six months conscription and apparently all my service for the last six years at school, given *almost* voluntarily, is to be of no avail whatsoever.

At the end of May, when the 50th Northampton Anti-Aircraft Battalion invited him to enlist in the ranks as a Volunteer Reserve, David reluctantly accepted, hoping that sense would prevail and war with Germany would be averted.

On June 8, after thirteen and a half hours' flight training, Charles was sent off on his solo.

Part II

Life in the Army

Chapter Two

A Sapper on a Searchlight – August 1939 to May 1940

'Conditions of life in the AA Command are more difficult than it is generally imagined even by the rest of the Army.... They are in little pockets all over the country, many of them under junior NCOs and miles from the nearest farmhouse. It is therefore a dull life and must often seem a meaningless one, full of petty and not so petty hardships and discomforts.'

'Roof Over Britain.' The Official Story of the AA Defences.
Ministry of Information 1943

At the end of July, David's hopes of returning to start his second year at Queens' were finally crushed. Great Britain was put on a war footing and David reported to the 400th Company, 50th Northampton Regiment A.A. Battalion for its annual camp. For someone who already disliked army life as much as David, he could not have chosen a more unsuitable branch to join.

On Sunday 13 August, he packed his bags for camp, his carefree life of an undergraduate to be replaced by the sparse existence of a new Army sapper. Rising at 03.15 he sat down to eggs and bacon with the family, before Charles drove him to the Drill Hall, Northampton. At 06.15, after roll call the Company left for Duddington Camp, five miles south of Stamford and which quickly acquired the nickname 'Camp Concentration.'

After a long, awful wait at Duddington I signed in and was issued with a gas mask and steel helmet. We were then loaded into a great lorry and driven to Wittering airfield at breakneck speed by complete lunatics. I felt sure that I was going to die before my detachment even got to our camp. My first impression was less than favourable, it being a small wooden hut situated in a wood at the southern perimeter of the airfield.

The searchlight detachment comprised eight men, an NCO and Whistle, the cook/odd

Army Form E.518

RESERVE AND AUXILIARY FORCES ACT, 1939.
TERRITORIAL ARMY.

CALLING OUT NOTICE.

To—

Name ..... *GREVILLE HEYGATE. D. A.*

Rank ..... *Sapper* ..... Army Number ..... *2100258* .....

Regt. or Corps ..... ROYAL ENGINEERS

In pursuance of directions given by the Secretary of State for War in accordance with an Order in Council made under Section 1 of the above-mentioned Act, you are hereby notified that you are called out for military service commencing from *4.0 a.m. 13th August* 19 *1939* , and for this purpose you are required to join the *400* COMPA

50th (NORTHN REGT.) A.A. BN. R.E. (T.A.)

at ..... NORTHAMPTON ..... on that day.

Should you not present yourself on that day you will be liable to be proceeded against.

Cpthamb   major for

Stamp of Officer Commanding Unit.

Place ..... NORTHAMPTON

Date ..... *29. V. 39.*

You should bring your Health and Pensions Insurance Card and Unemployment Insurance Book. If, however, you cannot obtain these before joining you should write to your employer asking him to forward these to you at your unit headquarters. If you are in possession of a receipt (U.I. 40) from the Employment Exchange for your Employment Book bring that receipt with you.
You will also bring your Army Book 3, but you *must not fill* in any particulars on page 13 or the " Statement of family " in that book, and the postcards therein *must not be used.*

(593/2242) W1. 14345—673   0w 5/39 H & S Ltd. Gp. 399 Forms E518/1

Call Out papers for Sapper Greville-Heygate.
(Family Collection – Crown © 1939)

job man. It was situated half a mile from the main camp at Duddington. As soon as David's bags were stowed in the hut, he was put to work.

> My first duty was to collect water. This sounded quite an easy task until I discovered that the nearest supply of drinking water was to be found down a fifty-foot well, a mile away in Duddington village. I eventually delivered the filled tanks to our 'kitchen' which consists of a large canvas covering an open fire, an iron sheet, a saucepan and a kettle.

David took the opportunity to grab a second breakfast. This was followed by a two-hour spell of guard duty then he was ordered to make up his bed.

> Again, this seemingly simple task proved more difficult than it sounded. After collecting a horribly hard pillow and a very prickly blanket, I discovered that there are no beds. We are expected to sleep on the floor of the hut. While we were all grumbling about how great a hardship this would be, our vicious NCO called Corporal Amies came in. 'Sleeping won't be a problem,' he barked, 'because you have to be up for guard duty change every two hours anyway. After a few days of this, I can assure you that you'll be able to sleep anywhere, any time, without difficulty, but if I find any of you asleep on guard duty I'll make sure your life is not worth living.'

David drilled from 10.00–12.00 and followed this with two hours of guard duty, and in the evening, several hours of searchlight practise which he found quite enjoyable until a frantic phone call from the flight controller at Wittering demanded that they stop pointing the searchlights towards the airfield, having almost blinded a Blenheim pilot attempting to land.[1] David's first night was very disturbed. At 22.00 he went to bed exhausted, however sleep proved to be short-lived as two hours later he was back on guard duty from midnight to 02.00 followed by another two hours sleep then he was shaken awake once more for guard duty.

> *Monday, 14 August.* Back to bed at 06.00 completely shattered and out cold before my head hit the pathetic pillow but after only a half-hour's sleep I was again woken. I grabbed a mouthful of breakfast before being ordered to clean up the camp.

Thus an endless round of sentry duty and searchlight drills commenced until finally given time off, David, hoping that a car might make life a little easier, escaped camp and hitched a lift home. After supper, completely exhausted, he drove back to camp, but any idea of sleep was

'All quiet on the Kings Cliffe front.' Snowy White, David and Corporal Amies. *(Family Collection)*

dashed as they spent the next two hours chasing aeroplanes with the searchlight. At midnight they were warned that several dangerous IRA terrorists were on the move and they were to stay out on guard duty until 06.00.

Wednesday, 16 August. Back at the hut I fell asleep with all my clothes on, but was soon woken by Spud bearing a much-needed cup of tea. A couple of hours later I rose for breakfast. The others went back to sleep but I wrote up my diary which I hadn't had time to do before. Lunch was foul; the meat was practically raw, as it had been baked on a flat piece of tin over the open fire. Whistle, the cook, is lazy, dirty and ready to pick a quarrel with anyone. We all agree we must try to find a way of getting rid of him at the first opportunity. Luckily Spud, an experienced soldier from the Great War is always courteous and kind.

In the evening, David and his detachment, determined to perfect the use of the searchlight, caught many of the airfield's aircraft practising night-flying and landings. Naturally the pilots found this very off-putting and urgent messages were again sent from the airfield complaining that the pilots were being blinded by the light and ordering them to stop.

Thursday, 17 August. Spud looks after the huge old generator that we use to operate the searchlight. As I have never got the hang of wet shaving, Spud allows me to use the Lister generator once daily to power my electric razor. As it requires two men to turn the diesel engine I feel very privileged.

David snatched a few hours sleep before guard duty from 10.00–12.00 and again at 18.00–20.00 after which he took the corporal into Kings Cliffe, the village a mile or so south, for a drink to try to soften him up. Later, orders came through from Headquarters to say that a surprise air attack, involving 200 French bombers was going to go ahead. The French Air Force was to 'attack' Liverpool, Bristol, Birmingham, Manchester and Oxford. British fighter aircraft bearing lights were to intercept the 'enemy aircraft' and searchlight crews were to gain practise detecting these aircraft.

We sat up all night waiting for an attack. Two people fell asleep at their post with cigarettes in their hands, but they were woken by mates when they heard that Corporal Amies was on the warpath.

Early in the morning, they heard some planes flying over, but by then it was too light to engage them. However, the Daily Mail reported that the British air defences had been very efficient and although most raiders eluded the searchlights, a bomber was spotted at Blackpool.

'We had a great time using the searchlight on the Blenheim bombers.' *(Family Collection – Crown @ 1942)*

In the evening we had a great time using the searchlight on the Blenheim bombers flying at top speed with their navigation lights on. We got 29 targets out of 31. Guard 12–2 then 4–6.

On Sunday, David drove the twenty miles home, but was back by 23.00 hours for another round of night duty. Only one target came over and he described the guard duty from two to four o'clock in the morning as 'very sleepy hours.' He found time to get in a bit of shooting practise and managed to bag both a pigeon and a rabbit for the pot. After clearing up camp, he went on to Duddington for exercises.

We now have *live* ammunition for the machine-guns! After lunch I went to see the game-keeper to collect the paper. I stayed for a drink and admired his brown Labrador puppies. Luckily the night run was cancelled due to a thunderstorm so in the evening Steve, Spike, Whistle and I went down to the King's Head in Kings Cliffe where S was warned by the mother of his new girlfriend that she was only 16. The only other topic of conversation was about the threat of war.

I was just drifting off to sleep when there was a yell. 'Some guard corporal! The cook-house is on fire!' We all rushed out seizing the fire-buckets and put out the petrol stove that had caught fire and set the canvas alight.

After a good night's rest, David went to collect the paper in which there was much talk of war, and in hopes of a hot bath, visited the Goddards who lived at Duddington Manor.

We were due to be on the night run, however after getting ready for the Blenheim bombers, flying was cancelled due to ground mist and bad flying conditions. Then a car dashed up and after summoning the corporal at the double we were told that things were much more serious and that we were to be ready for action at a moment's notice with special air guards. We had had to wait to hear this message and the suspense was not too pleasant. We would not have been surprised if he had told us war had been declared, although there seemed little reason for it.

They waited up for the 23.00 news, then were on guard duty till 02.00. David sat in his car by the hut for about half an hour then pushed it down to the listener. They had not been there long when Lieutenant Bishton and his dispatch rider roared up on their motorbike. He rushed up to the hut with a message from HQ ordering them to watch all night for any aircraft without lights and to turn out if the HQ light went up. David stayed on duty for the rest of the night but saw nothing. After some sleep he had breakfast and went to 'Camp Concentration' for drill and a lecture on gas.

I had my first opportunity to drive the 6-wheeler Thorneycroft Army Lorry. I found it incredibly hard to change gear and pull the wheel round.

We had the best ever meal today, rabbit stuffed, or to be more accurate buried, in a sage and onion stuffing. Maybe the fire in the cookhouse has bucked up Whistle's ideas.

They got on with digging a six-foot rubbish hole and after tea, Steve and David drove off to Stamford to see the George Formby film 'Trouble Brewing.' They had

The searchlight detachment enjoying an Al Fresco lunch outside their hut. David is standing first left. *(Family Collection)*

just watched the newsreel when a message was brought in to say they were to return to camp immediately. They hurried out, causing a great deal of consternation to the other cinemagoers. Thinking it might be sometime before they would be able to visit a pub again, they stopped for a swift pint at a Phipps pub, then drove back to camp at great speed. On arrival they were surprised to find no one about except a sleepy sentry.

> We had to wait till the corps came back and then there was a hell of a row about ambiguity of the orders. I drove to the pub in Duddington and on the way back

Tedious hours were spent digging trenches. David is third from left. *(Family Collection)*

a silly idiot overtook me on a corner and I almost went into the ditch. Bed at 23.00 and slept till 08.00. The best night's rest I have had since arriving here.

In the early hours of August 24, Germany and the Soviet Union signed the Molotov–Ribbentrop non-aggression treaty and Hitler now looked towards Poland for his next land grab. In a last ditch effort to avert war, Britain and Poland signed an agreement of Mutual Assistance. They agreed that if Germany attacked either nation, the other would help defend it.

After a cold breakfast on the 25th, David's detachment filled in their B3 forms and everyone was set to digging the trenches. He was on guard duty when Cairns's batman came round with their pay. In the evening David cleaned his car and after a game of darts went to bed. All hoped for better news after Roosevelt sent a message to Hitler asking him to refrain from acts of hostility against Poland for a stipulated period in order that their differences be resolved.[2]

Over the weekend frantic negotiations were held to try to prevent the Polish situation worsening. Germany turned down a French proposal for face-to-face talks with Poland and demanded both the Polish Corridor and Danzig. President Roosevelt's appeal to Hitler met with little success, and the British sent a reply to Hitler's note, again expressing a wish for peace.

At 'Camp Concentration' we wore respirators for half an hour's gas attack practise. After lunch I went to Stamford to shop and had tea with Spike, Whistle and Steve. Later Mr Cairns came round with war orders. War tonight or not at all he says.

P.S. 02:00. No war yet and no lights seen.

On the 29th David madly drove home for a hot bath, listened to Chamberlain's speech and met Charles who had now notched up over twenty flying hours on the Tiger Moth. On the way back David reluctantly visited the dentist. He had a tooth drilled and filled without any painkillers and was sent from the chair with a mouth stuffed full of cotton wool. He never had much luck with his teeth or his dentists and throughout the war was plagued with tooth problems.

To ease the pain, I stopped off at the Haycock pub in Wansford and met up with some of the pilots from RAF Wittering. I found them cheery, welcoming and convivial – even after I admitted I was from the searchlight detachment.

Guard 10–12 and 4–6. Corporal Amies said that things were getting much more serious and we must be ready for action at a moment's notice but I am still hoping for a miracle that will avert war.

Poland also hoped that the war might be averted, but on the 30th, Adolf Hitler ordered German armed forces to prepare for an attack. The German radio reported that a sixteen-point peace plan had been put forward, but Poland refused to accept it. At dawn on Friday, 1 September, German forces invaded Poland from the north, south and west. During the day, the Luftwaffe launched air strikes on Warsaw, Lodz and Krakow. Many Polish units were overrun before reinforcements could arrive. The British Government demanded the Germans withdraw from Poland, announced a general mobilization, introduced censorship, air raid precautions and a blackout from sunset each day.

Not yet having heard the news, David was just about to set off for 'Camp Concentration' when Mr Cairns came round and told them that as they were such an intelligent lot they were to get a new sound locator with a remote control for the searchlight.

This searchlight was found in a scrap yard and rebuilt by The Garrison re-enactment group. (SAGH).

> Just before lunch I went off to Stamford to the garage to collect a battery for my car. The mechanic asked me, 'What do you think of the war situation now?' I replied I thought that there would be a war, to which he said, 'It's begun.' Puzzled, I went to the White Heather Café and ordered lunch. While waiting for it to arrive I read a newspaper report. The Nazis have crossed the Polish border and Stuka dive-bombers are attacking Polish airfields.

Shocked, David was finally forced to accept that Hitler never intended to stop at the Polish border. Feeling unbelievably depressed, he left the café just as an aircraft flew very low overhead. Terrified, everybody looked up. It was as if they expected to see German bombs or parachutists to come floating down into the street. After it had passed over, some people gathered into a tight huddle, while others hurried off to the shops to buy up what dried foods they could. Back at camp the mood was very calm.

> It was impossible to light a fire for supper as the wood was very wet and the petrol had run out. Ten of us heavily wrapped to the necks with our greatcoat collars up to our ears, others with caps over their eyes, or with steel helmets clamped on tight, sat around the table in the middle of the hut eating bread and marge. Come what may, war or peace, this is an experience worth having.

On Saturday, September 2, the German Army rapidly swept across Poland. The Polish Army put up a fierce opposition, but they were hopelessly outmanned and outgunned. Aerodromes and oil stores were bombed to cripple air and ground movement. The Polish Air Force fought with reckless courage, but over the next week, low on fuel, spare parts and pilots, it was virtually wiped out.

At Wittering, David heard that while Champ was on guard duty at Tixover, he saw a man in a field. He called out the guard and they crossed to the far side. Nine of the detachment went over to one corner and Champ to the other. On hearing noises he shouted, 'I think he's over here.' Hardly had he spoken when Champ was hit on the chest and shins with a crowbar sustaining three broken ribs. The others gave chase to his attacker, but gave up after four fields.

At 9.00 am on 3 September, Britain sent an ultimatum to Germany saying that unless German troops were withdrawn immediately from Poland, the two countries would be at war. No reply came and at 11.15am the Prime Minister, Neville Chamberlain made his sombre radio announcement that Britain was at war with Germany. Charles was ordered to report to Northampton Town Hall and was then told to go home and wait his turn for further training. Back at home he met their new evacuee Ronald Casemore[3], who had just arrived from London. Meanwhile David somberly noted in his diary:

A black day. Today we are at war with Germany.
'There is no man so foolish as to desire war rather than peace.
For in peace the sons bury their fathers, in war, fathers their sons.'

Herodotus.

The 'Phoney War' had begun and for many British people the pace of life hardly seemed to change. However, many of David's Cambridge friends were quickly mobilized, Neville Ussher, just back from annual training with the 5th Royal Inniskilling Dragoon Guards, was issued with a .38 pistol but no ammunition and put to work distributing gas masks.[4] Tony Nutting reported to the Leicestershire Yeomanry, Anson the Royal Artillery and Peter Storie-Pugh to The Queen's Own Royal West Kent Regiment.

Thursday, 7 September. Huffy and I were on guard by the searchlight 12–2 am. We heard noises as if someone was hammering by the Lister engine. Owing to our having no live ammunition, we have to rely on our bayonets in case of emergency and so we moved rapidly to where we thought the intruders might be. The noises ceased and we were just about to return when we heard heavy footsteps running away and we saw some dark shadows. I challenged. 'Halt! Who goes there?' There was no reply but a moment later three horses that had broken out of the field next-door trotted up. After Champ's adventures with would-be-wreckers I was ready for a scrap and I felt almost disappointed to find them equine intruders.

The news from Europe became bleaker and the strict blackout restrictions meant road accidents tripled in three weeks. David's good intentions of keeping a diary wavered and his letters home became less frequent. Along with many other men who found themselves swept up in a war they did not want, David felt despondent at being stuck in a tedious, unglamorous and unrewarding job. Public appreciation of the searchlight work was often confined to criticism by those who felt that the use of searchlights was likely to attract the attention of enemy aircraft.

It is highly likely that the tedium of this job will kill me off long before I ever see an enemy aircraft in my searchlight's beam. How I hate all the 'army nonsense', being told how to perform the simplest of tasks such as making beds, folding clothes and the endless marching and standing to attention.

Relief from the tedium came with David's regular visits to the Goddard's. Here he was greeted as a friend of the family and offered hot baths and delicious meals. These few hours away from the detachment were a welcome relief from army life.

In November he received a letter from Anson Howard.

The Provost's House, Coventry, 13/11/39.
Little did we imagine we would both be in the Army before the end of the year! I called in at Great Bowden on my way back from Cantab and heard all about you. I gather you are in a searchlight section living in a hut in Rutland and feeling rather bored, at least that is the impression. I thought you had got into the Northampton Regiment as an Officer. I imagined you strutting about in a lieutenant's uniform.... I went up to Cambridge to appear before the joint recruiting board in the hopes of a commission – I passed and am going to an Officer Training Unit as a 'gunner' for about 3 months whence I emerge as an Officer in the Royal Artillery. The whole business is a bit disturbing and rather annoying but it is wise to make the best of it.... Peter C is having a very pleasant time as one of four young men at a Woman's First Aid Depot, amongst dozens of – at least so he says – very passable girls of all ages. I enquired if he is going to join up. He wasn't quite sure just yet.... I heard about your evacuees and their pride in being with a family which owns 4 hunters and a tennis court and 2 soldiers! Think what an impression you'd make in your uniform! If you are ever around Coventry you're welcome for any meal.
                                                                 Yours, Anson.

By mid December, three British Infantry Brigades sent to France formed the British 5th Division and were deployed south of Lille along a fortified line. At Christmas David received news from University friends.

HQ Coy, 6th Battalion The Queen's Own Royal West Kent, Tonbridge, Dec 26 1939.
For some unknown reason after going down in June, I joined up in the TA in the ranks pending a commission and so I was called up halfway through August still only a Sergeant. I have been gazetted at last with seniority from Dec 1st 1938! This was I suppose due to that invaluable cavalry training received at Cambridge, anyway it makes me the second senior Subaltern of the Battalion and at present in the absence of my C/O I am in charge of the Company.
    This Battalion is almost completely officered by ex-Cambridge men, one from Queens', Allen by name. Peter Cruden[5] is still waiting to be called up, my informant on the subject Dick Matthews said that Peter applied to the Universities Joint Commission and they told him to hang on.... I have been having a hell of a good time so far in this war, the only fly in the ointment being the confounded petrol shortage. I think I shall lay my car up next year....
                                                          Yours ever, Peter Storie-Pugh.

Richard Osborn wrote that he had returned to Cambridge for a month before being sent to an ITW to continue his training:

I was sent to Hastings in company of many other CUAS chaps to be licked into shape. This process included a lot of marching, squad drill, some PT, several entirely irrelevant lectures and reminiscences and a lot of instruction in Morse code. We have all been sent home on 8 days leave following which quite a number of us are posted to Cranwell to start flying. It will be grand to get up again…. Most of our chaps are either from Oxford, Cambridge or London University so life while it lasts ought to be gay…. I see from your card that you're in a Searchlight Company. Keep the light on the night planes!

Merry Christmas, Richard.

New Year celebrations were dampened when rationing was introduced for bacon, butter and sugar, however on January 10, David's sister Marjorie married Bill Adler at Bowden Church. They had met in India in 1937 when Marjorie went to visit their aunt and cousins in Delhi, and Bill Adler was serving with the Welch Regiment on the North West Frontier. Severe winter weather set in at the end of January and as the thermometer plummeted, David's spirits reached an all time low. He wrote, 'The snow is so deep that the food lorries can't get through so I am now living on Lord Exeter's pheasants.'

Having finished his tank training in mid-February, Neville Ussher was posted to France to join the 12th Lancers. However, after arriving at Cherbourg, when asked his unit he 'naturally replied' the Inniskillings. Whereupon he was told to jump on a train and eventually arrived at their HQ in Mouvaux and stayed with the Regiment.[6]

In March, David received a postcard from Anson Howard who said he been posted to India and was to report for embarkation on March 10. Still studying divinity at Jesus College, John Earp wrote that this was a plum job and pictured Anson playing polo and spearing boar. All these letters set David thinking. Although as a mere Second Lieutenant, the Army did not require the independence of expression and thought that he desired, gaining an Army Commission was a way of escaping 'Camp

Marjorie's marriage to Bill Adler at Great Bowden Church. Charles is standing first left, David is at the back, third from right and Ronald standing far right. (*Family Collection*)

Concentration.' Hearing Anson's news finally persuaded David to take a more active role in deciding his fate.

> *1 April.* I'm thoroughly bored with the searchlight camp. Compared to the RAF, there is no excitement or glamour in the Army, just hard work, long marches and discomfort. So today, I put in for a Commission, if I have to be in the Army, I might as well try for a better job and as an officer, I feel that I will be able to contribute more to the war effort. I feel we must be optimistic for Mother and Father's sake. It's very hard for them having another war when they are not in their first youth and I think Ronald ought to take a less gloomy view of things for their sakes however pessimistic the silly chap feels inside.

David was cheered to hear news from Vivienne Lee, who was now a WAAF and learning to plot incoming planes.

> *The Grange, Heath and Reach, Leighton Buzzard*
> Dear David,
>   We have to pass a test, if we pass we go to Biggin Hill, if not, we have to go to some simply frightful training school and learn to wash up etc. so we hope to pass!! We haven't got our uniform but as soon as we have, we are given the awful berets and mackintoshes. If you become an officer, it will be too funny as I'll have to salute you!
> Love, Vivienne

While David was waiting for news of his commission, Gilbert Monckton and Neville Ussher were stationed with the 5th Royal Inniskilling Dragoon Guards somewhere in France. Peter Storie-Pugh with The Queen's Own Royal West Kent Regiment on the Belgium – French border, jotted a short note written about 10 May to give David a flavour of the conditions he was living in.

> *HQ Coy 6th Battalion Queen's Own. Date, day, year, lost count long ago.*
> I'm afraid I can't say much about our situation, work and general conditions because the censorship regulations are so very strict out here. We work desperately hard but the general comfort does not leave too much to be desired, taking everything into consideration. Our only relaxations at present are drinking and smoking and when the tobacco issue does not come, we just drink. We seldom have the time or surplus energy to do more than the occasional rubber of bridge, but the standard is not too high owing to the difficulty of having to read card values by the

COLDEST SNAP FOR 46 YEARS

THAMES FROZEN OVER

It can now be revealed that, during the cold snap which began in Britain last month—

London had twenty-five degrees of frost;

The Thames was frozen over at Kingston, and for eight miles between Teddington and Sunbury;

Temperatures in London were well below freezing point for a whole week;

Twelve inches of ice covered London reservoirs;

The snap was the coldest since 1894.

From north to south the country was in an icy grip, at Eskdalemuir, in Dumfriesshire, 21 degrees of frost were recorded on January 12, and a day later a similar temperature was experienced in Hampshire.

In London, however, 25 degrees of frost were registered at suburban weather stations. For a week the temperature hovered between 20 and 30 degrees Fahrenheit—from 12 to 2 degrees below freezing point.

Skating was general, the Serpentine and other London lakes being frozen over. Frozen pipes and tanks gave plumbers the busiest time for years.

The lowest temperature ever recorded in Great Britain was at Blackadder, Berwickshire, on December 4, 1879, when it fell to 55 degrees below freezing point.

During the coldest winter since 1894 the snow was so deep that food lorries were unable to reach David's camp.

light of a single candle. The weather seems to be breaking at last, which will make conditions better, but of course, we can't expect much just yet a while…. My brain has completely given out writing this disjointed letter. Hope to write again soon….

Yours Peter.

On May 8, Andrew Craig Harvey picked up a draft of forty men from Tidworth, and arrived in France early next morning to join the BEF. His timing could not have been worse, for at dawn on May 10, Germany invaded the Netherlands, Belgium and Luxembourg. Crushed by news of the German invasion, Neville Chamberlain stood down and Winston Churchill became Prime Minister of a coalition government.

Hearing the news of the invasion, Neville Ussher and his Regiment packed up, and along with other BEF and French troops, crossed the Belgian frontier to reinforce their Army, but after fierce fighting on the 15th they were forced to retreat, the Netherlands surrendered and Brussels was declared an open city.

Charles was ordered to report to No.1 Initial Training Wing at Pembroke College, Cambridge and David received a letter from the Royal Military College, Sandhurst.

> *Wednesday, 15 May.* It seems that the Army has faith in my abilities to command for I've been accepted for Officer Training and will leave here at the end of the month.

In France, David's friends were desperately fighting for their lives. Gilbert Monckton's Troop was rapidly falling back, however in the thick of the fighting the immaculately dressed General Alexander, seemingly unaware of the hail of bullets, stopped at Monckton's trench and disapprovingly said, 'You ought to smarten up a bit. Get a shave, for instance, and the next time you pass a barber's shop – don't!'[7]

On the 17th, Andrew Craig Harvey, loaded with cigarettes and chocolate, drove towards Renaix in Belgium, passing many refugees fleeing west. The next day a Troop of the 2nd Armoured Reconnaissance Brigade, commanded by Gilbert Monckton, were attacked by a large force of Germans in armoured cars, on motorbikes and with anti-tank guns. Monckton was ordered to act as left guard flank while other units withdrew. After fierce fighting they fought their way out.[8]

After arriving at Bicquy, Andrew Craig Harvey set off with the Brigadier across country to the main road down which the BEF was retreating. He wrote that the sight of the road just before dawn was breaking was just as he always imagined it would look in a great retreat with,' wounded men limping in threes, some infantry asleep as they marched, trucks with holes all over them and full of wounded.' At the end of the day, they received orders to pull out, as the Germans were only four miles away. Craig Harvey crossed the last remaining bridge over the Escaud near Tournai.[9]

Near Doullens, the Germans attacked a roadblock commanded by Peter Storie-Pugh. After fierce fighting, in which he was injured, the Germans withdrew and skirted round his position. Storie-Pugh escaped, but was captured on May 20 and taken to a German Hospital.[10]

Ordered to the Forest de Nieppe on May 23, Neville Ussher came under heavy fire and took what cover he could, however his carrier was spotted by several large

German tanks. A shell passed through Ussher's vehicle and exploded; severely injured, he was captured by the tank crew.[11]

Back in England, Peter Conant was at Waterloo Barracks Aldershot, with No.121 The Honourable Artillery Company, and John Earp, just finishing his exams at Cambridge, was closely following news of his friends:

Hawks Club, Cambridge, 24 May 1940.
David, Don't let them take you off to be shot up. The poor fellows on the other side seem to be playing a game of mutual slaughter; it's awful when you think about it. Judging from the Obituaries, the Irish Guards must have been semi-annihilated, for so far a Lt/Col, two Majors and a Captain are reported dead among the Senior Officers alone….

Yours ever, John.

On the 27th, four days after Neville Ussher's capture, Andrew Craig Harvey, ordered to deliver a message, rode his motorbike down winding lanes with high hedges towards St Sylvestre. He passed several French soldiers cowering in a ditch before his motorbike was hit by gunfire. An officer jumped out of a hedge, waved an automatic at him and ordered him to put up his hands. Surprised at being shot at, he said in his best school boy accent, '*Mais j'ai cru que vous etiez Francais,*' whereupon the officer replied in perfect English, 'I am afraid we're Boches.'[12]

While the 'Little Ships' began the rescue of thousands of exhausted troops from Dunkirk's beaches, another friend was preparing for action. At dawn on the 28th, Tim Vigors was sitting in one of a dozen No.222 Squadron Spitfires warming up ready to patrol the beaches of Dunkirk. He wrote that his mouth was dry and for the first time in his life he understood the meaning of the expression 'taste of fear.' 'Up until now it had all somehow been a game, like a Biggles' book where the heroes always survived.…'[13] Flying over the channel and from some distance away, Vigors could see the billowing smoke from burning oil and streams of big and little ships heading for the Dunkirk beaches.

Spending a few days on home leave Charles wrote:

16 Flight, D Squadron, Pembroke College.
They say they are going to make us all work hard here, as we shall not be here more than 10 weeks.… How difficult it is for people to keep cheery when all the news is so bad, (I mean news of operations abroad.) The news from the Home Front is as good, as the news from Belgium is bad. I do not listen here although we have a wireless and I wish that other citizens could be kept as busy as we are here so they wouldn't sit and worry about external affairs, which they are powerless to do anything about anyway. The BBC ought to say less about the fighting. The only thing for people to do is work, work and more work.

Yours affectionately, Charlie.

Chapter Three

Officer Training Sandhurst – Army Officer at Portsmouth, June 1940 to December 1940

'Getting a commission is like changing a third-class cabin for a first-class cabin in a sinking ship – a change for the better no doubt, but not much help really.'
'One Family's War' – Christopher Mayhew.

On Friday, 31 May, David set off for Sandhurst. He was not going alone. His new companion was Rob, a beautiful golden retriever, given him by the Marquis of Exeter's gamekeeper.

Rob is boarded with some lovely people nearby; he can run about the woods, in the garden and be exercised out of the back gate onto the common. Their daughter Cathy fell in love with Rob at once, so I think he will be very happy there. Once I have my bicycle I will be able to visit him and walk him in the woods.

Quickly settling into life at Sandhurst, David's training was expected to last four months. Overlooking playing fields, lakes and woods, David's room in the New

After the searchlight hut, David's corner room in the New Buildings at Sandhurst seemed luxurious. *(Family Collection – Crown © 1942)*

Buildings seemed most luxurious after the sparse conditions of the searchlight '*detachment*'; he was even provided with the services of a batman.

> *Saturday, 8 June 1940.* Dinner is at eight and we have each afternoon off, 1–5 but we don't seem to have a minute to spare. Nobody who hasn't been under guardsman's instructions would be capable of believing what a rush everything is, but I am happy and proud to have the privilege of this training. A & B Company are line regiment companies with line officers. C & D Company are Guard Companies with all Guard instructors and are definitely superior. I am in D Company and our Company Commander is Captain Steele of the Coldstream Guards, four times runner up in the Army golf championships.

Also in D Company, Arthur Neil Soutar had been in the same searchlight battalion as David, but based at Oakham and Exton. He noted that the Guard training came as a very rude shock and he was put on Company Orders several times in the first week.[1] Their days were filled with marches, PE and parades, but with free time at the weekend, David visited his cousin Maurice Lovett-Turner.

> I took young Maurice out to tea today as his prep school is only just nine miles from here. He said it was the first time he had been out of school since his mother left for India and as it happened to be the Speech and Garden party day, when most other boys had gone out, he was even more pleased about it.
>
> When I arrived back I started reading 'I Bought a Mountain,' written by Thomas Firbank, who is in my platoon. It is about farming in Wales and I am sure Father would enjoy it.

Apart from parades and inspections, much of the cadets' time was spent in lectures, some more interesting than others. Firbank wrote that one platoon commander read straight from his books and they played a joke on him by sticking pages together, but he turned both over and continued to read without a pause.[2]

Having escaped from Dunkirk on one of the last boats, Gilbert Monckton told David that Andrew Craig Harvey may have been taken prisoner, but he sincerely doubted it.

> Gilbert believes Andrew was killed in action near Dunkirk a week or so ago and Neville Ussher, my friend from Queens', was in the same tank squadron, is also missing.
>
> The evacuation of Dunkirk has snatched victory from defeat and there are hundreds of troops camped on the heathland around here. Many are in a bad way, without rifles or equipment but we often see them swimming in the Blue Pool Lido.[3]

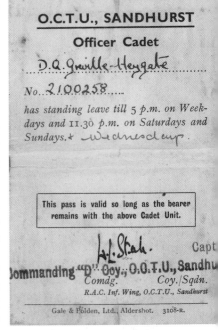

O.C.T.U., SANDHURST

Officer Cadet

D.Q. Greville-Heygate

No. 2100258

has standing leave till 5 p.m. on Week-days and 11.30 p.m. on Saturdays and Sundays. + Wednesday.

This pass is valid so long as the bearer remains with the above Cadet Unit.

H.L. Shah.   Capt
Commanding "D" Coy., O.C.T.U., Sandhu
Comdg.   Coy./Sqdn.
R.A.C. Inf. Wing, O.C.T.U., Sandhurst

Gale & Polden, Ltd., Aldershot.   3108-R.

Sandhurst cadet pass. (*Family Collection – Crown © 1940*)

D Company cadets, 1940. David is standing in the third row, fourth from left. *(Family Collection Crown © 1940)*

Rob ran away a few days ago, and while I was standing to attention on Morning Parade, Rob suddenly appeared. I saw him, but of course, I could not move. He went up and down the lines inspecting the troops then ran off, looking sadly abandoned before the parade was over and although I looked and called for him for a long time after, I could find no trace of him.

On 14 June, the German Army marched into Paris and the German High Command confidently expected that within a month the RAF would no longer exist as a fighting force and, in anticipation of the invasion of Britain, German troops were issued English phrase books. Goering ordered large daylight air raids on airfields and channel shipping to commence. With the threat of invasion looming large, David spent many tedious hours digging trenches at Reading, along routes to London, to defend against German tanks. Also working hard but enjoying himself, Charles wrote:

16 Flight D Squadron Pembroke College.
We are getting on all right and some of us, those with more flying hours than me, have already been posted to Flying School. I might be in the next batch. It's a good thing I did not bring a car here. They are quite useless and they try to make it impossible to drive it home, so many may have to be left behind by the unfortunate men posted to the other ends of the land….
                    Your affectionate brother, Charlie.

Friday, 21 June 1940. The police at Sandhurst found Robin today. He nearly went crazy when he saw me from his little kennel at the police station; he looks very well groomed and fatter.
    One of the saddest things about this place is the sight of the empty loose horseboxes and the riding school, which is now being used for tank exercises. The only person who rides on parade is the Adjutant. When we have battalion parade on Wednesday mornings he rides a fine black charger. His orders are

David with Rob, his golden retriever. *(Family Collection)*

Charles Greville-Heygate. *(Family Collection – Crown © 1941)*

so loud, yet so unintelligible that we often wonder if it is an order or the horse coughing!

With more men arriving for training, David was moved from his corner room to one further along the passage, and his new neighbours were an ex-correspondent of the New York Times and Hugh Fitzroy, the eldest son of the 10th Duke of Grafton. David was considering which regiment to apply for once he finished his training.

> There seems little chance of any leave for another two months but I hope to get some before joining up with my regiment. I did think of getting into the Scots Guards as it is not expensive in wartime but I have decided against that. I would rather be based in the country rather than the town and in the south rather than the north of England. If I knew Peter Pugh was still alive I should have tried to get into the same battalion but I haven't had an answer to my last letter and, as I know he was in France, I am inclined to fear the worst. I believe he was killed on May 20th about 10 days after his last letter to me. He was one of my closest friends at Queens' and I do wish he was here now.

At Sandhurst, officers who had seen fighting in Norway or France began to replace the older staff, and teaching methods became more practical. The cadets spent more time learning fighter tactics, and although David still found it difficult to give senior officers the deference they expected from the junior ranks, he came to admire these younger officers.

David received good news from Mrs Harvey who had refused to believe Andrew was killed. She had finally received a postcard to say he was a POW.

Charles passed the first stage of training and now at an Elementary Flying Training School at Desford, wrote to David.

C Flight, No.7 EFTS. 2 July 1940
I do not think I shall be allowed officially to visit Bowden, but I shall probably go once or twice 'unofficially' as you used to do. My quarters are a room in a bungalow, very cramped after Pembroke, which I share with Laurie King but there is a good Mess …
Your affectionate brother, Charles.

Richard Osborn, now training on Wellington bombers, commented that they were as heavy as a ten-ton lorry, but once flying they were beautiful to handle. He wrote:

RAF Harwell, Didcot.
I had heard of Peter Pugh from Peter C whom I met in London last weekend. It is very sad and makes yet another in the list of friends whom I have so far survive … If I have the chance of flying against the Hun before my time comes, every one of my planes inconsiderable bomb loads will have a name to it … I did a mild shoot-up of what must have been your place at Oakham one Sunday morning a couple of months ago. After a couple of steep turns over the place I shot up into a stall turn and came diving down at the parade ground – heading straight at an Anson! That rather shook me up, not to mention my co-pilot, so we took our old Oxford away before we did any damage.
Look after yourself. Yours, Richard

While David was finding life rather tedious, having been confined to barracks after several long nights on duty, Charles recorded his second 'First Solo' flight on July 10, just as the Battle of Britain commenced. At first light on the 11th, a call went out at No.226 Squadron for pilots to intercept incoming enemy bombers. On hearing the call, David's hunting friend Tim Vigors, still quite inebriated, having been out late drinking the night before, pulled on a dressing gown to camouflage his scarlet pyjamas and took off to shoot down the bombers.[4]

After studying hard, Charles passed his RAF tests and flew a navigation exercise to Cambridge, flying over hospital trains and tents full of wounded soldiers rescued from the beaches.

Now based on the North-West Frontier Province India, Anson Howard wrote:

Royal Artillery Mess, Abbottabad 1/8/40. Well here I am, a pukker Sahib, playing polo and drinking chota pegs.[5] I am in the Mountain Artillery, what used to be the Pack Artillery; we have to take the guns to pieces and put them onto the back of mules, which carry them up and down the hills of the NW Frontier. In addition to the mules, of which there are 120 in a battery, there are also 24 ponies, which we have the use of – as well as a charger of our own. About 10 of the ponies are trained for polo and I have taken up the game and find it thrilling.

Our existence is of such apparent comfort that it makes me feel an absolute cad. I should be in England and not out here.

One feels dreadfully remote from news of England here – even on the wireless it seems far away and like watching a film than listening to actual happenings. Whenever I hear of an air raid over the East Coast, I think of you sitting at the base of your anti-aircraft gun, well occupied. I would love to know what you have been doing in that time....

Yours, Anson.

On August 10, while hurrying out to fetch Rob, David tripped over a tree stump and twisted his ankle. The next day he played in the Company cricket match and scored 105 runs. However, after his ankle swelled up again, he was excused all drills, digging, PT and manoeuvres, but he continued to study hard. Meanwhile having passed all her tests, Vivienne Lee went to work in the Operations Room at Biggin Hill, an RAF station regularly bombed by the Luftwaffe.

Biggin Hill, Aug 13 1940.
David..., Life here has definitely been hectic just the last few days. They certainly seem to be coming over in much larger quantities and doing much more damage. We are definitely tired of Biggin Hill already. Mark is still at Paignton[6] and having a very good time, going out most evenings. He seems to think he'll be moving again soon to the next stage of his training....

Much love, Vivienne.

Bombs were also falling in the vicinity of Sandhurst:

We are being troubled slightly by the Jerries' crates coming over and dropping bombs around. The ordinary ones are all right, but these time-bombs are rather a nuisance, as houses have to be evacuated when they drop in the cabbage patch. The occupants have to look on from a safe distance and see the bomb go off and their house fall down like a pack of cards. One bomb fell about half a mile away in the village and three others in a town nearby. We saw seven German bombers go over today on their way back from a raid on Croydon. I think I shall have to write to Hitler and ask him to drop a time-bomb on the square outside, then we should all get leave until the thing goes off!

The RAF is doing marvellously. We saw about one hundred of our bombers going out on a raid on Italy; they looked absolutely grand. Later, the wireless reported that they all came back safely. A good show. Poor old Army, it plods along having much the hardest time and the most dull. As yet, it cannot do anything spectacular like the Navy or the RAF and, of all the branches, the infantry is the most boring, but someone has to do it, so it might as well be us.

It was now almost a year since David joined the Army, and the time spent training at Sandhurst was the longest stretch he had been away from home.

Dennys Scott came to dinner; he is at the Royal Artillery OCTU in Aldershot and looks pretty fit. He read in the paper that Peter Pugh, officially reported killed in action, is a prisoner of war. I do hope it is true.

We have such a nice new platoon commander called Basil Eugster, who won the MC in Palestine and the bar in Norway when a hand grenade landed on top of his tin helmet and exploded. A couple of months ago he had another lucky escape.

The MV Chrobry, a passenger vessel built in 1939 was being used to transport Allied troops to Norway and was sailing just off the Lofoten Islands. Amongst other troops the 1st Irish Guards were on board. Shortly after midnight on May 15 a German Ju87 attacked and set the ship on fire.

> Basil and the 30 officers on board the newly completed Polish liner were in the luxury cabins. He and a friend were chatting before going to bed when they heard machine-gun fire. They wondered if they ought to go up to see what was going on, as Basil's Company was providing guard and his friend was an Intelligence Officer. They just decided they should investigate when there was a colossal explosion that knocked them both out. When Basil came round, about half an hour later, he was lying in the debris with a raging fire only a few yards away. There were no beds left in the cabin, they had fallen through to the next floor. He pulled his friend out and they staggered off to find a way up out of the ship. They were trapped by wreckage on all sides, but managed to get through a dining-room window. They were then on the lower deck from the boats. Finding a rope ladder going up to the upper deck they decided to climb it, as the other end only went down into the water. However halfway up, they met about forty Poles coming down swearing. Basil tried to make them go up and they tried to make him go down. This impasse was finally settled when the rope broke and they all fell into the water. After a time, they were rescued by another ship.[7]

Having now notched up over seventy-four flying hours, Charles was posted to RAF Cranwell to fly twin-engine aircraft.

Cadets Mess. 18/8/40.
The College building is like a Palace and we could not believe that we were to be housed in it, and sat for sometime gazing at it across the vast lawn, rather overawed by its grandeur. Then we motored up and I walked up the steps. When I saw the 'Hall Porter' coming out to meet us I knew it would be alright…. The College is very full of traditions. I shall have to behave like an officer and a gentleman, but I think that I could not do otherwise when surrounded by such splendour. You seemed to be having a poor time of it when you last wrote. Mother mentioned in a letter that you haven't seen an egg for nine weeks!
Love, Charlie.

A few days later, after his solo test in an Airspeed Oxford Charles wrote again:

RAF College, Cranwell, 22/8/40.
The instructor giving me my Solo Test knew the Scott's very well as he used to go to Blakeney. He was busy talking about all these things as we went round. Result – I made a very bad approach and landing. I had to do another to satisfy him before he let me go off on my own. He said, 'Don't hurry, it's a fine afternoon

and you have three hours of fuel on board and the ancillary tank is full!' So that was that. These twin-engine trainers are very weird to land after Tiger Moths – try to do a three-point landing and the three and a half tons go down with a crash onto the deck, so wheel-landings with engine are the vogue. They were unpardonable when we were on Tigers. One 'First Solo' landed safely in a field of clover adjoining the airfield. He had thought it was the 'drome until he saw the wire fence looming up in front of him and put on the brakes. I hear the Flight Commander was furious, as the ground crew had to pull up some posts and take the wire down to get the plane back on the airfield. I do not suppose he would have minded so much if the undercarriage had broken on the aerodrome – that often happens – but the so-near-so-far idea of a perfectly sound aeroplane the wrong side of the wire was riling to him.

Michael West is here; he knew my friend Hilditch at Oakham School, as is Paul Baillon. I also met a friend of Douglas Edghill;[8] he said that Douglas had shot down a German aeroplane and got very embarrassed when his parents told people about the same in his presence!

Cheerio, Charles.

Ronald came over for a visit and took me out to lunch in his MG, which he drove at a terrifying speed and he took great delight in telling me that he hoped to be accepted by the RAF very soon.

Basil was in a bit of a state today. An Officer and platoon were lent to him for an exercise and when Basil positioned them, the Officer said that he would have to fire the mortar, as his men did not know how to do so and that his wireless operator had only a fortnight's training and didn't know how to work the sets either!

This inexperience in handling equipment was all too common. Thomas Firbank wrote that their course shot twice on the range and fired fifteen rounds with the Bren gun. 'We received the impression that the use of grenades and mortars was dangerous in practice, and that these weapons were to be reserved for emergencies of life or death.'[9]

A short time later, Ronald wrote to say that he was now an RAF officer and at 'Ops B' at Wittering. Delighted David wrote to his parents:

I told him to have a pint or two on me at the Haycock pub and look up Michael Watts Russell who lives near Oakham and is going into the Coldstream Guards. Michael often visits the Haycock on Saturday night. I met up with Charles Brodie Knight, William Bell and Robert Etherton.[10]

David's brother Ronald always drove at terrifying speeds! *(Family Collection)*

The Luftwaffe's tactic of bombing airfields was stretching the RAF to its limit, and on August 30, there were two attacks on Biggin Hill and thirty-nine people were killed.[11] The next day, the Ops Room also received a direct hit.

The German invasion of Britain was expected daily and rumours circulated about bodies of German soldiers being washed up on beaches. Plans were hastily prepared to warn of invasion and when it was judged imminent, the codeword 'Cromwell' was to be sent out. Later, when German Forces actually landed on British beaches, the church bells were to be rung. At 20.00 hours on September 7, the codeword was sent to Eastern and Southern Commands. Other Commands were sent the codeword 'for information only.' However, this caused much confusion and all over the country church bells were ordered to be rung.[12] Hearing the bells the Sandhurst cadets were alerted. David was once again urgently summoned from a cinema and Thomas Firbank hurried off to set up an anti-tank rifle in the upstairs window of a shop in Camberley.[13]

> *Saturday 7–Sunday, 8 September 1940.* We manned the roadblock all night, expecting the invasion, thankfully it turned out to be a false alarm. There was an awful raid on London and we saw ten Jerry bombers going over. At dawn with no sign of German troops, the stand-down was signalled and exhausted but relieved, we headed back to camp.

As the last weeks of David's course approached, training was stepped up, with night attacks, raids and a three-day march. These were interspersed with numerous enforced delays spent down the air-raid shelters. Meanwhile during a lull in the bombing raids Vivienne wrote:

> *Biggin Hill, Sept 9 1940.*
> We've had a hell of a time here. Being bombed to blazes for about the last fortnight solidly. Spending nearly all our lives in A-R Shelters. Quite frankly I've never been so frightened in all my life, they certainly do get you down after a while. Last night I lay awake for about four hours listening to the planes dropping their bombs and the Ac-Ac, each time thinking it would be us they hit next. …
>
>   Love Vivienne.

In an attempt to demoralize the population, the Luftwaffe turned their attention towards the capital, bombing the docks and the East End. While on Passive Air Defence duties, David watched a terrific AA barrage over London and listened to the dull boom of guns and exploding bombs.

> *11 September.* At 08.30 am the air raid siren went off again so instead of being in our normal shelter I spent the morning sitting in a wheelbarrow in the shelter under the Old Buildings, with the rescue parties. Another air raid went off at 20.30 so we had to rush out of the Mess and as I was still on PAD, I had to return to the basement, now somewhat cooler. The all-clear didn't sound until 04.30 in the morning so we had a bit of sleep on the concrete floor.

15 September. I spent the whole morning on a good Withdrawal Scheme, I was a section commander and it all went off rather well. Cycling back, Ken had a head-on crash with a motorbike and after flying over the top of both bikes, he fell on his head and broke his shoulder, luckily he had his tin helmet on. After lunch, with Bobby De Lautour[14] as platoon commander, we carried out a trench relief.

Saturday, September 21 was David's last day at Sandhurst and at the traditional passing-out parade the Adjutant rode through the building on his horse. David's attempt to pick a regiment in the south was in vain. Markham Nicholas Gentleman, Matthew Graham, Hugh Pritchard, John Peter 'Pip' Hutton and David were attached to The Loyal North Lancashire Regiment in Clitheroe.

On September 30, David drove north to the 50th Battalion of the Loyals and met his Company Commander, Captain Harry Allen who was six feet four inches tall and nicknamed 'Tiny'.

David Greville-Heygate. *(Family Collection – Crown © 1940)*

This is like a rest camp after Sandhurst! I am writing this in front of a large fire in our anteroom and our mascot, a tabby cat is stretched out near the hearth. We have an excellent cook and the food is better than Cambridge – except it leaves out the fish course. Today we had a goose, which was very tender and fell to bits when carved.

Every other day they marched three miles up Pendle Hill to the training area, nearly 2,000 feet high. It could be very windy at the top, but on a clear day there was a fantastic view all the way to the Irish Sea. Enjoying the fresh air and exercise, David tried his best to become a good Infantry Officer, but his heart was not in it.

Even the twenty mile march I made with my Company today seemed like a stroll in the country. The men sing excellently and my voice is getting used to the shouting. Last night we all went to the sergeants' dance. It was so hot we nearly melted. I was glad to get to bed. The five captains are very tubby, keep us in fits of laughter and Captain Allen is fatherly and kind. However, I do wish I could take more interest in Infantry work but it bores me, which is most unfortunate. I think I will have to push for some specialist work.

Writing to say that he would visit Clitheroe on his next leave, Charles asked about local pubs and fishing rivers. He also suggested some specialist work that might suit David.

RAF College, Cranwell.

I have put down for a posting to Army Co-operation as one of my preferences after leaving Cranwell. If you went into it, you could perhaps transfer into the RAF, as a chap who was in the Army before the war has just changed into Air Force blue and I understand he is lent to the RAF for the duration of the war…. I am now enjoying flying very much and as I now get no dual instruction except at night, we can fly in our own style for a change. We go in pairs in daytime except for formation flying, and it is nice having the company in the air…. Must do some work, so cheers.

Charles.

Charles did not get a chance to go fishing with David because after only a week at Clitheroe, David was sent to Portsmouth with the 10th Battalion.

I've been sent south to guard the docks and defend the coastline from invasion. After a sixteen-hour journey by night-train and coach we arrived at Portsmouth Harbour. It was such a clear day that it looked very pleasant in the late evening sun with little boats flitting past. I could even see the Isle of Wight. The barrage balloons added to the view, as they are wonderfully graceful and float upwards, glittering like silver in the sun.

Although David's first impressions were of a peaceful city, this was deceptive. With its large naval dockyard and industrial installations, Portsmouth was a prime target for German bombers. On 24 August it had suffered the worst bombing raid of any city except London during the whole of the Battle of Britain.[15] Although most of the

David's Portsmouth Dock permit. *(Family Collection Crown © 1940)*

officers and the Mess were based at the imposing Clarence Barracks in the centre of Portsmouth, David's new living quarters were at Portsdown School, Cosham.

> In peacetime it must have been a grand place to stay. The men have wonderful accommodation here in the rambling modern school on the hillside. Captain Pell is the only other captain in these schools besides my company commander. He was at Queens' Cambridge some time before me and is a good cricket, and rugby player. Pip Hutton is now my roommate and is going to marry Mary Radford in Nottingham Cathedral soon. We have only four officers up here, but we are quite satisfied as the remainder of the officers down at the barracks are having a rather sticky time of it. There are two Majors who wear monocles and they have completely dampened the Mess, people just use it as a restaurant and disappear after dinner to various hotels until bedtime.

A few days later while at Clarence Barracks, David met his first German PoWs and he was surprised at how different the men were.

> We have some wounded German airmen prisoners here. One is an Austrian, a gentle character and a great contrast to the other, a Prussian Hun. They are most complimentary about our aircraft and I wish Charles and Ronald could hear what they think of the RAF; it would make them very proud to hear what they think of the Spitfire!

The Army gave David an unintentional twenty-first birthday present by sending him to Woolacombe for a weapons training course. *(Family Collection Crown © 1942)*

A French ship has taken refuge in the docks and uses its guns at low level against the Luftwaffe, which causes everyone greater concern than the aircraft it is trying to shoot down. I quite like the sound of guns now and it is fun waiting for them; today one went off only about 100 yards away – a gun not a bomb. They haven't dropped any bombs since we came here.

Charles, nearing the end of initial training, wrote with news that everyone, bar two on his course, passed their Wings' exam. He said that Mark Lee had arrived at Cranwell a week late having been sent by mistake to an airfield in Scotland where they only flew Masters.

RAF College, Cranwell, 19 October 1940.
When we first came here, one of 11th course got lost and landed near Wittering where there is a flare path laid out, and the other night, one of 13th course got into a cloud at 2am and managed to cruise until 6am when his petrol was almost exhausted so he came down near Ripon. Very lucky not to be hurt! He's back here now – so you see, night-flying is quite as exciting as Father seems to think, although I won't get lost as I keep very close to the lights! But as we have had much fog, little night-flying can be done at present. I shall have lots more training after leaving Cranwell before going on any bombing expeditions. Must stop now as I have a duty to perform.
Yours, C.

Friday, October 25 was David's twenty-first birthday and he had good cause for celebration, for as well as receiving several telegrams from his family, the Army had unintentionally given him a most pleasant birthday present, a trip to Devon for a weapons training course. The next day along with Captain Jones, David caught the train to Woolacombe and reported to the Woolacombe Bay Hotel where they were to stay for the three-week course.

It was an excellent train and, considering it came from Waterloo, it was only half an hour late, very speedy and much to my surprise had a dining car. There are about ten RAF officers here and eighteen of us 'Army Boys.' The hotel must have been lovely until about three weeks ago, with nearly 100 bedrooms, a billiard room, great sun loungers looking out across to the sea and wonderful views over the bay.

1 November. In the evening I went over to Ilfracombe with Dick Arnold[16] and Briggs in the SS Sports car. After drinks we went onto a golf club dance at the Pavilion with the Joe Daniels Jazz Band where I met a charming girl called Rosemary Brooke Boone.[17] Her father is in the Royal Army Medical Corps. It was the best dance I've ever been to and we arranged to meet again.

Also on the weapon-training course was James Bysse Joll,[18] a fluent German speaker with the Devon Regiment who eventually transferred to the German section of SOE.

2 November. After talking to Joll I have now definitely decided to apply for a transfer, though what to I don't know. I think the Infantry is the most dull of all jobs. I shall tell the Colonel so when I get back, the more I see of it, the less I think I am suited to it.

While David was away, the Luftwaffe recommenced bombing raids on Portsmouth. On October 29, in two heavy raids, shops and houses were demolished or badly damaged and a high explosive bomb fell on the railway with thirty-nine casualties and three killed.[19] Harry Allen wrote that they had had many air raids; once while he was on a route march with the company, they took cover in a ditch and watch fifty aircraft fighting it out in the skies above them.

Finally commissioned at the beginning of November, Charles was posted to No.2 School of Army Co-operation to receive further training before being posted to a squadron.

> *Officers Mess, RAF Andover, 5 Nov 1940.*
> Don't you think I am lucky being here? I am enjoying it very much as it is better than Cranwell…. I have not seen much of the place yet and I have not flown yet but shall get a Blenheim and crew eventually; my own ship! No more trips as second pilot-navigator for hundreds of hours as on Heavy Bombers, which were my first choice. Blenheims are very fast aeroplanes, I didn't realize before. The other chaps give quite a good account of it…. Congratulations on your decision to apply for a transfer. If anything comes of it the Army will have lost a good man…. I met Paul Baillon[20] in a restaurant in Oxford and he was on his way home on a motorcycle for four days' leave. He is flying Spitfires a few miles away and has had to use his parachute once already but that does not worry him! He seems to have enjoyed it…. We had lots of banshee wailings this afternoon but did not see the enemy. It would break my heart if they were to blow up our Mess, it is so comfortable….
> Much love, Charles.

With a weekend off, David was keen to meet up with Rosemary again, so he checked into the Montebello Hotel.

> They are such a charming family. Dr Brooke Boone is a Major and I believe a cousin of the poet Rupert Brooke. He was one of the doctors with the RAMC during the evacuation of Dunkirk. They tossed a coin to see who should remain behind to look after the wounded and fortunately for him he lost. We went for tea at Holloway's café; afterwards we walked down to the harbour and back along the cliffs then went to dinner and a dance at the Pavilion and had a lovely walk home.

> *10 November.* I had arranged a round of golf with Rosemary but it was far too wet and windy, so we went for a terrific walk over to Hillsborough and on nearly to Combe Martin; everything looked so pretty and we stopped for tea at the Golf Club.

After an exciting weekend, David received devastating news about his favourite horse. Several months before, David's mother had asked if Tommy Webb, a soldier billeted in the village, could ride Brunette. David had been only too pleased to have her exercised.

Great Bowden, 10 Nov 1940.
David…, You remember my remark that animals gave us a great deal of pleasure but also a great deal of grief. You have already had that with Robin and now I fear you will be grieved to hear about Brunette. Tommy Webb went out for a ride on Brunette and was just trotting along the Langton road when a huge cattle truck came far too fast round the corner. It went straight into the back of Brunette and knocked her over. She fell on Tommy's leg and died almost instantly. Tommy arrived here cold, shivering and white, but apart from a strong cup of coffee, he refused any treatment. It was not his fault.

We went to tea in Harborough and on our way back an aeroplane seemed to be coming straight at us on its way to Bowden and directly afterwards we heard it close by, and it appeared from behind the hedge. Ronald came back later and said, 'Did you see us go over?' That's the second time he has frightened Dawson!
Your loving Mother.

I was very grieved to read about Brunette, I was particularly fond of her. I hope she didn't suffer too much.

We had the most terrific crash today and the ceiling fell down, I don't know why, fortunately no one was sitting underneath it. I went to Ilfracombe with Martin, an Irish polo player and after drinks and dinner at the Queen's Hotel I met Rosemary. We went to see a flick, 'Zanzibar', and after spending a few pennies in the amusement hall I walked her home.

Having spent two months at Wittering, Ronald was posted to the Ops Room at RAF Watnall, the Control and Administration Centre for Fighter Command's 12 Group which covered the Midlands, Norfolk, Lincolnshire and North Wales. The area included the industrial cities of Birmingham, Manchester, Liverpool and Coventry which were all prime targets for the German bombers. The next day on November 14 the Luftwaffe carried out a heavy and systematic bombing raid on Coventry; 1,000 civilians were killed and much of the city was reduced to rubble. Incendiary bombs fell on the Cathedral in the heart of the city. Anson Howard's father, Provost Dick Howard, along with a small team of men, fought bravely to extinguish the fires. In a BBC broadcast he said, 'Bomb after bomb, incendiary bombs fell…. Finally a group of three fell on the roof and the fire blazed up and we had no more sand, no more water, practically no more strength to go on.'[21] Even with the Fire Brigade's help, they were unable to prevent the Cathedral's almost total destruction.

After reading the news, David was worried.

Poor old Coventry, I hope Anson Howard's family are not injured or the two little girls that had been evacuated. Anson will be worried when he hears the news in India.

We had the practical exam in the morning, followed by a most interesting demonstration of platoon weapons on the beach; I fired in line with a tracer and completed the weapons' course qualifying with a B. In the afternoon, after drinks in a cocktail bar, I met Rosemary. Then we danced all evening at a farewell dance in the ballroom and we went for a walk. It was a grand evening

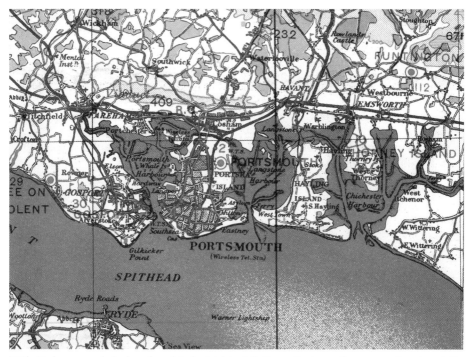

With its large naval dockyard and industrial installations, Portsmouth was a prime target for German bombers. *(Family Collection – Crown © 1943)*

with a lovely moon. My happy time is I am afraid drawing to a close. The people down here are so pleasant and the coast when one sees it through the rain is no less beautiful. This has been the happiest time of my life since war started.

This euphoria rapidly evaporated on David's return to Portsmouth.

Saturday, 16 November. I picked up my car and drove off, only to get a flat tyre. It was teeming with rain and I got drenched as the jack wouldn't work and when I got that working, the nuts had been done up so tight they wouldn't unscrew. It took me nearly half and hour for each of the nuts, so I didn't get home until about 11 pm.

David was further upset by a letter from his father regarding his intention to apply for a transfer to the RAF.

Great Bowden, 10 Nov 1940.
Dear David…, Please do let me know and get my approval before you make any changes. Your mother dreads having three boys in the Air Force, you are all the world to her. I will pay extra expense for the Cavalry or Guards but why not join the Royal Engineers, which will help you in the future?
Yours ever, Father.

David immediately wrote back to his father explaining his reasoning.

Dear Father..., I do not want to hurt you but as Tennyson said, 'Oh hard, when love and duty meet.' I am trying to get a post as an Air Liaison Officer between the Army and the Air Force. It will mostly be groundwork. It is hopeless to be stuck in a job I detest and I am more detrimental to the nation than a help. I am sure you would not want this state of affairs to continue. I might just as well go into air co-operation and perhaps spend more time in England than stay in this and go and die a lingering death somewhere in Africa, perhaps by March. Just because we are in England now in the Army, there is no reason to suppose we shall be here in two or more months. So if you are worried, I do hope you will think of the alternative.

Your loving son, David.

After attending his first month's interview, David, still in a black mood, led his platoon out on patrol.

Monday, 18 November. This is going to be one of the most awful months as I start on Portsdown Defence.

Oh ----! I had a bit of a row with Brigadier Underwood. I don't like the look of things.

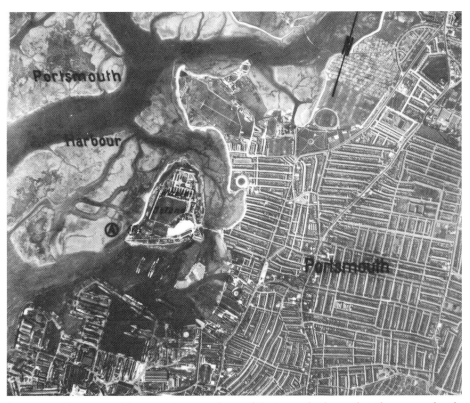

A pre-war German aerial reconnaissance photo of Portsmouth shows that they were already planning bombing attacks on military targets. *(NRO AIR 34/734)*

As I walked to supper tonight I heard a whirr, and a bit of shrapnel landed ten yards around the corner. I quite missed the air raids in Devon!

Thursday, 21 November. I must get an interview with the C/O, or write to the Air Ministry. I would almost rather be back on the searchlights than here. The shoptalk in the Mess drives me nearly crazy. We went out on an exercise at 10.00 and had a bloody awful day on Portsdown doing an attack. We spent a wet night in the woods and I had a very stiff neck by morning. How I hate this blasted job. If only I could get into the RAF. But of course there is only the usual answer from the Army; they've paid for your training so they won't let you go.

Saturday, 23 November. This is the most awful week that I think I have ever lived through. I've missed several days of my diary because I have been working almost non-stop and have had to catch up on it. I grab sleep in quieter moments and eat on the run. Unfortunately, the improved weather conditions have encouraged the German bombers to come over on seemingly endless raids. We've been defending the docks from the constant attacks by German bombers. There was a terrific raid and the anti-aircraft guns were firing like hell. About fifteen high-explosive and many incendiary bombs were dropped tonight. It was pitiful to see the widespread fires creeping across the town and heart-rending to hear the cries for help. The worst of it is that we are powerless to help, as we have no means of putting the fires out.

Finally, on the Sunday, David had a day off and he drove over to Andover to visit Charles. While waiting for him to return from a flight, David met Eric Hewson, Charles's roommate. They went to the Mess for a drink and chatted until he landed.

The Mess was very comfortable and the lunch delicious and it was grand to see Charles again he looks so well and thoroughly enjoying himself (lucky man!) We spent the afternoon looking in the hangars and exploring the intricacies of a Blenheim. I felt very at home with the pilots and aircraft and can see why Charles so loves being in the RAF.

The Mk IV Blenheim twin-engine bomber that Charles was now training on had a crew of three, a pilot, a navigator/bomb aimer and air gunner/radio operator. It was armed with a machine gun in the port wing, two in the turret and two rearward-firing guns beneath the nose.

Charles and Eric Hewson urged David to make a huge effort to transfer into the Air Force however many hurdles the Army put in his way. They all felt that it was a good time to try because the RAF was so short of pilots.

Back at Portsmouth there was terrific bombing and an Ack-Ack barrage but I am so used to them now they mean nothing. However I don't know if I will ever get used to Muffett for I've never heard anyone so noisy from the time he gets up to the time he goes to sleep and after.

Other people agreed with David. Muffett was described as a cross between Falstaff and Captain Mainwaring, a bear of a man with a bristling moustache and 'blessed with a voice that was difficult to ignore.'[22]

The interior of a Mk IV Blenheim bomber. *(Mark Murphy)*

The next day David took his first unintentional step towards a transfer to the RAF. The platoon was on an attack exercise and the Brigadier came round before David was ready, and finally his frustration with the Army blew up.

> After today's fiasco, my life in the Army may soon be nearing its end. I had a slightly heated conversation with the Brigadier. He bawled me out because I didn't stop my platoon's exercise on the arrival of a Flag Officer. In despair I snapped back, 'Heaven help the Army if this is how they operate. I am endeavouring to run a realistic attack here.'

The Brigadier was clearly taken aback by David's attitude and once back at barracks Major Stevenson summoned David and demanded an explanation. Stevenson said that the Brigadier had taken a very dim view of David's remarks, felt that he was not cut out for the infantry and not likely to make a good Army officer. David said he wished to apply for a transfer to the RAF and Major Stevenson replied that after David's behaviour, he sincerely hoped that he was successful.

> My God, I have never hated anything so much in all my life as this damned stuff we are on. I'm going to do everything in my power to get into the RAF. I shall stop at nothing. I have another three weeks of hell before I go to Clarence Barracks but it can't be worse than this. We marched over 100 miles last week doing schemes and we slept out last night. I thought the straw would keep me warm, but by 03.00 I was highly disillusioned.

One of David's University friends was also having a rough week. Peter Storie-Pugh, having escaped from a PoW camp and, after breaking his ankle while attempting to jump onto a moving train, was transferred to Colditz. Storie-Pugh's first impressions were daunting; he described it as 'a whopping great castle.'[23]

Peter Storie Pugh (left),Colditz Castle. *(With kind permission © P. Storie Pugh)*

December 5. Southampton had a bad raid last week and one of our companies is down there guarding time-bombs and cordoning areas off to stop looting. We have had some exciting raids this week. As I got back to the Mess, great whistles came and there were three colossal explosions just behind the school. It knocked the houses down but amazingly only killed one person. The craters of the bomb were only two yards from the edge of an Anderson shelter yet the four occupants inside were uninjured. A baby of just three months was not even crying when our people got there to release them. Martin[24] said how extraordinarily cool they were about it. There is a very strange sight, for a bicycle adorns the chimney of the next house; it looks like a huge stork's nest.

I just got back to my rooms, when there was a colossal explosion just down the road. Later we heard that the Carlton Cinema and a block of flats and shops which I had left only two hours before had been hit.[25] The whole place seemed ablaze and it was as light as day. The rain and weather saved us from any more attacks and within three quarters of an hour every fire was out.

Charles wrote a week later:

Andover, 12 December.
We've heard from Harry Butler that Jimmy Barker[26], my best friend at Cranwell, has been killed at Cranwell while night-flying in an Oxford. He was a good sort, but did not want to go on an Instructor's Course. He used to say that he wanted the war to end so he could go and climb Mt Kilimanjaro in Africa, and maybe he would have been killed doing that if it did not come to him this way.

I am going to fly in the dark tonight, first time in Blenheims. It will only be as passenger to see what they are like. We are doing operational training now, bombing, reconnaissance, photography etc, which makes flying interesting and I am getting more and more pleased with Blens and glad I got onto them.

C.

Chapter Four

The Blitz, Portsmouth and Tyneham:
December 1940 to April 1941

A junior Army officer is 'Told to cultivate self-reliance and initiative. Don't believe a word of it. The first is almost insubordination and the second almost mutiny.'

'Hints for Subalterns' by Guy Paget

At last, on December 14, David finished his monotonous training and drove to Clarence Barracks. His room had a view of the sea and there was an anti-aircraft gun just across the road from his window. David hoped that the gunner would not turn his elevation wheel the wrong way and land a shell in his room instead of on a German plane.

An anti-aircraft gun was positioned just across the road from David's room in the imposing Clarence Barracks. *(SAGH)*

Since I told Major Stevenson just what I thought of the Infantry and my desire to transfer he has been awfully pleasant to me. I hear when he was acting C/O he told the Brigadier off about being abusive to Captain Allen and myself. I must keep this quiet though; he is now the only man left in this joint for whom I have a certain awe. In the afternoon I went to Southampton and it was a pathetic sight. Most of the shops are shut and there are fewer houses standing than those smashed to pieces. Furniture and goods from the shops stand unguarded and unsalvaged on the roadsides although it has been over a fortnight since the big raid. One has to look for miles before one can find any shop still open.

That evening the guns went off and nearly shook David out of bed.

Monday, 16 December. I think I have wangled Xmas leave. Wouldn't it be grand!
    I was Orderly Officer today. Steve mounted guard at 08.30 and I acted as supernumerary on the clothing board with Major Peter Flower, he was immaculate with eyeglass and gloves and he picked up socks as though they were snakes!

The next day Charles again wrote:

Andover.
I have been bombing on a target today. The sea looked beautiful from 8,000 feet in the air. We got all the bombs into the danger area but not all of them close to the target! I had a difficult landing in a rainstorm the other day. The brakes were useless and the short grass and slippery mud gave negative grip and we slewed along the aerodrome sideways for sometime before stopping. (We go along side-ways quite often.) I have been taking photographs from the air, very interesting work.
    With the weather and other troubles with the aeroplanes, we only average an hour and a bit flying per day and what we do on the ground does not amount to much. I only got two hours sleep last night but I was not tired. We passed over Harborough Square but could not linger as we were off to Bury St Edmunds. The Hospital Trains at the railway bridges in Leicester Lane are black on top now. I expect they showed up on moonlit nights.
    My friend Paul has been reported 'missing believed killed.' I had hoped I was misinformed but now he is in the Casualty List. I never saw him at Andover as I expected to. I dreamt that I met Peggy and conveyed the news to her a few nights back….
                        Yours, love Charles.

(Paul Baillon was killed in a dogfight over Bournemouth by Luftwaffe Ace Major Helmut Wick. Baillon was the fifty-sixth and last aircraft Wick shot down for in the same dog-fight Wick was shot down by Flight Lieutenant John Dundas).[1]
    Just before Christmas, Richard Osborn wrote that he and his brother[2] were to be posted soon:

RAF Harwell, 19/12/40

David…, I've been here all the time getting more and more browned off with life in general. If you do transfer to the RAF, I hope for your sake you don't have to spend six months in a dead-beat hole like Harwell…. My other flying brother is flying out east any day now. He's not very keen about it, but I envy him being up against it out there compared with the prospect of Germany – with winter conditions and the ice worry…. I've done very little actual flying at the controls so god knows what I will be like when I go to a squadron. I shall be scared out of my pants in any case, but I daren't think what my flying will be like. Sometime ago, when I took over in an emergency, landing on a lousy night with 4–500 ft cloud base, I didn't save the affair. The plane dropped from 30 feet so we tried to go around again. The plane was flying like a brick and amongst other things I thought the air speed indicator was reading far too slow. When it was eventually tested and found to be OK, my hair stood on end at the thought of the speeds we were doing. We all got out OK but the plane was a mess. So next time you give about £25,000 to Lord Beaverbrook, tell him it's to buy a new Wellington to replace mine!

Merry Xmas. Yours Richard.

On Monday, 23 December, Portsmouth residents' Christmas shopping was spoilt when a German plane was shot down by anti-aircraft guns and a huge explosion ripped through Conway Street. It was thought that the bomber had been carrying a massive high-explosive bomb or several mines that it had intended to drop in the Solent.

It devastated a huge area and all the windows for a mile or so around here have gone. All that was found of the plane was a bit of the propeller in the Docks. The crew didn't stand a chance; what a waste of life all round.

David went home on leave and on Christmas Day heard Provost Dick Howard broadcast a sermon on the BBC from the roofless remains of Coventry Cathedral

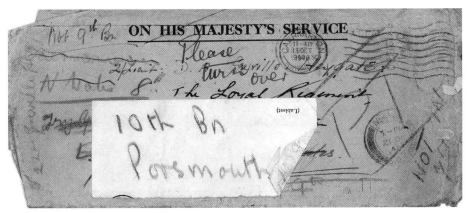

Letters followed David around the country before catching up with him in Portsmouth. *(Family Collection)*

asking the people of Great Britain to put away all thoughts of revenge.[3] In Burma, Anson Howard also listened to the broadcast.

2nd Derajat Mountain Battery R.A. (F.F.) Maymyo, 27/12/40
Christmas Day was two days ago and we had a very good time. The highlight of the day for me was hearing my father open the Empire Broadcast on the BBC. It was a weird experience hearing his voice; he came over very well too. But I had no idea that the cathedral at Coventry had been so completely gutted by fire, leaving hardly one stone standing on another.

I often wonder what has happened to all my friends in England. I would love to write to them only it is so difficult to know if they are still alive or not....
Yours Anson.

After leave, David arrived back to rumours that the battalion was to move to Tyneham, a village near Corfe Castle. New Year's Eve passed quietly. Little did the residents of Portsmouth know that just over a week later they would experience a bombing raid almost equal in ferocity to Coventry.

I very nearly got into communication with the Army about transfer of all fit men of any service to fly if they wished, as they could easily be sent back to their former jobs when they were wanted, and they would be of special value because of their new experiences. However, an Army Command instruction came out authorising the exact thing I was going to propose! So I put in my application for the RAF and Pip is thinking of doing the same.

In the evening Tiny and I went to the Queen's Brassiere where I met Pud Vigors[4] and a friend of Andrew's. There's a picture in Tatler of Tim Vigors with his DFC; he looks just the same, quite as mischievous, and I must write to congratulate him.

In October, Tim Vigors received the DFC for destroying nine enemy aircraft. His squadron had suffered heavy casualties; he twice crash-landed and openly admitted moments of extreme fear.[5]

10 January 1941. Dr Herbert has just come back from Ireland. He said how grand it was to see icing, cream and butter, no blackout, shop windows lighted up and cars with glaring headlights. Typical Irish, they had less petrol than us but they went on using it until it had all gone, then rationed it and though one can get coupons, one cannot get any petrol with them!

I can't think what's up. We have had no raids since I came back from leave. Still I mustn't complain. It is freezing here and the snow seems to have kept Hitler away fairly satisfactorily (so far).

David spoke too soon, for in the evening the Luftwaffe made its presence felt once again. The first raid started at about 18.00 when incendiary bombs started fires all over the city and David soon found himself in the thick of it.

There was the most terrific Blitz. It was rather thrilling while it lasted and I think I owe my life to the fact that the telephone from the police station to the barracks was put out of order. At about seven, just as Tiny and I were going over to inspect the barrack rooms the thing started. A terrific bomb fell towards the docks and showers came down all around then a blazing furnace started up fairly near. It lit up the whole town. Then there was a shower of incendiaries mixed with heavy explosives. We decided to postpone the barrack room inspection and went down to the basement instead. As we took cover, great showers of sparks came down all around. Once or twice, we thought the whole Mess was coming down on top of us, for it swayed madly as they were coming down 30–40 yards off each time. We kept going out to smother the incendiaries whenever we heard them come whistling down.

David was then called to the Commanding Officer and told to take thirty men down to Southsea Police Station to help them clear burning streets and shops. He said, 'Goodbye and good luck.'

From his tone, I felt sure that he didn't expect to see me again. We set off and it was like a scene from hell. Everything seemed ablaze, guns crashing and bombs whistling down. We tried to get along King's Road but a burning church stopped us because it fell across the road right in front of us. We finally managed to get to the station and we went out in various parties to help clear the streets, put out incendiaries and rescue people and equipment. Hanley's went up like a petrol dump and at Sears and Wells we stripped the shop models of their fur coats. It felt almost indecent, for in the fires' glow, the dummies looked very lifelike, but those coats alone must have cost about £4,000. I think my men

The aftermath of the raid on January 10. Handley's Corner 'went up like a petrol dump.' *(By kind permission of The News Portsmouth)*

must have saved about £20,000 worth of stuff. Only one of my men was injured, sustaining a broken arm. I released two Shetland ponies tied up by a burning stable and turned them out into the streets. We could have saved half the town, if we had had water, but it was not until they got the London Fire Brigade and the Brighton one that we could get water from the sea.

When David returned to the barracks, the canteen, Adjutant's Office, Orderly Room and the Mess were on fire, but the staff rescued most of their kit. David rushed to the garages where the C.O.'s car was already burning, but his was not yet on fire.

I drove it out and put it in the open, on the tennis court. Many incendiaries fell near it but were put out by all who had come from the shelters. The C.O. was upset, not because his car was a write-off, but because his best fishing rod was in the boot. They saved quite a lot of the Mess and we can still live here, though from the doorway of my room I can look out on open air. The firemen and civilians were wonderful but it was pathetic to see the hundreds of homeless families with babies, cats and dogs streaming away from the wrecks of what were once their homes. It was sheer devilry for they did not bother about bombing the docks, which are practically untouched. By midnight, the whole city seemed to be burning.

As well as most of the buildings in Kings Road, Commercial Road and the High Street being gutted, several churches, the power station, the Royal Hospital and the Guildhall were destroyed.[6] Over the next few days David and his men had little sleep.

Clearing up after the raid took several days. *(By kind permission of The News Portsmouth)*

Monday, 13 January. We cleared the streets and helped the homeless. They came back to collect whatever they could salvage from the smouldering ruins of what had once been their homes. But even in such terrible circumstances, they were able to make jokes. One publican, holding a smashed bottle of whisky, looked at the wreck of his pub and said, 'They can break our spirits, but they won't break our hearts!'

If there had been one person above ground to every three houses or shops then there would have been less damage as the incendiaries were easy to put out if one could get to them in time. We made a recce of the town. There was no looting I am pleased to say. Our barracks are without light, gas or water so I am writing this by candlelight. I am very fortunate that I only lost my camp bed, some underclothes, a sheet, a cane and a picture of Cornwall in the fire and I am shaving in cold salt water, which is very painful.

A new civilian fire-watching scheme is being put into force soon. The fires are easy to stop if they are dealt with at once but if left only 10 minutes, whole streets may be lost.

There is still no news from the RAF even though there is now a desperate need for pilots but I am still hopeful of success. Mother and Father dread having all three sons in the Air Force, but I told them that if I get a transfer I'll go like a shot. I have decided that to fight well I need to fight alone. I must get

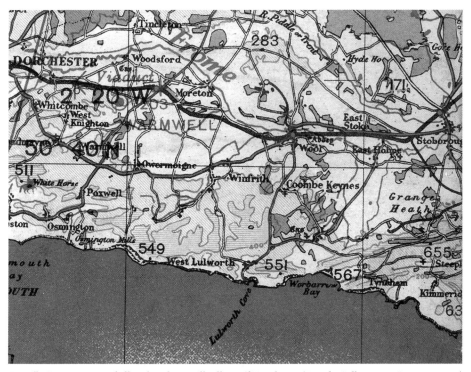

David's Company were billeted in the small village of Tyneham. *(Family Collection – Crown © 1943)*

an aeroplane and fight in it no matter what stands in my way, even if I have to resign my commission or desert.

While David was brushing up his Morse code, Vivienne Lee, having left Biggin Hill, was now learning the difficult techniques of scrambling and deciphering Army, Navy and Air Force codes at Oxford. She added 'Just for your peace of mind, we had a wizard time at Biggin Hill with lots of parties and dances etc and really, I was awfully sad to leave except I'd been there long enough, nearly a year.'

On 1 February 1941, the Company finally received the much delayed orders to move to Tyneham and frantically packed the sixty huge lorries parked on the barrack square in preparation for the move next morning. After dinner in the Mess, David met the Brigadier once again.

> I was feeling in good form, everybody seemed to be very glad about going and the Brigadier quite unfolded and was most pleasant. He had had a long chat with Winston Churchill and I think that had bucked him up. He was very nice to me and I have a feeling he thought more of me for having that row with him than if I had been silent, for he was more complimentary to me than to any of the other subalterns.

With all the equipment loaded onto lorries, everyone was worried as to what would happen if the Germans bombed the barracks during the night, but luck was with them. Rising early, everyone was packed into blacked out buses. The weather was fine as they drove in convoy through the New Forest; however by the time they reached Poole, the weather had turned very wintery. It began snowing hard and turned extremely cold. By the time they arrived at Tyneham, the wind and snow had developed into a full-scale blizzard, and of the nineteen troop-carrying lorries in the convoy, nine were stuck in snowdrifts or ditches and the hill road soon became impassable.

> Most of the men are to stay in the rectory so they are not badly off – that is when compared to the searchlights! The rectory was almost overflowing with The Queen's Own Royal West Kent, who are not moving out now until the morning,

The 'Loyals' were ordered to defend the Dorset coast from Lulworth Cove to Swanage. *(SAGH)*

as well as our Company, odd drivers and various other parties stranded by the snow. I was very pleased to see my car arrive several hours later, for all my goods and bedding were inside it. After unpacking we had lunch with the West Kent Officers. The hills are so steep and the snow is so bad that no one can get in or out of the village. The troop-carrying lorries, which were meant to be back in Weston-Super-Mare tonight, are still stuck in ditches.

Nestled at the bottom of a valley with rolling hills on either side Tyneham was a small isolated village close to the Dorset Coast. The village consisted of Home Farm, a Manor House and Rectory, as well as about a dozen houses, a small school and church. The sea and Worbarrow, a small fishing hamlet, was a mile south. The Army had requisitioned several of the larger houses and the officers were billeted with local residents.[7] Company Commander Captain Allen, second-in-command Lieutenant Higgins and David were billeted at Gwyle Cottage, home to Harry and Marjorie Grant. They found the cottage charming, and the furniture beautiful, having come out of the Grand Hotel in Swanage, but they were the only men in the battalion without electric light, hot water or gas.

The following day The Kents marched off carrying all their kit with them to meet the buses at the top of the hill. The rectory that looked so bleak yesterday has improved on closer inspection. It is a square house, very large for the village, with a tennis court and looks as if it must have been very jolly in peacetime. Battalion HQ at Home Farm is a lovely place, beautifully furnished. It has stables, its own electric light plant, central heating, a grand piano in the lounge and goodness knows what else.

David's Company was to defend the coastline from Lulworth Cove to Swanage. There was a small gun position, but at first they had very little in the way of weapons, equipped only with Canadian .300 rifles with thirty rounds of ammo each and homemade hand grenades made from old bottles filled with spirit.

Wednesday, 5 February. I am working harder here than anywhere else I've been, from dawn until 11 pm, trying to get things straight. As I am president of the Mess Committee I have to get the officers' food in. We can get fresh eggs but unfortunately, our cook can't make pastry or puddings so I'll have to get some instructions for him. In Gwyle Cottage, we had a Valour oil stove for cooking, but they asked for it back so now we have a petrol stove and the taste of petrol seems to get into all our food.

David met the Bond family who were still living at Tyneham House. Ralph Bond, the 'last Squire of Tyneham' was a local magistrate and Home Guard platoon commander, and had extended the offer of a permanent invitation to officers to drop into the house at any time if they wanted a bath.

The old lady must be nearly 90 and says she has met Mother and Father. They have a beautiful golden retriever and some good shooting land. I'll take my gun out if I get a chance and I do wish I had Rob here; he would love the walks and would be a great companion.

On Sunday, David drove along a steep road to Brandy Bay and his car was nearly blown over a precipice by the wind, for the roads were solid ice. The Army had commandeered the Duke of Somerset's summer residence overlooking the bay. David was most envious of the luxury he found there and for once even he was impressed by a senior officer.

> Brigadier Templer[8] is superlative. He was, some years ago, a Major in charge of one of our Companies under Colonel Collins. He gave the best talk or rather the most impressive that I have ever heard. He makes the officers go for a six mile run every week – including the Colonel.

During the week Peter Williams, one of the platoon commanders, went on leave, so David moved down to his room in a small cottage overlooking Worbarrow Bay.

> I am billeted with a spinster and her two nieces. Miss Ellis is one of those slightly old-fashioned ladies whom children love to spend their holidays with. She is very kind and cheery and I believe was in the USA until about 15 years ago, Anne, her niece is about 19, very jolly and a great country girl. Mary, the other niece is nursing, but is on leave at present. I thought at first that three women in a house are two too many! But now I think it has done me good, I am beginning to find things to talk about and I am not so shy.

Signed off sick for a week while recovering from a bout of flu, Charles wrote to David.

Andover, 14 Feb 1941.
Save us from spinsters if they are like Sylvia! (She's engaged now). Duddie is also engaged to Captain Steve Boycott in the Ulster Searchlights, which made me sad for a while. I told the M.D. I wanted to start flying again but I still have a bad cold and had a headache all day....

   We have ten more Army fellows here on No.24 War Course and I hope you hear something soon. Rowle said I ought to be ready for your C.O. with 'He's

Miss Ellis' cottage at Worbarrow Bay. *(Family Collection)*

acting entirely on his own initiative I believe Sir,' when tackled for enticing you from the Army to the RAF!

Although it is probably not the right thing to say, at the moment I am actually enjoying the war. I have had fun flying in and out the clouds like a goldfish in a rocky pool....

Take care, Love Charles.

On February 15, Private Norman Barnes of 'A' Company was accidentally shot dead on guard mounting parade, so after giving his soldiers yet another lecture on weapons' safety, David took the platoon for a run to Arish Mell, a popular bay for picnickers before the war.

We found an invasion barge (German[9]) on the beach. I love being down there as we can sometimes find shells, cornelian and amber in beautiful shades of red and brown. Revetting the trenches was the first task in both of the forward positions. Then we had live firing practise, we fired ten rounds from each weapon and threw one grenade. The coastline is grand and though it is only February, it seems like spring but I never feel quite safe at my position as the officer from the Engineers was blown up with the plans of the mines, but they have been re-plotted and another map is on its way. I think I know where they are all now but it is rather amusing taking a pace and not knowing if you are going up in smoke each pace further, it lends interest to walking!

Wednesday, 19 February 1941. In spite of all my warnings, Private Huskin of my platoon let off a round in the guardroom; luckily this time no one was hurt. We went out on a training march and threw live grenades, several of which failed to explode, which didn't give us the greatest confidence in their use in the event of an attack. Still it was great fun. Less amusing, we found a human foot in an army sock on the beach presumed to belong to the officer blown up while plotting the mines.

February 22 was a Red Letter day for David when a telegram arrived requesting that he attended an RAF interview. Charles dropped in for the day and after lunch they drove over to visit David Muffett at Brandy Bay. Muffett had just had a lucky escape from a minefield on his stretch of the beach. While checking his map for mine positions, an old fisherman came up to him to say that due to the stormy weather the sand had shifted them all and his map was useless. However, knowing the beach like the back of his hand, he could give him a rough guide as to where they were. Muffett quickly sent someone down to the beach to re-plot their positions.

Late in the afternoon, as it was still raining, Charles decided to stay the night, gambling on the next day being a 'no flying day.' They sat up until late, chatting. Charles went through questions he thought that David might be asked at his interview. Arriving back at Andover, Charles discovered that he had been required to fly, but his crew had covered up his absence saying that he was somewhere in camp but they couldn't find him. The Flight Lieutenant said that as long as Charles flew at some point in the day it would be fine and luckily it started raining again, and all flying was cancelled.

Along with Peter Hutton and Alfred Richard Howell, who were also invited for an interview, David rose early on February 24 and caught the train to Oxford. While waiting for the interview with the aviation board at the Old Clarendon Labs, David met a friend from Marlborough and one who knew Charles. After the interview and medical ordeal was over, they all piled into the bar.

> They are the nicest bunch of people I've met for a long time, almost like my old chums at Cambridge. I feel even more sure now that I am doing the right thing. I've accepted an offer of a lift home early tomorrow as I should like to see Father who has been quite ill for some time. I'll probably get into fearful trouble for going AWOL when I get back but I am past caring what the Army think of me!

The next morning the family were very surprised to see David walk in and his father cheered up no end. David arrived back at Tyneham in time to have dinner with two pilots from No.152

John 'Pip' Hutton. (*Tim Hutton Collection*)

Squadron. Eric Marrs and Dudley Williams[10] (Peter's brother) were stationed nearby at RAF Warmwell. Just a month earlier both had received the DFC for shooting down five or six enemy aircraft.

> *Saturday, 1 March.* Out on practise night manoeuvres. It was a foul night, with teeming rain, spray flying off the sea and a howling gale. On the way down near Corfe Castle our 3-ton lorry broke a small bridge and one wheel went over the side. We nearly overturned although we were only going about 3 mph. The lorry gradually tilted further and further over. We were very worried as we had no end of primed bombs and other novelties on board that could easily have gone up. Fortunately, we managed to right the lorry without any of the fireworks going off.
>
> One of the security officers, dressed as a German parachutist complete with swastika and steel helmet, drove his motorbike right through Wareham Corps. He was saluted and waved on by the Military Police and walked right into the Battalion's HQ. Here he confronted the Adjutant and balled him out about his soldiers' appalling lack of security. The officer turned the air positively blue with his language. 'God help us if the f…ing Germans ever get f…ing across the f…ing channel because it's f…ing clear from this f…ing exercise that the f…ing Army can't stop them!!'
>
> One of my men refused to carry out my orders so I am now involved in a court martial arising from it. It is rather aggravating for though it is not a crime that I have committed, one always has that guilty feeling that something will

crop up, which might be awkward. I am slightly nervous for, judging from the Law of England and the Manual of Military Law, I feel that unless I say the same thing about 20 times in 20 different ways including 'to wit', 'aforesaid', and 'the undermentioned person', I might come unstuck.

Nearing the end of his training and also encountering problems, Charles was relieved when a difficult decision was resolved:

Andover.
I had been hoping to reorganize my crew for although I liked my Air Gunner very much he was not very satisfactory. The Squadron Leader's verdict was that we must make mine (who I said was hopeless) do better. He said, 'We can do that, you and I can't we', and I had replied rather shyly, 'We can have a bloody good try!' This seemed to please him no end. However, it looked as though I should be a month or year on the job and I was saved this by his falling sick the next day. I was allotted another one who is much more intelligent. Sergeant Naylor is a very efficient new crew member; his original pilot cut his hand badly on a propeller and is off flying duty for sometime. Naylor is well over 6 ft tall and is very squashed in his small turret....

I telephoned a very nice WAAF officer, Josephine Pipon that I danced with at Marlow's on New Year's Eve and I took her to a Mess Ball. She is not unattractive, works at Upavon and I intend and hope to see her again so I shall be finishing at Andover as I started – jolly....

Yours, Charles.

While David waited nervously for the results of his RAF interview, Charles was posted to No.53 Squadron which was in the middle of a move from Thorney Island in Hampshire to St Eval in Cornwall. Here, as part of Coastal Command, No.53 Squadron was to fly patrols and anti-shipping operations off the French Coast. Coastal Command was also tasked with carrying out daylight raids on Brest, a heavily defended port used by the German Navy, to attack the enemy battle cruisers '*Scharnhorst*' and '*Gneisenau*' berthed there. These cruisers had sunk over twenty ships when they last sailed and the British Navy wanted them put out of action.

Over the next few days, Charles ferried aircraft down to St Eval and once settled wrote again.

Officers' Mess, St Eval, 18 March 1941.
David, you would love this aerodrome. My billet is a beautiful spot. I have a corner room in the Watergate Bay Hotel with splendid views of the coastline in either direction when the sun shines but every other day it seems to be foggy and wet. It does seem a long way from the centre of England. For example, I may mention that we have not yet had the morning papers and it is now five minutes to three. There are plenty of eggs, bacon and cheese in this district – and chips – so we sometimes go out to eat in the evening. They also serve the best teas in England, with hot toast, biscuits and cake. The flying at St Eval is more interesting than it was at any other aerodrome and I am thoroughly enjoying it. It calls for more skill as we fly in almost any weather. I am very

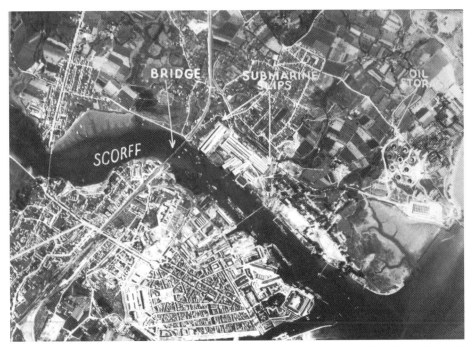

Lorient Docks. Charles noted in his Log Book, 'Weather stormy, low cloud but fine at Lorient.'
(SAGH – NRO AIR34/744)

proud of the squadron, especially when our efforts are mentioned on the BBC
bulletins or in the newspaper....

Blenheim flying is a most speedy and comfortable way to travel, a little jaunt
of 600 miles only took 3hrs 10min.... Must stop and go to sleep....

Your affectionate brother, Charles.

On March 23, Charles flew his first operational flight, an uneventful 'Bust' patrol
which was abandoned after an hour when the cloud lifted. With better cover on 27th,
Charles and his crew took off for Brest. Flying in at 5,000 feet, through light and
heavy flak, they dropped two 500-lb bombs on the depot ship the 'Condorcet,' an old
five-funnelled battleship, but the crew were unable to confirm if bombs hit the ship
as Charles took such violent evasive action to avoid being shot down.[11]

With privileged leave granted, David went home and everyone was delighted to
see him. After a few days rest he drove down to visit Rosemary in Devon. They went
for long walks, a film and a dance before David reluctantly returned to Tyneham on
the 27th.

I spent the day learning Higgy's job before he goes on leave tomorrow. I couldn't
find Muffett anywhere but eventually tracked him down in the maze of tunnels,
all at least 8 ft deep, that he has now dug, there's even an underground kitchen
and a latrine. I'm afraid that unless my transfer comes through soon I shall have

to do a lot more marching, but I shall be marching light, for my heart is in the RAF already!

On April Fool's Day, David received the news he had been impatiently waiting for when a telegram came through accepting him for pilot training.

Charles's 27th birthday was on April 4 and he was now flying in all weather conditions. On a convoy escort duty west of Ilfracombe, he flew figures of eight over the sea scanning for submarines and enemy bombers.[12]

Four days later, David attended a farewell party arranged for him by his men, and after saying his goodbyes he drove home.

Flying to Brest on another daylight-bombing mission on the 9th, Charles spotted a battle cruiser lying alongside the torpedo boat station. Dropping several bombs, he took violent action to avoid very heavy flak and was again unable to see if the bombs had had any effect. Flak, smashed his intercom and shrapnel went through the starboard engine casing, and out through the propeller. The first Charles knew of the extent of the damage was when the engine appeared to fail as his observer pulled on the boost handle. To add to their problems, as they were pulling away they were attacked by several Me109s. Naylor was unable to fire at them, as the rear-gunner's turret turned too slowly. Fortunately, the 109s did not press home the attack, and nursing his Blenheim home, Charles made a skilful landing with a punctured port wheel.[13]

The almost daily brush with death set Charles thinking of the future and knowing that there was a great likelihood that his aircraft would be shot down in the next few weeks, he wrote to warn the family.

St Eval, 11/4/41.
Dear Father…, Re the car: I always leave the keys in my rooms and the car will be safe there for a few weeks if it was left on the base. If I was killed or missing you would have various choices, even before Probate and the Officers here would help you all they could. You could either sell it, go down and fetch it, have it sent by train or hire a driver to take it home. The RAF would provide you with enough petrol coupons for the return trip I dare say. If I went abroad I would get 'embarkation leave' and bring it home. I have seen two British ships sunk by enemy action, it makes one realize the truth of the posters 'Waste means lives lost,' and one so admires the merchant ships….

Yours affectionately, Charles.

Part III

RAF Flight Training

Chapter Five

RAF Initial Training Wing, Cambridge: April 1941 to June 1941

'The British system of flying training is the finest in the world…. The aim is to produce pilots who can out fly and out fight the best pilots of any other nation.' 'Britain's Wonderful Air Force.' Editor – Air Commodore Fellows DFC.

The RAF celebrated its twenty-first birthday on 1 April 1939 and as the youngest of the three Services, it did not have the rigid conventions and customs of either the Army or the Navy. Huge responsibilities were placed on the young pilots and, as many flew solo or with small crews, independent thinking and self-confidence were recognized as positive virtues. This suited David's temperament, and having escaped the constraints and rigidity of the Army, he was determined to try his hardest to become a first-class pilot. In peacetime a pilot was taught to be a flyer first and then trained as a fighter. This training took up to two years, but with the desperate need for new pilots this had been halved. David was undeterred by the shortened syllabus, as far as he was concerned, the sooner he was flying the better.

The first stage of Air Force training was at an Initial Training Wing. Here the cadets, kept well away from any aircraft, were expected to gain a thorough knowledge of essential ground subjects, including the theory of flight, aircraft recognition, law, signals, the structure of command and most importantly, navigation.

David's course was made up of forty-four Army Officers and four other Officers. Two cadets shared a bedroom and a sitting room. Paired with Bewick Hack, David quickly agreed to move one bed into the sitting room to make two single rooms. He was delighted.

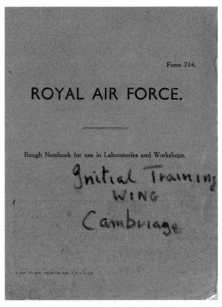

David's RAF ITW Cadet notebook.
(Family collection – © Crown Copyright.)

12 April 1941, No 2 ITW. It's grand to be back in Cambridge with a good crowd and at last I can write that I am in training to be a pilot. I'm in 'A' Flight, No.1 Squadron. We are based at Selwyn College not Jesus as I was expecting,

David found time to embellish his ITW notes with doodles. *(Family collection)*

but I mustn't complain about a little thing like this. There are about 40 on the course and they are a spirited bunch and like me, all are 'Army Rebels.' Although we are the first course to go through here we are being looked after very well with an excellent batman, excellent messing and hardly any restrictions. There is a completely different atmosphere to any I have found in the Army. I think the reason is fundamentally the superiority of the RAF over the Germans, also instead of being a subaltern who, when the day comes, can go ahead of his men into battle and it matters not if he is lost, here there seems to be individual care of each person.

David went to the King's Easter Service then walked through the cloisters and down to the river.

It seems a little strange to be back, for in spite of the war, Cambridge still has an air of peace about it. I think of Peter Pugh when I walk through Queens', Andrew when I walk by Trinity and of Anson down at Jesus College.

David hoped that he might meet friends when the undergraduates came back, but he didn't have to wait that long, for he soon spotted his old cavalry groom cycling past. They had a long chat before David walked up to the Union for tea and then went out drinking at the Baron of Beef in Bridge Street.

Monday, 14 April. Up at six, which was rather an effort after last night! The real work starts today. We have lectures all day, from 8–6, with an hour's break for lunch.

Charles, excited that David was at last training with the RAF, wrote a long letter with helpful advice about flying. He also hinted at the dangerous work he was carrying out.

St Eval, 16.4.41
I am thrilled by the important news that you are at No.2 ITW. It is a new idea sending Army Officers there. Now you are entering a flying career let me give you one or two bits of advice. It is rather terrifying having one's first few lessons. In peacetime the instructors seemed so fierce to me. Heyward – I think was really fierce. He had to take up a different job. Now Heyward taught me these things:

1. Stand up to your instructor.
2. If you don't feel you are suited to each other, ask the Chief Flying Officer to change your instructor.
3. Don't let your instructor hustle you. It is quite difficult getting dressed up in flying clothes with the parachute, helmet, goggles, headphones and safety harness. He will just have to wait till you are ready and be patient.
4. Listen to everything the instructor says, remember to carry it out. Things like cockpit drill. It may seem to be unnecessary, but it won't be.
5. Temper Dash with Discretion. Dash untempered claims many victims.
6. Watch your air speed. I have seen many pupils stall in Tiger Moths.
7. Take an interest in Theory of Flight and Engines, if they are on your syllabus. If the lectures are no good, talk to the instructors individually. Or better still the Engineering Officers. The technical men!
8. I never learnt a thing at aircraft recognition lectures, it all went in one ear and out the other. What I now know is from looking at pictures in Airplane and Flight every time I have a few minutes to spare, and of course from observation. I don't want to see any German planes in the sky as I am not certain I should beat them in combat and I don't ever expect an Italian one – there aren't many left. But if you want to be a fighter pilot you will need to be good at recognising aircraft – friend and enemy.

I must not sermonize too long.

My job at present is connected with *Scharnhorst* and *Gneisenau*, generally as the Germans know and the *Daily Mail* discusses the matter pretty freely so I hope I won't get court-martialed for telling you. I have an aeroplane of my own but it is damaged by cannon shell holes….

Yours Ever, Charles.

The undergrads came back in the middle of April and David met up with Johnny Earp[1] who was still studying at Jesus College.

He said that the last time he had seen me was when I was on the searchlights looking very dirty and quite an old man and I now looked as though I had just come back from a pleasure cruise and years younger! To my great joy I heard that Richard Osborn is at an aerodrome only five miles from here. If he gets back alright from night Ops I will meet him tomorrow.

While at the hairdressers, David was surprised to recognize the person sitting in the next chair. It was Peter Conant, now working with the Intelligence Corps and on a five-week German Interrogation Course as he spoke fluent German and French. Peter Conant was just as delighted as David to be back in Cambridge. In his autobiography he wrote.… 'Term was in full swing and I met many old friends, in fact it seemed like being back at University.'[2]

I used to wonder if the type of people I like had all been taken prisoner or killed, owing to the fact that they were so keen that they had gone overseas at once. Although many have gone that way, I have found that type again here. After meeting Peter Conant at the Baron we went on to a party with some very lively RAF types from Oakington, who were celebrating their rescue from the North Sea yesterday after their Wellington developed engine trouble. They had ditched in the sea and a trawler, the SS *River Spey* had spotted their rubber dinghy.

On April 16, Roy Elliott[3] and his crew from No.3 PRU were returning from a raid on Bremen when their bomber caught fire. Ditching the aircraft in the North Sea near Lowestoft, the crew of six, plus two extra passengers were picked up. Arriving back at RAF Oakington, Elliott and his crew met Lord Trenchard[4] who, hearing of their lucky escape, gave them a week's leave.

This has been the happiest week since the outbreak of war. We have some really grand chaps in this Flight. Ian Duffus[5] was in the same class at Marlborough College as Charles and Bob Cranston[6] was at Queens' with me; they are the tops! After lectures I met up with Peter Conant at the Union and we saw a grand exhibition of an Me109[7] in the Newmarket Weapons Week parade.

During the week, Richard Osborn invited David to a house-warming party at RAF Waterbeach. The first Wellingtons from No.99 Squadron had arrived a month earlier and were flying armed recces on German naval ships in the North Sea, as well as carrying out bombing raids on docks and industrial targets in France. Charles continued bombing Brest docks and on April 20 and 23, they again attacked the battle cruisers moored in the harbour.

Officers' Mess St Eval.
I have lots to tell you about this life of mine. I get so tired as it's ages since I had a good night's sleep. The work I do is very hazardous and therefore I love it. I never do anything risky when I can avoid it, but when circumstances lead me to it, it's grand. Do you remember we used to discuss this question of risk and

A Blenhem IV bomber flying over occupied France (SAGH © NRO Air 34/744).

feeling frightened when riding out to meets of hounds? Well I attempt to live each day as if it was my last in certain matters, such as answering letters and leaving my car key where it would be found! I find an added spice in life and appreciative sense of all good and beautiful things in the world. I am quite dead to the horrors of war and applaud a good bomber pilot even if he is German (couldn't done better myself!) and then add, 'May he crash in flames before he gets back.'

I went back over to Andover a few days ago and we had to leave at 5 am. I wondered if I should ever wake but then a miracle occurred for at 4.40 about ten bombs nearby woke me up, so I leisurely dressed! My luck has been amazing....

Must stop now, Love Charles.

Charles's belief that luck was on his side was echoed by many pilots, including Battle of Britain pilot, Peter Townsend. He wrote:

Some of us would die within the next few days. That was inevitable. But you did not believe that it would be you. Death was always present, and we knew it for what it was…. Some strange, protecting veil kept the nightmare thought from our minds, as did the loss of our friends. Their disappearance struck us as less a solid blow than a dark shadow, which chilled our hearts and passed on.'[8]

Newspaper reports began to criticize the RAF High Command on their policy of bombing Brest's port and shipping, so Wing Commander Cohen, a Senior Air

Liaison Officer to the Royal Navy, was sent to observe an attack on the docks to assess the risks and effectiveness of these raids, and to decide if it was worth continuing the bombing. A call was sent out for a pilot and crew to fly Cohen over Brest, and contrary to Charles's promise to his parents regarding risk-taking, he instantly volunteered to take this sixty-six year-old 'big wig' on a night attack. Serving in his fourth war, Lionel Cohen was not an armchair observer. Having already fought in the Matabele and Boer Wars, he had enlisted in WWI as a trooper, then transferred to the Royal Naval Air Service. Cohen founded the RAFVR and in February 1939 aged sixty-four, was commissioned as a Pilot Officer and took part in seventy flights as Observer and Air Gunner. When asked why he insisted on flying on operations, he told Admiral Dudley Pound, 'Without practical experience I could not offer solutions to problems,' and added that 'It was good for morale to have senior officers sharing watches with the young air crew.'[9]

On the 24th, Charles, Cohen and his crew flew over Brest Harbour through flak and searchlight beams. At 7,000 feet they dropped two 500 semi-armour piercing (SAP) bombs and three flares, and returned back to base without mishap. After this raid Cohen concluded that the bombs dropped were not heavy enough to be effective.

Another top official, the Secretary of State for Air, Sir Archibald Sinclair, visited Cambridge to observe the RAF/Army training unit in action. After watching David's group being put through their PT exercises, he made complimentary remarks about the pupils.

26 April. After lunch I drove home to find a letter from the Battalion Quartermaster requesting the return of items that I had forgotten to hand in. I made up a big package containing a valise, a haversack, one belt and revolver holder, a pouch, a water-bottle carrier, three straps, one mess tin and a waterproof cape and put it on the train to Corfe Castle – their carriage cost me a grand total of one shilling and ten pence. At supper, Father and I agreed that we should move the foals to the field in front of the house early next morning. I went to bed at 10.30 pm and at midnight four heavy explosive bombs landed near our house in the back field. There was a great smell of dynamite and the odd ceiling fell down. I raced downstairs and found all the back windows blown in and the backdoor hanging off its hinges. I opened the scullery door and poor Rob shot out through the kitchen and was up to Mother's room in a flash.

David went out to look at the damage. The bombs had landed behind the house near the paddock, the youngest foal was dead and the two-year-old had a bad slash down its side. Charnwood was trotting around, but David felt sure he must have suffered some internal injuries, for at least 250 lbs of explosives landed just the other side of the fence. Dinah, who was in the field in front of the house, was fine.

Mother said it is amazing the slates remained on the roof, the explosion was so near. It seems to be a very unlucky accident. The German bomber was either lost or having engine-trouble and decided to drop his bomb on any target that looked as if might be a factory. They probably had mistaken the indoor riding-school for something more important.

Bomb damage on the riding school behind the family home. *(Family collection – Crown © 1941)*

Leaving the family to clear up the mess, David returned to Cambridge to sit a maths exam in which he hoped to achieve a score of ninety percent. In the afternoon, after winning a doubles tennis match with Robert Cranston, they walked to Grantchester for tea by the river. The following day they visited RAF Duxford's Air Fighting Development Unit. Here a large range of aircraft were kept for tactical assessments. The list included a CR42 Italian Fiat Falco biplane, a Tomahawk, an Albatross, a Grumman Wildcat, a Martin Maryland, a Bristol Beaufighter, a Boston, a Havoc, a Gloster Gladiator and an Avro Anson.

> Some of our course took a flight in a bomber. It appeared black, menacing and heavy. I shivered at the thought of night flying over enemy territory for many hours, with the extra responsibility for a crew who would be depending on my flying skills to bring them home safely. Those who went up were rather perturbed when, scarcely airborne, it suddenly caught fire. The pilot took immediate action and cut his engines following the usual fire drill. They rapidly landed and all were safe. The only casualty was one cap, slightly burnt, which

was dropped as the owner escaped from the aircraft. The cap was rescued and returned to him. This has definitely put me off bombers.

There was no such mishap for those who wished to fly Spitfires, but the first sight of one in the hangar didn't impress David as much as he thought it would.

I was suddenly filled with an overwhelming feeling of dread and loneliness of being strapped very tightly in the cramped seat with its tiny cockpit surrounded by a mass of dials, buttons and all the necessary instruments and armament about and below. It appeared that there was scarcely any space for any other control and my worry was how to escape in an emergency, as I was so tightly packed in with the parachute harness.

David talked with the pilots and ground crew. One Spitfire pilot told them that that he still adored flying – even after crashing when a German fighter shot off his aircraft's wings as he was taking off. Thrown out of his aircraft he escaped serious injury as he had the good fortune to land in a muddy stream.

The camaraderie and informal manner between ranks is so very different from that in the Army. In the Ops Room I spoke to an Intelligence Officer who said that the Germans are making 4,000 Me109s a year. I had great fun and any nagging worries about my abilities to fly seemed to fade by the end of the evening. I'll need to put in 110% effort if I am to have any hope of becoming a pilot. Luckily, I love maths and this will be a real help with navigation skills, (navigation being the most difficult part of our training, at this time.)

David's mother wrote to update him on the bomb damage at home.

Bowden.
You would be surprised how quickly the backs of the houses have been mended. All the roofs are mended and the glass is in the windows again…. The foal is no worse Dawson says and is eating hay and mash, and loves being in the paddock where the sun shines. I think she misses the other foal as she keeps looking about. I think you should call her 'Dinahmite!' We will have Dinah with her, when her wounds don't require so much attention…. We had a large mock battle here yesterday. It felt quite dangerous to be about and see soldiers hiding in the paddock….
Your Loving Mother.

The results of the maths test came through and, exceeding his expectations, David scored 95%.

I just hope I do as well in the next two exams. I must work hard in the navigation for it means a lot. Also if I fail, I will have to sit it again and miss my week's leave. I have now learnt to identify more than forty different types of planes – it's not too easy unless one sees them. We all find the work most interesting and everyone is anxious to do well as soon we are to draw our flying outfits.

Meanwhile, No.53 Squadron turned their attention away from Brest for a while and flew further south to attack the docks at St Nazaire, La Rochelle and the oil refinery at La Pallice. After a raid on St Nazaire, Charles and his crew became lost and with their wireless out of action, they flew right over the barrage balloons at Southampton and Portsmouth before eventually finding Thorney Island where they landed safely. On the night of 8/9 May, Charles again flew over St Nazaire. He observed a new type of flak and became so annoyed by the searchlights that he dived from 8,000 to 3,000 feet to drop his bombs and incendiaries. When he went to pull up, he was completely blinded and flying by guesswork, he expected to hit the sea, for he was going so fast. The rear gunner's glasshouse cupola (gun turret) broke in and Naylor shouted through the intercom, that he'd been hit by flak, that everything was in a terrible mess of glass and that ammunition was flying about in all directions. Somehow once again Charles managed to fly back to St Eval and land safely.

At Cambridge, David attended various lectures; one was given by a fighter test-pilot about the Italian Air Force's bombing attacks on Essex and Suffolk, and another was about Fighter Command.

Sq/Ldr Smith said that Polish pilots, many of whom fled to England with their aircraft at the start of the war, admitted that they had a deep hatred of all Germans and this could, on occasions, make them rather reckless flyers. One Flight of three went out on a Sweep over France and on their return, one aircraft had almost no tail, the second had grass and a bit of hedge in the radiator and the third had high-tension cable wrapped round its propeller.

There was news from Scotland when Rudolf Hess was captured on May 10. It was rumoured that Hess was trying to negotiate a peace with Britain if it gave Nazi Germany a free hand in Europe.

Tuesday, 13 May. I just read the news about Rudolf Hess. It's all very puzzling, just what does he want? I wonder if Hitler is 'in the know' about it. That would be wonderful, but I think Hitler's price might be too high for us to accept and I for one wouldn't trust him an inch. I believe it more likely that Rudolf is an escapee from an impending purge of the party. There could hardly be a purge without Hess knowing and he does not like bloodshed.

Tobruk is holding out well. I do not think Libya is by any means lost yet, I am hoping we shall perform the same operation around the Germans as we did the Italians.

Meanwhile, having flown to Donges, east of St Nazaire, to attack four petrol storage tanks, Charles and his crew obtained a direct hit on one. The petrol tank went up with a terrific flash and the pilot of the following aircraft was so put off by the explosion that he had to make a second run-in to attack. Charles noted in his Log Book 'The resulting fire could be seen for over 100 miles.' However, he felt it was a fluke that they hit the tank as it was such a small target that pinpoint accuracy was almost impossible. Having heard about the bombing raids, David speculated that Charles might be in line for an award.

I met an officer from St Eval who said that a recommendation from the AOC often means a DFC though sometimes it is given some weeks or even months later.

Mother wrote that Dinah's chestnut foal died. I am very sad, as it had such a nice temperament and I thought it would make a good replacement for Brunette. It is amazing that last year I thought we had too many horses, considering the food production requirements, but after the bombing, out of the five horses we had, Dinah is the only one left.

Food production was also the theme for a Country Life Magazine article about growing grass for human consumption. David's father wrote and received a reply from Major James Branson, who had featured in the Pathé News and written pamphlets on the subject including, 'Grasses for All. An Unorthodox view on Diet and Religion' and a recipe book for using grass in cooked dishes.[10]

Headley Mill Farm.
I was very pleased indeed to get your letter and learn that you are interested in my advocacy of the use of grass as an article of diet for human consumption…. I came by the inspiration which turned me onto the experiment of using grass-mowings as an article of diet for myself while I was breeding and training polo ponies…. I have been actually trying out experiments on myself for over five years now, and with most conspicuous success…, and found that freshly mown lawn mowings are most nutritional…. I could send you a 3lb carton of ready-made lawn-mowings for £1 post free….
Yours J Branson.

With a weekend off, David went up to London with Kenneth James Gibbons on May 25. Gibbons had been at Sandhurst with David and also transferred to the RAF.

I was very agreeably surprised at the state of London, Big Ben still looks fine. We went to the Trocadero then to Grosvenor House for an Officers' Club tea dance in the ballroom below the ground. I ran into Tom Ridpath[11] and he told me that his brother Mike has just got his commission and has joined him in the Grenadier Guards.

Meanwhile although flying dangerous missions, Charles was clearly loving squadron life.

St Eval, 25 May 41.
My wireless was smashed by a bomb blast, but it still looks ornamental! I had 48 hours leave and went to Andover. Charlie Naylor spent his leave with his wife. She gave me breakfast and lovely watercress and egg sandwiches (plus chocolate cake) for the return journey and asked me to look after 'Charlie' for her, which I assured her I would. We got lost in a maze of country lanes and only found our way out by means of a pocket compass…. That night I flew and when I got back to an aerodrome in the south of England I had been up for twenty-six hours! (Not up in the air you know up = out of bed.) Our little war here at St Eval goes

After a 'brilliant daylight flight' over Brest Harbour Charles was awarded the DFC. (© *The Illustrated London News 1942*)

The battleships *Gneisenau* and *Scharnhorst* docked in Brest Harbour. (*SAGH – NRO AIR 34/744 Part II*)

well and we don't care what happens in the Near East or the North Pole! I have done over 100 operational hours now, 130 in all since joining the squadron....
Love Charles.

The reason for Charles's mood was soon clear when on May 26, the national newspapers announced that 'An Unnamed Raider' had been awarded the Distinguished Flying Cross. It was unusual not to publish the recipient's name, but they reported that 'The Hero of Brest' had flown 'a brilliant daylight flight' over Brest to attack the German Battleships. Later, The London Gazette published the full details of Charles's award. 'On 9 April 1941 this officer carried out a daylight reconnaissance of Brest in order to ascertain whether the enemy cruisers *Scharnhorst* and *Gneisenau* were in port, and to attack them. By skilful use of cloud cover, he succeeded in obtaining photographs and dropping his bombs over the target. His aircraft was severely damaged by anti-aircraft fire. He was attacked by two enemy fighters but, by skilful manoeuvring he succeeded in reaching cloud cover while his air gunner resisted the attacks of the fighters. Subsequent examination of the photographs showed the bombs falling well within the target area. Pilot Officer Greville-Heygate has since carried out another reconnaissance over Brest obtaining valuable photographs.'[12]

I'm very proud of my big brother as the DFC is only awarded for exceptional courage or devotion to duty, while flying. He told me that not so long ago he had volunteered to fly over Brest with an Intelligence Officer. I do hope he doesn't take too many risks and takes care of himself and his crew.

Charles was given two weeks leave and at the weekend the whole family were home to congratulate him when he arrived back complete with his DFC ribbon. Charles and David had a long talk about flying and David jotted down notes of their conversation.

Charles said he saw things differently now. A change in outlook takes place in airmen in warfare. The bombing of houses that, when it first started and he was still in the training stages seemed abominable, now seems perfectly understandable. A German pilot, balanced between life and death, for he may be fired on at any moment by guns or fighters, does not waste time on sympathy for Englishers. He is concerned with two things, dropping the bombs where they do some damage, even if unable to find his real target, and getting back safely to ground at base. A job requiring no little thought and skill. The same principle applies with bombing ships. In fact Charles said that the more he flies the more he loves it, but on long trips it could get very tiring and he needed to have all his wits about him.

David told Charles of his hopes to fly single engine planes as he didn't want to be responsible for the lives of a crew as well as his own. Charles explained that this was all a matter of teamwork and required complete confidence in your crew.

On one attack on Brest at 7,000 feet a direct hit was obtained by Charles, he was aiming at one ship and hit the other. This hit was checked by his camera. Enemy fighters then attacked his aircraft, which put his instruments out of action. He was given 48 hours leave after one daylight attack on the battleship but when he returned they asked for another suicide stunt. Neither Fighter Command nor PRU would take the photos urgently needed so he went over at 3,000 ft. Charles said that he has lost quite a few good friends already as the Blenheim is not really the best aircraft for the job but they can take a lot of flak before they are shot down.

They chatted on late into the night, then Charles became serious and said he had kept all his paperwork up to date and made a will.

For a while I couldn't think what to say but before the silence got too long, Charles laughed and added that they always take a rubber dingy when they are flying and if they have to ditch in the sea it might be several days before they are picked up. If they were taken prisoner nobody over here would know for quite some time so I wasn't to write him off too quickly.

Late on Sunday night, David reluctantly returned to Cambridge.

Final Exams! Aircraft Recognition I got ok – except for the Hudson and I mistook a Maggy for a Tiger!! The Law and Admin exams today were quite easy. I got 100% which I was really pleased about as I swatted up for hours yesterday. Our syllabus finishes tomorrow and nothing remains now to impede my progress towards becoming a pilot…, except the dreaded navigation exam.

Some of British fighter and bomber aircraft David learnt to recognise. (© *The Illustrated London News* 1943)

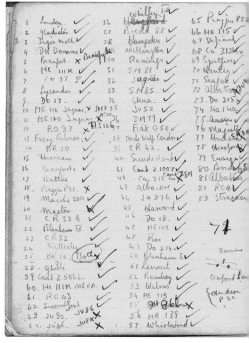

David's aircraft recognition test. (*Family collection*)

Friday, 6 June. The Navigation exam was a complete nightmare. The staff here said that it was the toughest one they had ever seen. I sweated out the day but at last found that I had passed. Thirteen of the group have failed, but as they are to be sent down to Devon for extra tuition I am almost jealous. It would almost have been worth failing the exam for a fortnight at Torquay and such a station, but I'm really looking forward to getting my hands on some real aircraft at last.

Having passed all exams, David was given leave until posted to an Elementary Training School. Mark Lee had returned home from Canada, so David and Charles drove over to hear all his news, then rising early the next day, David and Charles caught the train to London.

The fabric of the city is in rather a poor way but the people are cheerful and seem to carry on with their lives as best they can. Charles looked very handsome and many pretty heads turned as we walked down the street. It seems that everyone loves an RAF uniform and I felt very proud to be his brother. We looked in the shops and spent some time trying to buy things that are virtually impossible to buy elsewhere – in particular film and fountain pens and we collected a few things that Charles felt I might need as a pilot. Afterwards we had haircuts at Simpsons where the barber took a snip out of Charles's ear with a razor. While Charles had his photograph taken by Bassano, the court photographer, I looked at pictures of Royalty taken since Queen Victoria was a little girl. Then we lunched at the Trocadero, we ate roast duck, green peas and iced cakes. We booked seats for the George Black show, 'Black Vanities'[13,] but Charles would not take two seats in the front row because they make DFCs conspicuous, so we had seats four rows back. It was a grand show, Francis Day was very sweet and we both enjoyed it.

On Saturday morning, Charles returned to St Eval and four days later David drove north at the start of an eight-week course at RAF Sealand.

Chapter Six

Elementary Flying Training School, Sealand:
June 1941 to August 1941

'Instructors are the model of patience; though I am certain mine had considerably more grey hairs before he made up his mind to give me a solo test.'
'First Impressions of an E.F.T.S.' by J.R.M. Wingspan Magazine Nov 1940

Cadets who passed the ITW exams at Cambridge were divided alphabetically. Officers with surnames A-G were sent to Course 6, No.19 based at RAF Sealand, with David the last on this list. The others and the thirteen who had failed the Navigation exam were sent to Torquay.

RAF Sealand, near Chester in North Wales, was a heavily used grass airfield. The three-storey barrack blocks housed the large numbers of pupils (740 in 1941). Here, they would learn to fly in dual-controlled de Havilland Tiger Moth biplanes and would have to master take-off, landing, gliding, loops and rolls. They were expected to fly about ten hours before going 'Solo' and a minimum of fifty hours to complete the course.

18 June. I felt a little lost when I arrived on the aerodrome because everyone was so busy. It is a shame that my two best friends went down to Devon, however it seems a terrific place, comfortable and warm. The Mess is run like a first class

Course 6, No19 EFTS Sealand. Most 'Army Rebels' are sitting in the front row. *(Family Collection – Crown © 1941)*

hotel, it has a billiard room, a library – and best of all the bedrooms have running water! I have a good room to myself. The only problem I can see with the grass runway is that dust is thrown up by the slipstream of the aircraft. The last course went to Canada so there is a possibility that I could be sent there, I hope not, I should hate to be so far away from home and the family, and would feel that I was wasting teaching time on the voyage over. I just hope I can eventually get on to Fighters but talking to the Instructors I soon found out that the chances of becoming a fighter-pilot are very slim. Out of the fifty pupils on the previous course,[1] three have gone onto night-fighters, two on to day-fighters and three were turned down.

David soon met up with other friends as Harry Dent and Ivor Melvyn Evans arrived later in the day. They had an 'excellent tea' in the Mess and were desperate to get airborne, however aside from flying, pupils had at least two lessons of ground instruction most days. These subjects included meteorology, armament, law and administration, engines, signals and navigation. An article in the Cambridge I.T.W. 'Wingspan' magazine made it clear that their lives were about to become harder. 'Once at Flying School you haven't time to be impatient. If you're not flying, you are at lectures and if you're not at lectures, you are studying. Make no mistake about that! Gone are your long and short weekend trips to London; only on three nights a week are you free before 7:30, and Sunday is a day of work.'[2]

19 June 1941. We had hoped to get airborne today but instead we spent the entire day in yet more lectures as the flying instructors are booked off until Saturday. First, we had a talk by the C/O, mainly about taxiing accidents and our responsibilities, and then filled in our air-raid insurance forms. Next, we had a talk about navigation and ground studies, followed by a talk from the CFI re punctuality and our syllabus. After lunch we had a photograph taken of our group and went to draw our parachutes, which we will not have to use, thank heavens, except in a real emergency when we are supposed to exit the aircraft and count to three before pulling the large metal ring to deploy the chute. I sincerely hope I never need to use mine.

In the late afternoon they were free to look around the airfield. There was a mixture of aircraft at Sealand. The Tiger Moth was the basic trainer, but other aircraft on the base included an Oxford, a Lysander, a Beaufort, a Hart, a Blenheim, a Wellington, several Masters, Hurricanes, Spitfires and an Anson. David was particularly smitten by a beautiful looking Flamingo, the first all-metal aircraft built by de Havilland, which landed and from which several Brigadiers emerged looking very pleased with themselves. David's hostility for 'big wig' officers made him cynically note:

They were wearing thin parachutes and Mae Wests and were followed out by their batmen carrying their luggage. They had probably just come back from leave in Ireland on the pretext of business.

While David was finding his way around Sealand, Charles and P/O Antony Evan Hilditch were on patrol searching for shipping. Spotting a periscope and a nearby

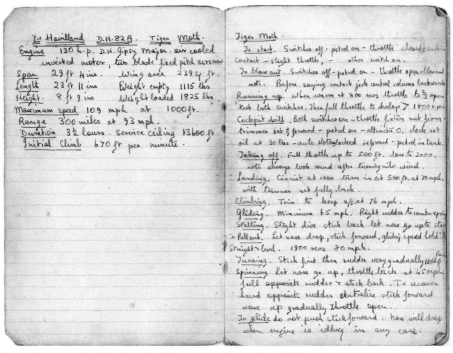

Time spent in the Link Trainer allowed pilots to gain instrument flying experience while remaining safely on the ground. *(Family Collection – © Crown Copyright)*

Tiger Moth cockpit drill. *(Family Collection – © Crown Copyright)*

boat crowded with passengers, they flew very low and close alongside. Charles debated whether he should sink it, but as the passengers were in civilian clothes and waved at him he decided against an attack.

Friday, 20 June was sunny with a slight breeze and very hot. David was up at 07.30, had a leisurely breakfast then strolled down for an armaments lecture.

> We are doing the Vickers again so I know all about it, followed by aircraft maintenance, 4-stroke cycle engines, which I did in car maintenance at Sandhurst. Also aircraft frames, theory of flight and controls, most of which I know already. Then we had a talk on rescue of aircrews from the sea. After lunch, we had a lecture on how to fold parachutes, and a talk on the Link Trainer, a flight simulator, which is designed to reduce instruction time needed in the air. The operators are able to correct the most basic pilot's faults before a sprog takes up an expensive aeroplane. We all had a turn and I entered the cramped box and had my first taste of 'flying' but it was so hot I nearly melted.

The Link Trainer was a flight simulator used to teach instrument flying. It had a hooded fuselage, a full range of instruments, short wings and tail and was supported on four bellows, which could be inflated or deflated and these movements were controlled by the pilot's control column. This saved valuable hours of instruction in the air, as well as aircraft losses and pilots' lives.

> After a quick tea, we went down to the hangars where we were shown over the Tiger Moth. There was a wonderful smell of oil, dope, canvas and fuel. We practised getting in and out and how to do up the webbing seat straps. Once comfortable, we went through all the controls and were shown what they do. In the evening the padre said we had already made a very good impression on the CFI.

Although studying hard, having failed the navigation exam, John Skinner[3] and David's best friend Bewick Hack appeared to be enjoying their time at No.13 ITW based at the Belgrave Hotel Torquay. Hack wrote 'I have done a bit of yachting in the bay.… It's very amusing to see so many here, however the Wing Commander is very good, he gives a lot of his time personally.' He added that the others who did not go to Sealand were also at Torquay and that they probably all would go to an EFTS Marshals at Cambridge when there was room.

On the longest day of year David was up at first light. It was a great day with clear skies and Sergeant Hillier and David went out to the tarmac with their flying jackets and parachute by 08.40, ready for their first flying lesson. His instructor, Pilot Officer Allan, showed Hillier and David the Tiger Moth controls, then after taking Hillier up it was David's turn.

> The great moment arrived as I strapped in and called for the prop to be swung, the engine started with a roar and we raced along the bumpy field and took off. My first thought was of how suddenly the earth dropped away. It was very warm and just such a grand feeling, especially when we felt as though we were falling. We went through lessons 1, 1A, 2, airmanship and controls. The 25 minute flight, took in the landmarks of the Birkenhead and Liverpool balloon barrage, the Welsh mountains, Chester, the Dee ships, Hooton Park aerodrome, the

Log Book page of David's first Tiger Moth flight. *(Family Collection – © Crown Copyright)*

Dee estuary up to the railway then along it until it came to two bridges, a big factory and then the aerodrome could be seen once again. Landing didn't look as difficult but I expected it is. Allan said it was very bumpy and flying was suspended in the afternoon due to bad weather so we had more lectures and a signals test for which we needed six words a minute. We have some grand chaps here in this flight and I feel rather a cad to be enjoying my job so much after quitting the PBI,[4] leaving friends still wading in the mud. Flying is absolutely grand, at least so far as it has gone which is negligible.

(Two friends also escaped the mud at the end of June when Peter Hutton and Richard Howell reported to Cambridge ITW).

With low cloud down to 500 feet, fog stayed over the airfield all the next day and David hung around on the tarmac till 15.00 hours before calling it a day.

Coastal Command had started the process of re-equipping Blenheim squadrons with more suitable aircraft and while awaiting their turn, No.53 Squadron was flying low-level attacks on enemy ships. On a Shipping Attack, once a convoy was spotted, the aircraft would come in low, drop delayed-action bombs before flying over the ship and checking to see if the bombs exploded on target.

Not all attacks followed this ideal scenario as Charles and best friend, but accident-prone Eric Hewson, discovered on a Bust patrol carried out on the 23rd. They spotted a convoy and both planes reduced their height to fifty feet. Charles flew over the ship, dropping all four 250 lb bombs. He later reported that they had glanced off the deck and failed to explode, whereas in fact one exploded above deck level as it hit the aft mast, killing and injuring several crew members and damaging the ship enough to warrant its return to Lorient for repairs.[5] Shrapnel hit Charles's Blenheim in the engine, wing and tail. Flying right behind him, Hewson's bombs missed the target. After losing contact with Hewson, Charles flew home alone. Hit by flak, 'Nine Lives' Eric Hewson jettisoned his remaining bombs, but after fifteen minutes, 'The aircraft broke in half and crashed into the sea from a height of 10 feet.'[6] Hewson and his crew, Sgt A.R. Dawson and Sgt W.G. McCorkell all managed to get into the lifeboat. They were finally picked up by a French fishing trawler after spending three days adrift at sea. Eric Hewson offered the fishermen 100,000 francs to take them to England, but the captain said he was unable to do so as he didn't have sufficient fuel. They were taken to France, handed over to the Germans and sent to Stalag Luft III and Stalag Luft VI.

Monday, 23 June. My first lesson when we eventually got going was on straight flying, but it was very bumpy, with a 25–30 mph wind. On the first trip it seemed quite easy but the next proved more troublesome. Taxiing was not too easy in the wind so we started sideways and the turns that had seemed to be easy proved tricky but I managed to cover gliding, climbing and tail trimming. I was very loath to come back to land, I love flying and am beginning to feel more at home in the air. Allan says it is a big step in flying for one lesson and I have made a big improvement in this lesson, even though there is so much to remember – what with rudder, control column, revs, speed, trimming, etc.

News came through that the Germans had launched 'Operation Barbarossa', a surprise attack on the Soviet Union and everyone followed the reports carefully:

There is exciting news about the Germans invading the Soviet Union; they already claim to have shot down 67 German planes. Let's hope Hitler finds that the Russian bear has a thicker coat and sharper claws than he expects.

I was over at the tarmac by 08.30 and it was grand to be first up, although it was quite cool at 3,000 ft. For the first half-hour I did turning, gliding and a little bit of landing and take-off. On my second trip we covered climbing and then I experienced the most extraordinary queer sensation in the stall. The sea looks pleasant from the air, although I'm usually so busy looking at the instruments, that a quick glance is all I can take, otherwise everything goes wrong and as a beginner it takes ages to put it right again. I get muddled with the trimmer stick and when climbing I find it difficult to keep the speed constant.

The Spitfires here are a bit of a nuisance as they are so well camouflaged that it is difficult to see them, they go so fast (compared to a Tiger) that they come out of the blue very suddenly. Later while talking to one of the staff pilots about the speed of the Spitfire, as compared to the Tiger Moth, I was told that on the previous course a pupil was hit by a Spitfire and the pilot hadn't really noticed the Tiger Moth – until it crashed on the railway.[7]

Hearing the news of Charles' DFC, Richard Arnold, who had been on the Southern Command weapons course with David wrote from 9 SFTS RAF Hullavington to congratulate him on his transfer to the RAF.

It must be in your blood as your brother has done so well … I am still in the same place and still the same rank although I am the most experienced ex-military officer (at least from an active service point of view) on this Station … I look back upon the three weeks at Woolacombe as the most enjoyable time I've had since I got back into uniform.

Yours ever, Richard Arnold

David received a letter from Vivienne Lee who was now working just twenty miles away at the RAF Embarkation Office in Liverpool, and they arranged to meet up. Later, woken by heavy gunfire on the city, David thought for a moment that he was back in Portsmouth and he lay awake for a long time listening the raid.

Luckily we had a boring lecture in the morning so I didn't need to concentrate too hard, but I had rather a large lunch and this proved to be a bad thing because straight afterwards we did spins. Flying in a spin is most unusual, the nose of the aircraft goes up, speed slackens until one seems to be balancing on its tail and the aircraft feels as though it is at the top of a swing. Then the nose drops with a sinking feeling which is hard to describe and the earth spins faster and faster,

53°41'N. 06°42'E.

This low-level attack on an enemy ship was similar to flights carried out by Charles. *(C1939A © IWM)*

then up comes the nose again with another swinging sensation. Fortunately, I managed to hang on to my stomach.

The second trip, practising landings and take-offs was not as difficult as David had imagined, but he was still not confident in anything – except his instructor as yet. Back in the Mess, David told Allan that he hoped to fly single-engine fighters. Allan replied that only about four percent of his students would be good enough to do that and walked off before David dared to ask him what he thought of his chances. He wondered if he should set his aim a little lower and try for fast twin-engine aircraft and join Charles' Squadron.

On June 26 two No.53 Squadron Blenheims took off on a shipping patrol in the Bay of Biscay. Charles was flying PZ-Y with observer Geoffrey Troup and wireless operator/air gunner Charles Naylor. New Zealand pilot Dennis Herrick was flying with observer Gordon Gahagan and wireless operator/air gunner George Wells. Off the Brittany coast they spotted three German anti-submarine vessels. With Herrick following close behind, Charles turned in to attack the ships. His bombs dropped a few feet short of one vessel and his aircraft was hit by fierce flak. Herrick's bombs also missed, and hit by flak, one engine caught fire. Neither aircraft returned to base, however, several enigma messages sent from the German ships were picked up and decoded by Bletchley Park. The ships had reported that they were attacked by two aircraft, both of which were shot down and they had picked up a seriously wounded airman.[8]

Unaware of his brother's unfolding drama, David had another lesson in Tiger Moth No.42.

I held the nose down a bit far the first time. Circuits now seem easier, for one can follow the canal and get a guide from the main road. I love landing but do not feel so confident with take-off yet, the control of rudder is my weak point. I flew for an hour and landed on the other aerodrome as there were a lot less planes about. I did one emergency landing in the next field, though I did not touch down and then some low flying but it was very bumpy over the factory.

27 June. After lunch we were flying again. I climbed to 4,500 ft and was told by my instructor to keep the throttle open owing to rarefied air. It was getting quite cold. I was shown what to do in event of a fire and how to abandon the aircraft. My instructor then switched off the engine and put the aircraft into a dive, there was a terrific whistling of air and scream of wires while I was pressed to the back of my seat and we hit 170 mph before the engines restarted. On my second 30 min flight of the day I did take-offs and landings but I felt that with winds of 35 mph it was really too gusty.

David was right to be cautious. A pilot from another flight dipped his wing on take-off and tipped his aircraft onto its nose; luckily neither sustained much damage. On Saturday there was low cloud at 300 feet, but it cleared by mid-morning and David went up to practise circuits and bumps, which his instructor thought were rather poor, so they went round for another try.

I was determined to bump, I levelled out to make landing about 10 feet above the ground, but in the take-off I pulled the stick back too quickly and I couldn't keep straight. I am still finding it very difficult to master landing and take-off – but so are most people. I hope I will get on alright, but there is always the worry before you go solo, for if it takes too long now in wartime, they haven't the time to spare to persevere with the people who don't pick it up quickly enough.

After tea, Harry Dent, Robert Cranston, Neville Day and David drove to Chester to watch a film.

Monday, 30 June. Not a great start to the day, the sausages for breakfast were not too good and I got a big ticking off for bad circuits, but I got better as the day went on and Allan thought it wouldn't be long before I could go solo. At times, when I get a couple of things wrong I wonder if I will ever be able to fly. We went up to 4,000 feet and did some spins from stall turns. I have now got in 6½ hours flying and Allan is leaving soon but I hope not before I go solo. Monty[9] who has flown before did his solo test and passed.

Most pilots looked forward to their first solo flight, Tim Vigors wrote of his, 'There are moments in one's life which remain in one's memory so vividly that even over half a century later they are as immediate as ever they were…. I was so full of emotion, anticipation and above all, an utter loneliness combined with a wonderful feeling of freedom.'[10] On July 1, it was David's turn.

I did 45 minutes of circuits and bumps, the landings were quite good and the take-offs not too bad then Allan suggested I try a solo test with P/O Horsborough. I did two circuits then saying, 'Off you go,' he climbed out of the cockpit and I went for a ten minute solo flight. It was grand to have a plane under one's

David took his first solo flight in a Tiger Moth after eight and a half hours. *(SAHG)*

own control and I did a good landing but then found a bump and the wing hit the ground, which I was rather cross about. I am the second person in my flight of fifty to go solo and I felt very pleased with myself as I have only flown 8½ hours–10 hours is the norm before attempting a solo.

David's elation did not last long for once back at the Mess, he picked up his post. There was a letter and a parcel from home. He opened the parcel first and, along with the binoculars he had asked his mother to send him, there was a short note. 'Father and I are getting over the shock a little and we are still hopeful that we may hear that Charles is safe somewhere.' David realized that the unopened letter also from his mother had been sent several days before the parcel. With a heavy heart he opened the letter.

27 June 1941, Bowden.
I am so sorry to have to write to you with such dreadful news but we have just had a telegram to say that Charles was reported missing on the 26th of June. We are trying to get more news but this is all we have at present. I will write as soon as we find out more details….
Your Loving Mother.

David sat down in one of the chairs feeling stunned. A few people came over to congratulate him on his solo, but he was unable to say a word for quite sometime.

Poor M and F, what they must be going through. Poor Charles, he is such a grand chap to have for a brother, I pray he is safe. I keep telling myself not to panic. He may have been able to land somewhere – if he just had a shell through his engine – or he could be in a dinghy out at sea. Was he on convoy duty or had he gone back to attack the battleships at Brest again? Was he flying alone or with others? If so, did they see his plane come down?

David went to bed early, but unable to sleep, he got up and wrote home to his family.

Thank you for your brave letter. The news is, I'm afraid, a thing we had all feared and prayed might not happen, yet somehow one felt that our family's immunity from suffering in this war could not last for ever. I do want you to be hopeful and optimistic for there is a great deal to make us believe that he may have been picked up

Newspaper cutting of Charles' DFC award and report of him being missing. *(Family Collection)*

by a French boat or come down safely in France. The Germans seem to retain the news of prisoners a long time. Andrew was reported killed and people even confirmed it, and it was so long that everybody except Mrs Harvey believed he must have been killed, and then she heard he was a prisoner. My friend Peter too was missing and then presumed killed, and only after about five or six months did they hear he was a prisoner. So keep as cheerful as you can and do not worry any more than you can help, and perhaps things will turn out well. I wish I was home to help you a bit.

It was ironic that I should have been the first person in this flight of 50 to go solo in eight and a half hours and then to come back to the Mess and read your letter. Please do not worry about my flying, at the present stage it is not dangerous – and even if after my training anything should happen to me, I should like you to know that I would rather have done something well and helped the cause we are fighting for, than to have a cushy safe job and have scraped through by avoiding things. I assure you that my chief fears, in fact I hope my only fear in flying is the worry it may cause you.

Very much love, David.

P.S. Please never wish I was back in the Army for it is the last thing I want both for personal reasons and for national ones – if that is not too high fluting.

Unable to sleep, David was completely exhausted by the next morning, and after twenty minutes of dual flying he was sent out solo to do practise turns over the river.

I was given No.74, a pig of a plane which flies with the right wing down at about 30°. It was very misleading and the instruments didn't seem to work and I wondered if I would ever be able to get the aircraft back down on the ground safely. I found everything difficult and flying does not seem quite so friendly any more after yesterday's news. I couldn't stop worrying about C when flying, and it does take one's concentration away from flying on instruments.

David went round the airfield several times before he managed to make a half-reasonable landing. As soon as he was out of the aircraft Allan bawled him out about his dreadful flying and lack of concentration. David told him about Charles and how worried he was and said that being in the air was the last place he wanted to be at the moment. Allan completely changed his attitude and was most understanding. He said, 'I know how you must feel, but you really need to get back in the air straight away to regain your earlier confidence.' So, reluctantly David climbed back in the aircraft with him. They went straight up and did some aerobatics, low-level flying and climbing turns, and feeling more confident, David was sent up solo once more.

I flew much better and made a good landing. I am rather scared of Allan as an Instructor, but I like him very much.

On receiving the news of Charles, Ronald had returned home for the weekend to give some moral support to their parents. He updated David on the news and tried to remain positive about Charles's fate.

HQ No. 27 (ST) Group RAF.
It seems not impossible Charlie might have gained the coast of France or Ireland by boat or swimming, if he made a forced descent on the sea, or they might have landed in hostile or neutral territory, in either of which case they would presumably be taken prisoner or interned, and news would not be received for some time. So I decline to take an unnecessarily pessimistic view at present.

Mother and Father are bearing themselves with great courage, especially Mother, which is a relief, as I generally feared the effect on them if he should meet misfortune. Nevertheless it is a grievous blow to them, and no doubt you also feel the same intense distress and shock that I feel. But there is comfort in the fact that so many of those reported missing in the war have eventually been accounted for, as prisoners of war or interned. Some have been at sea for many days and survived....

Your affectionate brother, Ronald.

David received a copy of a letter sent from the Air Ministry officially informing his family that Charles' aircraft had failed to return to base after an air operation. The Commanding Officer of No.53 Squadron also wrote to his father.

Dear Mr Greville-Heygate,
I should like to convey to you my deepest sympathy and also the sympathy of all the Officers and Airmen of this Squadron, on the sad occasion of your son being reported missing. It is a loss which I personally feel very deeply, and also one which is a severe blow to everyone in this Squadron. Your son was one of our best and bravest pilots. I met him before he came to the Squadron and watched the development of his operational career from the start. From the beginning he looked as if he was going to turn out well above the average and when the opportunity came to do a job of outstanding merit he did it with fine courage. You probably know the whole story of the operation for which he was decorated so I will not repeat it. It was a fine piece of work and the whole Squadron was, and always will be, very proud of him, men of his calibre are not come by every day....

Your Obedient Servant, Squadron Leader Brown.

Six days after Charles was reported missing, No.53 Squadron moved from St Eval to Bircham Newton near Kings Lynn to exchange their out-dated Blenheims for the Lockheed Hudson. No operations were flown for several days while they learnt how to handle the new aircraft. Once operational, they began flying shipping recces between the Dutch Islands and fiords, and as a result aircraft losses were reduced.

I flew another solo flight today and my hours are increasing rapidly. Stunting loops are fantastic, although it felt most extraordinary to be hanging upside down, four inches off the seat, with the earth 4,000 ft below one's head. I was glad I was strapped in tightly as it was very bumpy.

David's mother was now desperately worried about him flying, thinking that she might lose him too; she hoped that he would return to the Army. However, this is the last thing David desired, for although very tired, he was beginning to enjoy flying once again. After a visit to Sealand, Cambridge ITW Instructor Sydney Robert James Addison wrote to David to say how sorry he was to hear that Charles was missing.

Selwyn College, Cambridge.
So far as I could gather, the 20 "A" Flight chaps are doing well and giving the Army an admirable name for keenness and hard work…. Congratulations on your solo effort. You didn't know it before but you were my pick for 'No 2.' Denny was an obvious first choice, having flown before, but you were a shot in the dark and I rather praised myself on my judgement! I don't think there is any point in rushing one's first solo, but it's good to hear of you doing it so quickly nevertheless. I was allowed to take the controls for 10 minutes on the way home and felt quite a fellow! We had a lovely run home more or less hedge-hopping all the way….

Sincerely Yours, Robert Addison.

On July 9, Flights and instructors were swapped around. David's new instructor was Battle of Britain pilot, Flight Lieutenant Edward Brian Bretherton Smith. His No.610 Squadron Spitfire had been shot down on August 12 1940, after being involved in a dogfight with a dozen Messerschmitt 109s. The London Gazette reported 'His aircraft was hit by two shells, damage being inflicted near the cockpit and petrol tanks. His aircraft caught fire and, although enveloped in flames, he successfully abandoned his aircraft.' Badly burnt, Smith was rescued from the sea, and hospitalized for some time.[11]

My new instructor seems very nervous and I hope this is due to his harrowing experience of being shot down and ditching in the sea, rather than to my lack of skill as a budding pilot! I did a 40-minute dual, doing forced landings. We saw some little children and a farmer in a nearby field who waved and I could see the happy expressions on their faces as they played and we waved back, much to their joy. Loop the loops is one of the easiest things to do in an aeroplane.

Thursday, 10 July 1941. As we took off, Smith asked if I would like to fly night-fighters when I finished my training. After some quick thinking I said I would, but as we landed I thought it was rather too important decision to make – with time and both feet firmly on the ground – so I told Smith that I am still considering what I might like to do after finishing here and I am not so sure about night-fighters.

Each time I come into the Mess I glance at the telegram board and I'm sure I will be waiting for the telegram to say Charles is safe for at least the next six months.

David's father had been unwell for quite sometime and the loss of Charles was almost more than he could bear:

My Dear David…, I am so sorry I have not written to you before but am sure you will understand how terribly I have suffered in the loss of Charles. I did not realize he would be taken so soon. He never mentioned his work to me, I think because he did not want me to be worried. I ought to have got the names and addresses of the crew of his aeroplane for, if either of them are ever heard of, that might help us; also not knowing any of his friends at the aerodrome leaves us solely dependant on the official letters….

Your loving Father.

After reading in the news that Charles' WAAF girlfriend, Josephine Pipon[12] had been killed by enemy action on July 8, David wrote home.

How sad Josephine Pipon's father must be for not letting her go to Egypt.

Vivienne invited me up to play tennis and I went via Neston and Hoylake to Liverpool and under the marvellous Queensway Tunnel for 1/6. The slums at Liverpool are appalling, unblitzed and blitzed, the people of twenty or so look

RAF Map of Chester, Liverpool and Sealand. (*Family Collection – Crown © 1942*)

about forty and the old ladies look about one hundred and fifty! What a lot of improvement could be done in this world if this wasteful war wasn't going on.

Trying to gain further news of Charles, David wrote to Eric Hewson, but received a reply from Flying Officer Leonard John Maxwell Bunce, No.53 Squadron's Adjutant, who wrote that it was his unpleasant duty to inform David that Eric Hewson was missing, but added that if David was keen to join the squadron they would be extremely pleased to have him. 'I suggest that when you arrive at your Service Flying Training School you should put in an application to join 53, stating that your brother was at one time with them, and continue to pester them until they post you to us. In the meantime it would be necessary for you to ask for twin-engine training after E.S.T.S.'

Although David would have been very happy to join 53 Squadron, just a week later he received news of his next training post.

Friday, 18 July 1941. Great news! I am to fly single-engine fighters, I can't wait. I leave Sealand on the 30th and after a week's leave go onto Tern Hill Service Flying Training School flying Masters. As we are practising map reading I flew over to Tern Hill and Shawbury then as my instructor is buying a house in Wales we flew over to see it. We do not waste time doing this sort of thing for one has to practise map reading and instead of going round in circles we go to some interesting place. By the end of this course we have to fly about 50 hours and I've done about 45 while others have only done 15 or so. I love this life, what a change from the Army!

At this point in their training, pilots began to feel confident about flying and this posed a particular problem, for confidence with limited experience meant an increase in accidents. On July 24, David witnessed a Hampden hit a Tiger Moth head on, they spun to earth and both Instructor Sergeant Frederick Wescott and Second Lieutenant Ian McColl died of their injuries.[13] David noted other accidents in his Log Book.

Margate landed his Tiger on top of another, he escaped unhurt but wrote both aircraft off. Lawrence Holt-Kentwell[14] bumped his wheels on top of a hangar on the way down but still made a near perfect landing.

Losses were not confined to trainee pilots as on 24 July Eric Marrs, the No.152 Squadron pilot David had met at Tyneham, was shot down while flying close escort for Hampdens bombing the battleships *Scharnhorst* and *Gneisenau* at Brest.

We have had by far the best half of the course. The rest of the ITW lot who were in Devon have now gone back to Cambridge and they will not find it as comfortable as here. They will have to take a sandwich lunch out to the Marshall's flying field by bus each morning, go back for dinner and out again for evening flying.

The news is more cheering these days, when we think of the ragged army coming back from Dunkirk just over a year ago and we seemed up against the world. I think Hitler must beat the Russians or fall. The burning policy must be pretty awful, advancing through smouldering ruins all the time, it's bad enough going through bombed towns and villages. Just think of 9,000,000 men in the Russo-German battle, it certainly is a gory world but I suppose it always has been with each generation fighting, not for the 'Glorious Future' they like to think they are, but to preserve the past they loved and consequently to a great many a cause lost before they start, for the past is dead and things can not go back to what they were.

At the end of July, David wrote to friends in his old battalion. He received no reply from Clitheroe and thought they must have been posted abroad. However, a letter arrived from the 10th Brigade at Mill House, Lulworth. Hoping to transfer to the RAF, George Robinson[15] wrote asking about the type of maths questions asked in the RAF test so he could swot up beforehand. He added 'I expect you have passed your Solo by now and are doing things like spins and stomach turning slow rolls.... Please write soon, it's awfully boring down here.'

Meanwhile, Mary Hutton wrote of Peter's training.

University Arms Hotel, Cambridge. 25/7/41.
I have been down here a month now with Pip who is at the ITW! I expect it is the same as you did (course I mean). He is working so hard, he's frightfully keen in fact shows more enthusiasm than I'd ever imagined, not that I'd ever grumble!!! He is at New Clare, but he always has dinner and sleeps here. He does his exams next week so if you have any tips for him do let him have them. Then he has three days leave and following that, an elementary flying course here. I have not done any riding for a long time as Pip will be a proud father in September – can you imagine that?
Love Mary

P.S. I am at C Flight, No.1 Squadron, No.2 ITW Clare College and if I get through that flunking Navigation exam I go to E.F.S.T. in a few days. I hope you are able to wangle some leave occasionally and visit Rosemary. Best of luck old man....
God Bless, Pip.

David's course finished on 30 July; eleven men had been suspended, 1 LAC was transferred to No.8 Course and two Army officers, Robert Drummond and Humphrey Gilbert, were retained for further flying instruction. Of the remaining officers and airmen, nine officers were sent to 5 SFTS Tern Hill and eight to No.12 SFTS Grantham. Two sergeants went on an Instructor's course and the rest were shipped to Canada.[16]

At the beginning of August, David's parents received an official letter that again gave them renewed hope that Charles might be alive.

6 August 1941. Pilot Officer Charles Heygate was one of the most brilliant young officers it had been my good fortune to meet. Early this year he put up a magnificent show for which he was awarded the DFC and I looked forward with confidence to seeing him achieve rapid promotion and more distinction in the Royal Air Force. I was very sorry indeed when he failed to return from a shipping strike in the Bay of Biscay. Yesterday, I heard from Intelligence sources that Herrick, the pilot of the second aircraft on the attack, which also failed to return, was a prisoner of war although injured. This, I think, must give us a little fresh hope for your brother, although we must not build our hopes up too high….

Group Captain Arthur Pethick Revington

While on leave, David took the train up to RAF Bircham Newton to pick up Charles' car and to try to gain more information about Herrick. Hilditch showed David around a Hudson (which David thought looked complicated to fly) but had no further news. After driving home, David received a telegram cutting his leave short by a week, so cancelling plans to visit Devon, he packed up ready to report to Tern Hill the next day.

Chapter Seven

Service Flying Training School, RAF Tern Hill, Flying Masters: August 1941 to Sept 1941

'Aeroplanes are not in themselves inherently dangerous but they are unforgiving.'
'Spitfire. A Test Pilot's Story,' Jeffrey Quill

No.5 Service Flying Training School was based at RAF Tern Hill near Market Drayton in Shropshire. Its role was to teach pupils to fly single-engine aircraft, and by the end of the course, they were expected to fly almost automatically to any given point, in almost any weather condition. If they passed, they were awarded their Wings. Teaching time was split between flying and ground instruction in navigation, meteorology, bombing and reconnaissance. The two-seater Miles Master, affectionately nicknamed the 'Maggy', was used to teach instrument, night and formation flying after which they progressed onto the single-seater Hawker Hurricane.

The fifty pupils on No.65 Course were a very mixed bag. There were ten Army Officers; David, Peter Biggart, Charles Roger Boyce, Leonard Buck, Wriothesley

No.65 Course. Sitting L to R – Stephens, Day, David, Evans, Biggart, Duffus, Denny, Buck, Miles, Berry. *(Family Collection – Crown © 1941)*

Denny, Donald 'Bert' Draper, Neville Day, Ian Duffus, Melvin Evans and Peter 'Jerry' Miles. Ramo Digamber Garware was a university graduate from India, and Govert Steen was a battle-experienced Royal Netherlands Air Force pilot. Leading Aircraftman Count Franz Ferdinand Colloredo-Mansfeld was the son of an Austrian diplomat who had studied at Harvard University and enlisted in the RAVF after the annexation of Austria.[1] There were three Frenchmen; Sergeants Gouby and Sayers were Free French Air Force pilots and Second Lieutenant Louis Ricard-Cordingley, son of marine painter Georges Ricard-Cordingley, had studied Law before escaping from France. The rest of the cadets were RAF Corporals and LACs.[2]

In spite of their best efforts, David's best friends, Harry Dent and Robert Cranston failed to gain the standard required to train on single-engine aircraft.

Arriving on Thursday 7 August, David was pleased with his first impression of the station.

> The Mess is quite palatial. It looks across the cricket ground towards the flying field with the Wrekin standing behind. Goodness knows how much it cost, for each bedroom has hot and cold water laid on. There is a billiard room and the sitting room is equipped with radiograms and internal microphones for ordering drinks etc. There are several tennis and squash courts and to cap it all, at the Hawkstone Park Hotel there is a private golf course with lovely woods, lakes and fishing and the officers can use it for the princely sum of 10/6 a quarter.

David soon met up with Ian Duffus, but having taken advantage of the ambiguous telegram ordering them to report on 7/8 August, Roger Boyce and Donald Draper

Cadets SFTS Tern Hill. No.65 Course. Good friends, Boyce and Draper, kept in touch with David throughout the war. *(SAGH – NRO AP11-F540)*

did not arrive until the following day. However, it is possible that Donald Draper was late as his younger brother, Flight Lieutenant Gilbert Graham Fairley Draper, a Spitfire pilot with No.41 Squadron, went missing after an operation on the 7th. Their first day was filled with various talks. Working hours were 'pretty stiff' and the two inexcusable crimes were landing without an undercarriage and low flying, which had caused a number of write-offs. At lunch, Donald Draper told David of his brother's lucky escape the year before. On 30 October 1940, Gilbert Draper's No.41 Squadron Spitfire was attacked near Ashford by Luftwaffe Ace pilot Adolf Galland.[3]

> Crashing his aircraft, Gilbert sustained a serious head injury, but fortunately an eminent brain surgeon on his way to another accident, saw the crash, raced to the scene and took him to hospital.

In the evening, keen golfers Draper and David went down to join the golf club and were mystified when asked for an extra threepence for the sheep fund. Thinking it was some kind of raffle they asked what this was, and the Membership Secretary informed them that it was an insurance premium against killing a sheep whilst playing on the course.

> *Saturday, 9 August 1941.* The Navigation Instructor seems a bit of a bounder, but is quite amusing. He is always telling stories and using the most awful RAF slang…, 'shooting a line' and 'putting up a black.' There was much talk about the 'fighter boys and glamour boys,' and 'There I was upside down in the cloud, f--- all on the clock and still climbing,' and lots more about pranging a kite and low flying. We then spent the day doing cockpit drill for the Maggy and there are no end of dials, levers and knobs.

A much more complicated aircraft than the Tiger Moth, the Master had a variable pitch airscrew, flaps, brakes, a retractable undercarriage and a top speed of about 225 mph. Fighter pilot William Dunn commented that 'It was a hell of a lot "hotter" and much more advanced' than anything he had ever flown before. Mainly wooden, it had a doped fabric cover. 'The wings were covered with plywood sheeting which, after a rain or period of damp weather, would actually wrinkle a bit from the wetness…, this had no effects on the Master's flying capability, but it did cause the pilot to wonder if perhaps the soggy aircraft might not come unglued in flight.'[4]

> We all lack any confidence in flying at the moment, but perhaps that will come all too soon, although flaps and undercart make things more complicated. It is not easy to land without wheels, although it is done now and again, and I don't understand how you can forget because there are great red lights showing and a hooter screams at you if you throttle back to land when they are not down. We have all been severely warned that those who forget to put the undercarriage down and then land on their bellies will be court-martialled. After lunch, I went down to Dispersal to start flying. The Master feels grand and no rudder is needed to turn but it has a vicious stall and I felt as though we were flying at a colossal speed which was rather unnerving. Comparing a Maggy to a Tiger is a bit like riding a Shetland pony on the leading rein, then getting on a bad-

tempered racehorse which goes so fast that it feels like you are out of control. The difficulty is the number of switches and instruments, about fifty-one in all.

Coursework kept everyone very busy; every other day, lectures finished at 17.00 hours. One week they flew from 06.00 to 13.00 hours and the next week from 13.00 to 20.00 hours. Night flying was extra. If very busy, or in bad weather when the grass airfield was flooded, flights were sent to nearby airfields such as Childs Ercall. Pupils would often be bussed over to Cosford, twenty miles south which had a slightly less muddy runway and was often used for circuit and bump training.

Tuesday, 12 August. There is a silence pact at breakfast which all the pilots try to keep to but Ian compared the noise of the Masters' engines warming up to wild beasts being uncaged and starting to roar. 'Like lions waiting for their next meal.' Today we had to be up at 04.30 to take a bus over to Cosford which is the most awkward aerodrome but serves a very good lunch!

An article in the Times was printed on August 13, with the headline 'Famous Pilots Missing.' It reported the loss of 'Legless' Douglas Bader, 'Sawn-off Lock' and added that a third DFC pilot, Charles Greville-Heygate was also missing.[5]

Up again at 04.30 David flew for an hour with Flying Officer Geoffrey Walter Harding[6] before attempting a rather disastrous solo test with Pilot Officer Falconer.

I was so busy concentrating on other things I forgot to put the wheels down. I felt such a fool, but Harding only said that he hoped that I wouldn't forget again. Then I soloed in the Master. The engine – a Rolls Royce – is most confidence inspiring and it sounds like a sewing machine or an electric motor as it makes a lovely purring whine.

We have no end of French and Dutch pilots. Netherlands Air Force pilot, Govert Steen, in our squad is awfully nice. When the Germans took over the airfields, they were terribly polite to the Dutch pilots and allowed the officers to walk around in uniform and look over the German planes. Govert got a job in a Fokker factory as a labourer, pinched a plane and flew to Britain. He has had to learn flying our way here, though he has flown over 1,000 hours.

When Holland was invaded, Govert Steen destroyed two German aircraft before being shot down and was unable to fly again as all serviceable planes had been destroyed. On 6 May 1941, Steen and several others managed to steal a Fokker T-8W twin-engine seaplane moored in the harbour and fly to England.[7]

Free French pilot Ricard-Cordingley is most amusing. He had a crash on landing today but thankfully neither he nor his aircraft was too badly damaged. He escaped from France in 1940

Dutch pilot Govert Steen, the battle-experienced Royal Netherlands Air Force pilot. *(SAGH © NRO AP11-F540)*

and he told me that the aerodromes were full of planes but there was no petrol in them, for if ever a plane was left unguarded with fuel in the tank for more than a minute it disappeared, either to North Africa or England.

French pilot Second Lieutenant Louis Ricard-Cordingley.
(SAGH © NRO AP11-F540)

Louis Ricard-Cordingley escaped from Toulouse in France on June 22 1940. Ordered to guard a Caudron Goéland, (a French commercial aircraft) while the pilot, who had come from Vichy France, went to see the station C/O, Ricard-Cordingley and several others NCOs from the flying school jumped in and took off. The pilot, Sergeant Didier Béguin, wanted to fly to North Africa, the others to England. They pointed out that they would be shot if they landed in Vichy North Africa in a stolen plane, so crossing the Channel and short of fuel, they landed in Devon.[8]

Donald Draper finally heard that his brother was alive although suffering from slight burns having bailed out over Merville in France and captured at Fruges on August 8.[9]

A Dutch pilot over from Grantham says that Charles Barton had a mid-air crash in his Oxford which caught fire. He was thrown clear on hitting the ground and only broke his leg. Flt/Lt Lord,[10] our Training Flight Commander said that the Oxford is a beast to fly whereas the old Anson is grand.

In a letter to David, George Hugh Cavendish Emmett, learning to fly the Airspeed Oxford, agreed with Lord. 'The tame looking Oxfords are not as tame as I imagined and we are having one crash a day and a cadet written off yesterday. It needs two men and a boy to level them out when landing.'

Harry Dent, now at Grantham, was not enjoying flying Oxfords either.

No.12 SFTS, Grantham.
David…, I'm afraid there is very little chance of my ever arriving at Tern Hill, or even flying SE[11] engines at all. However, I shall keep on trying and if SEs are completely out of the question I shall try hard for day Beaufighters…. We have all soloed in Oxfords now, average 6 or 7 hours. As with Masters, they are rather frightening at first, and not only at first.

We have rather a lot of low cloud here, which is liable to come down over the aerodrome at any moment. I lost myself in cloud the other day and when I eventually got out I could not find the aerodrome for half an hour. I was scared stiff.

David's great friend Harry Dent flew on the first 1,000 bomber raid, on Cologne. *(By kind permission 214 Squadron Website).*

This place is very comfortable and the food is excellent…. We have lectures and flying alternate mornings and afternoons, as at Sealand. Do you have to learn the bombsights and similar piffle or do you miss all that as fighter boys?

I am hoping to see Eller and Evers[12] tomorrow.

My regards to the boys.

All the best, Harry.

PS. The 'old-unds' sends their regards to the 'glamour boys.'

David was still finding flying the Masters tricky:

While flying steep turns from 9,000 feet I observed a completely circular rainbow and I thought I was getting the hang of the Master. Then I got overconfident and nearly crashed through a wire fence while doing a powered approach without flaps – I had left the throttle open by mistake. Today in lectures, we were told that if a Master has not recovered from a spin at 4,000 ft it is about time to bail out. This caused a smile, as Bert D (Killer) had only got out of one at 2,400 ft yesterday. Apparently an unmodified type!

Wednesday, 20 August. One of the Free French lads was killed today while trying too steep a turn; it appears he had been chasing another plane and spun in from 250 feet.

Free French pilot Corporal Emile Laurent on Course 63 had met up with another pilot and started unauthorized low-level flying. Laurent was on the tail of the other aircraft when he lost control and crashed at Sheriff Hales.[13] On August 21, Jan Plesman, a Polish friend of Govert Steen arrived for Course 66 SFTS. Son of Albert Plesman, the founder of KLM Airline, Plesman had been training with the Dutch Air Force when the Germans invaded Holland. He cycled from The Hague to Spain and flew on a KLM commercial flight to England in May 1941.[14]

Saturday, 23 August. Yesterday we got out of signals early so I caught the 17.45 train home. Ronald was also on leave and we agreed that M and D seem a lot better and are beginning to deal with the uncertainty of Charles's disappearance. They've had some good news from Douglas[15] who is now a Colonel. My train was delayed and I reached Stafford quite late, only to find my car parked at the back of the garage blocked in by two buses and three cars and I caused a terrific commotion trying to get it out.

As training became tougher, news of cadets being killed continued. FFAF Sergeant R. Sayers was killed in a crash near Bridgnorth.[16]

The engine of the French lad's Master cut while night flying. He crashed and I'm afraid he's in a critical condition with a fractured skull and several other injuries. I don't know what his chances are. Ian Duffus had a letter from his wife to say that Jack Hall had been killed; he was keen on becoming a pilot but only managed to get observer.

News of another death came on August 28 when Peter Henry Albert Pickering crashed near Stafford.[17]

I was up flying up at 04.30 with P/O Foster for an Instructors' navigation test. Then I did a 40 min solo in Master N7935 which 'India' Pickering crashed later in the day. Rumour has it that he was low flying but if a crash occurs that is usually what it is put down to. As I was the last person to fly the Master before him, I was called to attend the court of enquiry held by Wing Commander Dennison, the CFI. He had a marvellous little chrome model of a Master in his office in the Control Tower. I reported that I had not encountered any problems with the aircraft.

Thursday, 4 September. We had no flying in the morning so Ian and I went to see the CGI to ask for a day off at the weekend. He said the whole squad would have tomorrow off. So after flying in the afternoon with aerobatics – though visibility was not particularly good – Bert, Ian and I rushed off to Crewe, we just had time to park the car and I caught the 18.50 to Rugby and home.

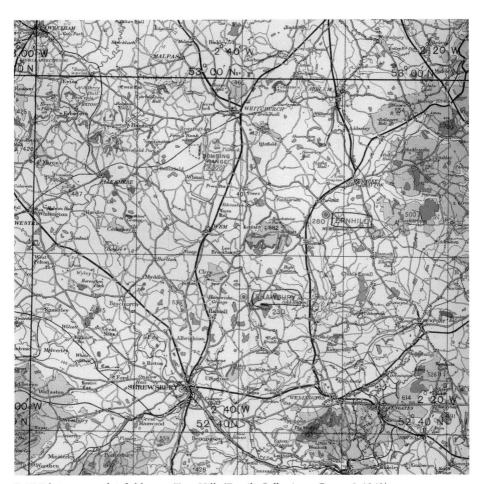

RAF Edition map of airfields near Tern Hill. (*Family Collection – Crown © 1943*)

Taking the train to London the next day, David found the Cumberland Hotel was full, so he booked into Oddenino's in Regent Street, a well-known meeting place for Polish pilots, which advertized itself as 'the Centre of the World.'

> Oddenino's is not up to much for a London Hotel but it doesn't matter, as one doesn't spend much time inside. I saw a show at the Prince of Wales, and then had dinner at the Trocadero with a Canadian Medical Officer. He is rather horrified at the lackadaisical way the English are taking the war when the country's very existence is at stake. He said that the Canadians hate the Japanese even more than the Germans and are longing to fight them and he thinks they may well have to soon.

Flicking through the September 3 Issue of the Tatler, David spotted a photograph of Colditz POWs. One chap immediately caught his eye, it was Peter Storie-Pugh, 'Looking like a convict but still smiling.' By the time this picture was published, Storie-Pugh had already unsuccessfully attempted to escape from Colditz via a tunnel in the canteen and was planning his next attempt over the roof. He devised a code which enabled him to write freely to his family, and the War Office was able to send escape material, for example money or maps, hidden in various innocent looking items such as gramophone records or playing cards.[18]

A few days later Melvyn Evans and David went to a dance in aid of the Red Cross at Broughton Hall, a half-timber house taken over as a school. However, booked to fly at first light the next day, they reluctantly left early.

Colditz PoWs. Peter Storrie-Pugh, sitting first left, 'looking like a convict but smiling.' *(With kind permission © P.Storie Pugh)*

Thursday, 11 September. Up at 04.30 to fly but the weather was rotten, very misty with low cloud so I took the Master up to 10,000 ft. I emerged into a land of sunshine above great soft carpets of glinting white clouds that stretched as far as the eye could see and then disappeared into a bluey-mauve haze where the blue sky merged into the cloud on the horizon. It was quite the most enjoyable experience of flying to date. The only problem was how to get back down to the ground. Without a wireless, it has to be done by compass and guesswork. After steering a north-easterly course through 6,000 ft of cloud, I emerged straight over the aerodrome; I was most impressed by my navigation skills. It is one of the most pleasant things about flying, being able to go and see the sun, even if it won't come to see me on the ground.

The food in the Mess has improved 100% now that it has been taken over from the civilian contractors who have had it for the last three years and the subscription is still only 2/- a day which is cheap for an RAF Mess. Jim Mollison,[19] the husband of Amy Johnson, was in here last week and I think he is flying planes from America.

Towards the end of the month, David received several long letters. The first was from Flight Lieutenant Robert Addison.

Jesus College, Cambridge, 18 September 41.
If you can get a line to Barton give him my congratulations on his lucky escape. It's a joke really, as I'm always told that straps should always be properly done up and presumably he wouldn't be here if he'd kept to the rules! It's great fun hearing from you all again as you say, you are the first of the A.O.s[20] to go on singles, barring one from the first flight. There have been a few since, from Marshall's and quite a lot onto night-fighters.

By the way I saw Hack in London the other day; he went to Booker (21 EFTS) and is now on Oxfords at Cranwell. Had a complete write off on a Beaufort as something or other didn't function, and his undercart wasn't down. Plane a write off and no one even got a scratch!

Must shut up now. Yours, Robert Addison.

Harry Dent also wrote with news of old friends from ITW.

Grantham, 21 September 41.
Thanks a lot for your letter, I'm glad you are all beginning to like Masters. You seem to have an excellent system of flying.... Our course seems to have every type of accident that is possible but fortunately, the only officers embroiled were Barton[21] who is improving steadily and Bunny[22] who had to land without an undercart. Otherwise we have had one cadet killed and various others forgotten undercarts, spun into the ground on landing, and in numerous other ways managed to put planes out of commission. Most of us have finished our night flying, but the weather has held up our cross-countries so that we are only half way through them. Ken Gibbons is a little bit behind through a recurrence of his ear trouble, but I think he will catch up. Davis who is in the next course has

been grounded for low flying over his old aerodrome and there is some talk of a court martial, although I hope it won't come to that.

We have been asked for our preferences and I shook the CFI by telling him mine is single-engine fighters. He has recommended me for flying Fighters (twins presumably) but the possibilities are not very great because very few go to Fighters from here.

I saw Dennis Evers[23] and (W)Ray Eller a few weeks ago and Dennis was over here playing rugger the other day…. We are starting exams this week (I suppose the same applies to you.) At the moment we are all in a 'flat spin' about it. We don't seem to know nearly enough…. My regards to all the Glamour Boys. I may get to see some of you at a Fighter OTU….

All the best,
Harry and the Bomber Boys.

The last letter was from Captain Allen, now training at the Camouflage Development ITC[24], before being posted to Egypt or India. He wrote:

Farnham Castle.
I often think of those pleasant days at Clitheroe, those detestable weeks at Cosham and the excitement of Pompey. And I shall never forget our operational role at Tyneham. Everything that happened at Tyneham stands out clearly, possibly because we had more time to reflect. The Mess was very homely and matey amidst a cold hard world. Worbarrow was eternally pleasant and Kimmeridge a bleak wind-swept area.

There are 21 of us here, 18 are artists and their drawings make me look positively ham-fisted but I am absolutely revelling in it…. Do you still move about with all those aids to comfort? Primus, hot water bottle etc? I'm terribly glad that you like your job. You were so determined to get it.

Yours ever, Harry T. Allen.

Towards the end of September the weather started deteriorating and the two-shifts-a-day flying rota was changed to one starting at 08.00, and continuing to 20.00 hours. Pupils on David's course began to prepare to fly the single-seater Hurricanes.

We are supposed to be getting Hurricanes soon, which will be marvellous and I've started learning the cockpit drill. It is perhaps the finest single-engine plane in the world and will be grand after the Master as it is much more reliable and I believe much safer.

Thursday, 25 September. Night flying postponed. Garland's engine cut and he crashed into a house, both house and aircraft burst into flames. Garland was pulled out of the plane and was taken to hospital with slight burns.

According to G.B. Garland's accident reports, he was flying solo in a Master practising steep turns, spins and forced landings when he overshot the airfield and selected an unsuitable field in which to land. He opened up, but hit a house and crashed near Denby church.[25]

The barracks, RAF Tern Hill. *(SAGH – © NRO Tern Hill ORB AP1)*

Less than two miles from the airfield at Hinstock, George John Howard D'Silva also crashed, but was not so lucky.

Friday, 26 September. D'Silva went into a spin in a Master at about 8,000 ft. He almost pulled out of it at about 300 ft, but the plane didn't stand it and he dived into the ground.

When David felt he was perfect on the Hurricane cockpit drill and had done it blindfold, he was tested by Squadron Leader William Arthur Toyne.[26]

The Squadron Leader gave us an exam on the Hurricane cockpit drill. Fortunately, the others who went in first told me what questions he was asking so I was prepared for some of the more awkward ones which came up. Night flying is postponed until Friday. Basil Marshal's Hurricane engine cut and he attempted a forced landing but he clipped the hedge with his tail, the aeroplane overturned and thrown forward. He cut his lip.

Chapter Eight

Flying Hurricanes at Childs Ercall:
September 1941–December 1941

The Hurricane was 'an engine of war…, far less tolerant of faulty handling and needed more room to recover. A mistake at low altitude could be fatal.'

'Time and Chance. An Autobiography.' Peter Townsend

In 1941, Childs Ercall, later renamed RAF Peplow, was a relief landing ground about six miles south of Tern Hill. The small village of Childs Ercall lay just to the north of the grass runway, and it was from this airfield that David took his first flight in a Hurricane.

The Hawker Hurricane Mk 1 had a Rolls-Royce Merlin III engine and a maximum speed of about 340 mph. Sammy Wroath, the Hurricane RAF test pilot reported that 'The aircraft is simple and easy to fly and has no apparent vices.'[1] However, for a young, inexperienced pilot it was another matter, and it soon became clear that the next few weeks' training would prove to be the most difficult so far.

Tuesday, 30 September. An Awful Day. We started Hurricane flying today. I got up early and caught the bus over with several others at 06.15 for a whole day's flying at Childs Ercall. Neville and Ian were to fly first but after climbing into their Hurricanes it was discovered that Ian's aircraft had an internal cooling leak so Neville was to go off alone. While waiting for my turn P/O Foster[2] and I went off in the Master to practise some low flying. Landing forty-five minutes later I asked Peter Biggart, who was looking very pale, if Neville was back yet. He said, 'Neville's in the deck.'

Master and Hurricane training aircraft at Turn Hill. (*Family Collection*)

His engine had cut about 100 ft from the ground. He hadn't jammed the nose down and consequently it stalled. His Hurricane did a quarter spin straight into the ground and it caught fire and burnt out. Neville was thrown clear but broke his neck and died instantly.

This was the beginning of a series of misfortunes in quick succession. Jerry, Monty and Roger were sent up in the Hurricanes, in a rainstorm. Roger landed hard on one wheel and his undercart gave way and he bent the propeller. Jerry got to Tern Hill, did a heavy tail landing, lost his tail-wheel and dipped a wing. Monty got down OK.

I took one up feeling sure that this was my last time on Terra firma. Take-off was difficult; the Hurricane's nose is so long that you can't see in front of you. I zigzagged down the runway checking out of the side-cockpit window for obstacles and took off. After take-off I had difficulty raising the undercarriage as one has to change hands on the stick, at a critical time, to operate the retractable undercarriage selector lever.[3] When actually flying, it felt a beautiful aircraft to control. The Hurricane responded well but problems arose when I tried to land. Approaching the airfield at Tern Hill, the Hurricane seemed to have no desire to slow down for landing. I overshot the runway and had to fly around for another attempt, with the same result. I began to wonder if I was ever going to get down; I did three overshoots but then made a perfect landing. After an hour and a quarter I returned to Childs Ercall and landed perfectly there too.

Everyone was pleased to see David return, for they feared that he had also crashed, having taken such a long time to get back.

We are such a close group that the loss of Neville seems too heavy a burden to bear. Neville had not been himself for sometime and I'm afraid his nerve had gone a few weeks ago. It was rotten luck, his first trip in a Hurricane and the engine cutting like that.

Wednesday, 1 October. We returned to Childs Ercall and the first misfortune of the day happened when Bert accidentally put his arm through the bus window; he had to have several nasty cuts looked at and arrived later bandaged up at various points.

I took up a Hurricane, a De Havilland Type *(Mk I revised)* in the morning and it seemed to take an age for the flaps to come down. I didn't like it at all. The weather got bad so I landed early. By lunchtime we had all flown successfully with just a few ropey landings, except Peter Biggart and Ian Duffus who didn't come, I think their nerve has gone. At the end of the day, after another 50-minute flight, I was more accustomed to the extra speed and power. I feel more confident now and think that the Hurricane is safer than the Master.

Tony Hilditch wrote with news of No.53 Squadron:

St Eval.
We are getting used to the Hudsons now and most of us like them very much. As you say they are rather heavy but you get used to it and if you have enough

strength you can throw them round in a quite surprising way. They are very suited to our present job – long anti-submarine patrols…. I shall not be surprised to hear that you have been put on to Army Co-op on Tomahawks and if so I should be very interested to hear something about it. As you know, we were once supposed to be Army Co-op ourselves and I should like to hear the latest developments.

Yours, Tony.

At Liverpool Docks, Dennys Scott embarked on the 'Dominion Monarch' and set sail for Singapore.

Thursday, 2 October. The chocolate I ate before I took my written Wings' exam was most delicious; our exams included Signals, Airmanship, Maintenance, Armaments and Navigation. They were very easy except for the navigation paper, but Professor 'Plumb Line' put me straight on that and I passed.

Not everyone was finding things so easy. Ian Duffus was beginning to show signs of the strain and in the evening David had a long talk to him in the 'Stormy Petrel' the local pub just outside Tern Hill's gates. Duffus told David that he and Peter Biggart[4] had decided to give up flying and go back to their Regiments. They remained at Turn Hill doing odd jobs around the station until rejoining the Army. David was glad as he didn't think Ian was really cut out for flying, especially as he had a wife and children to think about. David met up with Duffus again at No.35 Recce Wing where he was posted as an Air Liaison Officer.

David was pleased to meet up with Robert Drummond[5] and Humphrey Gilbert who, having stayed on for further training at Sealand, now arrived for Course 67. Ex-Hollywood make-up artist Humphrey Gilbert already had a reputation as a practical joker, but later when posted to No.609 Squadron, he quickly gained further acclaim for crashing aircraft. In July 1942 he crash-landed his Typhoon and a month later was concussed during a forced landing. Unfit to fly until the end of the year, his C/O Roland Beamont vividly remembered the squadron's Christmas party. Gilbert on a horse – with a pretty WAAF on pillion – rode through the front door of Doone House and up the stairs, the horse leaving a number of steaming 'gifts' on the way up to the first floor. Seeing Beamont, Gilbert slid down the banister saying, 'Just parking my horse Sir,' and disappeared into the bar. Later when a pilot was required for target-towing duties in Palestine, Gilbert seemed to Beamont to be the obvious choice.[6]

Ex-Hollywood make-up artist Humphrey Gilbert gained a reputation for crashing aircraft. *(SAGH – NRO AP11-F540)*

Needing to notch up about twenty-five more hours flying time, David's course were now flying Masters and Hurricanes up to four times a day.

The trouble is the weather is rotten so we are getting very little flying and we wait around all the time. Toyne is such a nice Squadron Leader. He is the most refined and reasonable individual it has been my fortune to meet in the RAF service since I started my training at Cambridge. He went through the Battle of Britain, has the DFC and was stationed near the place where my days in the ranks were spent.

Vivienne Lee wrote with news of Mark, who was now flying shipping patrols in Beauforts.

RAF EO, Liverpool, Oct 9.
I had definitely thought of going to the Middle East but everyone was so against it that I just hadn't the courage to do it all myself without the moral support, anyway I think the work is as important here and I have given up the idea now. Mark, by the way, is on Ops now and stationed at St Eval in No.217 Squadron.

I'm amazed you are flying Hurricanes so soon. Gosh it must have been a bit terrifying the first time. You sounded rather fed up but I believe Mark hated the hanging about waiting for night flying, it certainly must be pretty awful....
Vivienne.

Hearing the news of Neville Day's death, Flight Lieutenant Robert Addison wrote:

Jesus College, 4/10/41.
It was with deep regret that I heard of the death of Neville Day. Such a good chap. I remember his grin. Keen as mustard. But I hope that the rhythm of your training has not been too badly interrupted. If I may say so, as a non-flying man, you must make this sort of sadness a lesson, in the sense that only constant vigilance will do. I don't want to preach, god knows, but it is so important that you excellent fellows should not fall by the wayside in training. If it is any cheer, except for poor Hall, this is the first death in my own 150 AOs....
Yours Sincerely, Robert.

On the clear but cold night of October 11, David flew seven night landings with Flying Officer Foster then three solo before going back up with his Instructor for one more. Catching a few hours sleep, he started flying again in the late afternoon. Childs Ercall was misty and he drifted badly in his dual landing, but managed six further solo landings. The rest of the week David flew cross-country flights to Hereford, Pershore and Sealand, and also gained an hour's aerobatics and spinning at 1,000 feet.

Crashes and accidents were now regular occurrences. William Vocking was killed night-flying at Chetwynd on 17 October, having put his flaps up at a hundred feet instead of his undercart and on the 22nd, Sergeant Maurice Delecray, a Free French pilot in a Master flying on No.64 Course was also killed.[7]

At morning lectures there are more and more empty places, the bills for wreaths mount up, letters of sympathy have to be written and funeral parties have become part of our routine.

Airmen's losses around the base were not confined to the RAF. During an air raid on Wednesday, 22 October, a German JU88 was shot down. Two crew members bailed out near Market Drayton, however Oberfeldwebel Herbert Datzert and Feldwebel Eric Neukirchen, unable to escape the aircraft, were buried with Service Honours at the nearby church of St Peter and St Paul, Stoke-on-Tern.[8]

> I can't understand the mentality of some English people. This week two German airmen walked into the village and knocked on the door of a house. A sleepy head poked out and growled, 'What do you want?' When the owner heard they were Germans he said, 'Oh do come in and have a cup of tea!' A very different reception awaited me when my car was locked in a yard today and someone had to get up to undo the gate.

October 25 was David's twenty-second birthday and he had hoped to get home, but he was not granted leave. News of David's old Battalion arrived in a letter from Peter Williams.

> *10th Bn Loyal Brigade, Corfe Castle, 26/10/41.*
> After returning from Wimborne we went to Swanage where we stayed for just over three months erecting that bloody scaffolding most of the time, and then we moved to Kingston, my platoon to Seacombe the most desolate spot in the Battalion area. – Two Nissen huts, a cook house and a hut for myself into which you can just fit a camp bed and a table.... You may have heard Dudley's friend was reported missing. He was shot down off Brest when they went over as fighter escort. They lost a sergeant[9] the same day, the latter was reported a prisoner. Dudley is very fit and now in Norfolk and seems to spend a lot of his time over Holland and Northern France....
> Major Hickson is now on RAF Liaison, Muffet is now a Captain.[10]
> All the best. Peter Williams.

Advanced Formation in a Hurricane behind my instructor Flt/Lt Lord and another pupil, the clouds were grand. I am now really enjoying flying and it has become almost second nature to me. This has been the most pleasant week's flying I have done for many weeks. Hurricane aerobatics above the clouds is good fun and a pleasant pastime. Flying is a real pleasure now whereas it used to be a Terror! I love flying the Hurricane and can't wait to get into the air. They are glorious planes and except for Spitfires, I believe they spoil you for flying anything else. It's hard to describe the sense of excitement. You get dressed up in parachute harness, helmet, goggles, oxygen

During a break in training David poses with his Hurricane. *(Family Collection)*

mask and microphone, then struggle over the tall side into the small cockpit; I don't know how some of the larger chaps manage. Once settled down, you clip up the Sutton harness, RT fitted and tested, then the electric start is plugged in and the great engine roars into operation. After running up, chocks away, all gauges and switches tested, brakes off, you taxi out to the boundary of the field, turn into the wind all set for vital actions and open up gradually. The aircraft shoots forward and accelerates at a terrific pace. Then off it comes and the ground rapidly falls away below. The fields and houses shrink away. Any little touch on the controls causes the Hurricane to react instantly in any direction. You may shiver because it can get a little draughty up here even with the hood shut for although it is warm on the ground, it can get quite cold at 9,000 ft. After practising your skills, you reluctantly head home, not ever wanting to land because you feel more at home up there than you ever thought possible.

Not all the pupils at Tern Hill were finding flying as easy, and another pupil, LAC Brian Napoleon Lee, was killed on the 28th. In all, five pupils were killed in October, one from Course 64, one from Course 67 and three from Course 66.[11] David noted in his diary that on October 30 the French pupils had 'a field day' at Childs Ercall.

One in a Master, landed with the undercart up, which broke our course record as we hadn't had one to date. Another, in a Hurricane, tried to take-off in coarse pitch and went through a hedge. He had looked at FINE fully back and the modification label had come off and it was now, as usual, fully forward. A third, in very bad weather, landed his Hurricane near Dispersal and with his wing took away a Master's undercart then just missed another Hurrybox. He then hit the bowser tractor before finally stopping on the wet ground with no brakes.

By the end of the month all No.65 Course pupils had covered the syllabus, passed the Ground Exams satisfactorily and gained the required flying hours. David's total was seventy-one hours on the Master, ten and a quarter hours on the Hurricane, with ten hours in the Link Trainer. Expecting to be awarded his Wings he was surprised to be given a week's leave instead. Harry Dent, who had already received his Wings, wrote with his news.

Officers Mess, No.20 OTU, Lossiemouth, Scotland, 7/11/41.
David…, We received our Wings on 21 October and went on leave for a fortnight. We then suddenly had our postings. John Finman and myself here on Wellingtons, Bunny to Upper Heyford and Ken Gibbons to Bicester…. I am at last resigned to bombers and shall try to get into Stirlings eventually. Apparently the next few weeks consists entirely of ground subjects. We are not due to fly for three weeks but they are rather behind and I don't really expect to start for months. It is dammed cold up here and the Mess is not too good but we are amongst a good crowd of officers, most of whom are Canadians.
Bunny went to Monty's wedding and also went to see Ian, when he was on leave. Wray told me that he saw you in town….
All the best, Harry.

At home, David found Ronald also back on leave. He was working with No.27 Signals Training Group at Cirencester, but itching to get back to a Fighter Station. Disappointed after the excitement of hearing that Herrick was a POW, the family were finding it hard to keep on hoping for good news, and approached by an artist who offered to paint Charles's picture, they all agreed it was a grand idea.

Reporting back to Tern Hill, ready to be sent on to the next stage of his training, David found that although there was to be no more flight training, there was still no news of when their Wings' presentation was to take place.

6 November. I arrived just in time for tea. Nobody seems to know when we leave here or where we will go but everyone is looking much better for their leave. Jan Plesman has been up in London, meeting up with hundreds of Dutch friends and had spent about twenty-five pounds! Louis Ricard-Cordingley went for a cruise up the Scottish Coast in a steamer, he met a Professor at Edinburgh University who asked him to stay whenever he liked. Melvyn went to Worthing to see his old Battalion where he has two brothers then went home to Aberystwyth. Monty came back married to Topsy Gray from Pinner and I hear he's been in great trouble for not asking Groupy's permission first. He has to do orderly officer duties and gets no leave for some time. There is rather a good picture of them in the Tatler.

After dinner in the Mess, coffee in the lounge and a game of billiards, David had a long talk to Polish pilots Jan Plesman and Govert Steen.

Plesman is posted to Spitfires at Hendon. Lucky chap! In London, he met a Pole who was wild, having waited four months in England doing nothing and he wanted 'to pull the trigger on hundreds of Germans.' He has tried all he can to get to Tobruk but he is 35 so too old to fly. Another Pole reported, 'I flew to Berlin and back and stooged around for a long time and never had a shot fired at me, till I reached Portsmouth on the way home where I was greeted by a terrific barrage.'

Jan can't wait to fly over his home when he gets to a squadron and intends to drop hockey balls and pictures of his Queen there. He thought it would be grand for morale and that the news would spread around the Netherlands like wildfire, starting with one Spit dropping two hockey balls but by the time it got to the other end of the country it would probably be 500 Spitfires and a thousand hockey balls! The reason for the hockey balls is his old club were running very short before he left and they would know who was flying over.

Talking of propaganda I think the Free French will be able to do quite a lot in that line. Each Sunday at 11 am the Huns have a great parade through the streets of Paris and he thinks a squadron of Spitfires clearly marked with the Cross of Lorraine by the side of the roundels (red, white and blue now) would be a good show especially if the Huns ran for it.

Steen told David that when Germany invaded Holland there were few civilians who thought invasion was likely, but the Government knew and the Air Force was ready. Steen flew up to intercept the Luftwaffe bombers and shot down a Ju88 from a dive

David felt a glow of pride when he received his pilot's wings. *(SAGH – © Crown Copyright.)*

attack on his tail. He also had a dogfight with an Me110 and, as his Fokker G1 could climb better, he shot it down, but was accounted for by several others on his tail. Steen dived away with no engine and force-landed.

As there were no more planes available, he got a machine gun and defended a canal road. An American car came along at about seventy miles per hour with six paratroopers in and he shot the driver, the car swerved across the road, hit the curb and flew straight over on its back in the canal. They shot all but two, whom they captured.

On Monday, 10 November, Oldfield told the pupils that he had good news for them and would tell them at the passing out party of ground staff, pupils and instructors in the evening. David arrived with Louis Ricard-Cordingly and Melvyn Evans.

There was a terrific noise and sound of many queer instruments being played but still no definite news had come through from the Air Ministry. The next day we turned up at the hangars at 9 am, had our Log Books stamped up and passing out chits signed by a number of people. After lunch we went down, expecting to be awarded our Wings, only to be told that we were to stay at Tern Hill for another week. Some had already put their Wings on their uniforms. Poor old Garware looked so proud in his Wings and Sgt's stripes but was told to take them off again. So glad I hadn't put mine up. Garware[12] told us his woes, his father, an Indian, made a lot of money and owns a car factory. G's father gave two Spitfires to the British Government, sent G to England to join the RAF (which cost £1,000) and yet G cannot get a commission although he has a degree from Bombay University. With a lot of bad feeling in the camp, Melvyn, Bert and I drove to Whitchurch and hitched a lift into Chester with a commercial traveller. It was a nerve-racking drive as he had only started driving three weeks before. Sharing a room, we spent an uncomfortable night at the Royal Oak.

At last on November 19, No.65 Course finally received their Wings, and David officially became a Pilot Officer.

So many men have been drawn into a Service to obtain a coveted uniform or emblem and now in 1941, when the deeds of the RAF are proclaimed, there are few who do not feel a glow of pride when they first appear in public wearing a pair of Wings. I am no exception.

Of the fifty pupils, Lieutenant Duffus and Lieutenant Biggart returned to the Army due to 'Loss of Confidence', Lieutenant Day, LAC Pickering, LAC De Silva and Sergeant Sayers were killed in flying accidents, and LAC Vere-Holloway was unable to reach the required standards. They were assessed as 'Above Average' for both Navigation and General, and 'Average' in Instrument and Night Flying.[13]

Back at home, David found it difficult to settle.

> I will be glad when my leave is over and I go onto an OTU. However I can now go hunting as Father has a sweet polo pony, Goldfinch, that played for England several times, I was worried that it may have a docked-tail especially as we have always been so critical of the Walkers with their docked tail horse but it was fine. 'The laugh would have been on us,' as the Americans would say. Riding him is like driving a Bentley after an Austin Seven or flying a Hurricane after a Tiger Moth.

As well orders to report Old Sarum, David received a batch of letters written on December 1. Both Melvyn Evans and Donald Draper wrote that they were posted to Old Sarum, and Melvyn added, 'I only hope that we don't fly Lysanders – rather than Tomahawks. I hope you and Bert are coming along as well and indeed it may be that all the old gang may turn up, for A.C. was my 3rd choice.'

After a crash in a Tiger Moth, Richard Osborn spent over a month in hospital with concussion.

RAF Chipping Warden, Nr Banbury, Oxon, 1/12/41.
The other fellow got two black eyes! The Tiger was just two seats with us sitting in them, while all the other minor fittings such as engine, wings etc were scattered around. But that finished me for Ops, I only had 2 or 3 trips to do before my 200 hours and I must confess I was getting pretty tired after 31 trips and 5 months at Waterbeach.... I went to Harwell and got comfortably settled there in the Anson, flight training navigators, when after three weeks they rushed me off to this mud hole. I took a very poor view of the whole show. Here I am, in an Operational Flight and risking my neck with the newly formed crews....

Yours, Richard. [14]

Captured in Singapore, Dennys Scott spent the war as a Japanese POW. *(With kind permission of Lucie Johnson)*

Now thousands of miles away from home, Dennys Scott and his Regiment disembarked in Singapore. Their timing was terrible, for the following week two waves of Japanese bombers launched a surprise attack on the American's Pacific Naval base at Pearl Harbour, Hawaii. They sank six US battleships and sank or damaged over one hundred other vessels. The Americans were shocked by this unprovoked attack. On night-duty, Ronald received a signal, stating that Pearl Harbour had been attacked, but unaware of where it was and therefore failing to realize its significance, he placed the message into the pending tray to deal with in the morning. Finding the signal the next day, the Station Commander was absolutely furious with Ronald for not waking him.

By late afternoon on December 8, when Britain and America declared war on Japan, the whole world knew the importance of the Pearl Harbour attack. Pondering on the intensity of the attack, David wrote home.

What a terrible thing these Japanese suicide torpedo bombers are. What is the answer to it?

Chapter Nine

Lysanders Operational Training Unit, Old Sarum: December 1941 to February 1942

'The Army Co-operation pilot was quite a different animal from the Fighter pilot: he was an independent character. Being in Army Co-operation was like a rather special club.'

'Mustangs at War,' Roger A Freeman.

O ld Sarum Airfield was opened in August 1917 for use of the Royal Flying Corps and the airfield on the outskirts of Salisbury, Wiltshire was close to the Army training grounds and camps on Salisbury Plain. In September 1941, it became an Operational Training Unit (OTU) for No.41 Army Co-operation to teach the highly specialized skills required of an Army Co-op pilot. The course was between seven and eight weeks in duration and pilots were expected to work every day of the week.

David drove down to Old Sarum, stopping en route at RAF Chipping Warden to meet Richard Osborn for lunch. Having returned from the Middle East after quite a long period of air fighting, Richard's brother Andrew was also an instructor there. Both were sporting DFCs.[1] At Marlborough, David met Hugh Craig Harvey who said his brother Andrew had been at Oflag VII-C in 1940, and had now moved to Oflag VI-B. (Here he shared a hut with John Peyton, and with several others they dug a 255-foot long tunnel, but before they could escape it was discovered by the Germans).[2]

9 December 1941. I stopped in at the Polly Tea Rooms. The tea was good and the cakes were up to their usual standard. Mrs McDougal recognized me and let me buy some that had been reserved for teas. She said that early on in the day they had all kinds to sell. It wasn't too bad a drive except for the last few miles across Salisbury Plain, which was difficult in the blackout. It was good to meet the old gang who were already here. The Mess is comfortable and very different to all the others I have been in, a very good spirit. Many people here are wearing khaki uniforms and I am allowed to wear either, so I'm going to wear khaki in the daytime and change to blue at night.

In the Mess, David met up with Peter 'Jerry' Miles, Monty Denny, Donald Draper, Roger Boyce, Gordon Buck and Melvyn Evans and nineteen year-old Peter Erskine Vaughan-Fowler who was also at Old Sarum.

Army Co-op pilots carried out a huge variety of tasks, mostly flown behind enemy lines. On an Artillery Reconnaissance (Arty/R), pilots identified targets to attack,

Oblique and vertical photos of Andrew Craig Harvey's home taken by David. *(Family Collection – © Crown Copyright.)*

CAMOUFLAGE INSTRUCTION CHART Number VIa AIR PHOTOGRAPHS—Army Signatures

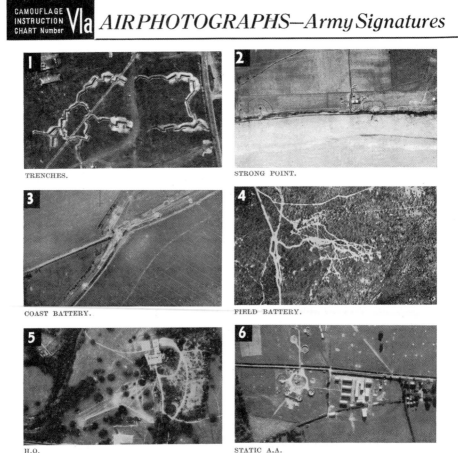

On a Tac/R, Army pilots photographed trenches and gun emplacements. *(Family Collection – Crown © 1940)*

directed Artillery fire towards enemy positions and gave instructions to correct the gunner's range. When flying a Tactical Reconnaissance (Tac/R) they observed and relayed information about advancing troops, enemy movement, trench, road and bridge defences and gun emplacements.

On photographic operations (Populars), pilots located and photographed enemy targets, such as radar masts and coastline defences. Photographs could be taken from two different viewpoints. Vertical photographs, mainly used for mapping or confirmation of hits, were taken from any height. Oblique photographs, taken from a low-angled viewpoint gave good indication of an object's height and size. This required the pilot to 'hedge-hop', flying as low as fifty to a hundred feet, and pilots had to take care to avoid trees or power lines.

It took a lot of practise to perfect the art of aerial photography. In a letter to David, No.16 Squadron pilot, Douglas Wills 'Sammy' Sampson, wrote of the difficulties of using the Lysander's camera viewfinder. 'The minute gridded glass viewer was at about the limit of vision on the floor, if not lost to sight under dropped pencils, bits of old maps and the remains of airman's buns from the NAAFI's wagons. I personally found this unmanageable and am sure it was specified by some Teutonic mole in the Air Ministry.'[3]

Other Co-op duties included picking up or dropping messages, flying army supplies or personnel, and later these tasks were expanded to include anti-shipping patrols (Lagoons) and daylight, low-level, air-to-ground attacks of enemy positions. (Rhubarbs).

> We met Wing Commander Fuller,[4] the C/O, as well as the Adjutant and Chief Ground Instructor. Then we went down to pick up a Mae West life jacket and a small packet, which is a self-inflating rubber dinghy, which will be added to my parachute. The spire of Salisbury Cathedral will be a useful landmark as I'm told that in low foggy weather it sticks up out of the sea of cloud. Monty, Melvyn and I went into Salisbury and had drinks at the White Hart, the Cathedral, the Red Lion and supper at the Officers Club. I said to Monty that I was bound to bump into someone I knew and sure enough at supper I ran into Greville Selby Lowndes. He is now in the Grenadier Guards and told me that, Michael Harvey, John Jameson[5] and my great friend from Sandhurst, Robert Etherton, are all in the battalion. I'm hoping to meet them all next week.

In foggy weather the spire of Salisbury Cathedral proved a useful landmark. *(Family Collection – Crown © 1941)*

Meanwhile in Singapore, David's friend, Tim Vigors, now C/O of No.453 Squadron, was facing difficult times. Force Z, a British naval squadron led by HMS *Prince of Wales* and HMS *Repulse* had been ordered to intercept a large Japanese invasion fleet. As No.453 Squadron was designated the Fleet Defence Squadron, Tim Vigors suggested that six of his Brewster Buffalos provide air cover during daylight hours, however, Admiral Philips was in favour of maintaining radio silence. It was only when Japanese bombers located Force Z and began to attack that Vigors finally received orders to scramble. Eleven pilots took off…, 'but it was too late: when Vigors arrived, *Repulse* had gone down, *Prince of Wales* was sinking, and there was no sign of Japanese aircraft.'[6] Later Vigors bitterly commented, 'I reckon this must have been the last battle in which the Navy reckoned they could get along without the RAF. A pretty damned costly way of learning.'[7]

On December 11, Italy and Germany declared war on America and the USA immediately responded by declaring war on the two Axis powers, calling them 'savage and barbarous forces.' The next day Butterworth Airfield on the east coast of Malaysia was the target for Japanese aircraft. Vigors took off, but he was quickly shot down. After bailing out, he saw Japanese planes coming in to attack him. Remembering advice given to him in the Battle of Britain, as he descended he collapsed his parachute several times. Hit in the thigh, Vigors escaped serious injury, and landed in a forest on Penang Island. He was rescued by locals and eventually evacuated to India.[8]

Although the war in the Far East was going badly for the Allies, David noted that there was better news in the papers from the Russian Front:

Saturday, 13 December. It would be marvellous if the Russians could knock the Germans right back to Germany. They certainly seemed to have saved Moscow, Leningrad and the Crimea for the winter at any rate.

After breakfast I reported to 'A' Flight, took a good look around the Lysander and had my solo test at last. Mother calls them horrid planes that look like beetles. In one way she is right, as Lizzies look slow and heavy, but I soon found that they are easy to fly and are perfect for Co-op work.

The two-seater Lysander had a Bristol Mercury engine, its high wing gave the pilot good visibility and it was able to take-off and land on small fields or unprepared short runways. An observer sat in the rear cockpit and acted as machine-gunner. The aircraft had forward-facing twin Browning guns in each wheel fairing, and Lewis guns for the observer.

After the heavy rain, it is amazing that the airfield is not muddy; I suppose it must be

The Westland Lysander's high wing gave the pilot all round visibility. (*SAGH © Illustrated London News*)

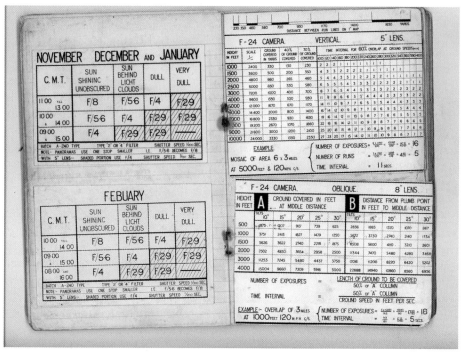

Aircraft camera settings. *(Family Collection – © Crown Copyright)*

the chalky soil. The Lysander has been unserviceable for a while but at last today I had my second flight which I enjoyed. In the evening, I went into Salisbury to the White Hart for a drink with Pip and Mary Hutton. Pip is down here for a few days' leave.

The next day David went to Boscombe Down, home to the Aeroplane and Armament Experimental Establishment (A&AEE), a research facility for testing aircraft. In one of the hangers, David spotted an odd brown aircraft with the nose, engine, cockpit and tail all in different sections. Only the wings were clipped onto the fuselage. Asking what plane it was, he was told that it was the new North American Mustang. David remarked that he sincerely hoped that he wouldn't have to fly one as they looked likely to fall to bits very easily.

Unable to get home for Christmas, David's family had to celebrated without him.

Christmas Day. I was flying yesterday and so sorry to miss the carol service from Kings College. I had a quiet Christmas here on the base, as I was Duty Officer. I thought I would offer so that one of the married types could go off to see his family. I listened to the wireless in the morning then as tradition dictates served the airmen their meal. It was an excellent repast all beautifully decorated.

Christmas lunch was so good it even received a mention in the No.41 OTU Operations Record Book. 'In spite of the difficulties imposed by wartime catering, it was found possible to serve all personnel with an excellent dinner, including turkey, pork, plum

Army Camp, Salisbury Plain. Co-op pilots were trained to take low-level photographs of army positions. *(Family Collection – Crown © 1941)*

pudding, mince pies, beer and ten cigarettes per head.'[9] On Monday, 29 December, David had a pleasant surprise.

> Tiny Allen phoned from the Watch Office having received the letter I had written when I had the flu. He is now a Staff Officer G3 Camouflage and was waiting to fly off somewhere. I went over to dinner at my old Corps HQ and had a long chat with a great deal to talk about. It was so good to meet people keen on and content in their work. Allen said he enjoys every moment of his job and I told him I was in my element too. I am glad I joined Army Co-operation, I'm enjoying it immensely, especially the low flying which is exciting although it requires a great deal of concentration.

David was saddened to hear from Vivienne[10] that Mark Lee had been killed on December 9, when his Beaufort crashed off the Dutch Coast.[11]

> *Tuesday, 30 December.* I am sorry that Mark has been shot down, what rotten luck after he had had his leave cancelled, for otherwise he would have been at home. However, he was on a particularly hazardous job and it was as I feared when no phone call came that Sunday.

Prompted by a Christmas greeting from David, Harry Dent wrote:

Lossiemouth, Scotland, 6 January 1942.
David…, The news I have for you is mainly pretty foul, but I'll try to give you the best first. Most of the boys are at Bicester. Bunny Emmett and Paddy Boyle went to Upper Heyford on Hampdens but managed to switch to Blenheims at Bicester[12] where they found Bob Lancaster and Ken Gibbons. I believe that some of them have nearly finished and are expecting to go (Middle) East…. John Firman and I found ourselves in this god-forsaken refuge of the dammed in the hinterland. Our course put up an all time record by being here for 8½ weeks without once going up. We expect to be here for another three months by which time I shall undoubtedly have gone quite mad and bitten a Group Captain or something equally futile. I have been examining my past life pretty carefully, but I can't find anything sufficiently heinous to warrant consignment to this misbegotten arctic swamp…, By the way, do you remember Phillips[13] who came to you from us with love; did he pass out of Tern Hill?
Yours ever, Harry.

A week after Christmas, David hoped, as part of his cross-country and navigation flying practise, to land in the field at Bowden. However, things did not go as he had planned.

I flew north with Sergeant Spencer and flew only a few feet above the house but my plan failed, the paddock was apparently unoccupied and hardly a soul could be seen, so I didn't alight, I can't understand it at all. I will have to find out what went wrong or find another perching place. I shan't be able to get home now for about six weeks.

During January, he continued training on cross-country navigation, low-level dive-bombing, night-landings, formation flying and taking evasive action. By now the

A steam train passing Army Camp 3365. *(Family Collection – Crown © 1941)*

family knew the chances of Charles turning up alive were very slim, and on January 16, an official letter arrived concluding that he was now 'Presumed dead.'

Another friend's death occurred on January 26 during a Spitfire training flight at No.57 OTU Hawarden. Louis Ricard-Cordingly collided with Polish Spitfire pilot, Flying Officer Roman Suwalski. Ricard-Cordingly bailed out of his plane, but too low; his parachute failed to open fully.[14]

After two months training the 'Army Rebels' were finally split up. David and Peter Miles were posted to No.16 Squadron, Melvyn Evans, Donald Draper, Gordon Buck and Roger Boyce to No.4 Squadron based at Clifton near York, while Monty Denny remained at Old Sarum as an Instructor.

Part IV

Operations with No.16 Squadron

Chapter Ten

RAF Weston Zoyland with No.16 Squadron: February 1942–May 1942

'The skill of the photo reconnaissance pilot was incredible; they were among the best pilots in the Air Force…. How they could take the photos they did is astonishing when you remember they were taken in combat, and often being shot at….'

Allan Williams, Curator National Collection of Aerial Photography.
Independent on Sunday, 23 November 2009.

No. 16 Squadron, a reconnaissance squadron working with Army Co-op, was stationed at Weston Zoyland, about four miles from Bridgewater, between the villages of Westonzoyland and Middlezoy. The small, grass aerodrome had a wire-mesh runway with a hangar for maintenance. In the orchard next to the airfield was an assortment of huts that served as HQ, Dispersal and Army Liaison offices. There was also a mobile darkroom where photographs could be developed and printed. Nearby, in the village of Othery, Townsend House was used as a Mess, the local hall served as the NAAFI Canteen and bar, and the pilots were billeted around the villages.

Othery, with Weston Zoyland airfield in the distance. The large square farmhouse on the left was David's billet. *(Family Collection – Crown © 1942)*

Army Co-op squadrons normally comprised twelve aircraft and crew (fifty per cent of whom were ex-Army officers) and a large supporting team of ground staff. No.16 Squadron had around 25 officers and 150 ground staff whose roles included fitters responsible for engines, and riggers for the airframe, Air Liaison Officers, armourers, electricians, radio-operators, batmen, catering and photographic staff, clerks, drivers and medical personnel.

At lunchtime on 11 February 1942, David arrived at No.16 Squadron and soon met up with other 'new boys' Peter 'Jerry' Miles and Ian Dixon Baker.

> After a drive over the lovely countryside of Somerset I arrived in the peaceful village of Othery about three miles from the airfield. The War seems to be very far away. The Commanding Officer lives in a caravan near the Officers Mess and we are all billeted in cottages here. My billet, Elm Tree Farm, is a small house, a five-minute walk from the Mess and the room is nice but very cold. The retired farmer and his wife, the Thatchers, are very pleasant and let me come into the sitting room in the evening. There is no electricity in the village so we use oil

Othery Village. *(Family Collection – Crown © 1942)*

lamps, there is also a water shortage and the water is off for considerable periods during the day. I was very cold last night and so I looked under the quilt. I found a considerable mixture of a large towel, a blanket and a bundle of chintz curtains, or so it would appear, so I have borrowed a blanket from Jerry who has too many. I had thought we might be somewhat isolated as the Squadron is detached from the airfield. I was correct, but I wasn't sufficiently prepared for it. I tried walking back from the airfield but soon decided that I will bike in future and my car will also be a useful asset for trips further afield.

No.16 Squadron chiefly flew Lysanders, however, the squadron had a variety of other aircraft including two Tomahawks, two Fairey Battles,[1] a Proctor for communication duties, a Tiger Moth for flying staff around the country, and a Miles Master for instrument practise. While other Co-operation squadrons were in the process of converting from Lysanders to Curtiss Tomahawks, No.16 Squadron decided that, with its inadequate firepower and lack of armour plating, they were not the right aircraft for the job, and decided to continue to fly Lysanders.

There are some very good types here. Alastair Maclay[2] left his farm in Scotland twelve months ago to volunteer to fly. Tony Davis,[3] my Flight Commander, is from a similar background as me, he studied engineering for a year at Magdalene College, Cambridge, then went into the Army before transferring to the RAF.

We have a real country existence but I think it will be a trifle muddy until spring comes. We feed in the Mess and, considering the water shortage and oil cookers, the food is remarkably good. Charles would have loved it here, it's all very unofficial.

After heavy fighting, news finally came through on 15 February that the British Forces in Singapore had finally surrendered to the Japanese. One of the soldiers captured was David's friend Dennys Scott.[4] In his speech Winston Churchill described the fall of Singapore as 'the worst disaster and largest capitulation in British history.'[5]

While Scott was being led off to a POW camp, David was flying the Lysander whenever the weather and aircraft repairs would permit.

I had a grand day flying over some of my favourite pieces of England under ideal conditions. I saw small ships steaming out to sea and wondered where they were going and what dangers they would run into. I lunched at St Eval and was interested to see what sort of place it was as Charles said so little about it. Tony Hilditch had left two weeks ago,[6] however I met a chap who said that Herrick had died in hospital shortly after being shot down so it seems likely that we will never find out what happened to Charles. It's the not knowing that is the worst part.

I listened to Churchill's speech. He is very clever and I am so sorry that he has to answer for others' mistakes and to answer for those scandalous individuals who corrupt the mind of the public with destructive criticism regardless of the facts. He said that people should not abuse the privilege of free speech and constructive criticism. Exactly what I hoped he would say.

Ilfracombe was one of David's favourite places in England. *(Family Collection – Crown © 1942)*

As the squadron was not yet operational, David continued to hone his cross-country and map reading skills, flying a combination of tours of southern England to Plymouth and St Eval, ably helped by his air gunner Sergeant Goode. They also took part in several Tac/Rs and air-to-ground firing exercises.

At Clifton Airfield, No.4 Squadron's 'new boy' Gordon Buck was also practising air-to-ground dive attacks, while his gunner Flight Sergeant Boyd fired at the target. On one of these dives, Buck failed to pull up in time and his Lysander hit the ground. William Malins saw the crash. 'I watched the aircraft breaking up as it slid nose first along the ground.' Sgt Boyd was pulled from the wreckage alive with minor injuries but Gordon Buck was killed.[7]

Upset at the loss of their friend, two letters arrived from No.4 Squadron. Melvyn Evans wrote:

Officer's Mess, RAF Clifton, York. We were all upset by Gordon Buck's untimely death on Tuesday.... Luckily his air-gunner escaped with minor injuries and will soon be out of hospital. This has cast rather a slur on an otherwise very auspicious introduction to the squadron. The officers are very friendly and all in all a pleasant crowd. We very soon settled down and are comfortable in billets scattered within ½ mile of the aerodrome. As regards its geographical position, the aerodrome is even more convenient in its proximity to York than OS to Salisbury. This (you will now no doubt be saying) must suit a person of my erotic instincts very nicely.

Yours, Melvyn

Donald Draper, who also witnessed the accident, said it had been very hard for his wife and child and added, 'We all arrived here safely on the day appointed, except for Vaughan Fowler! The weather has been awful so we have had very little flying.' He wondered if Weston Zoyland was as bad as the rumours; 'I should hate to think that you are unable to have a bath!!'

At the end of February, with the new clothing rationing due to come in, David, Alastair Maclay and Tony Davis took the opportunity to spend an afternoon in Taunton buying clothes and other essentials.

> I am finding it difficult to shave, as wet-shaving in the mornings in cold water is slow and painful so I brought a battery for my electric razor. I thought I had finished with that when I left the Army, for it is only for use when there is no electric light. We finally have two baths installed in the Mess but soap is almost unobtainable and I don't know what I would have done if I hadn't had a stock of it.
>
> I am annoyed that I lost my small fountain pen, the only one I have left is definitely a wartime model and it just drips ink everywhere.

Being a country-based squadron, staff had less places to spend their free time, so a range of activities were offered. Land in the central camp area was given over to an allotment for growing vegetables, and early morning PT sessions, arranged especially for Officers and NCOs, were held by the appropriately named, Corporal Cramp.

Pistol firing could be practised at the Butts, and one day 'Sammy' Sampson heard a thrashing whoosh as a low-flying Lysander disappeared behind the Butts. 'The C/O said a few penetrating words including a dire threat about low-flying.' Back at the airfield it was noted that the Squadron Leader's aircraft had a broken landing-light. 'He was not on view for a day or two and we junior officers were never informed about the murky details.'[8]

Pilots caught up in the thrill of flight often ignored these dire threats. One cold February afternoon, ALO Patrick 'Pat' Furse had a memorable flight with 'Mac', who flew low over the flooded area near Glastonbury 'to make the wild duck and geese get up and fly with him.'[9]

Towards the end of the month David noted two fatal crashes in his Log Book, the first on February 21. No.268, a tactical recce squadron, often working with No.2, 4, and 16 Squadrons, was on an exercise off the coast of Swanage. However, No.501 Spitfires were mistakenly sent to intercept them. Flying Officer Chris Hawkins's Tomahawk was damaged by cannon fire, and on reaching the coast he attempted to land but hit a tree.[10]

Next day, the second crash occurred when Ken 'Smoothie' Booth collided with Flying Officer Gerald Musgrove from No.247 Squadron. Booth was carrying out a gas spray demonstration, unaware that Musgrove was attacking a bridge near Totnes. Booth's Lysander caught fire and Musgrove's Hurricane crashed into the River Dart at Totnes Race Marsh. [11] Booth, Musgrove and Flight Sergeant Gordon were all killed.

Sunday, 22 February. I packed up Ken's personal belongings today. I am beginning to realize that I have entered a new life, for being a pilot is a life in itself. Each morning there are empty places in the Mess. I realize that if I am to do my job properly I must concentrate solely on flying. I must not look to the future and must live one day at a time, for now my life is, at most, only 50% my own. From now on, I will place my life in fate's hands. I no longer find death so terrible. It is too commonplace, an event that has lost its terror. I do not want to die, but if I crash, well, that is that.

No.16 Squadron pilots worked closely with the Army on a variety of training exercises, sometimes involving the local volunteer units. These soldiers were not in the regular services, being too young or old, medically unfit or in a reserved occupation. They defended targets such as factories and patrolled beaches or fields where Germans might land. On March 8, David, Alastair 'Mac' Maclay and New Zealand pilot John 'Wendy' Wendelken were sent on an exercise with one of these units.

I had a bit of a prang today while on an Exercise with the Taunton Home Guard. Wendy, Mac and I were ordered to act as German aeroplanes attempting to land troops on Cheddon Down in the Quantocks. We were to make a few low-level attacks on the Home Guard, drop several smoke bombs as a screen and then land in the next field. The Home Guard's orders were to stay hidden, allow us to land and then let us have it with their popguns. As I dropped the last canister for the smokescreen, Wendy and Mac went ahead and landed safely. I was coming in behind them to land, just over a little bank about 5 ft high. I was just about

A Lysander on a training exercise with the Home Guard. *(H4209 – © IWM)*

to put my wheels down when I saw twenty or so chaps lying in the grass. When they saw where I was intending to land they jumped up right in front of me.

I quickly opened up the throttle hard to pull the nose up but this caused the tail to drop slightly and I felt a small bump from the rear. I thought that I must have hit one of the soldiers. The control column felt very sticky and the elevators didn't seem to be working at all. I could just wiggle the tail-actuating wheel back and forward about 1/10th of a turn, so using throttle adjustments and tail-actuating wheel I managed to stay at about 200 ft and I nursed the aeroplane round in a large circle at about 100 mph.

Knowing that the Lysander was handing in a curious way, and that he was not going to make it back to base, David decided that he had better get down as soon as possible. After checking for more bodies, alive or dead, he landed somewhat heavily in the field, bounced fifteen feet, landed, bounced once again and finally on the fourth bump landed. Goode was having a terrible time, as he did not know what was going on. They both clambered out and looked over the aircraft, David realized with relief that the bump he had felt was caused by catching the rear wheel on the top of a raised ditch which had jammed it against the elevators.

A somewhat shocked Home Guard Captain hurried up. I told him that if this aircraft had been an enemy troop carrier the Captain would have wiped them all out, at the minor cost of a few of his own men. The Captain was most apologetic. Then Wing Commander Stansfeld came over and said, 'What a disgraceful landing and in front of the Home Guard of all people.'

I told him to look at my landing wheel. He was quite shocked and said, 'Good god!'

Wendy and Mac also came over to see if all was well then, after checking their own planes, they flew back to report. The Home Guard Captain offered to give Goode and myself a lift back to base, which we gratefully accepted. We stopped on the way at a farmhouse and the Captain gave us a real Somerset cream tea, with scones, strawberry jam and cakes to follow. The damage to the Lizzy was almost nil and, as it was not my fault, the C/O seemed to think I had done some quite good flying.

Wing Commander Wolryche Stansfeld wrote up an accident report. 'Pilot Officer Greville-Heygate considered returning to Weston Zoyland but the aircraft was handling in a curious manner and he decided it would be advisable to land as soon as possible. He completed the circuit and landed at 15.45 hours.

David damaged his Lysander's tail-light avoiding troops who jumped up in front of him as he was landing. *(SAGH)*

The landing was heavy. I consider Pilot Officer Greville-Heygate took the correct action and executed a skilful landing under extremely difficult conditions.'

However, Group Captain Arthur Flower of HQ 36 Wing was rather more critical of the whole exercise. 'The arrangements for the exercise were obviously rather lax, inasmuch as the soldiers were allowed to get in the way of the aircraft during its approach. Reality in training is desirable, but not to the extent of endangering life or aircraft.'

In March, No.239 Squadron, made up by merging pilots from No.16 and No.225 Squadrons, flew down to Weston Zoyland for an air-firing exercise. The day before his twenty-fifth birthday, New Zealand pilot, James Grevatt, crashed into the cloud-covered, high ground.[12] David noted:

> *Friday, 13 March.* Wing Commander Donkin[13] C/O of No.239 Squadron is staying in the Mess. Today Grevatt, one of his pilots was killed in the Quantocks.

A week later, Ronald came down to visit, eager to experience David's flying ability first hand. After taking him for a flight in a Tiger Moth, David gleefully wrote:

> I decided to show off my best aerobatics but on landing after 20 minutes Ronald got out of the aircraft looking very green and told me that he didn't think he would fly with me again. This pleased me immensely!

The next week, David carried out a gas spray and smoke-screen demonstration for the Williton Home Guard, which went without a hitch, but one flown by Douglas Sampson did not go quite as planned. 'My most successful gas spray was on a convoy but not – I admit – the correct one. The troops were on a nice straight open road, out of their lorries and having lunch. Fortunately I don't think they identified the A/C!'

During March, David's time was spent formation flying with Ralph Erskine 'China' Young, air-to-ground firing at Stert Flats and practising evasive action skills with Tony Davis. This involved making a steep turning dive and pulling out at the last minute. Douglas Sampson gave great thought to the outcome of such an action between a Lysander and an Me109, and decided that the 109 pilot may eventually become so dizzy that he would fly home in a bad temper.

> *Friday, 27 March 1942.* I can't quite fathom whether I'll be getting leave or not. It all depends on how many pilots will be away from the squadron.
>
> Mac, Pat and Jerry and I went in the ALO's car to Dartmoor to watch a demonstration at Oakhampton of Fighter Aircraft v Tanks and Transport. We had a great journey down and afterwards went to Exeter and spent the evening there. We watched the film 'Dumbo' about a baby elephant with very large ears which I enjoyed very much. It is a Walt Disney triumph.

While in Exeter, David met up with Rosemary who was now a WREN and working at Devonport. They met Edward Burkett 'Teddy' Wigg[14] from David's old battalion who was surprised to see him, as he had been told that David's name had appeared in the Times' Casualty List. Later, David met up with some of the men who were still with the Loyals.

Higgy said that I was the last person in the world he expected to see walk through the door as he had heard I was dead. I then met up with three men who were in my platoon and was most gratified to hear them say that they were talking about me in the NAAFI just the day before. They said things were not as they used to be and they longed to be back at Tyneham again. Then I met all the Officers who were left (not many); the others – and that would have included me had I stayed – have gone abroad. I have been lucky for I would also have been there if I had left Sandhurst a week earlier.

Teddy heard from one of them who is wounded and a Japanese prisoner, the others are missing I believe. It was rather a sobering thought that I could have been out there. It is strange how fate plays such an important hand in one's life.

(The 5th Battalion, re-designated the 18th Battalion Reconnaissance Corps, had been posted to reinforce Singapore arriving just in time to surrender to the Japanese.)

While on leave, David received a letter from Harry Allen who was relieved to hear that David was alive and added, 'Life for me has expanded a good deal with the improvement in the weather. People still have to put up with my lectures of course and, although they occasionally show signs of claustrophobia, I don't mind so long as they don't actually pass out.'

In the March 28 issue of the 'Illustrated London News,' David spotted an article about Colditz which included a sketch of Peter Storie-Pugh; David was also pleased to hear from Melvyn Evans and Donald Draper who had settled well in the Squadron.

No.4 Squadron, York.
Northern Command seems fairly persistent in demands for photographs Tac/Rs, R/T tests, container dropping and 'beat-up' etc, so one's flying is consequentially very interesting – a fact which makes me all the more pleased that I have finished up in A.C. Command.

Last week VERY pleasantly spent on detachment with an Arty regiment in Norfolk (Hunstanton). We provided Arty/Recce sorties for them (which was very successfully carried out on the whole) and shared a Mess with them. The latter was in a grand country mansion – Hunstanton Hall – and it was a pleasing pastime to go for walks in the park before the day's work began or after tea….
Cheerio for now, Melvyn.

Donald Draper added, 'By the way, Vaughan Fowler has gone off to more important work on Lysanders! I understand that two went from your squadron and that they were returned owing to shortage of night-flying hours…. I have heard (about 4th hand) that you gave yourself a nasty shock by banging your tail-wheel on a fence. It seems to me, I may be wrong, that there is very little future in doing that as a hobby!'

Peter Vaughan-Fowler's 'important work' referred to a call that had been sent around the squadrons for Special Duties pilots. These duties would involve landing agents and supplies into enemy countries and required very accurate flying, the ability to navigate at night and land in small fields by torch or moonlight. This signal had asked for experienced volunteer Lysander pilots with at least 250 hours of flying experience, but in error had omitted the word, night.[15] Several pilots came forward from No.4 and No.16 Squadrons, only to be turned away as they did not have the required night-time flying experience. Vaughan-Fowler, six hours short of a total flying time of 250 hours and with limited night flying experience, also applied (after hastily borrowing a Tiger Moth to top his flying hours to 250.) Amazingly, he was accepted and on October 26 1942, he carried out the first of seventeen successful clandestine landings, ferrying agents and members of the Resistance into occupied France.[16]

On April 6, Easter Monday, David flew an hour's night-flying and there was such a fine moon that he could see for about ten miles. However, his engine sprung an oil-leak and by the time he landed, he was covered in oil from the knees of his battledress downwards.

> My batman made a fantastic job of removing the oil and it looks almost like new again. I don't know how I would cope without his excellent services as he is so attentive to all my needs.

After a week's leave, David stopped in London to try to buy a few things and he took a taxi to Regent Street.

> I had just enough time for a refusal at Kodak's, there was no film there at all, whether cine or ordinary!! So another of our luxuries gone.
> At Taunton I collected my car from the garage and for the eight days I paid – after a struggle – just 2/6d. The garage owner wanted me to have it for free as he has a son in the USA in the RAF.
> At the Rose and Crown I met China Young, Tony Davis and the doctor.[17]
> Mrs Lee gave (sold!) me a plate of bacon, eggs and chips. Back at my billet the door didn't catch properly, the cat got in and ate our week's cheese ration, which was a great pity.

While David had been on leave, Ian Baker and Peter Miles had flown up to Clifton and heard that Roger Boyce had been killed. Taking off from Doncaster on April 11, the No.4 Squadron de Havilland Dominie crashed, killing William Giblin, Squadron Leader Inglefield and Roger Boyce.[18]

Donald Draper wrote that although pleased to see Ian Baker and Jerry Miles when they dropped in, but was sad to report the death of Roger Boyce. He said that Boyce's wife had just moved to York and he had had to break the bad news to her. 'We are hoping to come and see you as soon as we are rid of some Army exercises. I notice you say you have landed at your 20th aerodrome. My list is well over 20 and 9 types of plane flown!! Line! Try and get up here one of these fine days! I will stand you a beer (maybe)'.

It was not just the RAF that was losing men through accidents. Four days later there was an unfortunate incident at Imber Down on Salisbury Plain.

10 Group had been instructed to arrange a tactical air exercise with tanks, lorries and dummy soldiers, and 5 Corps of Southern Command was put in charge of the live shoot in front of official observers. With bad visibility for flying, the exercise was postponed a few days, and due to a misunderstanding about numbers of aircraft required, several No.175 pilots did not take part in the rehearsal. One of these was an

inexperienced pilot, American Sergeant William John Andrew McLachlan, new to the squadron and who had only fired his guns three times.

On April 13, although the weather was better it was still hazy, and the pilots were attacking into the sun. Sixth in line for the attack, McLachlan saw the aircraft in front of him turn, dive and straighten out before he lost sight of it. He dived in and let off two short bursts of fire then, seeing people running, he realized that he was off-target and had mistakenly shot into the midst of the observers.[19]

> Some of our pilots went to watch the exercise. The Generals were all sitting there and as the firing came awfully close to the spectators, our people threw themselves flat on their faces and the Generals were looking over at these nervous people when they suddenly realized they were actually being shot up. One of our pilots had been lying down with the peak of his service cap digging into the grass and when he got up a bullet had gone through the back.

Twenty-five officers and men were killed including Brigadier Grant Taylor OBE MC and Captain James Roland West MC. Seventy-one men were injured including Brigadier Vere Gordon Stokes. It was not the first time Stokes had been under fire, having won the MC and Bar during the First World War, when he assumed command of two companies and led 'both successfully through a heavy enemy barrage.'[20]

Douglas Sampson added that the incident with the Hurricane pilot who 'mowed down a line of VIPs in a demo ground attack, caused a certain amount of promotion in the Army, but created little new goodwill towards aviation.'[21] McLachlan was killed ten weeks later when his Hurricane was shot down near Cherbourg during an attack against a minesweeper.[22]

Later in the year the Army, almost unintentionally, gave the RAF pilots a taste of their own medicine when they arranged a demonstration of a live artillery barrage. Douglas Sampson, selected to observe, wrote:

> The Army wanted a chance to impress the RAF 'flyboys' with their firepower so a few pilots were taken up to Larkhill Artillery Ranges. Near the target area the RAF was grouped on the reverse side of a wide, shallow gully, short of a tank hulk. A very tall Brigadier with a red hat…, posted himself with tannoy nearer the target…. 'Now Gentlemen,' he said, 'You will experience the terrifying effect which the poor old Hun will have to put up with,' and he called for gunfire.
>
> Personally I could never become fond of the atmospheric disturbance caused by 5.5 projectiles in flight, still less the uproar when they arrive nearby. Our group appeared less happy and were reducing their silhouettes to a minimum when a pair of shells landed with the most unpleasant noise about 50 yards from us and nearer to the Brig. This was closely followed by others. We were all doing what we could in the way of tunnelling while flat on the grass and we heard the Brig (via tannoy) call for ceasefire. But with great efficiency there were four more on the way. Thank goodness only one troop was off. When the wonderful silence was noted, heads came up. The chap, in whose back I had my head, showed me his hat. The wire cut and all the stuffing was coming out. All this time the Brig had been upright and fully exposed, mike in hand, and the

Lenny, Sammy and Old Mac in 'the delightful little Mess' in the orchard at Weston Zoyland. *(Family Collection)*

ADC one pace to the rear. He was now wearing a hat without a peak. It looked like an old-fashioned pillar box with a red band but I didn't hear anyone laugh.'[23]

Once back at the Mess they all ordered very stiff drinks.

Now living at Leasingham Manor in Lincolnshire, Mary Hutton wrote that Peter was night-flying Oxfords at Cranwell and their son Timothy was growing up fast. Delighted to have made so many good friends in the RAF David wrote home.

No.16 Squadron is full of wonderful people, all of us Army rebels who have had rows with the Army, and it is such a wrench when friends leave, I have just heard the news that we are going to lose Pat our charming ALO and it is hard that he should have to go at such short notice. I don't know where he is going for he was only told yesterday and had to be off at lunch time today.

The Air Liaison Officer's job was of particular importance to the pilots. With information from Army headquarters of Allied and enemy positions, the ALOs briefed pilots before they flew out on a recce. They could request them to look out for specific targets or observe transport movement and the pilots could relay information back as a brief message while flying, but on landing they would be fully de-briefed by the ALOs, who passed on information gathered to the Intelligence Staff. Any aerial photographs taken were developed on the airfield and sent off to be analyzed with scientific precision. By 1945, 90,000 photographs and negatives were sent daily to the Central Photographic Interpretation Unit based at RAF Medmenham in Buckinghamshire. Colonel Roy Stanley a US Intelligent Officer noted, 'There was no point in asking a man to risk his life, then not getting every bit of information that the film contains.'[24]

Flying up to Clifton aerodrome on April 24, David briefly saw Melvyn Evans and lunched with Donald Draper. On his return to Weston Zoyland he heard news from Monty Denny, now a staff pilot on Tomahawks, Harvards and Mustangs.

> Jerry went over to Old Sarum and saw Monty Denny, he has a good flat and is very happy. Mac's mother back from India has brought back quite a lot of things, including chocolate. Mac gave me a milk block and it was quite strange tasting peacetime chocolate again.

On leave in April, David met up with Marlborough friend, Anthony Patrick Mahon, who was working as a code breaker at Bletchley Park on German Naval codes,[25] then went to Yeovilton to meet Rosemary, based at HMS Heron. Here the RNAF Fighter Direction training centre taught aircraft control from ships, however, due to a shortage of radar and planes, ingenious and inventive ways including the use of ice cream tricycles as aircraft, were used for training practise.[26]

> Rosemary seems very happy doing the same sort of work as Ronald at Wittering and except for the food she has no grumbles at all. She is very full of the Senior Service already but I told her that if anybody had the excuse to build an aeroplane before Noah built his ark we would be the Senior Service but she didn't seem to agree.

After extensive testing, both at Duxford Air Fighting Development Unit (AFDU) and Boscombe Down's A&AEE, the ideal aircraft for Army Co-op arrived in the shape

No.2 Squadron often flew on exercises with No.16 Squadron. *(Family Collection)*

of the American P-51 Mustang. The reports concluded that although the Allison engine was underpowered for high-altitude combat, at low-level its performance was excellent and the Mustang soon began replacing both the Lysander and the Tomahawk. Built in America, it was shipped in pieces across the Atlantic and re-assembled at Speke, Liverpool.

Tasked with delivering new Mustangs to the squadrons, Flying Officer James 'Jimmy' Jump Davies recalled his first flight.

> I had seen one at Duxford and climbed all over it but it had no handling notes. O'Farrell[27] and I were flown over to Speke in an Anson to pick up a Mustang to deliver to Viscount Acheson, the C/O at Bedford. We took off from Speke into fog over the river and I didn't know that I ought to have locked the tail wheel. I did a perfect take-off and thoroughly enjoyed myself, it was a wonderful aeroplane, so easy to fly right from the start. Then we got to Bedford and O'Farrell landed first and I came into land afterwards and I did the best landing I'd ever done. I didn't even know that I was down and when I taxied in I felt a little ashamed of the fact that they thought what a brilliant landing I had done for my first time and I remember saying that it was a very easy aeroplane to fly.[28]

Going back to Speke to pick up Mustangs for No.16 Squadron, it was quite late by the time the aircraft were ready to fly, but they decided to take a chance and set off for Weston Zoyland.

> However, the weather was bad, it was getting rather dark and we had no radar in the planes, we managed to nip into Shawbury, for the night. Unfortunately, Shawbury forgot to make a note to inform flying control that the Mustangs had landed and we were reported missing. We took off very early the next morning and we set the Air Raid warnings going at Bristol. We were greeted very warmly by all the chaps who were waiting to see a Mustang.[29]

David, who had been doubtful about the Mustang the first time he had seen it, soon changed his mind once sitting in the cockpit.

> *Sunday, 26 April.* It is a really glorious aircraft in every way and you get a great view from the air. The cockpit is large and comfortable but it does get very hot. The range is enormous; two tanks hold enough fuel for about 4 hours flying. The only drawback is that, like the Hurricane you can't see a thing in front of the nose when the tail is on the ground. At take-off and landing you have to guess where the edge of the runway is. But once in the air, visibility is excellent and it fair zips along at about twice the speed of a Lizzy. It may not look as beautiful as a Spitfire, but it has a 1,150hp, liquid cooled engine and is the fastest Army Co-op plane in the world.

The Mustang was solidly built with a much longer range than either the Spitfire or the Hurricane. Wing Commander 'Roddy' Davenport noted that 'It was rather like a big, solidly built American car; it had bags of torque from a very smooth engine, it handled well and had a low-level of noise in the engine.'[30]

'The Faithful Steed'. No.2 Squadron Mustangs. *(Family Collection – Crown © 1942)*

For reconnaissance work, a camera was fitted, pointing downwards at an angle behind the pilot, and accuracy was ensured by lining up the target with a mark on the trailing edge of the wing.

With the arrival of the single-seater Mustang the pilot's work increased, for he now had to act as both pilot and observer, so they usually flew in pairs. The lead pilot, would concentrate on taking observations and photographs, while his No.2 would fly behind to keep him covered and look out for enemy aircraft, and sometimes friendly ones as well, as the Mustang was the first British fighter to have square wingtips and from certain angles it looked similar to the Me109. In the hope of preventing mistakes, a series of visits to RAF Fighter Stations were arranged to show the comparative silhouettes of the two aircraft.

We now have an ALO from the Northampton Regiment to replace Pat, he has been in Iceland for months and it is most amusing to hear what he has to say about the Americans over there. They got on very well together but still liked to poke fun at one other. The Americans used to laugh at official radio procedure e.g. 'Hello Base B4 calling, are you receiving me over,' and the answer, 'Hello B4 base answering, receiving you loud and clear, over.'

The Yanks say, 'How are you getting me this morning Casanova? Go ahead,' and the pilot replies, 'Getting you good brother,' or words to that effect.

Devey[31] said that when the Americans first came to Iceland he heard from a very high official that the American didn't mind beating off any attack on the USA but didn't think that the States would ever join in the war themselves. At first when they heard on the radio that Japan had attacked them, they were all completely stupefied for about a day, they just couldn't believe it, but they really

Jerry Miles and 'Sandy' at Weston Zoyland. *(Family Collection)*

settled down to things when they were in the war and a complete change came over them.

After the Mustangs were allotted, David delivered one of the old Lysanders to an airfield north of London. On his way up, he landed at White Waltham and dropped in a large photo with the Duty Pilot and met the Commander-in-Chief who was taking the photograph back with him. David then took the tube into London, but found all the hotels were full. However, sometime before, Jan Plesman had recommended a place he stayed at when visiting London.

> I remembered that I had jotted the name in my diary so I took a taxi to the address which was just behind the Ritz Hotel and I was in luck as there was one room left. My bill was 15/- for a room with private bathroom, breakfast in bed, telephone and electric fire and as I get £1 for staying away on duty it will help to pay for a short holiday. It is a very useful place to know and I think they recommended it to Allied pilots. I had an excellent dinner at the Trocadero and appreciated it fully as I'd had an early lunch and no tea. I saw a review after dinner and finished with a quick drink at Oddenino's American bar in Regent Street. I usually call in there as it is a meeting place for the Dutch pilots and I had met Govert Steen there last time I was up. This time the girl behind the bar said Jan Plesman had only just left about two minutes before and I searched several other places including the Berkley and the Piccadilly but unfortunately couldn't find him.

The next day, before heading back, David did a little shopping hoping to buy a new fountain pen:

Although the fountain pen maker Swans are not making any more for the duration of the war they are repairing their own, old ones. Fortunately I had a piece of an old one, it had no nib, no cap and no tube but they repaired it so now I have the equivalent of a new pen, worth about 18/6 – if they were obtainable – for only 6/-.

No.16 Squadron held a dance the next day and David had asked Rosemary, but she was on duty, so he took Amathe Meyer, a cousin of the Somerset County Cricket Captain, Jack Meyer.

On May 17, ITW friend, Ronald Arthur Duce[32] was killed when he overshot the runway at Snailwell whilst trying to land a No.268 Squadron Tomahawk. Opening up the engine to make another circuit, it stalled at 200 feet and crashed into the ground.

On the same day Harry Dent wrote his last letter to David.

Stadishall, Newmarket, 17 May 1942.
It was grand to receive your letter which followed me all round the country and to hear how all the others are fairing. I would love to come and visit but I doubt I could put a Stirling down on your aerodrome if it is purely fighters, but if you ever have a chance do come up here.

I'm glad to hear you are pleased with the aircraft you are flying. As you can guess after all this time I have been assigned to flying bombers and working at night like a cat burglar. However I have managed to get on to Stirlings so I am doing a spot of damage.

Bob Cranston went to Bicester with Bunny, Ken Gibbons, Paddy Boyle and Dennis Evers; as far as I know they are all now in the Middle East on Blenheims except Bunny who was very unlucky. He had some back trouble due to an ancient kick in the back at rugger and after about a month of it the RAF decided it was not their business and bowler-hatted him.[33] He's had an operation and a lot of pain and I think when it's all over in a few months he'll go back to the Army.

Don't worry if this letter blabbers somewhat I'm always tired these days; I guess I wasn't cut out for night work….
Yours ever, Harry.

There had been a long tradition of keeping pets, mainly dogs, on RAF Stations and No.16 Squadron was no exception. In addition to Peter Stansfeld's Alsatian, Ian Morrin was looking after a Golden Retriever that had belonged to a pilot who had been killed, and there was a 'six-toed kitten which could grasp things just as though it had hands.' David was delighted to be asked to look after a puppy for a week or two until Viscount Acheson[34] could collect him.

He had left Sandy with the vet in Bridgwater and Peter Stansfeld asked if I would look after it, as he noticed I was not antagonistic to his Alsatian, Ffumf, as some of the other members of the Squadron seemed to be. I suppose it is because Ffumf always growls at people and rarely takes any notice of anyone but his owner. This is quite unusual as most dogs belonging to someone in the services become general pets. However, Ffumf seems to taken a liking to me for some reason.

Sandy is a very pretty, six month old cocker spaniel, but as he has terrific ears I have nicknamed him Dumbo. His manners are excellent and he is very obedient. His only trouble is that when he came he was almost a skeleton and so now he's always completely ravenous.

On a free Sunday David, John Tattersall and Sandy went to Burnham-on-sea, about fourteen miles from the airfield, for a walk and a round of golf.

Tatts was an accountant in peace time and I think he's very plucky to take up flying age 31. We played 10 holes but there was a great wind around the course which made things harder, then we had great games on the beach with Sandy who couldn't quite understand why drinking the sea water made him so thirsty. When we got back I listened to Mrs Thatcher playing hymns on her harmonium and it somehow fitted with this beautiful Sunday afternoon.

In an attempt to severely demoralize the German people, Sir Arthur Harris planned the first 1,000-bomber raid over Germany, and although he had only a little over 400 aircraft with trained crews for front-line operational work, 'he did have a considerable number of further aircraft in the conversion units…. This secondary Bomber Command strength could be crewed by a combination of instructors, many of them ex-operational, and by men in the later stages of their training.' On May 30, Harris ordered the attack and over 1,000 aircraft were dispatched.[35] Churchill was prepared for the loss of a hundred aircraft but in the event only forty-one were lost. One was Harry Dent's. It crashed about thirty miles northwest of Cologne and all eight crew members were killed. After reading the news David wrote home.

Fancy over 1,000 bombers over Cologne in 1½ hours, the city must have been almost erased.

At the end of May, No.16 Squadron completed their Mustang conversion period and low-flying practise. Having been taught to fly very low, very fast, to avoid German anti-aircraft guns, David took part in 'Exercise Pigeon,' a five-day, low-level recce exercise with the Army's VIII Corps.

'Low and Oblique.' Factory chimney near Basingstoke taken during a training exercise. *(Family Collection – Crown © 1942)*

Chapter Eleven

In the Orchard at Weston Zoyland:
June 1942 to October 1942

'I had a sense of being in a close community. The pilots call one another by their
  Christian names.'

'Men of the RAF,' William Rothenstein 1941.

With the coming of summer and the worsening petrol situation, No.16 Squadron began moving back into tents in the orchard on the edge of the airfield. Many visitors commented that despite the tents, No.16 Squadron was the best in the Command. Sir William Rothenstein, commissioned by the RAF to tour various RAF Stations and draw portraits of the men working there, had visited No.16 Squadron the year before and noted the relaxed, open manner of the squadron. 'Instead of the usual close offices, work was carried out almost in the open. The various flights and sections, assembled in tents, huts and lorries, made an attractive picture under dappled shade of apple and pear trees, and alongside hedges. All the units, the C/O's office, the signals, electric generators, kitchens, photographic sections are mobile.'[1]

When the petrol ration was reduced David bought a motorbike. *(Family Collection)*

On June 1, David flew up with other 16 Squadron pilots to Snailwell, Sawbridgeworth, then Ipswich, for a Tac/R beat-up exercise for Eastern Command. Visiting No.2 Squadron's Mess at Great Hyde Hall, David remarked:

Our Mess will be a slightly less grand affair, for when we return we move it into the orchard. We shall still live in our billets but will bicycle up each morning at 8 am and stay up there the whole day.

However, once back at Weston Zoyland it was not long before David and the other pilots moved into the orchard too.

Our tents are already littered with parachutes, Mae Wests, Irving suits and outside I can hear Vera Lynn singing on the radio – although I am not keen

The C/O and pilots of No.16 Squadron, June 1942. Stansfeld's Alsatian 'Ffumf' takes pride of place in the front row. *(Family Collection – Crown © 1942)*

on her myself. Sandy has become a great favourite and is threatened with kidnapping by everyone he comes across!

I've taken over the job of Mess secretary, which takes up a good deal of time, but I still find time for swimming, tennis, golf and even the odd game of cricket.

On June 5, yet another friend was killed. Govert Steen was shot down on a sweep with No.129 Squadron near Octeville.[2] Ten days later, Anthony Greenly, John Devey, Peter Miles and John Tattersall were posted to the newly formed No.170 squadron, and though still based at Weston Zoyland, No.16 Squadron threw a leaving party for them. Two days later Mrs Stuart, 'The Tatler' society reporter, took photographs of the squadron officers for the magazine. Over the next week, David was kept busy flying air-to-ground and air-to-air firing exercises, while several No.16 Mustangs flew down to RAF Harrowbeer to work with Plymouth Defence.

23 June. I took Sgt Simpson down in the Tiger Moth and went on to Plymouth in the staff car. We had a lovely drive over Dartmoor eating strawberries all the way, before flying back to Weston Zoyland.

During the exercises at Harrowbeer, Wing Commander Peter Stansfeld suffered a bad crash. He later told David what happened:

I was coming into land and I suddenly saw chaps taxiing onto the runway. I thought I must go round again and let them take off. As I was going round the thing blew back and the carburettor caught fire and I was left about 200 ft up, facing Dartmoor or whichever moor it was, with nothing on the clock! I was too low to bail out, so I tried to edge round to make a crosswind landing, which eventually I did, but just as I was getting over the last line of trees, the engine stalled and I went in from about 50 ft.[3]

As Stansfeld's aircraft dived towards the ground, his wing hit a stone wall and pieces of the Mustang spread over a considerable distance. 'I was thrown through the roof. If it hadn't broken up I would have been alright but I pushed the roof open with my face and then broke my hip on the way out. I landed just outside the Officers' Mess and the first chap to come up was the station doctor who was having lunch, thank god!' A few pilots also ran over expecting the worst, but were amazed to find Stansfeld alive, still in his seat on the grass, with pieces of aircraft scattered all about him. Although known for its great cockpit strength, Stansfeld was lucky to survive.[4] Badly injured, having broken his hip and nose as he was thrown through the cockpit canopy, he was still conscious and amazingly managed to say hello to Douglas Sampson, who wrote, 'With some other reluctant bods we went to view the results and were amazed to see Peter still in his seat, apart from his aircraft, still conscious and with heart-tugging courage saying, "Hello Sammy." He could hardly smile but I think he tried hard.'[5]

Stansfeld continued, 'I saw my driver Corporal Brimbal…, and all I could say was "For god sake take care of my dog." before being taken off to the RAF hospital in Torquay.' David wrote:

> The C/O has had a bad accident, he is seriously injured but not on the danger list. He is remarkably cheery and can even joke about his injuries. He has a very strong constitution and I think he will get quite well again.
>
> As I write this, poor Ffumf is very lost, he misses the C/O and growls at anyone who goes near the chair where the C/O usually sits, but he is eating which is good and is looking fit and is becoming less fierce as he is looked after by different people. Sadly Sandy is leaving here soon, everyone will miss him dreadfully as he's been quite a character.

Blenheim Palace – the birthplace of Winston Churchill. *(Family Collection – Crown © 1942)*

Squadron Leader Alexander Glen Pallot, David's old Flight Commander at Old Sarum, took over as temporary C/O for three weeks until 'He was demoted again to second-in-command when the Air Ministry realized he was an Auxiliary Air Force officer and refused to allow him to have command over Regulars.'[6]

Tony Hilditch wrote with his news and added, 'I now have a Flight in No.53 Squadron and am acting Squadron Leader. The promotion has been rather sudden and takes getting used to. I am at present on home leave, but I have had a telegram saying that I am posted overseas and so my future movements are a matter of great doubt.'

While on leave on David went to London.

Sunday, July 12. I had lunch at the Trocadero as it opens at 12.00 and most of the others don't seem to open until 12.30 pm now. I suppose it is something to do with the 5/- restriction for meals. I then went down to Taunton, standing in the corridor, for the trains are always packed on this line. There were two very pleasant American pilots whom I had a long conversation with and I was considerably surprised, with both their comparative modesty, and also with their respect for the RAF, its aircraft and systems. One is coming over to lunch one day when he gets out of hospital.

After tea at the Castle Hotel in Taunton I rang Rosemary and we spent the evening looking around Yeovil. She looks extremely well and is doing a particularly interesting job and they are now allowed to change into civilian clothes when off duty which is a great reform.

While David was away, No.170 Squadron left Weston Zoyland and Wing Commander John Roderick 'Roddie' Davenport arrived at No.16 Squadron. This proved a popular appointment.

Davenport, our new C/O, was in the Army before he transferred and was a Flying Officer in this Squadron when war broke out. We all like him very much and he is very friendly, sociable and was the son of the bursar of Marlborough College. I often think how fortunate I was being posted here as we all get on so well together. Roddie soon gave me a nickname 'Immaculate Heygate,' as I always fly in my service dress rather than battledress which I don't like very much.

This neatness in dress did not apply to David's hair, which was longer than regulations required and he was known for having an untidy wisp that he would flick back at regular intervals.

'Immaculate Heygate'. *(Family Collection)*

Cranmore Tower on the Mendip Hills, Somerset, was a familiar landmark for the No16 Squadron pilots. *(Family Collection – Crown © 1942)*

No.16 Squadron now had twelve Mustangs and two in reserve, and although the pilots loved flying them, they suffered from several mechanical problems. The first from the tail-wheel, which was in the slipstream of the radiator and could overheat, and on take-off and landing, they were prone to bursting. In consequence, Mustang tail-wheels were always in short supply. Wing Commander Davenport recalled, 'Some bright lad of ours overcame our problem by discovering that the tail-wheel of a Beaufighter was the same size, so we laid in a generous supply of these before making it common knowledge.'[7]

The other, more serious problem was from the hydraulic system, which failed due to the stresses put on it. On 16 July, while landing at Yeovilton, Ian Baker had an air failure with his hydraulic system, and overshooting the runway he wrecked his Mustang but escaped injury. Eric 'Chunky' Chegwin, who had flown the aircraft before Baker, reported that he had not noticed anything wrong with it on his flight, so David was asked to investigate the cause of these failures.

The Mustang hydraulic system investigation is most interesting but it takes up a lot of my time with much drawing and writing involved. However, today I escaped to play cricket against Marlborough – their last match before Lords – as part of Meyer's team. I hadn't held a bat for two years but managed to stay in for a quarter of an hour and made it to tea. Meyer is chief of the local A.T.C. and has a school[8] at a lovely house near Street. His cousins, mostly girls, act as mistresses, secretaries etc and they are a very pleasant crowd. We go over there for bathing, riding, golf, cricket and tennis.

I've been rechecking all the Mess accounts and I have managed to get the deficiency down to -11d. I've also been going the rounds paying the billets, if they get 1/- too little they scream at you but if you pay them too much, mum's the word. I've found quite a nest of racketeers in a small way.

We all miss Sandy as he has now flown back with Lord Acheson and he really did look beautiful when he left here, his coat was glistening like a mirror. It seems very quiet without him.

Later, David received a letter from Acheson, now based at No.51 OTU Twinwood Farm, to thank David for looking after Sandy and added, 'He survived his first flight exceedingly well in fact he seemed most interested in everything which was going on around him. I hated taking him away because you had become so attached to him. But I promise that if and when he has puppies you shall have the best.' Several days later a very fine silver beer tankard arrived, inscribed 'D.A. Greville-Heygate RAF from Sandy.'

On Monday 3 August, William Gilliland, Douglas Sampson and David travelled up to Edinburgh together on duty. They found the Scottish people friendly and the food outstanding. With time on their hands, David climbed up to view the castle while Gilliland and Sampson sat on the wall at the bottom claiming that it was far too hot for walking. Back at their hotel they were surprised to find Tony Davis and John Turner, on forty-eight hours' leave from 'Exercise Dryshod.' This exercise was held at various locations in Scotland to train troops in beach assaults and landings. After taking the Flying Scotsman back to London, David returned to Weston Zoyland at the weekend.

Sunday, 9 August. I do wish Charles was here with the Squadron, he would have loved it. Gillie, Tony and I played cricket on a field about 200 yards from Glastonbury Abbey. We were the only Officers playing and were the top three scorers. We like to do well so the airmen aren't able to say 'Oh, we have to have the Officers play but we would do better without them!'[9]

While reading through 'Country Life Magazine' David was surprised to see that Elisabeth Jardine daughter of Major General Jardine[10] was reported to have married Flight Lieutenant John Sharpley, the squadron's doctor. David wrote to his parents.

Country Life magazine printed a picture of Elisabeth but there must be some mistake as I don't think she and John are married, for they certainly were NOT a week or two ago as he has been posted and is now onboard a ship.

On 19 August 1942, the Dieppe Raid was launched. Around 6,000 troops, supported by 237 ships and landing craft of the Navy, and 74 squadrons of aircraft, attacked the German-occupied port. Intended as a 'hit and run' attack they planned to seize and hold the port for a short time and to use airpower to draw the Luftwaffe into a large battle. However, meeting much stiffer resistance than expected, they withdrew, leaving as many as sixty per cent of the troops killed, wounded or captured. The RAF lost 106 aircraft to the Luftwaffe's 48.[11]

As a raid, Dieppe was an expensive failure, but it highlighted several deficiencies in RAF training, and it was clear that Army Co-op squadrons needed more operational fighter-training. As a result No.16 Squadron was affiliated to No.12 Group, Fighter Command and a programme of Shipping Recces and Strikes was authorized.

On the same day as the Dieppe raid, No.4 Squadron flew to Weston Zoyland to join No.16 Squadron for an armament practise week and David was delighted to spend time with Draper and Evans.

> The Dieppe raid seems to have been quite a big show. I'm glad to see that Mustangs are getting a share of the news now. The Daily Mirror stated that Spitfires, Mustangs and Hurricanes took part.

Mustangs were rapidly making a name for themselves. The Daily Express reported 'Mustangs usually hunt in packs of two or three and are increasingly hated by the German soldiers in Northern France,' and added that RAF pilots thought they were 'Wizard.'[12] Another article commented, 'They are sturdy, capable of standing up to almost any punishment. It is not uncommon for them to come back with evidence that the tops of trees or telegraph wires have been flown through.'[13]

David spotted this stately home south of Salisbury. (*Family Collection – Crown © 1942*)

On a flying visit over his house, David was pleased to see both his mother and Marjorie out on the road waving, while Rob ran up and down the lawn barking madly.

> I expect the Mustang would have appeared as rather a streak to them, although I was purposely flying slowly (for us) so I could see more. I didn't go down too low in case I knocked Mrs Clarke's tiles or chimney pot off! She doesn't like low-flying aircraft, especially the Lancasters – after the bomb in the field she gets frightened – but I've told Mother it's better she had the odd fright than we lose a bomber crew over France from lack of practise.

After a mosaic mapping exercise in the Lysander, David and Corporal Budd stopped for tea at RAF Pembrey. Corporal Budd met his brother who was working there, and David was pleasantly surprised to meet his old roommate Bewick Hack whom he had not seen since ITW, and was flying Spitfires.[14]

While having tea, David heard of an interesting incident that occurred at the airfield in June. Lost after a dogfight, Luftwaffe pilot Oberleutnant Arnim Faber mistook the Bristol Channel for the English Channel and thinking Pembrey was a French airfield he came in to land. An airman waved him to dispersals then, surprised to see the German markings, grabbed a Very pistol and took the bemused Faber prisoner. This was a huge piece of luck for the RAF; there had been plans to steal the latest model Focke Wulf 190 from Germany to test its potential and here was one presented to them in perfect working order.[15]

At the end of August, two new pilots, Eric Martin and Arthur Richard 'Kip' Kemp, arrived and September 7 saw the start of 'Exercise Mars,' which involved the Army's 3rd Division. David flew several Tactical and Photographic Recces between Weston Zoyland and Oatland Hill. On a navigation exercise the next day, David headed out into the Bristol Channel.

> I flew to a point beyond Lundy Island and down to the Scillies which, worryingly, I failed to find. On the way back visibility became very bad and I returned on a reciprocal course but less 30 degrees and found land again much to my relief. I was extremely glad to make it back to base without hitting anything.
>
> In the evening Elisabeth Jardine and I saw a good film called the 'First of the Few' about the life of R.J. Mitchell, the designer of the Spitfire. It was really worth seeing, nothing bloodthirsty about it and excellently written and acted.
>
> Elisabeth is suing Country Life for the statement about her being married to John Sharpley. She has had nearly a hundred wedding presents already and has been put to endless trouble. As John is overseas he can't help, and being only a private she hasn't much time to spare – she is still not commissioned even though her father is of such high rank in the Army. It is surprising how few girls in the Forces seem terribly keen on getting a Commission.

On September 16, David was delighted to see Ian Duffus who arrived at No.16 Squadron for an 8 Corps signal exercise. The next day 'B' flight pilots consisting of David, Richard Pughe, Eric Martin and Alastair Maclay were sent down to RAF Colerne to improve their Fighter and Night Flying techniques.

No.16 Squadron Mustang UG D AG431. *(Family Collection – © Crown Copyright)*

While attempting a low flying unofficial 'beat-up' in a Master III, Sergeant Kenneth Adcock hit a tree at Street, Somerset. Adcock and his observer, Sergeant Bates, were killed. David's turn for an accident came that evening.

I had a slight mishap night flying. I took off along the ill-lit runway into the darkness with cloud at 600 ft and this is where my troubles started. It was pitch-black, the weather was terrible and I was finding flying on instruments near impossible. I thought that discretion was the better part of valour and I decided to get back on the ground as soon as possible so instead of doing a four-leg circuit, I did a turn around, watching the lights so as not to lose sight of the airfield. As I approached I got the green, permission-to-land light and came in straight away. In rather a panic, I forgot to put my undercarriage down. I held off for a seeming age, it didn't settle at all but I wasn't going round again into that murk, then there was the most unpleasant grinding noise. I felt a scrape and a terrible clattering as I did a belly-flop landing on the airfield. There was a hell of a row and sparks of

P.O. Prune's definition of a good landing is one you can walk away from,

'A good landing is one you can walk away from.' Pilot Officer Prune Tee Emm training magazine. *(Family Collection – Crown © 1943)*

colour everywhere and then the horn started to blast when the engine finally stopped. The second-in-command was in a terrible state, as he was still above me in the lousy weather, and now couldn't get his aircraft down. The airmen took my plane off the runway and he eventually landed. He said. 'I can't believe what a stupid thing you have done, but bother the aircraft, you and I are both down, both standing and alive, let's go for a good drink and forget all about it.' I am going to get a rocket in the morning and am more than a little worried that I will be grounded.

Next day, David met with the C/O who said that the mechanics had looked very carefully at his aircraft, but couldn't find any faults with the undercarriage. He then asked David if the undercarriage lights had been showing on his approach. David had to admit that he had not seen them, as he had taped over the light with sticking plaster. The early Mustangs were not modified for night flying and the green undercarriage light was so bright on the instrument panel that it played havoc with pilots' night-vision. Putting sticking plaster over the offending light was a simple and effective method of dealing with dazzle. However, while this solved the problem of loss of night-vision, the undercarriage up warning light was rendered useless.

After hearing all of this C/O Davenport was jolly sporting. He warned me not to do it again and said, 'Oh David, you of all people to do this! I would never have thought it but I know you would never have done anything stupid intentionally. As you know there is a new penalty for pilots who do stupid things and damage aircraft, a sort of disciplinary camp, but if I send you there I know you'd be bolshie, whereas you never are here, so I will just say don't ever do that again. I guess that's what we can expect of sprogs like you if you're only given ten hours to convert to the Mustang.

Sammy Sampson awarded Barney Gilliland the 'Iron Cross First Class for one Mustang (nearly new) Confirmed'. *(Family Collection)*

They gave me a red endorsement card for landing with the undercart up so I count myself very lucky that I was let off so lightly. I shall be very careful of cockpit drill in future.

Davenport later noted, 'It had to be remembered that in those days cockpit drill was in its infancy!'[16]

On 22 September, Gilliland crashed his Mustang when he overshot the perimeter, and Douglas Sampson wryly noted that their short-landing expert Barney[17] was to be awarded 'the Iron Cross for one Mustang (nearly new) Confirmed!'

As it was becoming damp and cold in the tents in the morning, David moved back to the comparative warmth of Elm Tree Farm. Also on the move was Jan Plesman as No.167 Squadron started flying shipping recces and intruder missions. Plesman was particularly pleased to move south as autumn set in.

London, Oct 42.

David…, I am sending you a small note to let you know I am not in Scotland any more. I have been posted to Ludham…. Of course it is not 11 Group but still it is better than being up in Castletown for the winter. Many told me that you had been at Oddenino's. I think I came the same day. If you are coming up to Ludham please let me know in advance so I can make sure not to miss you. How are you doing yourself?

All the best…, Jan.

The North American Mustang painted by a Polish Mustang Pilot. *(Family Collection – 1942 Artist unknown)*

A week before David's birthday, Pilot Officers Cecil Ernest Franklin and Douglas Sampson set off on a low-level Tac/R exercise with an Army unit near Blanford. Having just been posted from 41 OTU this was Franklin's first chance to demonstrate his flying skills, but unfortunately at the end of the exercise he flew into a hill. Douglas Sampson noted that he had not seen him go.[18] The resulting enquiry concluded that there was an error in judgement of his height. As a result of his death, No.16 Squadron decided that all new pilots, many of them who came direct from Training Units with only ten to twelve hours Mustang conversion flying time, would be trained further as soon as they arrived.

On the 18th, *The Times* reported on a daylight attack carried out by No.5 Group. Eighty-eight Lancasters attacked the Schneider armament works at Le Creusot. The raid lasted just seven minutes and caused severe damage to the factory which manufactured guns, ball bearings, locomotives and armour-plate; six other Lancasters attacked the transformer.[19]

When I was on leave I was very cross on hearing Mrs Clark complaining so bitterly about the 4-engine Lancasters that fly over her house. It really does make me writhe inwardly when I hear people condemn unreasonably and I couldn't say that I expected a big show from them soon. I told her that they need to practise over here before operating that way in France. I hope she read in the paper today about the 94 Lancasters which bombed the Schneider factory in France in daylight and 93 returned. An amazing feat! The one that was lost they think was blown up by its own bombs it was so low. Now here's my point. If they had not been practising over Bowden that day maybe only 73 or 63 might have returned. Better someone frightened at home than ten lost in France.

Chapter Twelve

On Operations at Middle Wallop and Exeter: October 1942 to December 1942

'The Mustang would buffet just above the waves almost like playing ducks and drakes; it was indescribably exhilarating and against all the rules of flying discipline, but nobody seemed to care, there was still a war on….'

'Spit and Sawdust' George Hassall Nelson-Edwards.

RAF Middle Wallop, six miles southwest of Andover, had a long, grass runway with both permanent and hutted camps on site. Tactical Recce squadrons were sent here for Fighter Affiliation and Operations Training, and in October it was the turn of No.16 Squadron. 'A' Flight pilots, Anthony Davis, Douglas Sampson, Patrick Taylor and William Gilliland, went first, followed on the 19th by 'B' flight, consisting of Richard Pughe, Eric Martin, Alastair Maclay and David. Here they were met by the legendary Battle of Britain pilot, Wing Commander Tommy Dalton Morgan, one of the few single-engine day fighter pilots to shoot down bombers at night. Wounded several times, he received the DSO, DFC and bar.

Wednesday, 21 October. Tommy Morgan with the Spit Wing has taken us in hand and is training us in fighter tactics, something we have not been taught before and we are thankful for his useful advice and help. Our main job is to take photographs and get back without getting involved with any fighting, but if we are, it would be a good idea to know what to do.

The large new building here reminds me of a hotel, it seems that each chair belongs to somebody and

Tony Davis, Pat Taylor and Gillie Gilliland in their RAF bell tent. *(Family Collection)*

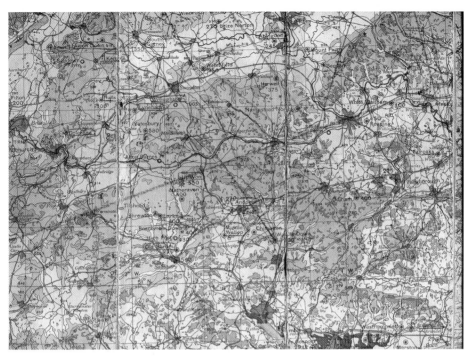

Map of Andover and Middle Wallop. *(Family Collection – Crown © 1942)*

one never quite knows whether to offer a chair by the fire to a lady or not. The WAAF Officers live in the Mess and it surprises me that the fighter pilots never seem to notice them at all, one or two of them are not unattractive. At times it is rather trying but it must be as difficult for them too, however they have their following of ground stooges and brown jobs in particular. The fighter boys are a good crowd and we are getting on well with them. Bill Griffiths[1] who was on my course at ITW is also here. What with the Mess being so cold and the babble I can't concentrate tonight, I shall have a bath and go to bed early.

The next day, *The Times* reported the death of school friend, Peter William Jarrett, an observer with No.115 Squadron.[2] In the evening David arranged to have dinner with Pip and Mary Hutton who were living in Andover.

As I was heading off I saw a very windswept ATS[3] who asked for a lift and I was amazed to discover that it was Elisabeth Jardine who was in great form.

I had a most pleasant evening catching up on all Pip and Mary's news. Pip – who was just the most discontented man in the Army I ever met with of course the exception of myself – has been transformed. Mary says she hasn't heard him grumble since he joined the RAF.

As part of their training, 'B' Flight began flying operations and on October 24, David flew his first Op.

Mac and I few over the Cherbourg Peninsular, trailing up and down the coast hoping to get some German planes to come and play but it was probably for the best that we saw no sign of any enemy aircraft. Eventually, as we decided to call it a day and head home, right out of the blue we were jumped on by a couple of our own Typhoons, who mistaking our square tipped Mustang outline for Me109s started to let rip with all their guns. Mac and I waggled our wings frantically to show our markings and fortunately they stopped firing before any real damage was done. It would have been the height of bad luck to have completed my first hour of operational flying and been shot down by my own side.

In the afternoon, I went back up for some aerial combat practise with Spitfires from No.501 Squadron.

The next day, Eric Martin also had a narrow escape and David was especially pleased to see him land safely at Andover.

After the excitement of yesterday I had almost forgotten it was my birthday until I received my presents. They very nearly came to grief, as the pilot who flew them over here from Weston Zoyland, hit a barrage balloon cable on route. He arrived here badly cut about and his Mustang came in with a lot of its tail missing. Marjorie sent me some chocolate which she knows I am always keen on and now with the rationing in full force, it seems to give it an added attraction.

We have been having an extraordinary selection of different types of weather here and this afternoon we did formation flying in pretty foul weather and pelting with rain. I needed all my concentration to keep in line. We spent the rest of the afternoon playing shove-halfpenny, billiards and squash.

'Wendy' and Eric Martin pose next to the 'ghastly' Nissen hut. *(Family Collection)*

In the offensive, 'Operation Torch', Allied troops landed in North Africa and after the El Alamein victory, Churchill gave one of his finest speeches and ordered church bells to be rung. However, not all the war news was as good, as the Germans took control of Vichy France.

> *Sunday, 15 November.* It was grand to hear the bells ring, it is a very small village with quite a large church but today it was very full. It is also cheering to see signposts back up. I wonder what the French Fleet will do, the Germans are so cunning that they may try and get it by trickery if it doesn't leave Toulon soon.

Before choosing the D-Day landing beaches, the Joint Planning Staff needed low-level photographs of the entire length of France's coastline. No.16 Squadron was tasked with photographing the coastline from the Cherbourg Peninsular, the Channel Islands and St Malo to the North Coast of Brittany, and on to Brest.

When trained, 'A' and 'B' Flights would take it in turns to operate from Exeter. Wing Commander Davenport wrote, 'The plan was to operate with pairs of aircraft at sea-level on shipping reconnaissance and in addition to take oblique photographs of the French coast…. The outward leg was flown at speeds of 240 mph, with as lean a mixture as possible, and when near the French coast speed up to 280 mph.'[4] Battle of Britain pilot George Nelson-Edwards, whom David would meet at Hawarden, later wrote, 'I found flying the Mustang 1 on low-level reconnaissance nothing if not exciting. We used to head out for the English Channel at nought feet, following the contours of the countryside, and then skimming over the waves at 'deck level,' as we sped towards the French coast full throttle…. The Allison-engine Mustang was almost untouchable at five hundred feet but on the climb it rapidly lost power and was a sitting duck at altitude.'[5]

Bad weather had made Weston Zoyland a sea of mud and without hot water or electric lights it had become quite unpleasant, so David was pleased when on November 18, it was the turn of 'B' Flight to set off for Exeter. For the next few weeks, as well as flying over a dozen shipping recces, they would take hundreds of photographs of the coastline.

> Today we flew down in formation to Exeter. On landing it was discovered that my Mustang's airscrew was damaged so Chunky[6] flew me back to Weston Zoyland in the Proctor where I picked up another one.
>
> My billet is a very nice single room in the Rougemont Hotel with a gas fire, hot and cold water and an excellent bed. Tony Greenly brought down my wireless so I'm now listening to the BBC orchestra playing for the Forces. I have asked Mother to send me my khaki putties as Tony wants a pair and I am only too glad to get rid of my old ones.

On November 20, David carried out an hour and twenty-minute shipping recce over the English Channel to Iles Sept, east to Ile de Brehat and on northeast to Guernsey. There was no sign of enemy aircraft and he returned without problems. The next day the weather was not so good and, owing to lack of cloud cover, after an hour, David and Wing Commander Davenport returned without completing the recce.

Saturday, 28 November. We have been kept very busy here. On Wednesday Tony Davis and I spotted three small ships, twenty miles east of Brehat, sailing west. Yesterday I flew over lovely, sunlit St Brieuc Bay and today Mac and I flew a Lagoon over Ile de Batz, Ile de Vierge and over Pontusval lighthouse before returning safely.

I see in the paper that John Paget and Jimmy Wrinch[7] are promoted to Flying Officers. Jimmy was at Rosslyn House with me. It is good to know one can get promotion as a prisoner of war.

At 09.50 on November 29, Alastair Maclay and Rosser Patrick Taylor also took off on a shipping recce from Exeter. Maclay was an experienced pilot and Taylor was a young but enthusiastic one. They headed south over the British Channel and at 10.40 they were called up, but no reply was received from either pilot. They did not return and David was devastated at their loss.

A BLACK DAY. Mac and I were to do a dawn Recce near Ile de Batz, but at the last minute I had been asked to fly a Rhubarb later in the day, so Pat a keen new sprog, took my place as Mac's No 2. I fear that they have collided at low-level but we hope that one or both of them may have managed to bail out or ditch in the sea.

Alistair 'Mac' Maclay and Squadron Leader Kirkwood 'Kirk' Curry were both shot down while flying on Operations. *(Family Collection)*

Tony and I went up at midday and we searched Guernsey, Jersey and Brehat, but could see no trace of them. To make things worse, on the way back we were jumped by Hurricanes who mistook us for German planes. We are all very quiet in the Mess tonight but I am still hoping to hear good news.

The good news never came and it was widely assumed that they collided, however at the time they were lost, two Luftwaffe pilots reported shooting down Mustangs. *Unteroffizier* Herbert Gumprecht claimed his sixth Mustang shot down, at 10.41 and *Unteroffizier* Friedrich May, who had previously shot down a Boston and Beaufighter, claimed a Mustang at 10.43 NNW of Morlaix; both pilots were from the Luftwaffe Fighter Squadron 8 JG2.[8] The next day, David and Wing Commander Davenport again flew over the area, hoping to spot some sign of Mac or Pat, but they saw nothing.

I had another sleepless night, I wish it was all over because as war progresses my generation seems to grow smaller and smaller and those that are left are mostly abroad or prisoners.

Events of this sort left their mark on squadron pilots, and they tried to find ways of coping with loss of friends and the possibility of being killed. Douglas Sampson was reluctant to tempt the 'Distributer of Good Fortune' so kept no diary and read no serial stories. Writing to his parents to hint about the nature of his work, David tried to prepare them for the possibility that he too might be lost.

Dear Mother and Father. I expect you will be surprised to see that I am down in Exeter. However I am not sorry at all as it is most unpleasant at Weston Zoyland where we are up to our ankles in mud and miles from a town with no hot water and no electric light.

I think I need to tell you that I am doing a certain job which is rather similar to Charles's – though not nearly so dangerous and in an aircraft far more fitted for it. So I just thought I'd mention it. I have been on the job for some weeks and I consider it less dangerous than my days at Tern Hill which were certainly much less pleasant. I love it down here and it is good to be doing a job which is of some use after doing three years training of one sort or another.

Anyway don't worry. I hope to get my leave in 29 days from now, so I won't be home for Christmas. I wonder if you can get crackers, I have failed to find any here. When I get a chance I'll try and get up for a day to RAF Bruntingthorpe, if it is open.

Don't let Father go running around farms without a coat nor do too much snow shovelling when it comes.

Your Loving Son, David.

For the next few days David flew a variety of anti-shipping patrols off Ile de Batz, Sept Iles and Brehat with Pilot Officer John Valentine Stuart-Duncan. David also had a mock dogfight with No.312 Squadron Czech Spitfire pilot, Pilot Officer Jaroslav Novak who was later killed on 14 May 1943 attacking enemy shipping at St Peter's Port Guernsey.[9] On December 6, with Stuart-Duncan as No.2 they spotted an oil

Porspoder Lighthouse from 300 feet. *(Family Collection – Crown © 1942)*

No.16 Squadron pilots huddle by the stove while waiting for the weather to clear. *(Family Collection)*

patch on the sea between Exeter and Ile de Batz, which was later confirmed as coming from the 'Penylan', a British destroyer sunk by E Boat S115 on 3 December, while escorting Convoy PW257.[10] After this operation, David returned to Weston Zoyland.

On December 12, Flight Lieutenant Tony Davis and Squadron Leader Kirkwood Currie[11] flew out on a Lagoon and Photo/recce. Near the Île de Batz and turning to make a photo run they were attacked head on by two Fw190s. Highly regarded by the Luftwaffe, these aircraft could out-dive and out-turn the Mustang, and after a short dogfight, Davis returned home alone having lost contact with Squadron Leader Currie, who had been shot down by *Unteroffizier* Friedrich May.

> As overworked pilots we are living on our reserves of nervous energy and life has taken on a different form. No longer is death terrible. It is too commonplace an event and it has lost its terror. We do not want to die because there are quite a number of things we wish to do after the war but if we crash that's that. There are times when one wants to live particularly strongly, especially just before going on and just after returning from leave for there are many good things in life as yet untouched and undone.

Highly experienced No.31 Squadron pilot, Squadron Leader Kenneth Frederick Mackie was posted to take Currie's place. In Burma he had received the DFC, having dropped supplies to troops holding out in a border garrison outpost and for 'courageously landing his aircraft on rough ground, and rescuing twenty-three people.'[12]

Now also promoted to Squadron Leader, Richard Osborn had been at RAF Breighton in York since May in an Australian bomber squadron. He wrote that the four-engine bomber he flew was definitely 'the bomber of the RAF'[13] and continued, 'I've been here since the end of May and Sq/Ldr in charge of a flight but in all that time I've only done 15 Ops – due to many various reasons. Still I just recently reached my 1,000th flying hour and celebrated it on the lousiest trip ever – all cloud flying, ice and one dud engine. My other RAF brother, Andrew[14] is unfortunately missing. He left Chipping soon after I did, but wasn't really fit for Ops. Still he had a crack and went missing at the end of August. We've heard nothing but personally I don't expect we'll hear anything more than the 'presumed' soon.'

Tuesday, 22 December. Last night our new Squadron Leader, Tony Greenly, Hamish Stothard[15] and I went to see a film, but it had just finished so we went to tea at the Castle Hotel Taunton instead.

Sgt Shobbrook and I flew down to deliver a turkey to Exeter and when we arrived back at Weston Zoyland, we heard rumours that, as it is to be rebuilt, we are to move to Andover. It can't come too soon, we have had the most awful weather with terrific gales and we are wading in mud.

Just two days before Christmas, Donald Draper had a serious accident when his aircraft struck a concrete mixer left on a runway extension. The official accident report stated that the mixer was unlit and difficult to see in the dark.[16] The Mustang was a write-off, and seriously injured, Draper was taken to Rauceby Hospital.

David reflected on his second Christmas away from his family.

I do hope my parents aren't too upset and have a good Christmas – for considering the state of the World today we really have a great deal to be thankful for – a retreating German Army both in Russia and in Libya.

Hamish Stothard, David, Tony Davis and Hugh Barber (out of roof). *(Family Collection)*

1942 has been a very happy year for me and I feel far more content now than I did at the beginning of the year – still in England but no longer bored and embittered.

Mary Hutton wrote with news that Peter was going overseas as soon as the weather improved. He was to ferry an aircraft from 10 Overseas Aircraft Delivery Unit at Lyneham to North Africa.

29/12/42, Andover.
David…, I hope you had a good Christmas. We had a wizard time. Pip got five sick days' leave after flu – starting last Tuesday till this am (Monday) so it was well arranged. He is now at Calne (Wilts) a perfectly awful place, the drome is at Lyneham and it's hell trying to get from there to here and vice versa. We wished you had been at Wallop on Saturday as we had a bit of a party and would have liked you to have been there…. Now for my bombshell, Pip is going overseas. He had embarkation leave just after you went back to Weston Zoyland, and I think it is more or less a matter of the weather now as to when. Isn't it foul? I'm hoping the weather will stay bad for a while.

All the best…Mary.

Chapter Thirteen

Andover, Ford and Exercise Spartan: January 1943 to June 1943

'A reconnaissance pilot is one of the most highly trained of modern fighting men. He must be able to: fly and navigate, fight if necessary, take photographs, observe and understand what he sees, and report accurately. All this must be done at once and alone.'

'Air Recce, 35 Recce Wing RAF.' HQ First Canadian Air Force.

At the beginning of January the runway at Weston Zoyland was to be rebuilt, so thirteen aircraft from No.16 Squadron flew in formation to RAF Andover. Here they met up with many old friends from No.170 Squadron. All leave was postponed due to the move, but David finally arrived home, minus his suitcase

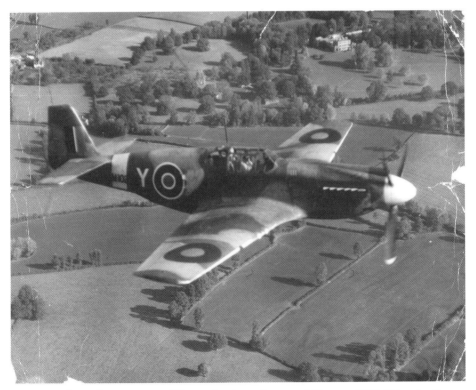

Mike McGilligan flying Mustang 'Y' over Southern Command Taunton 1942. Taken by Barney Gilliland. *(Family Collection – Crown © 1942)*

which he had lost on the train. His sister Marjorie and new niece Carol were also home.

> The loss of the suitcase is a severe blow. I had hoped that it would turn up but now after many fruitless hours of enquiries I fear that it is stolen. I am particularly worried as my Flight Log Book was in the suitcase and I feel sure that I will get a rocket from the C/O when I report it missing. I also lost all my negatives and the photo album which is very distressing. I couldn't get Carol the rattle for Christmas and, as brown paper and string is so hard to get, I had brought everyone's presents down with me.

On January 15, a No.4 Squadron Mustang suffered engine failure after low-level aerobatics. Undershooting his landing, George Hindmarsh hit a lorry and crashed onto the perimeter track. He escaped injury, but the lorry driver was killed. Hindmarsh and David became good friends at Hawarden.[1]

On 23 January, Richard Osborn flew his forty-eighth and last operation of his second tour. After an attack on Dusseldorf, his Lancaster was attacked by two Ju-88s, two of his crew were killed, and although severely injured, Osborn managed to ditch the aircraft at Warns. He spent the next three months in hospital at Leeuwarden and while there was visited by Wolfgang Kuthe, the Luftwaffe pilot who had shot him down. Sometime later, Kuthe brought his C/O, Helmut Lent – a top scoring Night Fighter Ace to visit, and their conversation was somewhat limited but courteous.[2]

Back from leave, David flew to Weston Zoyland for air-to-air firing practise. For these exercises an aircraft pulling a drogue[3] would fly up and down a line off the coast. Pilots would shoot at the drogue and the numbers of hits per pilot/gunner recorded. A drogue pilot's job was thought to be one of the least glamorous in the RAF; it was boring and occasionally dangerous, and so drogue-towing duties were often given to pilots as a form of punishment.

With his first shoot, David failed to hit the target drogue with any of his 400 rounds, but after checking the sights he found that they were slightly off. Over the next few days he increased his accuracy from four and a half to twenty per cent.[4]

> I heard of a drogue-towing pilot at Watchet (*an anti-aircraft gunnery range in the Bristol Channel*) who was appropriately named Pullin. He had once been a test pilot of an autogiro, but he claimed that it was such a dangerous thing that he was determined that it would never return to base. While on a flight, he dumped the autogiro in the sea, sufficiently close to land so he could swim ashore but deep enough so it couldn't be recovered. As punishment for this he then flew as a drogue pilot.

Facts seem to bear out David's story. On April 16 1941 a Cierva Autogiro (AP508), impressed into the Special Duty flight, was ditched in the sea near Seaton by Pilot Officer Raymond Aubrey Pullin. The subsequent inquiry reported that it 'Sustained an engine failure in flight,' and with insufficient revs to maintain height it alighted on the sea and sank immediately. Although an experienced pilot with about 1,000 hours flying time, around 450 of which were on autogiros, Pullin seems to have taken a somewhat 'laissez faire' attitude to flying. The month before, on March 25, at the controls of another Cierva C30A (V1186), he attempted to take-off up hill with a full load plus a passenger, and the autogiro ended up on its nose. The following year, on September 14, 1942, on a Rhubarb in the Bruges area, his No.239 Army co-op Mustang was hit by flak and he was forced to land in a field near Wissenkerke. Sent to Stalag Luft III, his Mustang was displayed with other captured Allied aircraft in Paris.[5]

With bad weather making living conditions at Weston Zoyland unpleasant David was glad when the air-to-air firing exercise was finally over:

> I had had quite enough of Weston Zoyland, especially when it rained and blew an 80 mile gale. I thought we were never going to get back to Andover but the weather cleared up and we flew back as fast as our wings would carry us. It is good being back with so many old friends – six of them who left us last summer.

David was also delighted when *The Times* reported that Major Antony Greenly was engaged to Diana Gibson.[6]

> Tony commits himself! I'm so glad, we get on particularly well together and he is an asset to the squadron. Sadly in spite of every attention Tony's little spaniel puppy died. The vet thinks he sat too near to the fire and burnt his head and eyes. Within three days of being a happy fat little puppy he was almost a skeleton.

Making a flying visit over his house, David was spotted by Marjorie and Carol.

> Bowden.
> It was very exciting to see you flying over the other day, it was tantalising to know you were inside that rushing roaring metal bird and not to be able to see you – I like the look of it tremendously – I wonder if we shall have aeroplane shows and gymkhanas in the air after the war, the show-ring 50 miles in length! Perhaps by then, they and the tanks will have exhausted the world of oil and petrol and we shall be back to the stately and leisurely days of the 'horse drawn conveyance' once more! It's rather amazing where everyone is getting their ponies and traps from. In Harborough, one sees the Pearson's bay, the Saunders's pony and several others. I wonder if the Heygate's chestnut will take her place amongst the shoppers one day. Take care of yourself….
> Marjorie.

At the end of the month, John Stuart-Duncan and Geoffrey Baker were posted to No.170 Squadron. Within five months, both pilots were killed. In February, No.16 Squadron received several Curtiss Tomahawks and Spitfires to allow pilots to gain experience with these aircraft. David recorded his first Spitfire flight on February 5.

> After checking everything was OK I climbed into the cockpit, switched on the starter and ignition switches, gave the priming pump a couple of squirts and pressed the starter button. I taxied down the runway and after getting the thumbs up took off. It was very exciting. I found that although it is not as forgiving as the Mustang, it is a most impressive and exciting aircraft to handle. I flew for an hour and was very loath to come back down to earth.

Less impressed with the handling of the Tomahawk, David hoped he did not have to fly them too often. This view was also held by test pilot, Neville Duke. In his autobiography he wrote, 'My first impressions of the Tomahawk were not very encouraging after being used to a Spitfire. The performance of the Tomahawk seemed poor and its rate of climb slow…, when I came into land I did the normal three-point Spitfire landing, ground looped and ended in a heap.'[7]

On 6 February, Pilot Officer Denis 'Nobby' Clark and Flying Officer Charles Oliver Potter were sent on an Arty/R course. Charles Potter had arrived in November from No.41 OTU. He was well liked but young, and his inexperience caused a tragic accident which sent shock waves throughout the Squadron. Wing Commander Davenport recalled, 'It was an ideal day to let the junior officers have a go at controlling some live 'shoots' by the 20 pounders of the Artillery.' After a successful shoot, Potter noticed soldiers drilling on the Larkhill barrack square and fatally decided to beat up the squad from behind. The only person to see what was about to happen was the Instructor, he realized that something very serious was imminent. He bawled at the top of his voice to the squad to fling themselves flat on the ground and promptly did so himself. Unfortunately one less agile soldier did not react fast enough.… As Potter pulled out of his dive and went into a climbing turn his aircraft sank a little and his wingtip touched the fellow on the top of his head. When all the others had recovered and shakily got to their feet the awkward man stayed down.'[8] Distraught, Potter returned to base.

> Potter flew back to Andover in a terrible state with a damaged wing. We are all very upset and it has caused great distress here. Unfortunately he has had to be put under close arrest which is the worst thing they could have done.

Charles Potter was court martialed and reduced to the ranks after pleading guilty to 'an act in flying which caused the loss of life to a person.'[9] Three days after this unfortunate accident Geoffrey Russell Baker, returning from his first operation with 170 Squadron as No.2 to Peter Miles, was killed when he crashed into the sea off Selsey Bill.

Later, David received news from Rosemary Boone.

> At last Rosemary has heard from her father, he is in hospital in Libya or Egypt at the moment, I do hope he will recover. Rosemary also writes that little Jennifer swallowed her identity disks and they thought that they would have to operate to retrieve them. Fortunately they were recovered naturally sometime later!
>
> I have been running the Flight on my own and have not been able to take any time off but my room is pretty comfortable with a small fire and I have spent the evening listening to the radio.
>
> Totting up my Mustang to date, they come to 155 hrs 10 mins and my personal Mustang AM226 'K for King,' shining sky blue and grey is the precious and jealously guarded treasure of A/C Jacques, my rigger.

A pilot became very attached to his allotted aircraft and it was often considered to be a personal possession. This attachment was also felt by the Riggers and Fitters. Rigger Ron Parnell wrote of an aircraft usually flown by Eric Martin or Richard Pugh. 'I

'Readiness.' Jimmy Jump Davies, Gillie, Stuart, Mike McGilligan and Mickie Gibbo. *(Family Collection)*

serviced 'H for Hector' from new and always polished it with Gunk hoping to get a few extra miles per hour out of it at crucial moments. Every time it went out on Ops I painted a little camera on the side of the cockpit.'[10]

On February 16, new pilots, George Roberts and James 'Jimmy' Jump Davies arrived. Roberts, who trained in Australia on Masters, was not enamoured with the Mustang and pestered everybody till they transferred him on to Spitfires with No.453 Squadron,[11] and Davies recalled arriving at Andover early one afternoon.

> David was the first person I met. I was feeling rather sorry for myself as I didn't want to leave No.2 Squadron and I felt that I was being landed there rather out of the blue but they made me very welcome even though I was reeking of whisky, (I carried a little glass whisky flask with me in case of emergencies and the glass had broken in my haversack while I was driving down.) The whole car, a little Standard 8, whiffed of it. I had been posted as Flt/Lt on Ops but for a while I was rather a spare wheel as Dick Pughe decided I wasn't going to fly any of his aeroplanes. I was there to replace Chegwin who had given up flying and had been posted away to do ground duties. No one talked about him.[12]

David wrote about this reluctance to talk about pilots who gave up flying.

> There are times when every pilot wants to stop flying after some particularly horrifying occasion and some pilots lose their nerve completely. We don't blame them but we prefer to keep quiet about it.

'Exercise Longford' was carried out in February and No.16 Squadron operated with 38 Division against the Guards Armoured Division. While pair-flying a Tac/Recce at 6,000 ft with Richard Pughe, David had a lucky escape.

'Mad Hatters tea party.' Bastow, Pugh, Gillie and Greenly at RAF Andover. *(Family Collection)*

On completing the sortie and diving through the mist I lost sight of Richard's aircraft so I continued to dive down. Suddenly I spotted a field a bit too close for comfort and only just managed to pull out of the dive seconds before making contact with the ground.

Having earlier made contact with a concrete mixer, Donald Draper, still recovering from his collision, wrote:

Rauceby Hospital, Sleaford. There is very little future in ramming unlighted concrete mixers on runways at night. I have been completely absolved of blame which is slight compense …, I had a letter from Melvyn posted in Gibraltar on his way to North Africa. He went to Spain on a visit and was not impressed by a brothel! I am still having some trouble with concussion and headaches and I have a scaphoid fracture of the left hand which is a very slow job. The scars on my face are healing. The photographs of the accident make me realize how lucky I was.

Best wishes, Donald.

On 27 February, No.16 Squadron pilots flew to RAF Ford for 'Exercise Spartan,' one of the biggest Army/Air Force exercises ever held in England. It was designed as a full-scale rehearsal for the invasion of Europe using air-to-ground co-operation, putting into place lessons learnt from the Dieppe raid. 'The scenario was that the Allies had landed in Europe, established a beachhead with air superiority and were about to breakout.'[13] The Airfield System, in which three squadrons were grouped together as a Wing was to be tried out, and the exercise area was divided into two opposing countries, 'Southland' and 'Eastland' with 'Westland' as a Neutral country. Ten Army divisions and an Air Force were allotted to each side.[14] Although looking forward to the flying, David was not so happy about the accommodation.

We are confined to camp along with No.170 Squadron, who are also using this aerodrome and the only downside to this exercise is the mobile conditions. This means that we are to live in tents while at Ford and although the weather is unseasonably warm for February, I am sure it is still going to be a cold and uncomfortable fortnight. I remember only too well sleeping out with the Army when I was down at Portsmouth and I again thank the foresight that impelled me to leave them when I did.

From the RAF's point of view, 'Spartan' was also a chance to test the efficiency of Co-operation squadrons living under mobile battle conditions. To make the exercise as realistic as possible, umpires judged each squadron's performance. One of these judges was Squadron Leader Laurence Irving, a Hollywood set designer, WWI pilot and now a Senior Intelligence Officer of the newly formed 35 Wing, responsible for Army/Air Force Co-operation.[15] At the end of each day the results of the pilots' operations were recorded in their Squadrons' Operations Record Book. This was divided into two sections.

i)   Form 540 was a daily 'Summary of Events,' typed in the Adjutant's office. The length and poetic content of the information rested entirely on the official in charge, thus some Squadron ORB entries would be impersonal and precise while others would show an eloquent, humorous or more detailed style.

ii) Form 541, comprised of 'Details of Work Carried Out.' Entries on this form were filled in from notes written after the return of each pilot from Operations. These entries (usually typed up monthly) recorded the pilots' observations or experiences of their flight.

Pilots also kept a personal record of their flights in Log Books. David kept two copies; the unofficial one was filled with notes, photographs and newspaper cuttings. This was highly disapproved of, as pilots were actively discouraged from keeping any form of diary.

During 'Exercise Spartan' David recorded in his Log Book, eight Tac/Rs in the Northampton and Aylesbury area, two air tests and a contact patrol. David met Flight Lieutenant Richard Vivian Muspratt[16] who had been a staff pilot with No.53 at Andover before moving to No.140 Squadron.

Muspratt said Charles was a quiet but excellent pilot and gave me news of Charles's other friends. 'Tubby' Grant[17] his old C/O, has become a Group Captain at the Air Ministry and Brian Bannister[18] was killed in an ordinary flying accident. What hard luck after all those trips against the enemy.

Due to a clerical error, the number of RAF personnel catered for on 'Exercise Spartan' was underestimated and so food at Ford was sparse. As resourceful as ever, Douglas Sampson volunteered to fly a Proctor to Weston Zoyland to pick up a cargo of fresh eggs. On returning to Ford, fully laden with his precious cargo, he made a very careful landing to ensure that they remained undamaged.

The Primus has been in constant use lately and the eggs were most welcome.

Today I flew a contact patrol in search of a lost armoured division in lovely weather; there has not been a drop of rain here for 10 days now and glorious sunshine, though there has been a cold wind at times.

In his report Major C.P. Stacey stated, 'The weather was exceptionally fine; no rain fell and the manoeuvres were conducted under the pleasant conditions of the English springtime. The nights, however, were cold.'[19]

The Southland army was attempting to seize Huntingdon 'the capital of Eastland' as rapidly as possible and No.16 Squadron pilots were sent up to support the advance and to find enemy armour in the Banbury–Bister area.

9 January. My aircraft developed engine trouble near Towcester so I had to made a forced landing at Westcote.[20] While waiting for repairs it was judged that I was able to evade capture and return to my lines.

A small mutiny took place on March 12, when the No.16 Squadron pilots refused to fly the unreliable Tomahawks, saying that the engine often failed even after being serviced. David, one of the pilots in this mini revolt, recorded the incident.

Oxford, with railway line and canal in the distance. *(Family Collection – Crown © 1942)*

We told Roddy that we wouldn't fly them because even when they come back from Burtonwood after maintenance, they can go wrong in a few hours. Today, Roddy Davenport said, 'There is nothing wrong with the Tommies and you must fly them because it is not up to you to say what aircraft you fly even if you do think they have rotten engines.'

Davenport decided to prove to everyone once and for all that Tomahawks were safe. So suited up and strapped in, he took off. He flew around the area doing some aerobatics then came into land. As he approached Ford, the watching pilots saw an untidy cloud of black smoke pour out of his now silent engine. Everyone held their breath, but Davenport made a skilful forced landing on the airfield to much loud applause from all. He quickly got out of the aircraft and went to inspect the damage. There was a huge hole in the crankcase where a piston rod had come right through the casing. 'You are quite right,' he said, 'These Tomahawks are not fit to fly. I am not going to have one on my squadron.'[21] David was jubilant.

> TOMMIES GROUNDED! The grounding of the Tommies is a mini victory for us pilots – a piston rod came through the crank case with Davenport up and he made a skilful forced landing, guessing speeds as the instruments were in French kph.

'Exercise Spartan' concluded at midday Friday, 12 March and was deemed a success. However, No.16 Squadron's 'casualty list' was rather alarming.

- Davies shot down twice by flak.
- McGilligan belly-landed after aircraft damaged.
- Gibbons suffered severe concussion.
- Sowerbutts wounded by shrapnel and also missing after an attack by hostile aircraft.
- David shot down by Flak and also landed behind enemy lines but evaded capture.
- Mackie, Martin and Kemp missing.

On the plus side it was judged that they shot down several enemy aircraft.[22] The final report concluded that air support was vital to the success of any battle and recommended that Army Co-operation Squadrons should be merged into a new Tactical Air Force.[23] Fifteen aircraft flew back in formation from Ford to Andover at the end of the exercise.

> It looked most impressive from where I sat and I hoped it looked equally good from the ground. It is great to be back in solid buildings after the freezing tents we have had to endure for the last 15 days. The Serviceability of 'B' Flight has been most commendable. Six aircraft were serviceable out of seven, every working day, working on dawn to dusk readiness.

Back on Ops, while carrying out a Popular near Avranches on March 25, David and John Sowerbutts misunderstood their instructions and flew over inland France for about ten minutes without incident.

> On the way back I took some good oblique photos of Mt St Michel and the coastline. We also sighted a convoy and stopped in at Middle Wallop to report its safe return. At 2 hours 15 mins this was one of my longest flights so far.

While 'Spartan' had been in full swing, Peter Hutton and his crew had taken off on March 4 to ferry a Blenheim to Gibraltar where they were to await further instructions. However, off the north west Portuguese coast, near Povoa do Varzim, the engines failed and they ditched in the sea. Attempting to get into their dinghy, it capsized, leaving them with a long swim to land. They were greeted by a large crowd who gave them food and took them to the Fiscal Police. After sometime, the Blenheim, which all had expected to sink, floated ashore. Worried that the aircraft's machine guns were pointing directly towards the shore, the crew were hastily taken back to make the guns safe. They were interned for almost a month before being flown home on May 27.[24] David was intrigued to hear of Peter Hutton's unexpected return.

> Pip who went overseas last month is back already and I have arranged to go over there for dinner this week to catch up on all his news. As Dick is on leave, I am Acting Flight Commander and leading the Flight in formation practise and Fighter Tactics.
>
> I have bought the most wonderful car, an Alvis 17 Silver Eagle, 4-seater drop-head Coupe for the princely sum of £135. Hugh had seen it at Anna Valley Motors and asked his father to pay for it, but he refused. I asked Father if he would buy it for me instead and amazingly he agreed.

At the beginning of April, David attended a Beam Approach Training course at Thruxton. BAT was an instrument-only approach to an airfield. Two fixed narrow radio beams were transmitted and only when approaching directly along the runway's centreline would the pilot hear a continuous tone and know he was on the right landing path. During the five-day course, David flew to several local airfields using the beams' signal and was then granted two weeks' leave. Having read in the newspaper that Anson Howard was a POW, David called on his mother.

> When she produced a picture of Anson which arrived that day, I learnt with some relief that the Major A.B. Howard must have been another person with the same name, a curious coincidence. Mrs Howard said Anson had been fighting out in Burma for a long time but had just returned to India.
>
> As it was such a glorious day and as I heard that Dr Boone is now back from Tunisia I decided to dash off to Devon to visit them. The Dr is feeling much better but still on a chicken, fish and egg diet, so it's no wonder they had to send him back. In spite of being ill, the Dr said witnessing the start of 'Operation Torch'[25] was an experience that he wouldn't have missed for anything, when on a brilliant sunny day in the Mediterranean there were Allied ships, of all description, as far as the eye could see and not a German or Italian anywhere, until about ten hours later when torpedo bombers attacked them. Twelve were shot down within sight and no more returned. So the Mediterranean evidently can no longer be considered an Italian lake!

On April 15, David helped make the preparations for Tony Greenly's wedding.

> Tony, Gilliland, Hugh and I caught a train to London and met up with him at the Berkley Hotel, went on to a dinner party at the Embassy and stayed at Flemings[26] in Half Moon Street.

In the morning we strolled round London then met Tony's best man, the news correspondent, Robin Duff. He has such a nice voice, which I suppose obtained him his job at the BBC.

Robin Duff was well known for his radio broadcasts and in 1942 he had vividly described an intense bombing raid on London, and how St Paul's Cathedral survived as the flames leapt up into the sky all around.[27]

I met Peter Flower who had been my Company Commander at Sandhurst, then I heard a voice say 'Heygate, I don't believe it.' It was Doc Cunningham, Ronald's friend who is now at the Air Ministry. After lunch we went to St Martin-in-the-Field and had to wait for another wedding to finish; by a curious coincidence it was the C/O's cousin getting married, so he had to attend two running! Robin was an excellent best man, very business like. After the ceremony we drove to 59 Eton Place where I met Ronnie Monteith[28] who was at Sandhurst with me and is Tony's cousin apparently! It was a lovely wedding.

By March 1943, Intelligence Staff at Medmenham were learning of a new threat, that of Hitler's secret 'revenge weapons' programme and were carefully rechecking all

David received the DFC for this photograph of a German RDF Station at Porspoder. *(Family Collection – Crown © 1943)*

aerial photographs, looking for new or unusual building sites. No.16 Squadron was asked to take photographs of one site situated on the very north west tip of France, at Porspoder, thirty-six miles from Brest. Weather conditions made it difficult to approach the area, but intelligence was urgently required.

> *April 24*. Eric and I were sent up to take a photograph of a tower that the Germans are building. We were told to get photos no matter whether they were good, bad or indifferent. The weather was terrible and on the way I lost Eric but I continued on until, to my horror, I spotted an island. I couldn't see any islands on my map and wondered if I had somehow flown up the English Channel instead of down, but I didn't think I could have strayed so far off course. I wondered where on earth I was, then I turned my map over and there was Ushant off the Brittany coast, near Brest. I had missed the tip of France altogether. With great relief I turned and flew inland at about 2,000 ft. Spotting the tower I climbed to 4,000 ft and took a diving photo of the tower at 380 mph. The builders were still working on it and I could see a Frenchman and his horse and cart.

David flew back as fast as possible, apprehensive that the photograph would not be good enough, but he gave the film to a waiting dispatch rider, who took it off at top speed to be developed. Eric Martin, who had also got lost, was very pleased to hear that David had made it home safely.

> I was then driven up in a staff car with the photographs as the boffins wanted to question me about it. The first question they asked was what colour it was. Of course I didn't have a clue; at that speed all I was trying to do was to get a good photo. If I had been asked to make a note of it then I would have been able to answer them.

The tower proved to be a new German Radio Direction Finder Station.

Now flying with No.225 Squadron, Melvyn Evans wrote to David from Souk-al-Arba in Tunisia:

> *BNAF.* I suppose I can't talk shop on the grounds of security so that immediately eliminates any details of any real interest. I have often wondered how you have been faring at home. I expect you do the odd rhubarb now and then as Bert said he had been doing before he foolishly rammed the concrete machine! (Actually today my Number 2 rammed a donkey – fortunately without hurting himself!) Peter Tickner returned home some weeks ago with an injured back and perhaps you will already have seen him if he visited the squadron. He can give you all the story up to the time he left.
>
> Yours, Mel.

While with No.225 Squadron, ex-No.16 Squadron pilot Pete Tickner, force-landed his Hurricane in the desert. Injured and trapped in his upturned machine, Tickner 'was extricated from the machine by a local Arab boy after he had handed him the aircraft's fire-axe which he used to get Pete out of his machine – I think Pete was unsure initially what the lad would do with the axe.'[29]

Towards the end of April, Mackie, Pughe, Martin and David flew to Vierge to take photographs of the lighthouses, and then David flew a dicey Shipping Run to

Ile de Vierge Lighthouse taken from 400 feet on 28/11/42. *(Family Collection – Crown © 1942)*

Guernsey, Jersey, Iles Batz and Sept Iles with Richard Pughe, Eric Martin and John Sowerbutts.

> We flew low-level just above the waves and I had to keep my concentration and check my instruments all the time, as it was easy to misjudge distances and become disorientated. I didn't want to spend any time in a small yellow dinghy out at sea. On the way back, the weather worsened and nearing the coastline we hit very low cloud and zero visibility. Pughe, flying lead aircraft did not reduce speed below 290 mph and I was very concerned for us all. We could no longer see either the beach or the cliffs as they were shrouded in cloud. I lost sight of all the others, but by a stroke of good luck, we somehow all broke out of the cloud, missing both the cliffs and one another. Flying at about 50 ft and at 300 mph, we had passed right over the naval base. Luckily, there was no time for the guns to shoot at us. Usually if a low-flying aircraft is coming in the naval gunners have orders to shoot first and then check if the aircraft is friend or foe afterwards – that is if it's not already too late.

After a low flying aircraft demonstration attack for the Army Generals at Old Sarum, David met Ian Duffus but missed Monty Denny who had left for India. David also

A Rhubarb train attack on the Cherbourg peninsular, near Lessay. *(Family Collection – Crown © 1943)*

heard that Tony Hilditch had been awarded the DFC.[30] The previous year No.53 Squadron was flying Anti-submarine Ops from the USA and Caribbean. On August 15 1942, Hilditch and his crew spotted a U-Boat and dropped four depth charges. Seeing oil in the water they felt confident they had sunk or seriously damaged it. However, although U108 received a severe jolt and some light bulbs were smashed, it sustained no major damage. While these attacks caused little serious damage, they significantly helped to reduce the number of ships attacked in the Caribbean.[31]

On Friday, 30 April, David flew a Rhubarb with Davenport over the Rennes area; they shot up and damaged two trains, seeing great flashes as the engines were hit. They also both scored direct hits when attacking two barges off the Jersey coast, the larger vessel returning fire with a machine-gun, and about a mile west of Dol they were met by a lot of accurate German Flak. Briefly landing at RAF Ibsley to report to a Whirlwind Fighter Squadron based there; they then flew back to Andover.

Following the success of 'Exercise Spartan,' the 2nd Tactical Air Force was created. Wing Commander Davenport was posted onto 84 Group's 123 Wing, Wing Commander Richard Ian Mallafont Bowen took over as his replacement and two Spitfire pilots arrived to teach Fighter Tactics.

Tuesday, 4 May. Mackie led us on a Lagoon and we flew to a point ten miles north of Brehat and then ten miles north to Sept Iles, it was Bastow's first Op and the sea was very rough. We encountered two Me109s but managed to escape without damage.

Before he was posted to England, Canadian pilot Gerry Hugh Bastow had had a very lucky escape. On October 14 1942, heading home for embarkation leave, he boarded the passenger ferry S.S. Caribou. Halfway across the Cabot Straight to Newfoundland, the ferry was attacked and sunk by U-boat U69. Of the 237 passengers on board, Bastow was one of the 103 rescued.[32]

On May 16, it was the turn of William 'Wendy' Wendelken to be rescued from the sea. While low flying at zero feet over the sea, his engine developed problems. Climbing to 1,000 feet, he called Mayday and stepped out of the aircraft just as the engine stopped. Parachuting into the sea, he clambered into his dingy and after paddling for four hours he was picked up by a motor gun boat.[33] David noted that Wendelken seemed to have 'all the bad luck and a certain amount of finger trouble.'

The next day, David and George Roberts were sent up to the west coast of Scotland, for a Combined Operation Aircrew course.

We were advised not to fly up to Troon as the weather can get quite bad at this time of year so I took the train. It had no restaurant car and was an hour late. I then missed the train to Troon but managed to get a welcome meal at the St Enoch Hotel Grill in Glasgow while I waited for the next one. The first person I saw at the Marine Hotel was Group Captain Acheson who wants me to look after Sandy again as their house has been blown to bits and with his new job he is never more than about five days in the same place.

After meeting with Squadron Leader Wilson, David was shown to a very pleasant room with a grand view of the Firth of Clyde. Once settled, he took a walk about Troon.

The weather was very bracing and I loved the smell of the sea. I seem to know a large number of people in the RAF now. Ian Morrin[34] my old No.16 Flight Commander is here – he's now a Squadron Leader – and Wing Commander Carroll[35] my chief instructor at Old Sarum is also here, we got on so well together.

At breakfast the next day it was stressed that as civilians were still living in the hotel they must exercise the strictest caution, not to leave any documents about, or discuss any part of the course within their hearing.

The people up here are most friendly, except the hotel staff who do not really hide their ill feelings at having half the hotel full of RAF and Navy Officers. I understand this is because they had been told that they would be freed for their summer commitments, however, I expect it helped them in the winter when business was poor.

The timetable followed a series of talks and demonstrations. Naval Officer, Lieutenant De Frimes, gave a lecture about landing operations, stressing that the main objective of a Combined Operation was to place an army ashore on the enemy's coast in such

Shipping and coastline photo. *(Family Collection – Crown © 1942)*

numbers that it could secure the landing site. They had a lecture on assault landings and beach operations and after hearing about the merits of using a combination of well protected warships carrying large numbers of troops, and flat-bottom landing craft that could place troops on the beach, they went down to Troon Harbour to see ships and landing craft varying in size from 10,000 tons to a twenty-foot Alligator – an American amphibious vehicle that could travel at seven knots in water and twenty-five miles per hour on land.

During the course there was also a lecture on the Control of Aircraft in Combined Ops, a visit to the Signals School and a demonstration of firepower by the Bombardment Unit on the ranges at Dundonald.

I went for a terrific walk by the sea. I wish I had brought up my civilian clothes and a bathing costume it was so hot. Only a week ago they had considerable snow so we have been lucky. This course has been most informative and I have met some very interesting people. We had a talk about the Dieppe raid and heard how all branches of the services learnt a good deal about importance of Combined Operations from it.

On David's return to Andover, pilots from twelve Mustang squadrons prepared to take part in 'Operation Asphalt,' Army Co-op's last offensive before it was dissolved. To be nearer the south coast, No.2 and 268 Squadrons moved to Thruxton and No.4 Squadron to Warmwell. 'Asphalt's' plan was to attack selected targets and the rail system across Northern France, with each squadron assigned hinterland targets to attack. No.16 Squadron's target was a power station south of Saint Brieuc and Guingamp.[36]

Due to unsuitable weather on May 24, the operation was put on hold. The next day was as bad, but by late afternoon on May 26, although a bank of sea fog hung over the South Coast and Channel, 'Operation Asphalt' was set in motion. David's Log Book recorded a sixty-five minute operational flight.

Our task was to attack the power station on the edge of the lake from both sides at once. We flew to coast line abreast six A/C led by W/Cdr Bowen. Chaos. Cloud in hills. Squadron mixed up. Radio chatter terrific.

Twelve No.268 Squadron aircraft took off, but encountered thick sea fog at zero feet and they returned to Thruxton. Aircraft from No.168 Squadron also crossed over the coast but after about twenty miles they too turned back, but when ten No.2 Squadron aircraft hit a wall of fog at Kimmeridge, they were ordered to climb above it. However, three pilots, Flying Officer Norman John Miller, Flying Officer David Hirst and Pilot Officer John Beaton McLeod, failed to climb fast or high enough and they crashed into St Albans Head, Dorset. All three were killed.[37] Douglas Sampson wrote scathingly 'All the squadrons were to be massed in an attack to win the war. Warm fronts finally aborted the show but only after a squadron had lost at least one pilot, scraped off as No.4 line astern on a Dorset hill.'

At the end of May, Douglas Sampson 'borrowed' an aircraft and slipped away to Ireland to ask his girlfriend Jeanne to marry him. He described the two day trip as 'A slightly unofficial project supposed to be a navigation exercise.' However, it seemed

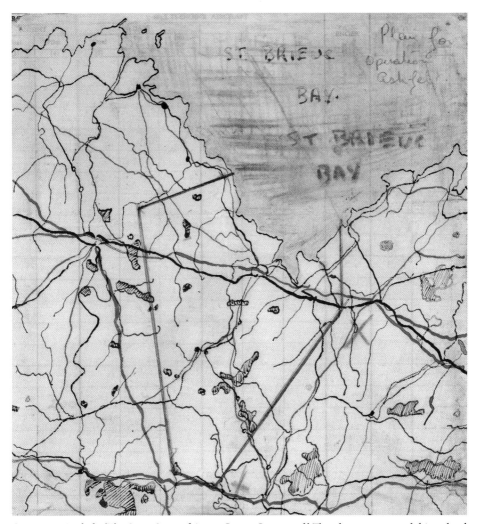

Operation Asphalt, 'The Swan Song of Army Co-op Command'. The plan was to attack hinterland targets in Northern France with twelve Mustang Squadrons. *(Family Collection)*

that Tony Davis had not fully understood Sampson's request. Fortunately he returned with 'some merchandise not seen for years, including bananas.... Before I could be informed of a mooted court martial, I had presented the aggrieved senior officer with exotic fruits etc and at the same time asked C.O.'s permission to marry. This is sometimes known as disarming! It was most effective, luckily for me.'[38]

May 29 was No.16's last day as an Army Co-operation squadron. After flying aerobatics in morning David, Mackie and Gerry Bastow flew an uneventful Interception Patrol from Swanage to the Needles.

While attempting a crosswind landing on 1 June, No.170 Squadron pilot, John Stuart Duncan, crashed his Mustang.[39] David noted in his Log Book:

F/O Duncan killed in Mustang going round again at Weston Zoyland after hitting bowser.

Later the same day, as No.16 Squadron was now affiliated to Fighter Command, David led the Flight over to Middle Wallop and for the next month the pilots studied Fighter Command organization, practised fighter tactics and beat-ups of gun positions. They were also tasked with intercepting German fighter-bombers that were attacking coastal towns at low level,[40] and Rhubarb patrols. David flew both Rhubarb and anti-Rhubarb patrols over Portland and the Isle of Wight, while good friend Gilliland received orders for overseas Air Staff Duties in North Africa. A farewell party was held in London before his departure and they all went to see a Terence Rattigan play.

> We had a grand day in town, amongst other things we saw 'Flare Path', the acting was very poor but some people seemed to enjoy it. Somehow that sort of thing doesn't go down on stage and when badly portrayed on the stage, it leaves much to be desired.

A mid-air crash at Middle Wallop on Monday, 14 June almost put pay to two No.16 Squadron pilots. Sampson had been on the Gunnery School course and was

No.16 Squadron pilots began training in fighter tactics. *(Family Collection – © Crown Copyright)*

detailed to fly combat practise with less experienced pilots. After being 'attacked' by Wendelken, he called to break off the attack. He recalled:

> I began gently climbing and turning to the right. Wendy settled in a span clear. I increased my rate of turn to head east and looked down to my left at Middle Wallop field – only a second – then with my side-vision before I turned my head Wendy's wing began to loom above the level of my cockpit. He had lifted his left wing and lost sight of me, I stopped my turn and reefed back the stick. His wing now looked like a house and he seemed to be in a steep turn but he slipped towards my aircraft. Just as I thought I was above his height there was a tremendous bang. The cockpit filled with white and grey smoke but this cleared as I called Wendy. [41]

Wendelken was going to bail out, but as he was not spinning, Sampson asked if he could belly-land at Middle Wallop just six miles away, which he did. Sampson also landed safely, and now able to look over his aircraft, he saw it had lost part of the nose from the leading wing-edge to propeller disc; his 50-calibre guns under the engine were bent and all his ammo had blown up.

> Wendy, already in debt to the Grim Reaper, had some luck today after a mid-air collision at 4,000 ft with Sammy's Mustang. Wendy's Mustang lost a large section of his wing – a portion of which fell near a local farmer but luckily missed him. They both landed safely and it was indeed fortunate that Middle Wallop has a grass runway that slopes uphill.

Several days later, Mackie and David flew a Rhubarb patrol over Avranches. They did not see any targets, but were spotted and chased back to the French coast at Cherbourg by two Fw190s; luckily they lost them and returned to base safely. A few days later on June 22, these roles were reversed when David was on standby for an Anti-Rhubarb patrol, hoping to intercept German fighters.

> We sat in the cockpit waiting for the green Very Light. When at last it was fired we took off in record time and I actually got to chase two enemy aircraft all the way back to within thirty miles of Cherbourg, but were not allowed to go any further. I wonder if they were the same ones we met the other day.

Chapter Fourteen

No.34 Photo Recce Wing – Hartford Bridge and Operation Holloway: July 1943 to Nov 1943

Recce pilots that 'didn't have stiff necks from all the craning didn't last long.'
Adelaide Daily Advertiser, June 2, 1994

With the demise of Army Co-operation, No.34 Photo Recce Wing was formed with Group Captain Lousada as C/O. and Wing Commander Stansfeld as Admin C/O. Now, as part of this new Wing, No.16 Squadron joined No.140 Squadron at RAF Hartford Bridge.[1] This large three-runway airfield was built in November 1942 on requisitioned land at Yateley Common. No.140 was to fly Mosquitos in day and night photo-recces, while No.16 Squadron was to slowly replace Mustangs with Spitfires in order to carry out high-level photo recces. As part of the reorganization, No.16 and 140's Air Liaison Sections were combined to form No.123 Section with Hugh Rigby in charge.[2]

Lent two Spitfires by 140 Squadron, one was soon put out of action after its tail was damaged by a heavy landing.

Sunday, 4 July 1943. This week, having finally packed up, fourteen of us flew to Hartford Bridge Flats. Sammy managed to upset Tony by landing the practice Spitfire from 50 ft like a Mustang. This landing was so awe-inspiring it merited many comments from the members of No.140 Squadron.

Ground crew unplug the electrical 'trolley acc' after starting the Spitfire's engine. *(Family Collection)*

To fly at high-level, pilots needed to be able to withstand the pressures involved, and No.16 Squadron pilots went to RAF Farnborough for tests in a decompression tank, which could simulate the effects of high-altitude flying. If a pilot failed to complete the tests, he was deemed unfit to fly on high-level operations. Out of the sixteen tested 'One fell by the wayside due to the bends…, and four were unable to sit out for the full two hours in the chamber.'[3] These pilots were Clark, Sowerbutts, Mackie, Davies and David, who was distraught at the prospect of having to leave the squadron:

> I have had a particularly harassing day today and I do not know now what my future will be. I am bitterly disappointed that I failed the test and am unfit for high-level flying. Sammy put my failure down to those who stuffed too much lunch. Now that circumstances beyond my control have arisen to complicate everything, I hope I can remain with the squadron until my promotion is due.
>
> I went for a walk with Eric Martin to try to forget it. However we talked shop all the walk so I didn't forget it at all. When we returned we decided to make some coffee, which was rather amusing; it was an event with a considerable risk of fire and scalding. Wendy came along, also a Canadian pilot dropped in, bringing tins of peaches, cream, boned chicken and other foreign cans with extraordinary things inside and so we had quite a celebration. I then asked to stay on and amazingly they agreed.

To celebrate its formation, No.34 Wing held a well-attended dance on July 23; the Wing Dance Band provided the music and the temporary Air Ministry building looked like a private ballroom in Mayfair.[4]

> Yesterday loads of old friends turned up as well as all four of our past and present C/Os – Stansfeld, Davenport, Bowen and Mackie. Ian Duffus and Tony Greenly also showed up and there was good food, a plentiful supply of wine and a large number of girls. We had a very jolly time.
>
> Today was Douglas Sampson's wedding, I flew down to Weston Zoyland but low cloud meant I had to return without landing. I was very cross that I had missed Sammy's big day.

On Sunday, 25 July, David and Denis Clark flew a 'dicey sortie' to obtain some urgently needed photographs of a tributary of the River Aure, near Bayeux. This was of great interest to Army Intelligence as it was just five miles south of the planned D-Day landing beaches of Gold and Omaha. They crossed over the English coast at Selsey Bill, but not long after, Clark's aircraft developed engine trouble and he had to return to base, David decided to carry on alone.

> I made landfall at zero feet near Port en Bessin. Cloud was 9/10ths, visibility 3,000 yards, just north of Bayeux, (well known for its tapestry) so I turned at the river and flew past Trevieres taking oblique photos of the stream at 1,000 ft for five miles. At times it appeared to go underground and was often only a ditch. No enemy aircraft were noticeable, but when the cloud broke I turned for home.

The weather turned warm and the pilots found a way to cool down while practising a useful new skill. About a mile from Hartford Bridge, Wyndham's Pool, a large man-

Dinghy Drill in the Muddy Puddle later proved very useful for George Holloway. However, Nobby Clark had some difficulty trying to climb into the dingy. *(Family Collection)*

made pond used as a swimming pool, proved a useful training ground for Dinghy Drill.

Thursday, 29 July 1943. It was so hot that we went down to the 'Muddy Puddle.' The dinghy inflated well and we cooled down as we practised getting in and making quick exits out when it capsized.

While the others watched on, Pilot Officer Roberts 'Buttoned up the weather cape in the correct manner and was capsized. His exit took five seconds which seems quite reasonable.'[5] Just a month later, this practise session was to prove especially useful to Flight Lieutenant George Holloway.

Finally some old Spitfires were delivered to the squadron and it was decided that 'A' Flight pilots would use them for high-level work. For the present, 'B' Flight would remain a low-level flight and continue to carry out Ops in the Mustang. David decided to find out just how high a Mustang could fly.

> *Saturday, 31 July.* I tried to take a Mustang up to 20,000 feet (their maximum limit) but when I got to about 19,000 ft it started to flap around alarmingly.

Later, four pilots including David flew over to Shoreham for air-to-air firing practise. David scored six per cent and eleven per cent, and top scorer was Tony Davis with seventeen per cent.[6] While there, Douglas Sampson, the 'gunnery genius,' had to admonish Australian pilot, Douglas Auburn Bleechmore, after the armourers complained that 'only half of each gun could be found after firing as he had fired off all his ammo in one burst.' When confronted, Bleechmore retorted, 'When I fire them, they stay fired.'[7]

As several new squadrons were due to move to Hartford Bridge, the pilots 'started the grim task' of laying the Sommerfeld tracking. This wire mesh track was rolled out and staked down on the field for fast construction of temporary runways or hardstanding. [8] The squadron pilots then moved into tents to practise living under mobile conditions and they remained under canvas for two months, but 'the Wing was never very happy in this sort of discomfort.'[9] Once settled, David wrote:

> The tents are once again littered with parachutes and the roar of engines are competing with the whine of some harmonious female from the radio within.

On Friday, 27 August, Denis Clark and Richard Pughe had a very successful 'train busting' sortie over the Brest Peninsular. Taking off from Exeter, they attacked a train twenty-five miles south west of St-Malo at Dolo. About five miles further south, they encountered another train. Pughe gave it a long broadside shot and saw people running for cover, and hits on the engine. After attacking an engine at Caulnes, they flew cross-country to the Rennes Redon line, shot up a train and saw sheets of flame rising from the fire cabin. Three more train attacks followed. South of Quimperle, Pughe had a 'heavenly shot' on an engine, stationary on a bridge, and in his excitement nearly flew into some phone wires before flying over the town and sending people running for cover. They continued on and attacked the next train in a cutting; again this resulted in smoke and steam. After Quimperle they shot up three more trains before returning home. 'In just over 2½ hours they had flown 550 miles and damaged 12 trains without encountering any flak or enemy aircraft.'[10] Several newspapers reported their successful sortie and David noted in his Log Book:

> Nobby Clark and Dick Pughe bagged twelve trains, a record number! I was there in spirit, as Nobby flew in my steed, 'K for King.'

George Holloway, Mike McGilligan, 'Wendy' Wendelken, Randy Ransley and Mickie Gibbons. *(Family Collection)*

The next day, two less successful train-busting operations were sent off. Richard 'Dick' Ransley and Ernest 'Gibbo' Gibbons found and shot up one engine, but reported back, 'Never had we seen a railway look so utterly empty.' Due to a faulty compass, Eric Martin and John Sowerbutts had even less luck. 'We crossed the French coast at Ile Vierge; an incorrect landfall…, and sighted the Brest balloon barrage. On appreciating that our landfall was hopelessly incorrect we abandoned the operation.'[11] Not to be outdone, Gerry Bastow and David flew a practise Rhubarb over Andover, Salisbury and Southampton, and claimed to have 'shot up' five trains.

> Dick Pughe and I then went over to a delightful club in Aldershot that he was a member of, having in peacetime served in the King's Own. The dance floor is reputed to be the best for dancing on in the South of England, beautifully springy! It had lounges, bars, dining rooms, two squash courts, ten grass courts and a cricket ground surrounded by trees at the back.

A series of events took place on Monday, 30 August, that started No.16 Squadron on the longest search and rescue mission of their war. Flying from Exeter, Squadron Leader Mackie and Flight Lieutenant George Holloway were briefed for Rhubarb No.4. However, things did not go as planned right from the start. They arrived too far west of their intended position, but found and attacked two trains before turning for home, crossing the coast at Ile Vierge. However, Luftwaffe fighter pilots of 8/JG 2 had been alerted of their presence. 'After seven minutes flying at approx 300 mph (about ten miles out from the French coast) the section was bounced by six Fw190s.'[12] One of aircraft was flown by Herbert Huppertz,[13] already credited with having shot down forty-eight aircraft. Mackie climbed for the cloud, instructing Holloway to do the same, but Holloway's aircraft was hit and unable to make cloud cover, he told Mackie that he was bailing out. However, after a further attack, Holloway ditched his aircraft in the sea instead. Circling in what cloud cover was available, Mackie requested a MAYDAY fix, then having done all he could, he flew back leaving Holloway alone in his dinghy.

Alerted to the fact that a pilot was down in the sea, aircraft from No.276 and 610 Squadrons, along with Mackie and Eric Martin, went up to search. When a pilot spotted a dinghy twenty miles north of the Ile of Batz, Mackie was able to confirm it was Holloway, but with dusk falling they lost sight of him. The next day, five more pilots from No.16 Squadron including David joined the search.

> 'Operation Holloway' gets underway. We flew down to Exeter in formation then at 12.25, Mackie, Pughe, Bastow, Davis, Wendelken, myself and two pilots from No.169 Squadron went out to search for Holloway's dinghy. We broke into fours and orbited left and right. Out of touch with the ground station we patrolled over Sept Iles and Iles Batz at 2,000 ft but no dingy was seen and we had to return after two hours. There were various Spitfires out doing strip searches and I'm sure it won't be long before the Jerries know that we have a man down.

Exeter ORB recorded the unfolding drama. 'Air Sea Rescue search was continued at dawn…. Six Spitfires of No.610 Squadron found a dinghy at about 07.00 but had to leave owing to shortage of petrol.' In the afternoon, eight Spitfires from No.616 Squadron led by Wing Commander Jack Charles,[14] who had himself been rescued from a dinghy just a month before, set off to search the area. They were attacked by eight Fw190s and in the dogfight, Flight Sergeant Ronald McKillop, Sergeant Paul Shale and a Luftwaffe pilot of 7/JG2 were shot down. Later, No.276 Squadron pilots, Flight Sergeant Edmund Sotheron-Estcourt and Flight Sergeant 'Pop' Ewans were out searching when Ewans heard a 'pinging' sound on his radio. Unaware that this was the German radar tracking them, he spotted four aircraft coming towards him. 'At first I thought they were Typhoons with white coloured engine cowlings. Rather unusual I thought, then hesitant and almost reluctant to think they could be Focke-Wulfs, never having met them before, I called out "Break!"'[15]

Flying into the clouds, Ewans saw the Fw190s attack Sotheron-Estcourt's aircraft, and Herbert Huppertz claimed a Spitfire shot down. When Ewans emerged from the clouds, the enemy aircraft had gone. Spotting an oil patch on the sea surface, he flew down and dropped a dinghy, vainly hoping that Sotheron-Estcourt had bailed out.

> Up again at 16.30 with Mackie and 6 other a/c to relieve No.616 Spitfire Squadron, we did a low search round Sept Iles and were twice attacked by Fw190s. We chased three back to the French coast but were unable to get close enough to fire. We then lost contact with No.169 Squadron and saw no sign of George or his dinghy so we headed back to base. My radio packed up and I ran out of petrol in one tank and I was flying on fumes in the other by the time I got back to Exeter after a two-hour flight.

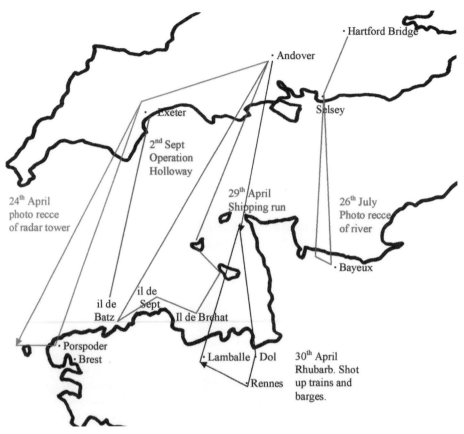

Some operations flown by David. (*SAGH*)

At 19.08, No.610 Squadron Spitfires found Holloway's dinghy and were relieved by Mustangs, but again it was lost in mist and darkness. On Wednesday, 1 September it was impossible to carry out any search due to low cloud.[16]

> We sat about chewing our fingernails, waiting to take-off, but the cloud stubbornly refused to clear so we had to accept that George was going to have to spend yet another night bobbing about on the high seas.

There was better news on Thursday as the search continued at first light with No.610, 619 and 276 Squadrons taking off, and just after 07.00 they found Holloway still in his dinghy 25 miles north east of Ile de Batz.[17]

> Great News! We heard that No.610 Squadron had spotted Holloway and were circling him. Four aircraft – Mackie, Davis, Martin and I – took off immediately to relieve them. We found the Spitfires guarding the dinghy and were joined by more Spits, a Typhoon and a Hurricane.

After dropping fluorescence into the sea to mark Holloway's position, two circled the dinghy, the other two patrolled up-sun, while short of fuel, the Spitfires headed home. A No.276 Squadron Walrus crewed by Flying Officer Ken Butterfield, Sergeant L.G. Badger and Sergeant R. Churchill set off. Ken Butterfield noted, 'Our customer was south-west of Bolt Head and a fair way out.' They 'Chugged into view, landed and picked up a grateful Holloway, who did not seem to have suffered too greatly from his three days in a dinghy, but who was extremely glad to see the Walrus.'[18] David and the others escorted the exhausted Holloway safely back to Exeter where everyone was delighted to welcome him home.[19]

'Operation Holloway' was a great team effort with 177 British planes involved in his rescue. Nine squadrons took part, flying Mustangs, Typhoons, Spitfires, ASR Spitfires, a Hurricane, a Walrus, a Hudson and a Swordfish.[20] However, three RAF and one Luftwaffe pilot lost their lives in this engagement.

> *Friday, 3 September.* It was fantastic to have Holloway back after spending 66 hours in the sea and I'm sure dinghy drill in the Muddy Puddle wasn't much of a preparation for the real thing. It was my first real close encounter with enemy aircraft. I am so glad I took an active part in what *The Daily Mail* called a real life drama. It was colossal and after four days of fighting we were rewarded by our pilot being rescued.
>
> I'm now certain that Charles was shot down at sea and I just wish I could have put in as much effort into finding him when he crashed as we did with George. I pray that he didn't spend hours floating in a dinghy waiting for a rescue that never came.

While Holloway thanked his good luck, Peter Hutton's luck finally ran out on September 9. Having recovered from his earlier ditching, he was ferrying a Wellington towards the Middle East when his aircraft vanished without trace over the Bay of Biscay. This time, after initially being reported missing, all on board were later 'Presumed Dead.'[21]

By the middle of September the overworked squadron Mustangs began to develop faults. Douglas Bleechmore crash-landed on the aerodrome, and John Sowerbutts was flying David's old Mustang AM226 to be de-rated, when it developed engine trouble and he too crashed. Luckily, both pilots escaped uninjured.

Now based at 130 Unit RAF Tangmere, Peter Miles wrote to David to ask about transferring back to No.16 Squadron. 'Do you think there's any chance, because if there is I'll try through the official channels.... Give me a good 'live' shoot recommendation to 16 and I'll buy you a drink or something.'

At the end of September David received rather surprising news.

> Rosemary wrote to say that she is to be posted overseas. I had always been opposed to her joining the Forces, but I admit that my ideas may be a trifle out of date. I tried to get her to take a Commission, but she found that she loved her job and up until recently a Fighter Direction Officer in the Fleet Air Arm was not open to WRNS. However, someone at the Admiralty must have recognized Rosemary's good work as it has now been made open to them and she was commissioned immediately!
>
> We must try to remain good friends and write often but with no strings attached on either side. What a topsy-turvy world when the women are the warriors and the men folk stay at home. But one cannot help seeing the

'All up.' *(Family Collection)*

humorous side of it and it is as Rosemary says a 'big adventure.' If she takes snaps of shooting tigers or riding camels I do hope she will send them to me. I wonder if she will meet Gilliland in Sudan, he was sent out at just the right time. I wish I could have gone with him.

I can't bear the thought of being 'chair-bound,' so I've asked to stay with the squadron for the time being and they have agreed, so will I continue to fly with them for a little while longer.

At the beginning of October, four pilots, including David, flew over to Shoreham for Air-Firing practise, however, they were thwarted when the drogue was shot away and were unable to return home due to bad weather. As David took off over the sea the next day, the main glycol pipe came off, his windscreen was covered and the fumes inside the cockpit became so strong that he was forced to make an emergency landing, down-wind, producing much smoke.

While No.16 Squadron attempted to get in as much high-level photographic practise before bad weather set in, Squadron Leader Kenneth Mackie was posted to No.2 Group, No.88 Squadron, 'because he liked flying nearer the ground.'

We are very sad to see him go, but the good news is that he is engaged, it's a fitting conclusion to Operation 16. He took me up in his Boston and I occupied the rear gunner seat as we carried out some fighter tactics and low-level flying. I'm so glad I'm not in bombers for, although Mackie is a brilliant pilot, I definitely prefer to be in the driving seat.

Later while trying to take photographs of Poole I was thwarted by low cloud. I took off and only once saw the ground again about forty minutes later so low was the cloud in these parts. Our Met people said it was clear at Barnstable so I nearly set off there but I got in just before it clamped right down…. Shaky do's.

After a year's absence on postings with No.140 and 4 Squadrons, Peter Miles was welcomed back.

25 October. My Birthday. It is great to see Jerry again, but we will only be together for a short time as I have finished my tour of Ops and am to be posted to an OTU at Hawarden. I do feel so very miserable at the thought of leaving so many good friends behind.

26 October. On the pretext of cross-country flying I dropped in to visit the family and picked up my fishing rod. I flew into Market Harborough and caught a lift home. Mother and Father were most surprised to see me. Father looks terrible; he is trying to keep the business afloat but only has half the staff and is missing Charles' guiding hand. Mother is frail and still struggling to come to terms with the loss of Charles and the added worry about the possibility of losing me too.

On one last detachment, David and Tony Davis went for a three-day convoy duty observation on the Destroyer 'HMS *Quorn*.'

We reported to Portsmouth dockyard and were welcome, on board by Captain Frederick Greville Woods and set sail towards Harwich.

In 1939, Lieutenant Woods had been posted as torpedo officer to the submarine '*Thetis*' which had sunk on sea trials in Liverpool Bay, with a crew of fifty and fifty-three observers on board. A coat of bitumastic solution had accidentally been dripped into a test-cock hole. Due to this faulty valve, and unaware that the bow cap of this tube was open, Woods opened the No.5 rear torpedo door. Sea water rushed in and flooded the forward compartments.[22] The '*Thetis*' nose-dived to the shallow

David and Tony Davis set sail with Frederick Greville Woods, Captain of HMS *Quorn*. *(Family Collection – Crown © 1943)*

seabed. Twice, Woods valiantly tried to shut the rear door of the torpedo tube, but the intense high pressures were too great. After thirteen hours and in hopes of organizing a rescue, Captain Oram and Lieutenant Woods exited via an escape chamber, swam twenty feet to the surface and were picked up by HMS *Brazen*. Two other men escaped, but attempts to raise the submarine were unsuccessful and ninety-nine were lost.[23]

On 31 October, David heard news from Melvyn Evans. He had been flying tactical recces with No.225 Squadron but, grounded due to dizziness, had left the squadron and was now working at the RAF Censor Office with the BNAF.[24] He wrote that his brother Eric had been killed fighting[25] in Tunisia and added he had met up with 'Ray Eller (Wing Commander) who was in the ill fated No.18 Squadron and was one of the three crews which walked back from the raid.'

The 'ill fated No.18 Squadron' had already suffered many losses of men and aircraft before moving to Canrobeit in Algeria. On 4 December 1942, the C/O, Hugh Malcolm[26] led an unescorted bombing raid on Chouigui airfield west of Tunis. They were attacked by a large number of Me109s, and one by one the whole squadron was shot down. Malcolm was killed, however Ted Holloway, Wray Eller, Ollie Brown and Norman Echess were able to walk back to base.[27]

At the end of the month five new pilots arrived from No.8 OTU to replace those unfit for high flying, while David and those unable to fly at altitude took their leave of the squadron. Flying Officer Denis Clark was posted to No.168 Squadron,[28] John Sowerbutts to No.170 Squadron and 'Jimmy' Jump Davies set off for No.140 Squadron, flying Mosquitos and taking night photographs with flash bombs prior to the invasion.

David reflected on his time with 16 Squadron.

Wednesday, 3 November. What luck I had to have so many friends to love and respect with this squadron. I have had some grand weeks and now it is my last day with them. I was given a good send off. My total flying time with No.16 Squadron is 508 hours, 60 on Ops. I don't think I shall get much flying at Hawarden as a Staff Pilot job is supposed to be a form of rest.

Who knows when the war may end; perhaps I will see Japan before I return to pick up the threads of life that I dropped on Aug 13th 1939. One never knows. There will be much work to be done and affairs to straighten before I can ever hope to set up a home of my own but I consider 23 to be quite young for a man.

Part V

Flight Instructor, Typhoon Training. Operational Flying in Holland

Chapter Fifteen

Flying Instructor at Hawarden and Poulton: November 1943 to August 1944

'On Rest 41 O.T.U. Poulton – Invasion Started. It would!!' F/O Eric Milne DFC
No.268 Squadron.
'ADJIDAUMO' 'Tail-in-Air'. The History of No.268 Squadron Royal Air Force
1940–1946. Colin Ford.

Along with Old Sarum, the RAF airfield at Hawarden near Chester, and the
neighbouring satellite airfield at Poulton, were the main bases for No.41
Operational Training Unit. These stations trained Army Co-op pilots until
disbanded, then switched to Fighter Reconnaissance training. At the beginning of
November, both Hawarden and Poulton started running refresher and conversion
courses for pilots on rest after operations.

The briefing room at No.41 OTU, Hawarden; Hugh Rigby pointing to the large map; David with his
back to the camera. *(Family Collection – Crown © 1944)*

On Thursday, 4 November 1943 David arrived at Hawarden as a Flying Instructor, just as No.84 Fighter Course finished their training.

> I was very sad to say goodbye to everyone at No.16, however, two others who failed the decompression test may come here later and I soon bumped into some familiar faces. Peter Morris[1] the Chief Ground Instructor was at Weston Zoyland with me, he found me a room and we had tea together. Squadron Leader Johnny Lucas whom I had met at Troon is Chief Flying Instructor, he is a delightful person and originally from Charles's squadron. The C/O is Brian Walford and only a Squadron Leader when he lived with us in the tents at Weston Zoyland, he's a Wing Commander now.

The Officers' Mess was based in New Hawarden Castle. This grand, mid-eighteenth century castle, was once owned by Prime Minister William Gladstone. David was impressed by the magnificent surroundings.

> What a Mess it is! How little did I think, when listening to Mr Jennings my old Marlborough schoolmaster when he talked of Gladstone, that one day I should be living in his castle! Perhaps I would have taken a bit more interest in that particular Prime Minister. The walls are hung with paintings by Van Dyke and Canaletto. The whole building is most beautifully furnished. There is central heating, a lift, a library, a billiard room, a grand piano and hot and cold water in all the rooms but I'd swap all this luxury, without a moment's hesitation, for a tent at Ford if I could be with the squadron again.

Over the next few days David met other ex-16 Squadron friends including David Rowcliffe, Gerald Scott and Ian Baker, who had just returned from the Middle East.

> Already I miss the atmosphere of the squadron worst than I imagined I would. I had just about got organized at Hawarden when they sent me to Poulton. The food is better but the accommodation not so good.

ALO Captain Hugh Barber[2] wrote from Andover to ask if David would fly down to talk to the FFA. He said that he had visited No.16 Squadron and was 'Sad to see the state into which the squadron has fallen. So many new faces and so few of the old and although I always thought that wartime brought many friends, I didn't realize how much they could mean. I'm no sentimentalist in such things but the truth was really brought home to me, like selling the family plate which had been in the family for generations.'

David soon found himself back at Hawarden and although he found the job found trying, he was to meet many experienced pilots, one of whom was George Hassall Nelson-Edward who flew with No.79 and No.93 Squadrons. In the Battle of Britain he shot down several enemy aircraft and was shot down twice himself. After one crash-landing he lost consciousness, and on recovering his senses, was amazed to see a large green parrot peering into the cockpit. Stranger still, the parrot belonged to a German who had escaped from the Nazis in 1936.

Nelson-Edward had arrived at Hawarden for training in aerial photography and had not flown Mustangs before, so David took him up for an hour's formation practise

SECOND D.F.C. IN HARBORO' FAMILY

TWO of the three airmen sons of Mr. and Mrs. R. Greville-Heygate, of Market Harborough, have now gained the DFC.

The first was Pilot-Officer Charles Edward Greville-Heygate, Harborough's first DFC, who was later reported missing, presumed killed, in February, 1942. His brother, now Flying-Officer David Arden Greville-Heygate, commenced his operational flying in that month, and has now received the same award.

The citation states:—

This officer has participated in operational flying since February, 1942, taking part in shipping and photographic reconnaissances and air-sea rescue patrols.

DIFFICULT SORTIE

In April, 1943, he completed a difficult sortie with great success. This operation involved a 200-mile sea crossing in adverse weather. Despite this, Flying-Officer Greville-Heygate obtained some excellent photographs. Throughout his operational career, this officer has set a fine example by his keenness and efficiency.

Flying-Officer Greville-Heygate (24) served as a second lieutenant in The Loyal Regiment in 1940, and was commissioned in the RAFVR in 1941. He was educated at Marlborough College, Wilts, and Queen's College, Cambridge.

Report of David's DFC award. *(Family Collection)*

before having a mock dogfight. In his autobiography, Nelson-Edward wrote that he found the Mustang easy to fly, but the photography a bit hit or miss, depending on the pilot's ability to navigate at both low-level and high speed. Once he had mastered this skill, Nelson-Edwards[3] was posted as C/O of No.231 Squadron and spent several weeks photographing V1 launch sites.

On November 16, The London Gazette announced that Richard Pughe, Antony Davis and David had been awarded the DFC for taking part in shipping and photographic reconnaissance, and air-sea rescue patrols. Congratulation letters soon poured in.

> I've had an amazing amount of letters and telegrams about my DFC. It is most gratifying to know that I have such good friends who sometimes think of me! It cheered me up no end and I know Charles would have been proud of me too.

Eric Martin wished David was still with No.16 Squadron so they could do a spot of celebrating. 'I imagine you are very cheesed off with the new job, particularly after all the frantic conversations with that Wing's posting.' Brother-in-law Bill

Adler, with C Company, 15 Welch, sent his congratulations and added 'Prudhoe in Northumberland is degrees colder than charity and they are doing their best to harden us up!' A delighted Pat Furse wrote, 'It is pleasant to see the ancient men of No.16 at last getting some of the glamour – there's been enough blood, sweat and whatnot. I see China Young[4] also collected one not long ago – but I am a bit behind the times nowadays. It comes from being classed as an Intelligence Officer! How do you like being a fairy godmother to incipient Prunes? As usual we remain fogbound and constipated and the days pass.'

Tony Greenly also could not imagine David enjoying life as an Instructor. 'It has come to my attention that 'Grovel Haybag' has been awarded a Distinguished Flying Cross – presumably for services rendered…. My only regret is that you and Tony did not get them earlier while I was still a 'happy man' in the squadron. It seems ages and ages ago since those carefree, and for me anyway, completely perfect days, but I find myself thinking of you all everyday; Zoyland, Exeter, Andover, Ford and so on.'

However, Donald Draper thought David would be 'very patient with the dumb.' Due to bad weather, David was exceptionally cheesed-off with the lack of flying, and this was not helped when thirty-four Mustangs were released for squadron use. To keep the pupils occupied, staff pilots were asked to give a forty-five minute lecture on a subject not covered by the syllabus. These experienced pilots had a wealth of experience to pass on. Flying with No.1 Squadron during the Battle of France, Roland 'Rolly' Dibnah[5] was shot down near Nancy in May 1940, but made it back in time to fight in the Battle of Britain. Transferred to No.242 Squadron, he flew with Douglas Bader and was credited with shooting down nine aircraft.

Having just returned from flying in North Africa with No.225 Squadron, Gerald 'Scottie' King Scott flew with No.4 Squadron in France in 1940 and escaped in a Lysander just as German tanks rolled onto the airfield. On November 27 of the same year, he had the unusual distinction of capturing Me109E Luftwaffe pilot, Wolfgang Teumer, after he force-landed at Manston. Scott rugby tackled him 'before he could fire off a flare into the cockpit.'[6]

When war broke out and having lost a relative[7] who had been a RAF pilot, George Hindmarsh took an Army Commission, transferred to the RAF and was eventually accepted for pilot training. After his first tour, Hindmarsh, with No.4 Squadron, said he was one of the five or six left.[8] Other staff pilots included Vasco Ortigao Gilbert, Albert Pollitt, Cyril Short and Robert Ireland[9], who was a Second Lieutenant in the Intelligence Corps before transferring to the RAF.

Desperate to get back to an operational squadron, David wrote to Robert Fender, recently posted to RAF Tarrant Ruston. Here, No.298 Squadron Halifax pilots were training to tow gliders. Fender quickly replied that he did not recommend David to come into his 'particular game,' however he sent his hearty congratulations and was glad to know that the fine work the Mustang boys put in had met with well deserved recognition.

Before Christmas, David went down to Hartford Bridge for a dance and met up with many old friends.

This job is meant to be a form of rest but I find it more tiring than the squadron. I am getting a little bored with the RAF in England especially as I am not getting enough flying, the weather is so bad with the fog and frost that we have not flown for well over a week and it looks set to continue. I went to a dance at Shotwick Hall and met two repatriated POWs who, having been captured in May 1940 were bitterly outspoken against the Germans.

The bad weather lasted over two weeks, but on December 19 it finally improved and the station ORB recorded that it was the 'first clear day for 17 days with a great deal of flying activity in consequence.' With the improved weather everyone seemed more cheerful[10] and on Christmas Eve, hoping he would not be missed, David went AWOL and drove home for his first Christmas with his parents in three years.

Boxing Day. On the drive back I picked up an airman who said he had been waiting for an hour and a half for a lift. Amazingly he turned out to have been one of my ground crew at Tern Hill in 1941. It was a great coincidence and he was very grateful for me stopping to pick him up for we saw virtually no other cars on the whole trip. I was pleased to note that my car's petrol consumption was very good and I wondered if it was due to the three moth balls that I had put in the tank.

(It is possible that by putting pure naphthalene mothballs into his petrol tank David might have got some increase in fuel consumption but they would have been of a very limited benefit.)

At tea, the C/O, Brian Walford asked where David was on Christmas Day, and he admitted that he had driven home.

Walford didn't seen to mind, he congratulated me on becoming a Flt/Lt and asked if I would like to attend some courses, to which I replied that I would be very keen to do so. There are two courses that I am especially interested in, both are based in the south of England. I am hoping they will be fun and a change of scenery, one is a Gunnery course the other a Fighter Leader course. This would be especially invaluable as it would qualify me as a fighter pilot and get me back on Ops again very quickly. There is no hope at the moment but if they send me off in the middle of this year I would like to go onto a Fighter Squadron.

On New Year's Eve, after a visit to Chester, David found Scott had been asked to test a Hurricane that had engine trouble in the air. However, on the ground it seemed to work perfectly well.

As Scottie wanted a bath, I said that I would do the test flight for him. He readily accepted my offer. At about 100 ft, the engine cut out completely. I immediately throttled back and turned sharply and the engine picked up again, but a second or two later it cut once more. I reduced the boost further, also the revs and I managed to get round the circuit and land safely. I taxied back and on arriving at the chocks an ambulance came roaring up ringing its bell. Luckily there was no need for it. Wing Commander Walford – who looks like Rex Harrison – and

CFI Johnny Lucas drove up in the car and congratulated me for landing safely. The Flying Control Officer said it was the quickest circuit that he had ever seen.

Having to answer many questions from several engineering officers about temperature, pressure, etc, David missed tea and rushed down to meet Elisabeth at the Grosvenor Hotel Chester for dinner.

> I was very impressed with her appearance, she was wearing a red dress borrowed from an ATS officer and had made a lace collar from her grandmother's antique hankie. We had such an interesting dinner party that we forgot that we were collecting another couple to take onto the dance so we arrived 45 minutes late. Renée bought along her 3 month old daughter and parked her with the WAAF Duty Officer. The dance went with such a swing we stayed until 2 o'clock.

The next day, David reflected on what the New Year might bring.

> It is only since I came here as an Instructor that I have felt the urge to write letters, diaries and read books, so once more on New Year's Day, I embark on another (and I hope my last) diary with all good resolutions and resolve to complete the record of 1944, which we are told may go down in history as one of the most decisive. For the first time since 1940, there is a general feeling of optimism and hope that this year we may see the end of European War. Myself, I am optimistic in public, when I think it to be discreet. I hope that by August, Germany will be forced to give up. However, it is a most unwise man who prophesies the future with as little knowledge as myself.
>
> I went into Chester to collect my tunic that I had the DFC and 1939–43 Star sewn on, then onto the Grosvenor Hotel to collect my greatcoat, which I had stupidly left there last night. I was unable to find it and was very upset because Charles bought it for me in 1940 and I have worn it ever since. I finally tracked down the Head Porter and he said that he had found it and put it by safely for me. I was most relieved and very touched when he said that he had repaired a small tear in the lining. He said that it was such a good coat that he felt he must sew it up before it tore further.

David wearing the greatcoat that he feared he had lost after a New Year's Eve party. *(Family Collection)*

Finally back in England, Melvyn Evans dropped David a postcard. Reclassified A4B, fit for ground duties, by the Medical Board, he was awaiting a posting and hoped David would visit him when he was settled. A few days later, David spotted a picture in the Tatler of another old 'Army Rebel,' Donald Draper. He was also delighted when he received a reply to his letter from Gilliland, who after leaving No.16 Squadron, was flying fighter-bomber support for the 8th Army in Libya, Malta, Sicily and Southern Italy.

No.250 (Sudan) Squadron. We never appreciated our luck or realized how happy we really were in No.16 Squadron. This is also a wonderful squadron. Our pilots come from Canada, Australia, South Africa, Rhodesia, New Zealand, England, Scotland, Wales and Ireland. We have the best C/O I could imagine. He is a SAAF Major. Honestly David we have a wizzo time…. One thing which would be better than 250, would be 'old' 16 out here.

Yours ever, Gilli.

Regularly shuttling between Hawarden and Poulton, David was never too sure where he would find himself sleeping each night, but by January 12 he was at Hawarden acting as 'B' Flight Commander on No.1 Tactical Exercise Unit, teaching pair-bouncing, and formation flying.

Having a Flight here means I am fairly busy once again. I have sole use of the Hurricane so I can fly around all the squadrons and find out the latest tactics they are using. This evening I walked through the park to the old ruined castle on the hill. The sun had set and the ruins against the sky presented a magnificent sight, its crumbling battlements silhouetted and sheep grazing in the moat. It was most idyllic and I wished I had my fishing rod.

We are now back in huts at Hawarden as the CFI said it is wrong for the senior staff to live in a castle while the rest are in huts on the field. Needless to say he isn't very popular at the moment, especially as it isn't his job to say where we should be living. I guess it is right that we set a good example to the rest but it doesn't suit me. I shall miss admiring the fine paintings of the Glynne family and of Charles I and II and wives by van Dyck, Sir Peter Lely and Canaletto.

In the evening, he met up with Elisabeth Jardine and they had a long heart to heart talk and, wanting to think things over, the next afternoon David cycled up the hill overlooking the countryside towards Chester.

It is my firm belief that no one has the right to ask a girl to wait for an unknown period of years without making friends with other men. One's youth is all too short but I think the war has deadened my emotions. Love complicates things, it means thinking of a future, without it

F/O. DAT DRAPER.

F/O D. A. T. Draper served in the London Rifle Brigade at the beginning of the war, and went to Norway with a special service unit. Later he transferred to the R.A.F., was the victim of a bad crash, but was eventually able to return to operational flying, and is now in a Fighter Reconnaissance squadron.

Old friend and 'Army Rebel', Donald Draper. (© Tatler)

we live or we die today. How can I plan for two or four years ahead when I find it difficult to plan my life two months ahead or trains two hours ahead?

Thursday, 20 January. It seems to be a month of dickey engines. I took a Mustang Flight down south to Heston but as there was fog on the ground completely obscuring the airfield we landed at Hartford Bridge. Pending clearance, Richard Garside said that his aircraft was running roughly and that the oil pressure was low. The duty crew ran up the aircraft and reported it as being OK for oil pressure, rough on mags, but safe to fly.

When visibility improved, David decided to fly on in Garside's Mustang. He ran up the aircraft on the ground and as everything appeared normal, they all took off to Heston. On arrival, David was twice sent round the circuit as other aircraft were landing, but on the third run-in, as he selected 'wheels down,' the hydraulic pressure dropped to zero degrees. He tried to pump flap down with the hand pump as he only had ten degrees, but nothing happened. As his wheels were only half down, the visibility was so bad and the aerodrome small, David decided to return to Hartford Bridge to land, being the nearest aerodrome with a long runway. Maintaining the ten degrees of flap, the oil temperature gradually rose with the drag of both flaps and wheels. On reaching the aerodrome, David lowered his wheels using the emergency method and indicated that he was in difficulties. Two squadrons of Bostons were in the circuit, but Flying Control allowed David to cut in and land first. The whole aircraft was by this time vibrating madly, however, David landed safely, but as he taxied back to the Watch Office he could hear loud unpleasant grinding noises. Fitter Ron Parnell remarked, 'The between-flight duty crew should have placed it u/s if it was rough on mags in the first place. I can imagine how hot the engine must have got with flaps partly down, wheels half down and radiator closed. Thank god the air-bottle was working OK for emergency lowering of the undercarriage. David was lucky indeed. The engine got so hot it could have seized up at any moment.'[11]

> While the aircraft was being looked at, I spent a most enjoyable evening with No.16 Squadron. Until one leaves a Squadron one little realizes the rut one has got into.

The next day, as the Mustang was still not airworthy, David took the train back to Chester.

> There seem to be too many pilots here at the moment and so I spent the day down at Poulton on a gunnery course. The upside of this job is that Poulton has a friendly easy-going atmosphere of a country airfield but I miss squadron life and I shall endeavour to be sent back onto an operational unit as soon as possible. Hopefully I'll eventually be sent somewhere overseas. I moved into Pontie's room, and am sharing it with Williams. Poor Pontie, he's lost two brothers in this war, his wife is about to have a baby and now he is due to be posted overseas. We also have another father in the Mess, for Homer Wolf[12] is now in possession of a son and most obligingly is doing SDO at night for us while his wife is in hospital.

Brown, Wolf and Scotty at Hawarden. *(Family Collection)*

At the end of January there was yet another reorganization, as there was a surplus of fighter-recce pilots. So they were split into three groups to learn advanced gunnery, army support, photography and navigation. One group was based at Hawarden, flying Mustangs, and the other two flying Hurricanes and Harvards at Poulton. David was sent to Poulton to act as Flight Commander of 'D' Flight, TEU, but almost immediately returned to Hawarden.

> I was simply wild today. To start with there were too many people in the Flight. Aircraft went u/s and pilots did stupid things. Then Elisabeth had already left the Mess when I rang up at lunchtime and there was no word from her to explain her silence. And then to cap it all the C.I. came round in the afternoon to say we were having a reorganization again and I was to act as a Tac/R Instructor. This work entails mostly office work with hardly any flying and no direct control over the aircraft. I feel a bit like a yo-yo, I am fed up with the perpetual movement and now I never unpack but just use my suitcase as a chest of drawers.

A Recce Instructor's job was mainly office-bound and duties included providing pinpointing exercises for use by ALOs, assisting the CFI in briefings for Tac/R sorties, leading pupils in discussion groups, and arranging swimming tests with Air Sea Rescue Instructors.

> In the evening, I phoned up Elisabeth to find out about her silence but was told that her Canadian friend had got on so well with Major Marat that he had overstayed his leave and they had all 'gone out on the town'. I went to a film but, unable to concentrate, went onto the Grosvenor where I met up with Fletch[13],

Paddy Roberts, Scottie and others. I had intended to get drunk but thought the better of it so returned to the Mess.

Here, David had a long chat to Paddy Roberts, one of the pilots on the course. He had joined the RAF in 1937 and, after postings in Singapore and Palestine, was with No.108 fighting the Italians. Returning from a sortie one day he spotted a petrol lorry abandoned about a mile from an Italian camp, and landing his Lysander close by, he set the lorry on fire. However, while taking off he tore a wheel off the aircraft on a stone. Frightened to tell what really happened, he agreed with his gunman to say that he had been attacked and shot up by an Me110. However, at the next Sergeants' party, his gunman blurted out the truth to his drunken comrades, the C/O soon found out and Paddy was awarded 'a black.'[14]

> *Saturday, 12 February.* I hope that I did not behave too badly last night, if so I suppose an apology is due. This is going to be most interesting as I have a lot to say to Mistress E when she returns.
>   Thick fog enfolded the airfield today so I gave half an hour's lecture to the flight ground crew. An unprepared lecture is rather difficult, I enjoyed it but one is rather inclined to jump from subject to subject and lose continuity.

David's movements between Poulton and Hawarden now came to an abrupt halt with an injury to his foot, and he was kept in sick-quarters for a few days. He then developed a temperature and a stiff neck.

> I am not used to this inactivity. If all goes well I should get home on Sunday. I have been making a huge effort in the reading line. I've been trying to read several books but have lost the ability to concentrate on a page for more than a few seconds.

As a Tac/R, David assisted the CFI in briefings and providing exercises for the pilots on rest or retraining. *(Family Collection – Crown © 1944)*

Hawarden is one big feud, all against all. The latest black was Johnny[15], who told the Group Captain that the American, Captain MacAlistair[16] had left without paying his Mess bill. The G/Capt. sent him a letter and received a reply today to say that he had paid his Mess bill *and* left £2 to stand drinks to other members of the Mess.

While in the Sick Bay, David received a letter from Melvyn Evans who was working at RAF Ford. 'As I am grounded, I'm afraid I won't be able to fly over to see you, but DO make it yourself. Bert did so 10 days ago and arrived in a PRU Spit XI. However he wasn't able to stay long, but it was very good to see him again. I am on a Flying Control job down here and will soon be going on a 6 week course at Watchfield before returning here for a month or so to 'pass out' as a competent controller!'

On February 26, as snow and the outside temperature dropped, David's temperature rose, he developed pneumonia and remained in sick quarters for the next two weeks. Recovery was slow but David was able to write letters to friends. Having been posted to a flying once job again, James Jump Davies was quick to reply.

'Sanford', Fleet, Hants. The hours of work are rather annoying being from 14.00 until I finish in the early or late hours of the morning. I am flying Mosquitos, a thing that I have been trying for, for some time, but never thought I would obtain. I heard news of Ken Mackie the other day. He is with No.223 Squadron.[17] From his address I have a rough idea where he is. I wrote him a long letter but I understand he is only allowed one airgraph a week to send away so I do not expect to get a reply.

Yours, Jump.

Monday, 13 March. I hope that today the doctor will at last sign me off as fit. I've caught up on all the letter writing that I haven't done in the last year. Fifty-two while stuck here, that must be some sort of record! Hearing that Gillie has been

'Gibbo' on his bike at RAF Poulton. *(Family Collection)*

shot down I wrote to his family telling them how much he was liked by all at 16 Squadron.

Sent home on leave, David took his father to watch the Rugby Services International, England v Scotland, at Leicester which they both enjoyed immensely. Arriving back at Hawarden, David heard that Tony Davis had been posted to the station.

> Lectures in the morning on Tac/R, then I cycled the seven miles over to Poulton to see Tony. He's a Squadron Leader at long last and has taken over the job of CFI there. Cycling back was hard against the wind on a very heavy bike, the last few miles were tough especially as one of my teeth is playing up.

In April, Squadron leader George Brian Walford[18] was posted overseas and Wing Commander Eric Plumtree[19] took over as C/O. Over the next few months David flew regularly between Poulton and Hawarden, teaching pairs-flying and practise Tac/sorties in the Hurricanes, and navigation skills in the Harvard or Proctor. One low cross-country flight with Harold James 'Jimmy' Chun was 'a bit dicey' as the engine cut, but fortunately it restarted and they arrived back safely.

During his time at Hawarden, David taught many pilots that he would later meet in Holland including Chun, Peter Critchley-Salmonson, Edward Holbech and Bruce Ford-Coates. David also managed to visit Ilfracombe.

> I spent my time walking about the harbour, chatting to the fishermen and buying lobsters for Rosemary's family. They told me that she hadn't lost her heart to anybody in Ceylon yet. On my way back, I dropped in on No.16 Squadron and met up with Sammy and other old friends, I am most envious of them as they are now flying every hour possible.

At 23.30 on 5 June 1944, after a delay due to bad weather, D-Day invasion landing plans were set in action. Robert Edward Vane De Lautour, who had been at Sandhurst with David, flew from Harwell to Normandy with the 22nd Independent Parachute Company. Their task was to set up a Eureka Beacon and light to help assault gliders find the heavily defended fortification of the Merville Gun Battery.[20]

The seaborne invasion commenced early on the 6th, and David's friend Peter Cruden was in the thick of the action, landing on Sword Beach at 08.40 with No.6 Commando. After attacking German troops in pillboxes and machine-gun positions, Cruden was shot in the shoulder by a sniper.[21]

RAF recce squadrons were kept very busy. Douglas Sampson set off for Normandy at dawn. 'On take-off the radio traffic was frenzied, with much yelling and maydaying. The Isle of Wight to Swanage was literally packed with ships. A sight to be seen once only and beyond description.' At Juno beach he noted that 'the artillery far exceeded the little contretemps at Larkhill, and at night the concentration of fire was frightening.'[22] The *Daily Mail* paid credit to the recce pilots, reporting, 'For 2½ years before D-Day, pilots of the Photographic Reconnaissance Wing of the 2nd Tactical Air Force photographed the Secrets of Hitler's West Wall.... No army ever moved into enemy-occupied territory with such a detailed picture before.'[23] No.16 Squadron aircraft had been fitted with new cameras with a film that crept, to avoid blur on exposure. This new technique took such detailed pictures of the beaches that one could almost count the barbs on the barbed wire. Jimmy Taylor later said that 'Every platoon commander had photos of where he was landing' and knew where the mines and other obstacles were.[24]

Other 2nd TAF pilots also witnessed the unfolding drama. No.168 pilots, supporting the beach landings, flew thirty-six Tactical Recces in eighteen hours, and Jan Plesman, flying with No.322 Squadron, provided close air support to the troops. Many of the pilots flying these missions had recently left Hawarden and those remaining behind felt they were missing out on something momentous.

I take a personal interest in the Invasion, especially as they must be using photographic material I took some months ago and I know the area the Allied Army are landing at intimately. What a sight it must be, I hope that the Jerries don't make too much trouble for our boys and that the weather improves or they will have trouble landing all the supplies they'll need. Good weather will be needed to make a success of the thing.

By the end of the first day, the Allied Armies had made successful landings and established bridgeheads on the Normandy Beaches. Two days later, returning from a sortie, Mike McGilligan was killed when his aircraft crashed near Redhill. The cause of the accident was unknown, but it was believed he lost control in low cloud.[25] David closely followed the army's progress inland.

The first wave of the Allied Invasion landed between Le Havre and Cherbourg. Today, Bayeux fell into our hands and to think that last year I was there flying over the river line. I'm so sick of paperwork and inactivity while friends are risking their lives over the skies in France, I have again put in for an overseas posting.

Over the next few weeks, ninety pilots finished their training at Hawarden. Some were posted straight to operational squadrons, others were sent to Group Support Units until the front line units required replacement pilots and aircraft.

Everyone was doing their part to help ensure the invasion was a success. ALO Ian Duffus had to deliver 6,000 urgently required photographs, gathered by No.4 Squadron, to General Crerar in Normandy. However, the bad weather made night flying impossible, so Duffus was taken by fast Royal Navy launch to Cherbourg and driven to the Canadian Army Intelligence Staff, where he handed over the information in time for the morning's attack.[26]

David's mother organized the making of swabs for the wounded. Requesting more, the hospital remarked on how beautifully they were made. She wrote, 'As I made most of them I was particularly pleased – I can make about four dozen an hour.'

Finally sent on a Training School course for junior officers considered suitable for promotion to Flight or Squadron Commanders, David spent three weeks studying leadership and discipline skills.

July 17. We are to work from 8.30 to 7.00 – quite a hard day – mainly studying law, regulations and procedures. I'm a little disappointed with Cranwell, I think this is because I had heard so much about it from Charles. The aerodrome and camps on each side, coupled with the flat country and lack of woodland or water takes away much of its attraction, however, inside the College it is very fine and most interesting and in the gallery there are pictures of German airmen presented by Goring. There is also a stout hall porter but I don't know if he is the same one that Charles wrote about.

At the weekend, Ronald drove David home where he found a letter from Gilliland's father.

Castlehill, Ballywalter.
David…, You must be one of Barnie's earliest friends. His plane was shot down while low-level attacking moving transport behind the German lines in Italy. He managed to get his plane up to 1,500 feet before she pinked out, he bailed out at a few hundred feet. He landed uninjured, except for some singeing to his eyebrows and eyelashes. A pretty close shave. He had previously been shot down and crash landed and was 48 hours unconscious[27]

Yours W.J. Gilliland.

On 31 July, Donald Draper and Flying Officer Hutchinson flew out on detachment to Plumetot, just north of Caen, where No.2 Squadron was based. They were then sent to search for a long-range railway gun which was holding up the Allied advance; this was the official version. However, in his biography Squadron Leader Laurence Irving wrote 'My nights were now sleepless, for at irregular intervals shells from some heavy

No. 89 COURSE.
TRAINING PROGRAMME.
22nd March to 28th March. incl.

Date.	0830 – 0915	0920 – 1000	1015 – 1100	1105 – 1200	1330 – 1400	1405 – 1445	1450 – 1530
Wednesday 22nd March	Adjutant. Arrival reports C.B.'s. Lecture Rm.1.	C.G.I. Opening address. Lecture Rm. 1.	Nav. Officer. Maps. Lecture Rm. 1.	Dental Officer. Inspection. S.S.Q.	NCO i/c Trng. Issue of knee-pads, notebooks etc. Lecture Rm. 1.	C.F.I. Flying regs. & Control. Lecture Rm. 1.	Signals Officer Description of apparatus. Signals Block.
Thursday. 23rd March.	Engineer Offr. Service Type 1. Lecture Rm. 1.	Engineer Offr. Service Type 2. Lecture Rm. 1.	C.F.I. Handling service type. Lecture Rm. 1.	Signals Officer R/T procedure & Discipline. Signals Block.	Engineer Offr. Merlin engines. Lecture Rm. 1.	Signals Offr. Practical in R/T cabinets. Signals Block.	Engineer Offr. Allison engines Lecture Rm. 1.
Friday. 24th March.	Engineer Offr. Written exam. Lecture Rm. 1.	Nav. Officer. F/R. Nav. Lecture Rm. 1.	Nav. Officer. Nav. Planning. Lecture Rm. 1.	Photo Officer. Air photography. Lecture Rm. 1.	Draw parachutes Parachute section.	By bus to Poulton.	To flights.
Saturday. 25th March.	Photo Officer. F.24 camera. Photo Block.	Commanding Officer. Air support. Lecture Rm. 1.	To Poulton.	P	L	Y	I
Sunday. 26th March.	Int. Officer. S.D. 158 Int. Room.	A/S Rescue Officer. A/S Rescue. Lecture Rm. 1.	To Poulton	P	L	Y	I
Monday. 27th March.	C.F.I. Instrument and cloud flying. Lecture Rm. 1.	Engineer Offr. Auxiliary systems. Lecture Rm. 3.	To Poulton.	P	L	Y	I
Tuesday 28th March.	Int. Officer. Escape and evasion. Int. Room.	Recce. Instr. Tac/R. 1. Lecture Rm. 1.	To Poulton.	P	L	Y	I

NOTE: From 1815 – 1845 hours on Friday 24th March and Monday 26th March, there will be P.T.

No 89 Course, No.41 training programme. *(David's Collection – Crown © 1944)*

gun burst over the beach not far to the north of us near Courcelles. At dawn I would wander about peeping enviously into the tents of my companions lying fast asleep like puppies blissfully unconscious.'[28] Draper and Hutchinson located the gun, hidden in a railway tunnel, and it was destroyed by a Typhoon Squadron. Thus, Irving's sleep was restored, but an exhausted Draper returned to England with gruesome stories of a lack of beer and sleep.[29]

Having finished his course at Cranwell, David drove back to Hawarden.

> Finding that there was nothing doing until Tuesday I slipped away to Devon, flying down to Barnstable, getting a lift to Woolacombe and a train into Ilfracombe. After an excellent dinner at the Montebello I paid a surprise visit to the Boones who asked me to stay for a second dinner which I readily accepted. The Boone's telephone bell never ceases. If anything goes wrong in Ilfracombe whether it be water shortage, Flag Days, evacuee children running away, discontented mothers, or transport to hospital, all come for settling to the Dr's. They must be quite worn out but there is no getting away until after the war. Today I went to the beach with the family and we collected a dozen jellyfish in a bucket. They caused considerable apprehension amongst the smaller paddlers, especially the striped one, which all present assured me was poisonous.

As more of David's friends set off for operational squadrons in France, Tony Davis was posted back to No.16 Squadron unexpectedly when Squadron Leader Atkinson, who had only taken over as C/O the day before, was killed by a Spitfire taxiing out of Dispersal.[30] Three weeks later, 16 Squadron moved to France, No.4 Squadron to Beny-sur-Mer and, after a short stop at 84 GSU, Desmond Clifton-Mogg[31] and George Hindmarsh arrived at No.2 Squadron in Bayeux.

Later, Hindmarsh recalled his time in France. 'They would ring up saying, can you check such and such a place to see if it is clear of German troops. Once they rang up and asked me to do something on the other side of Dunkirk. I asked, "Have we got Dunkirk yet?" They replied, "Yes," so I nipped over and got a very hot reception. I rang back to say that they needed to think again!'[32] Although German Forces held onto Dunkirk until 9 May 1945, the war on the Western Front moved steadily forward and by August 25, Paris was liberated.

At last, on September 2, David received orders to report to No.83 Group Support Unit to await an overseas posting.

Chapter Sixteen

Typhoon Training, Bognor, and Operational Flying with No.168 Squadron: September 1944 to December 1944

'Being a Typhoon pilot, that's pretty elite stuff.'
Harry Hardy interviewed by David Lesjak

R AF Bognor in Sussex had been built on agricultural land by the Canadian Royal Engineers in June 1943, and 83 Group Support Unit moved there in June 1944 with around a hundred Mustangs, Spitfires and Typhoons. Their role was to supply pilots and replacement aircraft to 83 Group's squadrons.

The Hawker Typhoon, the largest British single-engine fighter/ground-attack bomber, was a very effective weapon. It was universally hated and shot at by 'every German soldier in range'[1], and by July, more Tiffie pilots were required. However, pilots needed twenty hours experience on type before flying operations. Spitfire pilots were asked to convert to Typhoons, but unsurprisingly few came forward. Therefore,

Before joining No.168 Squadron, David flew twenty hours on Typhoons.
(Family Collection –
© Crown Copyright)

at the beginning of September, along with David, the pilots from No.168 Mustang Squadron arrived to gain Typhoon flying experience.

> I immediately was made to feel very welcomed; Bognor has an air of energy and excitement that was missing at Hawarden. I have met several friends already and one of the first aircraft I spotted on the airfield was AM226, my old Mustang. It has just been repaired after a crash and is due to go out as a replacement aircraft soon; it looks as beautiful as ever. (AM102 is here too)

The Typhoons was a brutish aircraft, weighing in fully loaded, at seven tons. Typhoon pilot, Desmond Scott, wrote that the engine snarled into life. Once airborne, Scott was agreeably surprised at its handling, but after an hour's aerobatics he landed drenched in sweat and exhausted[2] and Harry Hardy, a No.440 Canadian pilot commented that for the first few flights the Typhoon seemed to fly itself, with the pilot 'just going along for the ride.' With a 2,250hp engine, a four bladed prop and top speed of 400 mph, it was armed with four 20mm fixed cannons and could also carry eight 60 lb rockets. Although a formidable weapon, it had several faults; the cockpit often filled with dangerous levels of carbon monoxide, so most pilots put on oxygen masks as soon as the engine was started[3] The Typhoon was also notoriously hard to start, especially in the cold, and if the engine did not start first time, fire could take hold in the air-intake. Poor forward visibility made taxiing difficult, and the engines had such a powerful torque that they pulled hard to the right while taxiing. The day after David's arrival, while attempting a take-off, a wayward Typhoon knocked the wireless mast off the flight control vehicle and scattered groundstaff in all directions.

As the No.168 Squadron pilots had priority on flying time, David practised dive-bombing, pairs-flying and aerobatics in a Mustang III. One day, Marjory was thrilled to see David quite clearly in the cockpit as his Mustang banked steeply over their house.

A few days later, blinded by smoke, fumes and flames from an engine fire, Warrant Officer Davies attempted to land in David's old Mustang AM102, but he collided with James Parkin. Both aircraft were written off and Parkin was killed.

A welcome letter arrived from Rosemary Boone:

> *Colombo, Ceylon.* I am on duty at 8 tonight, not that there will be anything for me to do – there never is. But it will be a line that I do work sometimes; life in our world is very dull. We played with our first a/c about a month ago.... Night flying 'B' is cancelled. I hope that doesn't mean that I shall have to go to the Station dance. We have them regularly once a week – sometimes twice and I refuse to have to go more than necessary to cope with women-starved, half-tight men!
>
> Lots of Love, Rosemary.

David at last got his hands on a Typhoon (which the 168 pilots had quickly nicknamed 'The Club') and took it up for an hour's test, then later flew another hour and a quarter on turns and climbing. However, he was unimpressed by its performance.

> I flew my first Tiffie today. They are horrible, they shake like mad!

On September 20, after a two-week training period, the No.168 pilots flew back to Holland to commence operations. Squadron Leader Lambert,[4] who had flown the most hours on the Typhoon in the squadron, had just ten hours conversion time and David, who only had flown for three hours, was left to catch them up when he had a few more on the clock.

Although on rest at 34 Wing GSU, having completed his tour, when a request came through for photos of Wolfheze, Gerry Bastow offered to fly 'one for the road.' However, hit by flak over Arnhem, he crash-landed and hid in a ditch for three days. With help from the Dutch underground, Bastow evaded capture, staying several weeks with the Klooster family in Barneveld, before returning to England.[5]

Preparing for his overseas posting, David went to the dentist for a check up. It proved an unpleasant experience.

> Sitting in the chair, I began to wonder if it was such a good idea. The dentist had no pain-relief and no electric drill. Instead, he worked a very Heath Robinson foot-driven drill, with a loom thing that was made up of a big wooden wheel and several odd bits of string. The drill started and was left a second or two to get up to full speed then, as it drilled away at my tooth, it seemed to slowly unwind, like an old gramophone. As if this wasn't bad enough, once this torture was over, the dentist then got out his chisel and began digging away as if he had discovered gold. The painkillers that I had taken before I came in were not much help and soon wore off completely.
>
> I spent the rest of the day ferrying aircraft to our new base just down the road at Thorney Island.

As there were several operational squadrons flying from there, they quickly moved onto RAF Tangmere, three miles east of Chichester. Built during the First World War, the airfield had been extended in 1941 when two asphalt runways were added.

On October 2, No.168 Squadron moved to a winter base at Eindhoven, and with the colder weather approaching, Edward Kenneth 'Ken' Barnes[6] wrote asking for help to obtain a size 4 Irving jacket from the GSU equipment officer. These highly prized jackets were light, flexible, and the sheepskin lining provided good insulation.

> *168 Squadron, 143 Wing RAF, BLA.* I handed my Irving in before I left and didn't get one in exchange…. Then would you send it via the brown flight to me. I should get a receipt from them for it – or at least a chit for me to sign. It will make sure I get the goods. Irvings are too portable and precious to have flying around the continent unattached…. I hope you will be joining us soon – I shouldn't rush it myself but I would like to see you with us just to have a basin full of honours of war!
>
> Au'Voir Ken.

Finally ordered to report to No.168 Squadron on December 1, and not knowing how long or if he would return, David reluctantly sold his beloved car.

> My beautiful Alvis, which I advertised in *The Times* for £450, has been bought by a London chemist. I hope he will have as much fun with it as I have.
>
> I tore up my endorsement card given for 'Landing with the undercart up,' as I think that it might work against me overseas and as razors will be in short supply in France and Belgium I have decided to grow a moustache.

Before being posted to Holland, David reluctantly sold his Alvis Silver Eagle. *(Family Collection)*

After collecting extra kit from home, David headed back to Tangmere via a war ravaged London. V1 flying bombs had been falling on the city since June 1944. No.322 Squadron had been tasked with shooting V1s down and Jan Plesman claimed a personal score of eleven.[7] By September, the much more deadly V2 rockets were being launched, flying at speeds of 3,500 mph and giving little or no noise to warn of their approach, they devastated huge areas of London.

> The train from Harborough reached London at 17.20 and I went straight to the King George V Club for a quick supper. I then rushed to Victoria and found a train going to Chichester at 9 o'clock. As I was passing through the barriers I heard a swish, followed by a terrific bang. I didn't quite know what the swish was so I didn't move, but all the soldiers around me ran and my ticket was carried away with them. A soldier next to me said, 'That was one of those flying rockets. If they are closer one hears the bang first and most likely you'll be dead or buried under a pile of rubble.' I think it must have been some distance away and so the noise of the rocket was heard about two seconds before the explosion.

It was not just London that was experiencing V2s. In her weekly letter, David's mother wrote of a sighting.

> *Bowden.* Glad the bang wasn't any closer. Mrs Jackson told me today that her husband saw a curious thing like a huge lighted cigar going over the Fernie paddock a few nights ago. He stood still and expected to hear an explosion but thinks it must have travelled miles. A girl in Harborough said that several people had seen it too. Things of that sort seem to be attracted to the paddock.'
> Love, Mother.

Rosemary also wrote to David from the Fleet Air Arm Station, Katukurunda, Ceylon, and although enjoying herself, she had decided to apply for a transfer to a Fighter Squadron base.

On November 18, David drove down to Ford to visit Melvyn Evans.

We went out to supper with Brazilian inventor, Gilbert[8], who's married to a Yorkshire girl and is coming to No.168 Squadron too. The weather's been rotten for flying but I have managed to get up once or twice. There now seems little chance of getting home again before going to Holland so the sooner I leave the better, I am getting tired of hanging around here. My old friend Tel Vigors is in the Mess at Eindhoven and I am looking forward to seeing him again.

Based at 57 OTU, a Spitfire training unit, Eric Martin[9] was also hoping to be posted abroad to 16 Squadron. 'I saw Tony G[10] about three weeks ago and he says you sport a certain amount of growth on the upper lip, rather similar to an effort of mine; I'm afraid I can't quite picture it David…. Gerry Bastow I saw in London, he was just back in this country after a five week vacation on the wrong side of the Rhine.' Martin signed off 'I must sleep now, the pleasant champagne I had last night has left me rather tired.'

Having being repatriated to England and now convalescing from his injuries, Richard Osborn also contacted David.

Hazelrigg Hall, RAF MRU, Loughborough. As you probably know I was shot down in Jan 43, flying a Lanc home from Dusseldorf and in the process I got a dose of cannon-shell through my left arm. It was badly smashed up and took me nearly all my time in Germany to get healed. After 9 months they decided that I was a repatriation case – and I promptly got better! But I then had to wait till September before getting clear. I won't be allowed to bomb the Huns again and won't be fit for overseas for some time so I'll have to think myself lucky being a stooge somewhere.

Yours, Richard.

Eindhoven dispersal. This No.168 Squadron Typhoon L, was flown by David on 11 December over Wesel and Munster. *(Charles Brown © RAF Museum)*

At the end of November David flew ten minutes of local flying to top up his conversion hours to a total of twenty hours five minutes, and these were signed off by Squadron Leader Klersy,[11] a Canadian Spitfire pilot on rest from No.401 Squadron who was awarded the DFC in September 1944, having shot down two Fw-190s the day after D-Day.

Mrs Howard wrote that Anson, now a major with the 12th Poonch Mountain Battery, had finally seen plenty of action. Wounded while fighting the Japanese, he still carried a bullet in his thigh, had caught typhus and malaria in Burma, and almost five years after being posted overseas, was due home leave in March.

On December 1, David flew out to the Netherlands to join 168 Squadron, part of 83 Group, No.143 Wing. About thirty miles behind the Front Line, and shared with two other Wings, Eindhoven was a busy airfield as well as being 83 Group's vehicle and supply storage facility.

With the Germans retreating towards the River Rhine, the RAF now had almost total air supremacy and Armed Recces were regularly sent up to harry the German Army. No.168 Squadron carried out Tactical, Weather, Photographic, Artillery and Armed Recces; however the wintery conditions and a lack of aircraft made flying difficult. The Squadron's normal aircraft strength was eighteen Typhoons, however, at one point in November there were only six aircraft operational.[12]

David was warmly welcomed by many friends. The Mess on the outskirts of Eindhoven was on the ground floor of a Convent. The nuns, who had suffered great hardships under the German Occupation, lived on the top floor and in exchange for

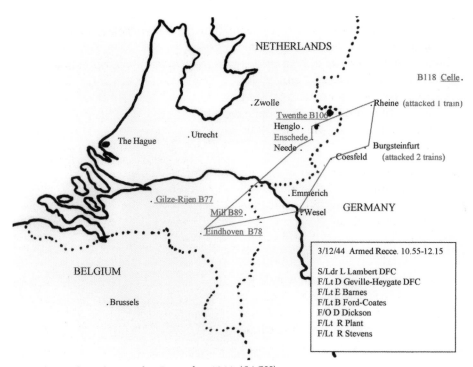

Plan of recce flown by David in December 1944. (*SAGH*)

food and supplies, they washed clothes and tidied rooms. Harry Hardy, also based at Eindhoven, recalled that each squadron had a classroom for their sleeping quarters with bunks lining the walls, leaving the centre of the room clear for activities.[12] David wrote home with his first impressions of life in the squadron.

> No.168 Squadron is a mixture of British, Australian and New Zealand pilots and they are all good types. We live in a convent and the food is terrible, we have high tea with marmite, marrow and meat mixed up and boiled sausages. The Dutch people have had a very hard time of it and all the shops are empty, there is no food at all.

Anxious to get some flying experience under his belt, David was soon in the air, but once up, was even more anxious to land.

> I took up a Typhoon for an air-test and formation patrol as No.2 to Derek Dickson. The weather was atrocious and I was very relieved to get down safely.

Armed with 20 mm cannons, the squadron was flying low-level armed recces, mainly lorry busting attacks and train-strafing. When attacking trains, the idea was to hit the engines to stop the train moving and then radio its position to a Mosquito or Typhoon bomb squadron, which would fly in and finish off the job.

On Sunday, 3 December, two armed recce missions were sent out. David flew in a formation of eight aircraft on the second recce as No.2 to Squadron Leader Leonard 'Len' Lambert. This time he found flying a little easier.

> The weather was a bit clearer today and we flew on an armed recce over the Wesel and Rhine area. As there was cloud over the area we flew east and caught sight of an Me262. Stevens[14] gave it a burst of gunfire but we did not see any hits. We then shot up two trains, which I was rather sad about, as they were such beautiful machines. Both trains and several trucks were hit and left on fire and smoking.

Strafing trains and trucks was dangerous work. 'Speed was your only ally… , you would pick up to around 350 to 400 mph and open fire at about 400 yards, you could only fire for about 1 second and only get away about 60 rounds.'[15]

In the evening I went to a wonderful concert at the Malcolm RAF Club but as we left a German pilot, obviously not a music lover, flew over with machine guns blazing. RAF personnel and civilians ran for cover until the danger passed. (He was shot down three days later.)

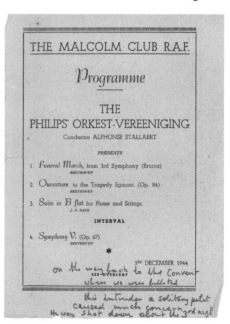

A musical concert given by the Philip's Orchestra at the RAF Malcolm Club, Eindhoven. *(Family Collection)*

The next day, David flew an armed recce over the Wesel and Enschede area, flying No.2 to Peter Mitchell. They ran into light and heavy flak, and then icy cloud. With full cloud cover, the trip was aborted and the formation split up and made their way back to Eindhoven. On landing, David crashed into another Typhoon.

> There were bomb-holes on the runway and Peter seemed to slow down very quickly as soon as he hit the runway and I found myself in danger of overtaking him. He then seemed to turn off too early and, seeing me coming, he stopped. I wasn't sure if I was going to chop him up or he was going to chop me up. Unable to miss his Typhoon I caught my port wing on his airscrew. Luckily neither of us was hurt and Mitchell was pretty decent about it, blaming the icy conditions. I will probably be given another endorsement – I guess it serves me right for tearing up my first red card.

Over the next few days, poor weather and a thick haze meant almost no squadron flying was possible apart from a patrol over a V2 site.

On December 8, David flew a thirty-minute testing patrol over Nijmegen as No.2 to Flying Officer Hussey. They did not see any Luftwaffe aircraft, but while away from the airfield, it was bombed. Luckily, the damage was not too great and they were able to land safely. David noted:

> For the last few days the weather has been dreadful. The Tiffie is a terrible starter and it is so cold that we have to keep them warmed up all night; they have to be started every hour or so.

Two days later, all aircraft were grounded, and to keep the pilots on their toes, they attended a variety of lectures. When the weather finally cleared, four pilots including David, flew a weather recce over the Coesfeld – Munster area, where they encountered heavy flak.

There were three main types of flak. Light flak from small calibre weapons would have to hit the aircraft to do any damage. Medium/moderate flak could explode on contact or be time-fuzed to create a shower of shell splinters. Heavy flak was often time-fuzed and, although the rate of fire was slower, could be grouped together.

David was very surprised when Rosemary wrote that she was married:

> *C/o R.A.N.A.S.I.O, Mail Office, Colombo.* It all happened so quickly that I had no time to tell anyone anything except send a cable home…. Tommy is a Lt Commander and a Wing Commander out here and we met first when I went, a brand new Wren, to Yeovilton. You may have come across him at Weston Zoyland from time to time – he was a Lieutenant in those days. David, the fact that I am married I hope makes no difference to our friendship we have always been the greatest of friends and I hope it will remain so.
>
> With love, Rosemary.

Rosemary could hardly have chosen a more experienced or more dashing a Naval pilot than Lieutenant Commander Thomas 'Tommy' Wade Harrington. He had served with the Ark Royal in Norway and Dunkirk, had taken an active part in the search for the Bismarck, and then with the Eastern Fleet, flown fighter-cover from the aircraft carriers HMS *Begum*, *Unicorn* and *Indomitable*, shooting down several Japanese aircraft.[16]

On December 16, a massive German counter-offensive was launched through the forested Ardennes region, its aim to advance to the port of Antwerp and split the British and American Forces. Taking advantage of the fog and snow which had grounded recce squadrons, the Ardennes Offensive came as a complete surprise to the Allies. The German Panzers broke through the American lines, and as they raced west, the fighting was some of the fiercest of the war.

By the 22nd the weather cleared enough to allow the RAF and Americans to put their air superiority to good use once again, and supported by the 2nd TAF, the Americans launched a counter-attack, prevented the Germans taking Bastogne and created a bottleneck through which only limited German supplies could be transported. With the better weather, No.168 Squadron was sent up to cover the area west of Dusseldorf and Cologne, and as far south as Prum. They attacked convoys, trains, tanks and other ground targets. Reading news of the German offensive and worried for David's safety, Marjorie wrote:

> Bowden.
> What horrible news for the last week (*but*) General Eisenhower's Order of the Day sounds as if things are not quite as black as one had begun to think….
> I hope you haven't been meeting the increased number of German planes….
> Yesterday it snowed hard most of the afternoon but, as the ground was so wet, it didn't settle. I thought of the poor bloody infantry in Holland and Germany and we are so glad to hear that you are at a good Officers Club and I hope that your nightly roof is warm and snow-tight. It will be a very good moment when we hear the front door open and you walk in again. We all miss you….
> Take care, Love Marjorie.

On Christmas Eve, as the German offensive reached its furthest point west, Derek Dickson attacked transport and flak positions near Malmedy in the St Vith area. Hit by intense light flak, he did not return, but everyone hoped that he had managed to bail out. Pilots said that flying in the Ardennes area at this time was very difficult, the flak was very accurate[17] and the German soldiers likened Typhoon pilots to highwaymen.[18]

By the evening, David's thoughts turned to home, and he was just settling down to listen to the radio when he was asked by Squadron Leader Lambert to fly an army officer to Brussels.

> For as many years as I can remember I have listened to the Christmas Eve Kings' College carol service and back at home I knew all my family would be listening and then they would give out the Christmas presents. I was very upset at the thought of missing any part of the service so I took a deep breath and said to the C/O that I couldn't recall disobeying an order from a senior officer but that I wish to do so now.
> He looked rather shocked. 'You will have to produce a very good reason for doing so.' I explained about the carol service and how much it meant to me. 'Well, this seems to me to be a very good reason, I love it too,' he said. 'Very well, I will ask another pilot to make the flight.' I was very grateful and thought that this made the service even more moving.

When the Met Office reported the weather was going to 'clamp down' on Christmas Day, many pilots decided to celebrate Christmas early. At Gilze-Rijen with No.2 Squadron, John Packwood recalled 'We all got pretty drunk. Then Christmas Day dawned bright and clear, we went down to the field and had to fly at dawn. I flew my sortie in the morning and got back down again. I was sitting around looking like death and Colin Maitland came up and said, 'For god sake, go back up to the billet before you die.... I was more or less threatened with a court martial if I was like it again on New Year's Eve!'[19]

No.168 Squadron flew three missions on Boxing Day, shooting up flak guns and trucks. Australian pilot Roderick Mackenzie's[20] aircraft developed engine trouble. While he flew back to base, the rest of the formation spotted a large convoy of vehicles which they reported to No.83 Ground Control Centre's mobile radar unit ('Kenway'). Ordered out of the area, James Perkins and Graeme Turner flew north east into heavy flak, but arrived back safely. Peter Mitchell joined up with a formation of Typhoons from 143 Wing, but Vasco Gilbert on his second flight of the day failed to return.[21]

Army lorries pass through a heavily bombed town. *(Family collection – Crown © 1945)*

Due to the shortage of aircraft, David had not flown since the 15th, while No.4 Squadron pilots, Donald Draper and David Rowcliffe, finally completed their second tours. A tour length for a recce pilot was about 200 hours operational flying or 80 missions completed; this figure gave Photo/Recce pilots approximately a one-in-three chance of survival, whereas a Typhoon armed-attack pilot's tour was 100 (usually brought down to 96) with at times, about a fifty per cent chance of survival.

A thick fog hung over Eindhoven on December 28, and all planned sorties were called off, so David took the opportunity to drive over to visit old friends at Gilze-Rijen airfield. Twenty-six miles north-west of Eindhoven, it was the base for No.2, 4, and 268 Squadrons. In Command was Group Captain Alan Anderson with Wing Commander Malins as Operations C/O.

David arrived just in time for tea – to many pilots an essential part of RAF life. Battle of Britain pilot Geoffrey Wellum fondly remembered sitting around the fireside in their comfortable Mess after the rigours of the day, and teatime was 'a ritual, a meeting with hot toast and unlimited cups of tea.'[22] As Canadian squadrons served a high tea at 18.30 hours, David had missed this luxury with No.168 Squadron.

> I've just had the most extraordinary bit of luck when I drove up to visit 35 Wing today. I was amazed as they were all sitting down in a beautiful Mess, taken over from the Germans, having tea and toast. I said, 'Oh you lucky things, how I long for an English tea and have tea and toast at 4 o'clock. I would give anything to be with this squadron.' George Hindmarsh immediately said, 'I'll soon fix it for you, we haven't got a new Flight Commander for 'A' flight yet. Come with me.'

David thought he was joking, but telling David to jump in his car he drove him up to the aerodrome. On the way Hindmarsh asked if he knew Anderson, and David said that he had heard of 'Mad Andy,' but had never met him.

> George said, 'Never mind, you are going to in a minute,' and at the Flight Office George knocked on the door, poked his head round it and said, 'Greville-Heygate wants a transfer.' He then pushed me in and shut the door behind me. The W/Cdr seemed unperturbed by my unexpected appearance and after a quick chat he said, 'Well, we do need a Flight Commander, Trevor Mitchell is leaving and we need a replacement. It is an odd way of choosing one but as you are here and I know your record you'd better stay. I'll send a signal through to your C/O grounding you until you are posted. I'll need you here on Monday so go and have a weekend in Brussels.'
>
> I couldn't believe my luck, I was so happy. I drove off in the car and I was so excited that I was not really thinking where I was going. Suddenly I saw a huge sign saying, 'YOU ARE NOW UNDER GERMAN OBSERVATION.'

In his excitement, David had driven north towards the Rhine by mistake. He quickly turned round and drove back to Eindhoven, still unable to believe his good fortune.

While David was on leave in Brussels, No.168 lost two more pilots. On December 29, Flight Lieutenant Roy Foster Plant[23] was last seen attacking a locomotive near Munster, but later reported as a PoW. Flight Lieutenant Ernest Gibbons, attacked by an Fw190, was killed when his aircraft spun into the ground.[24]

After forty-eight hours leave in Brussels, Tony Davis kindly offered David a lift back to base.

> *Sunday, 31 December.* We started off in the car but before long the roads were absolutely chock-o-block with traffic and at Bourg-Leopold we got stuck between the Americans going West-East and Monty going North-South, so Tony dropped me off. I walked a hell of a long way along the length of the tanks and vehicles and eventually caught a lift at the other end. There must have been at least thirty miles of tanks and vehicles stationary on the roads. If the Germans had any bombers left they could have wiped out both armies.

W/Cdr. A. F. Anderson, D.S.O., D.F.C.

David had not met 'Mad' Andy Anderson, until he was pushed through his office door by George Hindmarsh. (© *Tatler*)

At Eindhoven, David packed up his kit, said goodbye to new friends made with No.168 Squadron and, with just six hours fifteen minutes operational flying, David's days as a Typhoon pilot were over almost before they had started. A gentle, sensitive man, David had found that this form of fighting was not in his nature, and later when he saw first-hand the effects that the bombing and strafing caused to the German civilians, he could not feel anything but sadness for the waste and destruction the war had left in its wake.

Chapter Seventeen

No.2 Squadron, 35 Recce Wing, Gilze-Rijen – 'Bodenplatte' and 'Veritable': December 1944–March 1945

'I was posted to No.2 Squadron, 35 Wing, to join the happy band of vagabonds and live some of the best days of my life. 35 Wing was run with the minimum of red tape but the maximum amount of expectations. It was a glorious Rabelaisian existence where laughter and high living masked the unbelievable horror of war and sadness that surrounded our lives.'

'Rusty Memories' Peter Critchley. No.2 Squadron Archives

No.2 Squadron, part of No.35 Recce Wing, had arrived at Gilze-Rijen on November 23. This Wing consisted of 60 aircraft, 260 vehicles, 165 RAF officers and 1016 airmen, 41 Army officers and 135 other ranks. Made up of No.2, 4 and 268 Squadrons it also included 'four British Air Liaison Sections, an Army interpretation section…, two Mobile Field Photographic Sections controlling equipment which could produce 50,000 photographic prints in 24 hours.'[1]

Gilze-Rijen, one of the oldest airfields in the Netherlands, had been in Luftwaffe hands from 1940 until the end of October 1944. Built by a Dutch workforce, the brick living quarters were comfortable; there was a log fire in the dispersal building and it was considered very luxurious by the pilots. With permanent runways and aircraft bays hidden in pine trees, it made an ideal winter base.

David was warmly welcomed to the squadron.

I hope to settle in very quickly and will be flying on low-level Photo/Recce missions and reporting on German Army movements. We have all of Holland to cover from the Zyder Zee to the Rhine. This is divided into several areas. The Zyder Zee is the safest but very difficult to navigate especially when flooded. Arnhem and Nijmegen are OK but the Rhine, Calcar[2] and that sort of area have ghastly flak.

I am so glad to be off the Typhoons and I took up a Spitfire XIV for an hour to gain some experience on this type. It is a most exciting aircraft to fly but my tooth played me merry hell – so much for that dentist visit before I left England – but no doubt after a drink or two it will become numb.

I think the Spitfire is a very delicate and feminine aircraft, in contrast to the Hurricane which is definitely masculine. What luck to have flown three marks of Spitfire, the Mark I and V with the Rolls-Royce Merlin engines, and now the XIV with the Rolls-Royce Griffon engine.

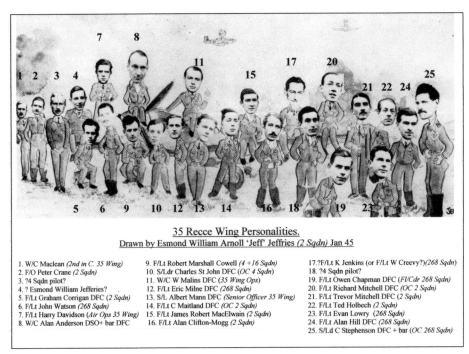

35 Recce Wing Personalities.
Drawn by Esmond William Arnoll 'Jeff' Jeffries *(2 Sqdn)* Jan 45

1. W/C Maclean *(2nd in C. 35 Wing)*
2. F/O Peter Crane *(2 Sqdn)*
3. ?4 Sqdn pilot?
4. ? Esmond William Jefferies?
5. F/Lt Graham Corrigan DFC *(2 Sqdn)*
6. F/Lt John Watson *(268 Sqdn)*
7. F/Lt Harry Davidson *(Air Ops 35 Wing)*
8. W/C Alan Anderson DSO+ bar DFC

9. F/Lt Robert Marshall Cowell *(4 +16 Sqdn)*
10. S/Ldr Charles St John DFC *(OC 4 Sqdn)*
11. W/C W Malins DFC *(35 Wing Ops)*
12. F/Lt Eric Milne DFC *(268 Sqdn)*
13. S/L Albert Mann DFC *(Senior Officer 35 Wing)*
14. F/Lt C Maitland DFC *(OC 2 Sqdn)*
15. F/Lt James Robert MacElwain *(2 Sqdn)*
16. F/Lt Alan Clifton-Mogg *(2 Sqdn)*

17. ?F/Lt K Jenkins (or F/Lt W Creevy?)*(268 Sqdn)*
18. ?4 Sqdn pilot?
19. F/Lt Owen Chapman DFC *(Fl/Cdr 268 Sqdn)*
20. F/Lt Richard Mitchell DFC *(OC 2 Sqdn)*
21. F/Lt Trevor Mitchell DFC *(2 Sqdn)*
22. F/Lt Ted Holbech *(2 Sqdn)*
23. F/Lt Evan Lowry *(268 Sqdn)*
24. F/Lt Alan Hill DFC *(268 Sqdn)*
25. S/Ld C Stephenson DFC + bar *(OC 268 Sqdn)*

No.35 Wing pilots and personalities. *(Family Collection – © Jeff Jefferson 1945)*

David was happy to have swapped the pit-bull temperament of the Typhoon for the greyhound speed and grace of the Spitfire. It was very much a pilots' dream plane. 'It had an indefinable quality of excitement about it, an unmistakable charisma, which greatly appealed to young and eager pilots, added to which it was the fastest and highest performing fighter of its day and most pilots wanted to fly the best.'[3] The Spitfire XIV could fly at over 400 mph and the Griffon engine produced over 2,000 hp. It had a five-bladed propeller, an f24 camera in the rear fuselage and was armed with two .50-inch machine guns.

David hardly had time to unpack his bags before the Luftwaffe launched 'Bodenplatte,' its last great aerial offensive. At first light on January 1, the Luftwaffe pilots flew low, and in total radio silence, to attack Allied Air Force bases in Belgium and Holland. At Gilze-Rijen, pilots and crews rose early for breakfast and briefings and by 8.30, four aircraft from No.2 Squadron had taken off. John Young and John Packwood flew northeast towards Apeldoorn, while Peter Critchley-Salmonson and Peter Green headed out to circle north east of The Hague.

Young and Packwood soon spotted a large formation of Ju88s, Me109s and Fw190s flying west, about two hundred feet below them. John Packwood later told David, 'I was No.2 to Johnny, he spotted them first, saying he saw a couple of Angels and I said, 'There are German aircraft down there.' There were so many flying at 200–300 ft past Apeldoorn. He then said something about wanting to have a go at them but, before we did Johnny radioed back to 84 Group warning of the enemy aircraft. Nobody was interested as far as I could see. So we dived down from the sun into the rear of the pack. I don't know what they thought we were doing, they must have been keeping a pretty poor lookout. The two of us came down in close formation from the sun.' Packwood lined up behind an Me109 and fired a five second cannon burst. 'I shot at this one. Just as well he didn't take evasive action as I wasn't very good at that…. I saw the tracer going slightly beneath him so I pulled the nose up a bit and the right-hand wing came off. Bang – straight down…. With all the bits flying around I thought I had shot myself down too. I didn't bother with the camera gun because you were always in for rude assessments if you had them on.' The 109 burst into flames as it crashed into the ground.

Meanwhile, Peter Critchley-Salmonson and Peter Green also reported seeing over thirty Me109s, three Ju188s and an Fw190. Still no air-raid alarm was sounded, and around 09.00, sixteen of the German fighters broke away from the main group to attack Gilze-Rijen. David found himself in their sights.

> The war may be nearing its conclusion but I don't think anyone has told the Germans yet. I was driving the jeep over to the Ops room just after nine this morning when the airfield was strafed by waves of Me262s, 109s and 190s. I saw the square wingtips and black crosses as one 109 came towards me, low and fast. It roared past, guns blazing, missing me but hitting the lorry following on behind, which was badly shot up. Luckily, the driver escaped with just a few cuts from flying glass. There was noise and smoke everywhere and several aircraft were hit.

Damage at Gilze-Rijen was relatively light. A few anti-personnel bombs were dropped, injuring several of the ground staff, damaging some buildings and destroying a Spitfire and a Typhoon. However, the Luftwaffe pilots did not get off so lightly. No.4 Squadron diary reported that the anti-aircraft guns shot down an Me109, an Fw190 and an Me262, and damaged five other aircraft.

Having baled out, Me109 pilot Hans-Karl Götz was captured and locked up in the Guard Room. 35 Wing's ORB also recorded the day's events. 'The aerodrome came under continuous air attack and ground strafing by jet jobs…. One Me109, whilst strafing the runway, hit the Mustang Flt/Lt Lyke had just landed, but only damaged the rear-end of the aircraft.'

Greater damage was inflicted at Eindhoven. Carrying out an air-test, a No.168 pilot, Howard 'Gibbous II' Gibbons, was halfway down the runway when the Luftwaffe attacked. Taking off, he turned steeply, shot the tail off an Fw190, but was almost immediately shot down by another. About forty aircraft were destroyed and many personnel were killed or wounded.[4]

Wing Commander Stansfeld was just getting ready for the day. 'I was shaving and looking out the window and suddenly I saw 109s going around the place like wasps. I couldn't believe it. It was about eight in the morning and they were attacking Evere airfield, which was near where I was billeted. I jumped into my car and raced to Melsbroek where I had left 34 Wing…. I saw little heaps of sort of burning Wellingtons and things.'[5]

Once the attack was over, Gilze-Rijen runway was judged fit for take-off and at 09.45, pilots headed out on Tac/Rs over Wesel and Arnhem. However, in the afternoon the hastily repaired runway was the cause of a tragic accident. Wing Commander Malins was watching as Leigh Woodbridge and Patrick James Garland returned from an Arty/R. As Garland landed, his aircraft 'hit one of the badly–repaired bomb-craters and bounced back into the air. In trying to correct his landing he gave the engine too much and the aircraft turned upside down and slid along the runway; he was killed instantly.'[6]

> It seemed as if the complete German air force attacked, it was too big an operation ever to be conceived or expected by our side. The Germans hit all the local airfields with everything they'd got left that could fly. Lefty Packwood shot down a 109 and Dave Mercer[7] a Ju188. Patrick Garland's death is particularly tragic as he was the last of four brothers to be killed, all had been in the RAF and his brother Donald had been awarded a posthumous VC in 1940.

The final tally for 'Operation *Bodenplatte*' was over 200 Allied aircraft destroyed or damaged and 11 pilots killed, however, the Luftwaffe paid a heavy price with over 170 pilots killed, wounded or missing and over 60 captured and it never recovered from the loss of so many experienced pilots.

A curious footnote to '*Bodenplatte*' was a Personal Combat Report made by John Douglas 'Joe' Stubbs. Pilots from No.168 Squadron were returning from a recce when Stubbs spotted six Me109s flying about 600 yards behind an unmarked Mustang and not making any effort to attack it.[8] Stubbs thought the Mustang was in German hands, however thinking it was being chased, Squadron Leader Lambert dived down through the 109s, and in the dogfight that followed, Stubbs claimed an Me109 damaged. (He was proved right about the Mustang's ownership; Lambert later met the German Colonel who claimed he flew the Mustang on a raid on Brussels.[9])

Over the next few days, snow that had fallen further south began to fall at Gilze-Rijen. On the 2nd bad weather grounded No.2 Squadron, but at Eindhoven the weather conditions were better and 'Joe' Stubbs was sent out to air-test a Typhoon damaged in the previous day's raid. While taking-off, the cannon access panel on one wing, which was not fastened properly, flew up, causing Stubbs's aircraft to spin off the runway and crash into Warrant Officer S.G. Jones's Typhoon, which was loaded with rockets. Both aircraft burst into flames. Jones escaped with severe burns, but Joe Stubbs was unable to escape his aircraft.[10]

> As there was no flying today I went to the dentist and got my tooth X-rayed. It proved to be beyond repair so it had to be extracted. It is a bit sore and I can't help feeling the large hole it has left behind with my tongue.
>
> *Thursday, 4 January.* I flew over to Eindhoven on an air-test; No.168 Squadron has had the most terrible time of it in the last few days and have been flying in appalling conditions. Five aircraft have been written off, Gibbous II was shot up at Eindhoven on the 1st and Joe Stubbs killed the next day. The only bit of good news they've had is that Derek Dickson is a POW.[11]

The next day, in perfect weather, David flew over the Dutch Islands, The Hague and Dordrecht, as Ronald Samuel Wolsey 'Ronnie' Kemp's No.2.

There was slight flak but we saw no shipping movement except for a possible moored E boat. About sixty men were heading north from Rotterdam, many of them on bikes but they scattered pretty fast when Kemp attacked them, causing them much confusion and some casualties. We also spotted a staff car, a light MT[12] and a tug which hastily cut the tow-rope of a large barge it was towing when it saw us approaching.

Marjorie wrote to David with home news.

Bowden.
David…, I listened to an account of the shooting up of aircraft on the ground on the wireless. I had hoped with all my heart that you were not one of those people coming in from dispersal. It's a good thing jeeps are quick off the mark. It is good to hear that you are enjoying life and I'm so glad you have a good Mess now…. Bill has managed to get off the Staff again and is expecting to go across the water anytime – he will probably get a few days' embarkation leave. I know he has felt more and more exasperated at being out of the battle zones for so long and I think he is glad now that he has taken the plunge. It doesn't often happen that one can choose whether to be a spectator or combatant….
Love, Marjorie.

During the first weeks of January, Allied forces pushed back the German units and, in an attempt to reach the banks of the Rhine, Allied Commanders, Montgomery and Eisenhower, planned a simultaneous assault. In the south, the US Army would launch 'Operation Grenade' and the north, a combined Canadian and British force would launch 'Operation Veritable.' While the British 2nd Army held the flanks from Nijmegen south, the Canadian 1st Army would advance through the thickly wooded Reichswald Forest, then head south and east to seize the towns of Weeze, Goch, Uedem and Calcar and finally advance toward the Rhine near Wesel. There were several heavily defended German positions on this route. Known as The Siegfried Line by the Allies, Hitler thought the 'West Wall' was impregnable; it bristled with anti-tank ditches, minefields and thousands of bunkers and gun-emplacements. There was also the Reichswald Forest and another defensive line from Rees to Geldern to be taken before the German forces could be pushed back over the Rhine.[13]

No.2 Squadron's role was to provide air-support to the Canadian Army, observing, photographing or attacking German troops and positions from Nijmegen to Venlo. 'Veritable' was planned to commence on January 12, however, winter weather closed in with a mixture of thick fog and blinding snow-blizzards. With the attack postponed, David was given a week's leave. He set off for Antwerp in the jeep, but it broke down and he missed his flight home.

It was most disappointing. The next day I was again delayed, this time with a puncture; however I finally managed to reach Antwerp and eventually arrived home in time for supper. As I was unable to warn the family of my homecoming they were very surprised to see me. The next day I borrowed father's car, drove to RAF Market Harborough airfield to get petrol, then I took Mother, Marjorie and Carol to visit Mary Hutton and her two boys.

The zigzag lines indicate positions of German trenches. *(Family Collection – Crown © 1945)*

Returning from leave, David discovered several new faces in the squadron as Tom Rayner, Frederick George, George Keith Malcolmson and Warren Blain arrived. Also posted to No.2 Squadron was Colin Dunford Wood, who at the start of the war had been in the Indian Army. On applying for a transfer to the RAF and knowing his eyesight was poor, he had memorized the eye-test chart and was passed fit to fly. He then flew in India, Burma and Iraq with No.28 Squadron before spending time at Hawarden. [14]

With the German forces rapidly withdrawing, the weather cleared and although the area was still covered in thick snow, 35 Wing began flying at full strength once again, however, David's first flight was not a great success.

22 January. George Hindmarsh and I set off on a Photo/Recce over the Reichswald Forest but his Spitfire developed engine trouble and after only half an hour we returned to base.

The next day, with flak over Arnhem, David and Kemp carried out a successful recce, spotting a long goods train with over fifty trucks and another with no engine. After

David in his Spitfire. (*Family Collection*)

bombing and cutting the rail there was not much else to report apart from a light field gun and tractor.

In the evening I listened to the Tuesday Serenade on the World Service but didn't think it such a good edition as the one I heard in Bowden. We get the *Daily Express* and the popular papers a few days late but rarely *The Times* which is a pity as people here like to do the crossword, but the *Country Life* magazines I brought back with me are wearing up well under the strain of continual reading. Ronnie Kemp brought me some writing paper when he was in Antwerp but I would really like to get to a town myself to get more paper, an account book, some elastic and several other things that I am running short of.

Apart from magazines and newspapers, letters from home were always welcome.

Bowden. Tuesday, January 23 1945.
We shall all be pleased to hear what kind of journey you had to London and hope you were able to get a good hotel with nice food.... Your father isn't well and spent a few days in bed. The best place in this weather.... Carol loves playing in the snow but nearly always cries when she comes in with cold toes.... We are all looking forward to your next visit....
With love, Mother.

Bad weather again closed in, with heavy snow falling at Gilze-Rijen, but finally American troops regained lines held before the start of the Battle of the Bulge. It had been a costly exercise with many casualties on both sides.

David flew several sorties over the heavily defended town of Arnhem. *(David's Collection – Crown © 1945)*

'Glider graveyard' in fields near Arnhem. *(David's Collection – Crown © 1945)*

Monday, 29 January. Yesterday snowstorms again prevented all flying but today it cleared enough to fly. After attacking a large truck near Arnhem and flying through light flak Chris Blundell-Hill's aircraft was hit but he made it back OK.

Wednesday, 31 January. Fog prevented flying so Pat Furse[15] came over and we had a most enjoyable evening with Charles Harris-St John[16] who is a born leader and C/O of No.4 Squadron.

January had proved a difficult month for flying with fog, mist, snow and bitter cold. David only flew six flights and the Wing's News summed up the last six weeks as one of many blank days with a snow covered airfield.[17] February started better and on the 2nd, Blain and David flew a recce of Arnhem, Apeldoorn and Deventer through both light and heavy flak. On returning to base, David found a pleasant surprise waiting for him.

Tony Davis flew his aircraft up to see me today. I was flying at the time but we lunched together and he went back late this afternoon. It was good to see him again and to hear that the old squadron is still a happy and efficient unit. He must be just about the perfect CO, a fine leader and a gentleman. However we are very lucky here and I have taken to this squadron very quickly. Tony is going to the ballet in Brussels, I wish I could go too as Robert Helpman[18] and Margot Fontaine[19] are dancing.

There was also news from David's sister.

Bowden, Feb. 3.
David…, I am sending the *Sunday Times*, there is a very interesting bit about a Spitfire pilot Flt/Lt Draper capturing an Me410 intact on an Italian airfield. I wonder if it is your Bert Draper.[20]

Father is much better and went down to the office again. He has been on the verge of a breakdown but seems to have made a remarkable recovery. We didn't tell you before as we thought it would worry you. A young Land Agent is coming to help him for two months, he seems very nice and has been invalided out of the Army....

Love, Marjorie.

On February 4, all German forces were finally pushed out of Belgium. Three 35 Wing recces were sent off to take photographs of stretches of the River Rhine. Squadron Leader Stephenson elected to recce a three mile stretch of the heavily defended river at Emmerich himself. To take the urgently required photos and in the face of intense flak, Stephenson's run was so low that he flew under several high tension cables.[21]

John Packwood and I are now sitting here trying to write letters home. He has been asking me what he can write about in his letter to his mother-in-law. I have found the same difficulty writing to my family – there is almost nothing to say unless one happens to go down the road in the opposite direction – but since we have not had cause to leave the daily path, another topic has to be found. I then remembered an incident that happened the other day when he was sitting on the hearth by the fire when the logs fell out. We have never seen him move so fast and we all decided that he would be no good at operational flying if he did that whenever he saw fiery flak coming up at him.

Flying a Tac/R in the Arnhem, Reichswald and Wesel area with John Packwood, they observed that the river appeared breached with slight flooding and saw no movement in the Reichswald Forest, but soon found themselves under attack by both friend and foe.

There was light and heavy flak over the area and my aircraft was hit. Then on our way back we were attacked by four Canadian Tempests of 83 Group and as our Spits are camouflaged for low-level flying I think they must have got the jitters and mistaken us for Jerries. Luckily, their shooting wasn't up to scratch and we managed to evade them and they were seen to land at Volkel.[22] I brought my Spitfire back with several small holes in the tail which were quickly mended.

Over the next few weeks the weather was cold with sunny skies and daily snowfalls, but then, just as 'Operation Veritable' was finally given the go-ahead, a thaw set in. This was bad news as the rain and mud would inevitably bog the ground battle down, and bad weather would ground aircraft. However, on the 7th the final plans for 'Operation Veritable' were distributed and that evening Wing Commander Anderson and Ian Duffus gave the pilots a talk on the forthcoming battle and explained what tactical and artillery recce missions would be required. At about the same time 900 Allied bombers attacked German positions along the Rhine. Cleve,[23] the 'Gateway to the Rhine,' was reduced to piles of rubble and the Germans, sensing a major attack was imminent, blew floodgates and winter dykes near Nijmegen.

At 5.00 am on Thursday, 8 February, 'Operation Veritable' blasted into action with more than 1,000 guns opening fire in one of the heaviest artillery barrages of the whole war. It was a busy day for No.2 Squadron; they flew both tactical and artillery recces. Polish pilot Antony 'Tony' Krakowski observed gun-flashes over Kranenburg, and New Zealand pilot George Malcolmson, who had only been with the squadron for nineteen days, set off on an Artillery recce over the Reichswald Forest area. Losing his No.1 in poor visibility and low on fuel, he was homed to Woensdrecht, but attempting to line up on the airfield his wing hit the ground and he was killed.[24] Flying further north over Apeldoorn and Arnhem, John Packwood and David were also hampered by low cloud and they returned to base after just twenty minutes.

> When the cloud lifted in the afternoon, Ronnie Kemp and I flew an Arty/R over barges on the Rhine. Communications were very good and we were able to confirm that the pontoon bridge that Ronnie saw earlier in the day was still intact. We spotted a train with fifteen flat trucks and about fifty barges. Several of these must have been packed full of arms and explosives as there was terrific fire and great destruction when they were shot up.

News came in that the attack had gone well, and Kranenburg on the north of the Reichswald Forest had been captured. Most pilots flew over the battle area and had seen immense activity from the guns.[25] Trying to photograph German troop and equipment movements the next day, David and Ronnie Kemp flew over the Reichswald Forest, Wesel and Rhine area. With smoke and haze over the area, observation was very difficult, although they saw that the ferries at Emmerich, Rees and Xanten were not working. At Wesel the barrage balloons were down, and barges, tugs and other light-craft were ferrying German troops and equipment to the relative safety of the east bank.

> There was much flooding but no sight of flak or any enemy aircraft but on my way back I was jumped by several Spitfires and my engine was hit and began to spray oil all over my windscreen, leaving me peering out of a black haze. Luckily I managed to get back to base.

As the Allies advanced through the Siegfried Line, Cleve fell and the Reichswald Forest was cleared. No.2 Squadron's flying tally during the period 6–14 February was excellent, flying about fifty missions, they destroyed several German vehicles and a Me109 was shot down by MacElwain.[26]

> I am trying to get to the dentist we have here, to get my teeth finished off, he is very good and has just returned from leave. The post seems to be rather erratic, I have only had one letter from Mother written two days after I left and I am unsure if any of my letters have got through.

Letters may have been delayed from England, but in the middle of February a letter arrived from Rosemary:

> C/o R.A.N.A.S.I.O, Mail Office, Colombo. It's early morning for me, in fact it's just turned eight and I am listening to the buzz and hum of aircraft, the scream of brakes and the natter of the millions of voices of people who have come to work! Belgium sounds as though it can still give quite a lot of fun. What a joy to look in shops and find an abundance of things there that they have to offer....

You must have had a terrible winter…. T's brother was in Manchester in the cold spell and says he awoke one morning to find even his breath had frozen on his moustache!

With Love, Rosemary.

By February 19, Canadian troops had cut the Goch-Calcar road, and Bucholt, between Keppeln and Goch, was captured. Two days later at Hummersum, twelve miles west of Goch, the 3rd Battalion Irish Guards was pinned down in atrocious conditions. David's old Sandhurst Instructor, Major Basil Eugster, was stuck in waterlogged open country and with fierce fighting, unable to advance further. With the wireless equipment bogged down, he calmly walked under shell and mortar fire to organize a withdrawal and rescued almost all his injured men.[27] Low cloud obscured David and Chris Blundell Hill's recce on the 22nd, so they could not fully cover the area, however, they attacked several trucks, three horse-drawn vehicles scattered on hearing their Spitfires approach, and at Zaltbommel they encountered accurate flak.

Recce photo of German defensive positions. *(Family Collection – Crown © 1945)*

As well as dodging flak in the air, David also found himself in the line of fire at the airfield. Gilze-Rijen was situated in what the pilots nicknamed 'Antwerp Alley' as V1s frequently passed overhead on their way to Antwerp. Anti-aircraft guns at the western end of the airfield often tried to shoot them down, but the V1s were notoriously hard to hit.

In the evening we had a surprise visit from Monty Denny, he needed a quick get away in the morning and wondered if he could stay overnight on the runway in his Mosquito. He asked me if it was safe to do so. I told him that we got lots of flying bombs overhead going to Antwerp and sometimes we try to shoot them down but they never land here. He asked again if it would be OK to sleep in his aircraft and I assured him it would be fine. However, in the middle of the night there was an enormous explosion as a flying bomb landed close to the Ops' Room. I hurried out to Flight Dispersals and found a very shaky but otherwise unhurt Denny. He fumed that I had misled him on purpose and from this I gathered that he was not happy with me. Apart from a rather shaken pilot, two Tempests and a Spitfire were damaged.[28]

Having finally escaped his staff job, David's brother-in law, Bill Adler, was posted to The 6th Royal Scots Fusiliers and dropping in to see David he was told that he had just missed him. He wrote:

I don't think I'll be able to get over again for sometime, we don't seem to be able to get about as much as your people. However, I saw a chap in your flight and he thought you may be able to come over tomorrow morning…. I've had a very good trip so far and seem to have got through much more quickly than most people. I was most impressed by the splendour in which you live and envy you a lot.

Yours ever, Bill.

David was unable to visit Bill the following day as he flew two Tac/Rs with Blain. In the morning, from Arnhem to Cleve they spotted an ambulance, but were again thwarted by cloud cover.

We flew to the Cleve, Wesel area in the afternoon but cloud had not lifted so we aborted the recce. Apart from spotting a white object, possibly a parachute, going through the cloud, the trip was uneventful. Having completed his tour, the squadron threw a grand party for Peter Crane.

Early on the 25th, Phase Two of 'Operation Veritable' codenamed 'Operation Blockbuster' began. Its objective was to take Xanten, the Calcar Heights and Hochwald Forest.

Our first flight of the day was aborted as there was a problem with Ken's radio. It was quickly mended and we took off an hour later and headed north towards Rotterdam where we spotted several small moored boats, a few cyclists and some pedestrians.

Heavy bombing destroyed many towns along the Rhine. *(David's Collection – Crown © 1945)*

No.168 Squadron was officially disbanded on February 26 due to heavy losses of pilots and aircraft, and the next day David flew an Arty/R west of Gooch to Weeze, and although the radio transmission was good and the guns were contacted, due to low cloud they were unable to carry out a shoot. Instead, David took photos of the River Maas from fifty feet, and in the afternoon with George Hindmarsh, flew another low level photo recce to Grave. Leigh 'Woody' Woodbridge and John 'Chick' Henderson were flying in the Geldern area when Woodbridge's aircraft engine caught fire. He bailed out, was picked up by a platoon of Marine Commandos and driven back to base. Everyone was delighted to see him return safely.[29]

28 February. The army desperately wants the series of photographs of the roads leading to Hochwald. So in the afternoon Blain and I went to retake photos of the Hochwald and Rhine battle area. We covered the area Cleve, Bocholt, to the east of Wesel and north of Geldern and spotted various moored barges and several MTs. At Veen, south east of the Hochwald Forest, it was very dicey with light, medium and heavy flak! We managed to come in low and fast and come out, almost in one piece with the photos as requested.

For the first time for a few days, the weather has given us a breathing space so I got down to writing some letters. Up till now I have been too tired to write in the evenings as our days are long and we often rise about 5 am. Just as I was writing home an aircraft shot down a doodlebug above me and a large crack appeared in the windows in front of me. My pen flew across the paper leaving a very large scribble on the letter y. I silently cursed the pilot for being such a fool as it landed about half a mile away. Let sleeping dogs lie or flying bombs fly I say – but I suppose better explode here than Antwerp.[30]

At tea-time I received a letter from Bill written on the 23rd. It has taken twice as long for this letter to come from just down the road as it does from home. Poor Bill, he was most impressed by the splendour in which we live, however we have our ups and downs too.

Venlo, on the Maas River, was liberated on the 1st and Ken Huskinson, and David set off to recce the area north, east and south from Venlo to Wesel. In varied weather with bright sun and hailstorms, they spotted four barges moored and more than ten pontoons on the south bank.

Krefeld Marshalling yard was very active, we saw several trains. There was moderate heavy flak, and at the eastern part of the area the roads were also very active.

David received several letters. Elisabeth Jardine wrote to say that she and John would be married as soon as he returned from India, and said that David's presence at the wedding would be 'absolutely necessary'[31] The other letter was from his parents:

Ripple effect of shipping on the River Rhine. *(Family Collection – Crown © 1945)*

Bowden.

We had sirens on two nights and began to wonder if 'blackout' will have to be begun again! The chickens are hatching out today and Carol was very excited when we showed her one. It is three weeks tonight since we set the eggs so I won't disturb her till tomorrow.... How uncomfortable to have explosions so near to you. I agree with your remark about 'sleeping dogs etc.' Marjorie has had nine letters from Bill but he hasn't had any from her. She thinks he is in Belgium. I wonder if the weather is cold with you, Bill says it is where he is....

Your loving Mother.

As the German Army was pushed back towards the Rhine, the mood in the Wing became one of mixed emotions. 'It was a day for Tac/R pilots to dream of..., every type of German vehicle was moving along the road,' however the pilots were frustrated because pockets of American troops had fought their way north so fast that it was difficult to attack German positions with a certainty that Allied troops would not be hit by mistake, thus large quantities of German equipment and troops were able to escape over the bridge at Wesel.[32] Over the next few days, between gaps in the cloud, David flew several recces west of the Rhine from Wesel and Duisburg to Krefeld.

3 March. The German Army is retreating over the River Rhine! We saw two MT, a camouflaged German tank and a group of twenty German infantrymen running through trees.

5 March. On a Contact Recce at Bonninghardt, once the low cloud cover cleared, we saw plenty of heavy flak and four German jets in the sun, which we turned to attack but they cleared off pretty smartish without returning fire when they saw us.

The Canadian and US Armies finally met near Geldern, and British bombers attacked the railways and roads, stopping further enemy traffic escaping. However, there was confusion between Army and RAF Intelligence as to whether any bridges were still standing over the Rhine; the Army believed that road and rail bridges at Wesel were down and 35 Wing pilots insisted they were still in place. At lunchtime on the 5th, Squadron Leader Maitland was sent off to settle the argument and reported back that the rail bridge appeared undamaged, the western end of road bridge appeared cut, up to eighty well-camouflaged MET were parked on roads and in farm buildings, and six miles upstream from Wesel ferries and barges were operating. He added, 'As might be expected, flak was intense.'[33]

Thursday, 7 March. The weather has closed down again and there was no flying yesterday or today but as we are now to move to Mill tomorrow, we have been kept busy packing.

Chapter Eighteen

'Operation Varsity', Mill, Holland, 7 March 1945–16 April 1945

'We are not going to be so comfortable as we have been most of the winter as we have no hot showers where we are now and are rather too far from Brussels, Antwerp, Ghent, Breda…, and all those other places we go on our weekly day off.'

35 Wing News Sheet No.60

At the end of the first week of March, 35 Recce Wing moved further east to B89 Mill. This airfield, hastily built by British engineers, had a runway 1,600 yards long, but only 33 yards wide. It was constructed of steel plates which made a deafening clanking noise when aircraft took-off or landed. Although it had good dispersal facilities and was close to the Mess, the Nissen huts lacked the luxury of Gilze-Rijen.[1] It proved an unpopular landing ground and was quickly nicknamed 'The strip that is never into wind.'

Friday, 8 March. After final packing we flew to Mill in the afternoon. This is a pig of a runway with a very narrow landing strip, running north to south, usually crosswind.

As No.2 and 268 Squadrons settled in, several old pilots returned; William 'Harry' Westbrook, Francis O'Neil, John 'Mossy' Moss, Joe Summers and John 'Junior' Varley rejoining after spending several months at Hawarden. Later, while the remains of the German Army crossed the Rhine, No.4 Squadron flew in to join the other pilots at Mill. Flying over the Wesel area several days later, Ken Huskinson and David confirmed that the last bridges were finally down.

It appears as if the Wesel battle is at last drawing to a close. There was lots of commotion and flak all over the area. We saw four Fw190s near Borculo and went in to attack but they broke away immediately. They don't come near these days unless they think you haven't spotted them.

Schwanenburg Castle, Cleve, was badly damaged by Allied bombing. *(Family Collection Crown © 1945)*

Delighted to hear of Bill's whereabouts, Marjorie wrote:

Bowden, 11 March.
Thank you so much for writing to say you had seen Bill and that he is looking
fine and comfortably housed. He said he most enjoyed seeing you. His own
billets seem to have been good and spotlessly clean and with such kind hosts.
How strange it must be for the nuns to have their precincts invaded with hearty
young men!! The Mother Superior told Bill that his French was excellent. I think
that pleased him. He says he is awfully lucky to have been posted to such a good
unit. It is so nice to know that you both have such good companions. It does
make all the difference in the world to one's happiness. I'm so glad to hear that
your 'old' squadron pilots are returning. You will enjoy seeing them again. I
suppose they are 'old' men of about 23 or 24. Well done re the elastic, Carol's
knickerbockers were in urgent need of support!
Love, Marjorie.

'Operation Veritable' progressed so well that by March 12, the British, Canadian
and American Armies finally reached the banks of the Rhine, and for a while No.2
Squadron turned their attention north to the Dutch Islands, Deventer and Borculo.[2]

Yesterday I flew a forward facing camera test with the camera mounted in an
empty 90-gallon drop tank, slung under the fuselage. Today for a change of
scene John Packwood and I flew a Shipping Recce and Strike over the Zyder
Zee. We saw three barges entering Stavoren, a trawler and several boats but no
flak or enemy aircraft.

On March 16, weather made flying impossible, so David and several others set off
for Krefeld, about fifty miles south east of the airfield. Although they had flown over
the area many times, this was the first time they had set foot on German soil. Sited
on the west bank with a bridge over the Rhine, Krefeld had a steel mill, railway line
and airfield. Before the war, with a population of more than 170,000, it had been one
of the Rhineland's most important cities. Consequently, it had been heavily bombed
and only captured on March 3 after fierce street-to-street fighting. Shocked by what
he saw, David wrote home.

We went into Krefeld to have a look around. It is terrible to see such miles of
desolation and the pathetic women, children and animals. Such misery and
waste – all for the sake of greed. It would be a good thing to leave some of it as
a warning for every nation.

The next day, David and Joe Summers flew over the occupied Dutch cities of Arnhem,
Deventer and Borculo and the German city of Emmerich, spotting a field hospital
and several moored barges.

There was heavy flak from Emmerich and we also took flak from a German
troop-train steaming northwest with about fifteen trucks. Many German staff
cars and motorcycles were heading east some of which we attacked but the
cloud cover made it difficult.

David was shocked by the bomb damage in the German town of Krefeld. *(SAGH – © NRO AIR34/742)*

David's mother commented on the effects of the Allied bombing.

Bowden.
I can quite imagine how terrible it must have been to see such misery....
Memories are short. I wonder what the young men who were fighting think of
Hitler now or if they still believe him to be some kind of god.
   One of the chicks died yesterday. I think the hen must have put its foot on it.
It is a pity as only six are left now and I think it was the one I peeled out!
Love, Mother.

While looting was forbidden by the Allies, the 'liberating' of the odd Nazi souvenir,
food, weapons and transport was universally accepted. Spotting something too good
to leave by the wayside, Harry Westbrook persuaded David to help with its recovery.

Harry and I went out to Calcar where we found a wonderful ex SS Officer's Opal
car abandoned by the side of the road. We decided that it would add greatly
to our mobility so we decided to liberate it with an explosive stick with the
result that I very nearly blew my hand off. We brought the car back in the three-
tonner but on returning to the aerodrome, my excitement was dampened when
I discovered that Sq/Ldr Maitland was missing, believed shot down. He had
gone on a trip that I would have flown, had I been on duty in the afternoon.

After lunch on March 18, Squadron Leader Maitland and Tommy Rayner had taken
off on a photographic recce from Emmerich to Elten. Having completed their first
run, as Maitland dived through the cloud on the start of the second, Rayner saw

intense flak bursting around his aircraft and tried to call him on the radio but received no reply. After searching the area, he returned to report that the Squadron Leader had been shot down. An eyewitness saw flak guns near Doetinchem shoot down 'a lonely Spitfire which had come low from the east.' Maitland bailed out, but too low, his parachute failed to save him.[3]

With Maitland's death, Squadron Leader Richard 'Mitch' Mitchell took over as No.2 C/O. Such a riotous wake was held that the contents of the Mess were wrecked. Hans Onderwater wrote that, 'Group Captain Anderson sent the pilots out in the three-tonner the next day with orders not to return until they had acquired new furniture and glassware.'[4] A similar farewell party had been thrown when Eric Marrs was shot down; No.152 Squadron pilots held a tremendous thrash in the Mess. 'When the party ended everything that would break was suitably disposed off, most of it thrown over the staircase into the hall below.' Surveying the damage the next day, the C/O thought that the Mess must have been bombed.[5]

Next morning, after a Tac/R to Utrecht, David set off to retake the photographs Maitland had failed to return with.

Up again with Warren Blain to take the urgently needed low-level 14-inch forward-facing photographs of the roads from Emmerich to Elten, flying at 1,000 ft at 400 mph, no flak or enemy aircraft were seen and good photographs were obtained.

The next phase of the Allies plan, to cross the Rhine, was split into five separate operations. 'Varsity,' was the codename for the airborne operation to help the 21st Army Group secure a bridgehead on the east side of the Rhine, and No.2 Squadron was to collect enemy intelligence before the crossing took place. However, difficult

Around ninety per cent of Emmerich was destroyed by Allied bombing. *(Family Collection – Crown © 1945)*

Smoke screen preparations for the Allied crossing of the Rhine. *(Family Collection – Crown © 1945)*

crosswinds at the airfield meant that it was almost impossible for them to take-off for several days. Finally, on the 23rd David reported:

> There is a noticeable decrease in enemy activity over the whole area although we spotted a train at Utrecht, reported its position back and it was pranged 11 minutes later by Spitfires of No.121 Wing. At the River Lek we saw some barges, some moored and others with Dutch flags painted on their back deck.

David's second sortie of the day was cancelled when a No.4 Squadron Spitfire caught fire on take-off. It burnt so furiously that it caused considerable damage to the runway.[6]

'Operation Plunder' commenced in the evening of Friday, 23 March, and in perfect weather and moonlight, the 21st Army Group crossed the River Rhine. By the early hours of the next morning, Allied troops had gained a number of crossings and a sixty-six mile smokescreen was set up to hide British and US Airborne Divisions sent to reinforce them. 'Once again the seaweed remained dry and all were thankful for another promising day.'[7] The *Evening Standard* reported, 'The South-east corner of England had a grandstand preview of the aerial crossing of the Rhine. From dawn onwards airplanes were flying in hundreds across the coast.' This air-armada was the largest single-day airborne operation of the war and included 1,572 planes towing 1,326 gliders, covered by 900 fighters and took about 3½ hrs to pass overhead.[8]

During the day, No.2 Squadron flew twenty sorties. Colin Dunford Wood and Nicholas Bowen flew north of Wesel and saw flak aimed at the airborne forces. Chun and Henderson counted over a hundred Hadrian gliders on an unfinished autobahn and over 1,000 parachutists in all directions. Further on they sighted about eighty gliders ready to cut off from their tows.[9] No Luftwaffe aircraft were seen by any of the Wing's pilots.[10] The enemy was overwhelmed in many places and as many as 7,000 prisoners were taken. Two days later, after flying with John Packwood, David reported:

> The first recce in the north of Holland from Amersfoort and Arnhem was uneventful; we saw very little traffic. In the afternoon we flew to Isselburg[11] in Germany and were met with slight flak from 88 mm guns. Totting up my total I've flown 34 hours on 37 Ops this current tour and I'm now due Easter leave.

The next day David again flew with John Packwood on a Tac/R from Utrecht to Hilversum and Apeldoorn. This area seemed more active than usual, and on their return they heard that Polish pilot Flight Lieutenant Tony Krakowski was

Gliders filled with troops and equipment were towed across the Rhine. *(Family Collection – Crown © 1945)*

missing. He was returning to base when his aircraft caught fire, and with no time to make a forced landing he decided to bail out. He later reported, 'I thought first of all that I was going to land on the spire of a church steeple; I just missed that and then I thought I was going to fall in the river which was nearby. Eventually I landed in a minefield near Kessel.'[12] Fortunately landing on the right side of the battlefield, he was returned to base the same evening.

Thursday, 29 March. I have had a few most frustrating days. My leave was postponed a day as there was no seats on the Dakota. It was then delayed again as there was no air travel, so I spent the night at 14 PTC.[13] At last I left at 9 am and was finally home at teatime.

On April 1, Chris Blundell-Hill flew a solo recce over the Harderwijk – Zwolle area and, hit by the anti-aircraft guns on railway trucks, he crashed into a meadow and was killed. Trevor Mitchell was posted to No.4 Squadron, and on his return, David was promoted to 'A' Flight Commander.

After the winter months and heavy demand on flying, the squadron's Spitfires began to develop mechanical problems, and they struggled to maintain aircraft, and once were down to a single serviceable Spitfire.[14] Peter Green, Joe Summers and Peter Critchley-Salmonson's aircraft all burst a tyre, so No.268 Squadron loaned them several Spitfire XIVBs.

As they retreated west into Northern Holland, the German troops put into effect a carefully prepared 'plan of demolition'[15] in order to flood as much of the country as possible, and David reported back on the extent of this destruction.

Peter Critchley-Salmonson's Spitfire burst a tyre on take-off, but fortunately he was not injured. (© *Grace Critchley-Salmonson*)

11 April. The flooding around Zwolle and Deventer is up to 4 ft deep and extends approximately ten miles by four miles north-east/south-east. We shot up a car and saw vehicles with Allied markings and a tank that we think was British.

While Allied tanks crossed a bridge built over the Ijssel by Canadian engineers, David and Ken Huskinson flew over Northern Holland from Groningen to Assen.

12 April. I can't think what has happened to all the German material they shipped back across the Rhine. They must be moving things at night now. It has been very quiet, there is

Bomb Craters near the Pontoon Bridge.
(Family Collection – Crown © 1945)

no flak and it feels more like we are flying on exercises in England, the only excitement we had was on returning to the airfield when I made a dicey landing with no brakes or flaps.

After finally capturing Arnhem, the Canadians met little opposition elsewhere in Northern Holland, and on entering Gorinchem the German Garrison Commander surrendered the town. However, amongst the celebrations there was also sadness with the news that President Roosevelt had died.

On April 15, American troops finally entered Colditz Castle and after almost five years and around twenty escape attempts Peter Storie-Pugh[16] was finally free. In Germany, General Dempsey's 2nd Army liberated Bergen-Belsen concentration camp. They were appalled by the conditions in which they found the 55,000 prisoners. By the evening of the 17th, the Canadian Army cleared Apeldoorn and in the 'Ruhr Pocket' more than 300,000 German troops surrendered.

Chapter Nineteen

Twente. The End of the War

'It is quite fair to say that nobody is in any hurry to leave TWENTE, unless of course the next move is to ENGLAND!'

No.2 Squadron Operation Record Book.

On Tuesday, 17 April, 35 Wing moved again, this time to Twente in Holland, four miles from Enschede and on the German border. Opened in July 1931, the German Army captured it at the beginning of the war and the Luftwaffe used it until 2 April 1945. The airfield was a great improvement on Mill, with an excellent Mess and brick-built buildings. The countryside around was pleasant with trees and hills in the vicinity, and being close to Enschede and Hengelo, this move was appreciated by all.[1] David however, discovered one or two disadvantages on the first night.

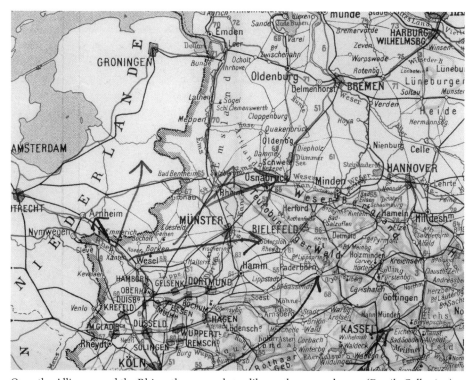

Once the Allies crossed the Rhine, they moved steadily north, east and west. *(Family Collection)*

We moved to Twente, an airfield taken over from the Germans. There are large murals on the walls and all the corridors and bedrooms are filled with bombs. The bomb disposal bods swear they are defused but we are not so confident that the experts have made a perfect job of it. It made for a less than comfortable first night's sleep.

The Wing's upbeat mood was helped by General Dwight D. Eisenhower's decision to cease all fighting west of Utrecht for the sake of the Dutch people.

Thursday, 19 April. In the afternoon Alex Steedman[2] and I carried out a recce over Gorinchem and Utrecht, but when my aircraft began streaming petrol we were homed to Kiwcke sur Mer (*sic*) by Symbolic.[3]

After a fifty minute return flight the next day, David at last flew the new Spitfire XIVB.

Friday, 20 April. On a recce with Sq/Ldr Mitchell we flew over Northern Germany, Jadebusen, Oldenburg and Delmenhorst. Most of the transport we saw was trains with steam up, some coaches with Red Cross markings on them, several barges and ships, and we were targeted by moderate, accurate and inaccurate flak.

As Soviet troops reached the outskirts of Berlin, David patrolled through low cloud.

21 April. Flying as Dick Lavington's No.2 we undertook a recce over Utrecht and Rotterdam with intense flak. It was a bumpy flight and I had to concentrate hard due to bad storms and ice clouds. Our chief job was to check the flooding north of Utrecht and the Zuider Zee. One part of the flooding extended for 1,000 yards and there were similar patches nearby.

A few days later, David took off for an Artillery Recce at Amersfoort with John Packwood, but when his radio failed, David flew on alone.

I spotted the target, and the gun positions were hit, but unfortunately a farmhouse was also hit and burnt out, which I felt rotten about, since there is enough damage and destruction here without me adding to it.

I have the use of a very powerful BMW at present, but it can't be left anywhere without a guard or it will be up on blocks and minus its tyres in a flash.

David's No.2 flying over the flooded fields of the Zyder Zee in Holland. (*Family Collection – Crown © 1945*)

The war was now reaching its final few weeks. On the 25th, as Soviet troops fought their way through the east of Berlin, 35 Wing received orders to cease operations over German occupied Holland. With all operations winding down, David was granted seven days leave. Taking a seat in a Dakota, he was flown home in a series of hops from Twente to Nijmegen, then Evere, Brussels and finally landing in Croydon.

> *27 April.* Mother and Father were very excited to see me and hear all my news. Father is quite unwell and my help is sorely needed to try to keep the business running. We are all now on tenterhooks awaiting the announcement of a German surrender and Victory Day. Father hasn't recovered from the shock of losing Charles and now hopes that I will be given compassionate leave as soon as the war ends so that I can take over running the business.

David was unaware that his father had already written letters to various officials requesting his release from the RAF. After nearly six years of fighting, the war in Europe reached its dying moments. The Grebbe Line was established in West Holland, and a temporary truce allowed food supplies to be distributed to the starving civilian population. As Bill Adler's Brigade reached the Elbe, Soviet Red Army troops captured the Reichstag.

Having been marched to Stalag VIIA, Andrew Craig Harvey and Philip Symington were finally liberated by American Troops on April 30.[4]

35 Wing News reported the Nazi empire was on the brink of collapse and Hitler had been killed. A signal sent from 21st Army Group ordered the 1st Canadian Army to cease offensive operations at 08.00 hours on Saturday, 5 May.

On his way back to Holland, David stayed the night in a jubilant London, and the next day the *Daily Mirror* reported, 'There are thousands of us in Piccadilly Circus. The police estimated that about 10,000 had filled the square and surrounding streets.'[5]

One of the thousands of people celebrating VE day was Daphne Whitehead, a WAAF plotter working at Bentley Priory. With a group of friends they wove their way through London's jubilant crowds to Buckingham Palace. 'We pushed and eased our way in till we were in a good position to see the red velvet draped balcony on which the royal family later appeared; the monument seemed to be covered with a mass of flies as people perched on the lions and figures. Every few minutes there was a terrific cheer, applause and laughter as someone fell into the water. A sailor and American at the top of the statues were trying to goad the crowd into yelling and shouting, 'We want the King.' Then there was a terrific roar as the Royal family came out, the King in his Naval uniform, the Queen in a lovely white evening dress and tiara, Princess Elizabeth in uniform and Margaret Rose in blue. Every time they waved to the crowd they nearly went frantic and yelled themselves hoarse.'

Afterwards, Daphne and her friends slowly made their way back to Trafalgar Square. 'The crowd were orderly, yet frantically happy. Sober yet yelling like mad. Tired but dancing, singing, marching all night. Nelson was picked out by the brilliant lights and stood proud, aloft and sombre. The Arch shone forth and fireworks and verity lights were ascending every few minutes off the top to the chorus of "Ooh" and "Ah." Rockets were swishing all over the place, one failing to rise exploded amongst the crowd. A final gleam of light was added by a girl leaning out of a top floor window gallery waving two lighted tapers.'[6]

VICTORY EUROPE DAY! I finally set off for Croydon and took a Dakota to Plantlunne in Germany.

Winston Churchill officially announced over the radio that Germany had surrendered unconditionally, and at Twente the celebrations started. 35 Wing ORB reported that this was the day they had long awaited. The Wing was given two days rest and 'Liberty Runs' were laid on, Antwerp being the main attraction. They also organized a firework display and dance with 'female partners' being provided from Enschede.[7]

David's mother wrote to David:

Bowden, 9 May 1945.
David…, We wonder how you got on in London when there was so much excitement and if you were able to go to the theatre or to bed! Just before lunch, Ronald arrived and we had quite a large party and all enjoyed it…. The village green had been decorated and the children had been given tea with all sorts of delicious cakes, buns and ices. Afterwards the children and all the grown-ups too, ran races and danced until midnight…. Only two names of Officers killed in *The Times* today which is very cheering and no one missing. What a relief it is that V Day has come, but the war in the East is rather a damper on one's spirits ….

We all send our love. Mother

PS. I wonder what happened to Hitler.

After VE Day celebrations. David and Frank Kenning relax in front of Twente's barracks. *(Family Collection)*

For the members of the Wing, the wild excitement of VE Day was soon replaced with an air of unreality and disbelief. 'It was a strange feeling a day or two later to go down to Twente airfield, where 35 Wing were stationed, to see Spitfires standing in silence in a serried line. Suddenly they seemed aware that their work was done and the urgency past: but in their silence they wore a quiet dignity and sober pride. They seemed to realize indeed that all was over more quickly than we did, who were unable to adjust our minds to the simple fact that the struggle was done, the conflict past.'[8]

Philip Symington arrived home much to the delight of his family. However, the declared peace doesn't seem to make much difference to our activities or future outlook. In fact, instead of finishing my tour by July, it looks as though I shall be here for ages, my next home leave is not for months.

In the evening we went to Almelo, to a club, but it was closed so we watched people dancing in the streets and processions of children carrying Japanese lanterns. It looked so pretty.

Saturday, 12 May. A very nice Royal Navy pilot, Lt Easy is with us at the moment and he knows Rosemary's husband Tommy Harrington as they were at Yeovilton together in 1941.

We had a very hot open-air thanksgiving service and it's a wonder we didn't all get heatstroke. This has been a week of flying in shirtsleeves followed by bathing in the lake and sun bathing. Quite pleasant and very hot, however they are asking for trouble for they are now demanding huge victory flypasts.

With the rest period over, 84 Group was ordered to carry out enormous victory fly-pasts over towns and cities in Holland, Belgium and Denmark. As well as 35 Recce Wing, 84 Group was made up of Spitfire, Typhoon and Tempest Wings with pilots from as far afield as Poland, France, Holland, Britain, Norway, Canada and New Zealand. Recce pilots, who usually only flew in pairs, had limited experience of flying in large formations, so they set about practising. With Squadron Leader Mitchell on leave, David led 'A' Flight's practise and later, thirty-six aircraft flew in formation.

A flypast over a parade of Canadian Army tanks and transport. *(David's Collection – Crown © 1945)*

Needless to say Wing practise was a bit of a disaster. Harry Davison, Freddie George and two of 268 pranged and when Mitchell came back he was furious. 'This is disgraceful,' he shouted, 'I go to Paris for the weekend and you stick my Spits into the deck like darts!'

Tuesday, 15 May. Another near disaster today. Togwell[9] never got off the ground at all as he overturned on take-off. Twelve of us from 2 Squadron flew over Utrecht, The Hague, Rotterdam and Amsterdam. In fact, we flew so far, that when we finally got back, practically everyone was running out of fuel and we were all trying to land at the same time before our engines stopped.

On the 16th, another fly-by was carried out, however, due to an emergency landing, several aircraft took off late and failed to catch up. In the afternoon, David photographed Arnhem and the Zyder Zee, and when flying was cancelled the next day, Trevor Mitchell and David slipped off to visit The Hague.

We dropped in to see Trevor's aunt, Baroness van Heeckeren van Walien and then met Willem Mandersloot – a young lad of about 17 whose father is a Professor. Willem showed us around the town, all the time asking questions about everything. We then went back to meet his parents who were living at an evacuation address in Laan in the centre of The Hague. They were hoping to return to their house on the coast in Scheveningen soon.

Saturday, 19 May. 84 Group Formation. We practised for Monday's display for VVIPs with No.268 and No.4 Squadron's sections.

Although this flypast was delayed due to bad weather, a new method of forming up was practised with each Wing given an orbiting point and joining the passing procession when told to do so by a ground controller.[10]

Rain did not stop the Wing playing cricket, and here they had an advantage over other teams in the form of Thomas Henry Wade, a successful pre-war Essex county

No.35 Wing pilots acquired a variety of cars. *(Family Collection)*

cricketer, and they scored a decisive victory over Enschede.[11] The match was well attended by the pilots who arrived in a variety of German cars.

Back in England Peter Critchley-Salmonson wrote to thank David for all his help.

The Royal Masonic Hospital London.
David…, I just wanted to tell you how absolutely grand it was being in your flight. Everything you could possibly do to make life pleasant and easy for us you did; and no doubt you still are doing and I can only say David that serving under you and Trevor made all the difference in the world to squadron life – and helped greatly in transforming what could so easily have been a tedious existence into some of the happiest days of my life; and for this – I, one of many, wish to thank you. It was absolutely grand….

How's the car? Has Harry crashed it yet – or is he looking for bigger and better things ? I have been flung into hospital with suspected dysentery and now they are talking about an operation. During the last ten months I have not been feeling too good – on and off – and I decided long ago that when I finished any tour I would get seen to – so here I am, and life is very pleasant and restful….

Meanwhile god bless and the best of luck … Critch.[12]

Brief home news also arrived in a letter.

Bowden, 21 May.
Ronald arrived for lunch time and is staying till Wednesday. Bill is here too; he came unexpectedly on Tuesday for about three weeks and is going away perhaps for eighteen months…. I do hope you will soon be in England again. Can't you talk to your C/O and tell him what a relief it would be to your father if you could get on with your exams to help him in his work?

Love, Marjorie.

David in his Spitfire XIV ready for take-off. *(Family Collection)*

On May 25, preparations were made for the squadron's move to Celle, and to demonstrate the RAF's strike potential to the German population, a fly-past was planned. This move into Germany was not looked forward to with any enthusiasm, and anticipating that there would be little chance to enjoy convivial company, pilots and crew took the opportunity to visit local Dutch bars before leaving friendly territories.

Last night we all went out, but overnight the flypast over Celle was called for and we were ordered into the air at seven, so I only had two hours sleep before leading the squadron on a modified group formation. Nine aircraft took part. On his return, Lavington, short of fuel overshot his landing and not wanting to risk going round again he ran out of runway and wrote off his aircraft. Fortunately he was unhurt.

Part VI

Post War

Chapter Twenty

Celle, Occupied Germany and Demob:
May 1945 to Nov 1945

Germany …, 'the land of empty beer gardens and non-fraternization.'
34 Wing Newsletter

Celle Airfield, twenty-five miles north-east of Hanover, was built in 1934 and was taken over by the Allies on April 11, 1945. It had not been heavily bombed, but the flying school destroyed all their remaining aircraft on the aerodrome before they left. The move into occupied Germany came as an unpleasant shock for both pilots and groundcrew.

Wednesday, 30 May 1945. After a hurried lunch we moved base and I had a lovely drive up here in a very powerful BMW and actually saw hills on the way. Celle has the most luxurious Mess that I have ever seen. It is on the lines of a country club with sun loungers, terraces, spacious halls and an incredible underground bar with wine cellars running for miles.

It was Goering's pet station and there is a great sculpture of him in one of the rooms but what a difference we see in the local population. The Dutch had all been so charming. Here the German girls from 2 to 30 are pretty and smiling but the German boys from 1 to 40 are scowling, round-headed and fond of spitting. Perhaps they think it insults us but as long as they spit at our feet and not at us I couldn't care less.

When the squadron was settled in, David was flown home in a Dakota for a week's leave. Arriving back on June 15, he discovered friends Ken Huskinson and Colin Dunford Wood had left the squadron. David's dark mood was intensified by the horror of hearing first-hand of conditions inside Belsen Concentration Camp.

We are just ten miles away from Belsen, which was liberated some weeks ago.

German Reichsbank 20,000 Mark banknotes. *(Family Collection)*

When the wind blows in this direction, you can just about smell the place. Several people went up to see if they can do anything to help and came back looking very pale. They said that the conditions are just too awful for words. The old camp has been burnt but about 20,000 inmates are sleeping in the guard's barracks. We hope the guards will not escape justice as they have lists of them all.

After his visit, Wing Commander Bill Malins wrote, 'Seeing the horror of the camp for the first time turned my stomach, but it justified every single day that I had spent fighting the war.'[1]

Judged on how many hours his pilots flew, the C/O, Richard Mitchell, a regular in the RAF, was naturally keen for them to fly as often as possible. However David, who had by now flown about 800 hours, felt that any pilot who did not want to make flying his career, should not be asked to further risk his life and this resulted in his reluctance to follow orders.

A paper Nazi flag. *(Family Collection)*

David was on leave in The Hague when this photo of No.2 Squadron was taken. *(Family Collection – Crown © 1945)*

We are all browned off and while the C/O is eagerly trying to get pilots into the air, I am doing everything in my power to keep them on the ground. Things are getting blacker now that the war is over. They no longer need to bribe us into the air so they have taken them away. Life is absolutely awful now that they have taken away our cars too; poor Harry is heartbroken. All further leave has been cancelled and we are isolated in one of the ugliest parts of Germany one could possibly find. And of course, as there is no fraternisation, we have no company. I am therefore taking the opportunity to start a correspondent course in Forestry, Agriculture and Botany and I bought a rather good microscope the other day and it should prove most useful.

Trevor Mitchell wrote to commiserate.

Life must be absolutely bloody now they have taken the cars away. One didn't realize it at the time but it was really all there was to do. Poor Harry must be like a fish out of water. Were the cars given to the Dutch civilians? I went to the S.M.O[2] about my back, which I wanted to get fixed up as it was by then very painful. This is the end of my third week in hospital at Weston near Blackpool!!! I spent fourteen days flat on my back then they put me in plaster from neck to hips so I can hardly do a thing for myself. As you've probably heard, a lot of redundant aircrew are being transferred into A&SD Duties[3] which I must try and avoid at all costs. A job like Guy's[4] would suit me fine. Ferrying abroad from this country. He's left Leics now and has gone to Filton near Bristol. He's been putting up innumerable blacks of late.' [5]

Yours, Trevor

When re-construction on the runway at Celle was started, all three squadron's aircraft flew to B150 Hustedt, seven miles north, and pilots were driven there daily. A full dress rehearsal was arranged before a Group Fly-past over Copenhagen and several aircraft, David's included, set off, but when the weather deteriorated they were ordered back to base. The next day, as the weather did not improve, it was cancelled. To keep everyone busy it was decided to have a salvage day at Celle. Everybody lent a hand to clear out all the cellars and attics of the buildings, as well as the piles of rubbish and wrecked German aircraft that were scattered all over the airfield.

In July, David's spirits were lifted with the news that the squadron was to fly to RAF Warmwell for armament practise. Twelve aircraft set off for England, but owing to bad weather, David and nine others only reached Osnabruck before being forced to return.

July 7. Our second attempt to fly home went well. We flew from Celle and landed at Gilze-Rijen, then on to Dunkirk and over the channel. After landing at Manston to refuel we flew over Dorset to Warmwell, bringing back memories of time spent there in 1941.

For the next ten days, David and the squadron practised air-to-ground and air-to-air firing. On the last air-to-ground shoot, David's guns failed to fire and his Spitfire was logged as u/s.

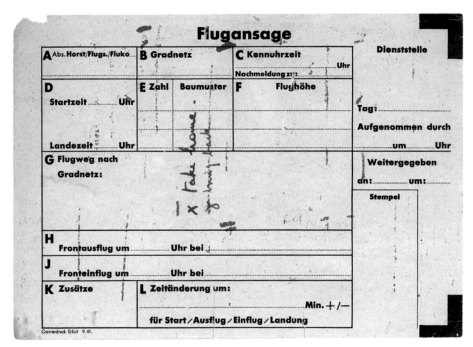

Paper was in short supply so David wrote letters home on the back of Luftwaffe flight forms. *(Family Collection)*

After a dance held in Dorchester on the 19th, which all the squadron pilots attended, nineteen aircraft flew back to Germany, however, as David's Spitfire was still being repaired, he remained behind.

> I flew to RAF Market Harborough in the Master with W/O Spears. Mother picked me up from the airfield as Father is still very unwell. It is clear that he cannot cope with the overload of work at the office so I will apply for a compassionate posting and am hopeful that it will be granted.

While at home, a letter arrived from Anson Howard[6] who was in England. 'I'm kicking myself for not looking you up a month ago. I thought of doing so but wasn't certain. If I had, we would have been able to meet. As it is, I'm afraid I'm off again to distant countries in the near future. I came home for 61 days leave which is very near its end now…. If you ever come out, I'll be in the 12th Mounted Battery or 32nd Mountain Regiment. I know it's doubtful our paths will ever meet but they might do.'

News also arrived from George Hindmarsh[7] giving David hope of early demobilization. 'They have found me a job at last. I'm assistant to the assistant adjutant and he knows as much about the job as I do as he's been on the job two days longer! Maybe things will be a bit better in Germany now that some of the restrictions have been lifted, it is to be hoped so. I've been enquiring about demobilization. I'm told that GD officers will be out in September so it looks a bit more hopeful.'

Things moved very quickly with David's application and on Monday, 30 July, he was ordered to report to 84's Group Disbandment Centre for an interview. David

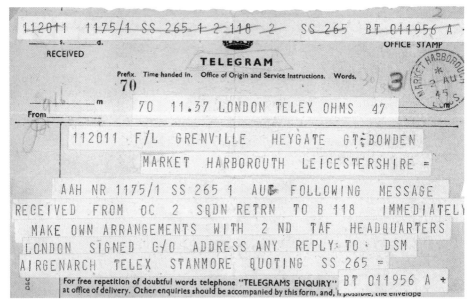

Squadron Leader Mitchell ordered David to return to Germany immediately. *(Family Collection)*

flew up to Worthy Down and Lasham and met with one of his oldest RAF friends, Donald Draper,[8] who informed him that he was owed two weeks active service extension of leave. However, this news was not conveyed to the squadron and David received a curt telegram from Squadron Leader Mitchell ordering him to report back immediately. After telegraphing that he would return on August 13, David set to work in his father's office.

> Everything is in such a state. At 71 and in failing health father is unable to manage the work on his own. I've visited Kelmarsh, Sulby Hall and seen Major Paget. Today I drove up to the airfield to get petrol then took Father to watch a Leicester v Northampton county cricket match. There was a terrific thunderstorm at midday, which stopped play for a while but eventually play was resumed and Northants won.

Early on August 6, an American B-29 plane dropped the first atomic bomb over Hiroshima. The blast levelled almost everything within a two-mile radius; 70,000 people were killed and 80,000 wounded. Three days later, a second atomic bomb was dropped over Nagasaki; up to 80,000 people were killed. In the face of such vast destruction the Japanese Generals finally accepted defeat was inevitable.

Unable to put off his return to Germany any longer, David flew back to Hustedt and on August 15, (Aug 14 in USA) Emperor Hirohito in a recorded radio address surrendered unconditionally. The squadron was stood down and two days' holiday was declared. A week later, David took up Spitfire 'K for King' for a thirty minutes flight over Celle, and on landing received the news he had been eagerly awaiting.

David with his Spitfire. *(Family Collection)*

August 22 1945. My posting to 84 G.D.C. just came through. Bloody fantastic!

As David was flown home, No.2 Squadron received the tragic news that Flight Lieuenant Tony Krakowski had been involved in a car crash. John Packwood wrote 'It was very bad luck. He was a passenger in a car driven by one of his Polish friends in Hanover. They hit a stationary lorry and Tony was killed. They had his funeral here – I've never seen so many Polish women before in my life.'[9] The whole squadron attended his funeral which was held at the airfield on the 29th and Krakowski was buried at the Military Cemetery at Celle.[10]

Emperor Hirohito officially signed the Japanese surrender and two days later David was posted to HQ Fighter Command, but moved straight on to No.19 Squadron based at RAF Molesworth.

John Packwood wrote that things were changing rapidly within the Wing with some pilots from No.4 Squadron transferring to No.2 Squadron.

Celle. Some people do really stick their necks out. I haven't flown at all since you left…. I had a cold which kept me off flying – and just as that was getting better a mosquito had the audacity to take an enormous bite at my face. It swelled up to a large size and I couldn't get my oxygen mask on. Unfortunately, it's all right now so I'm afraid I'll have to fly tomorrow – unless of course another mosquito does the decent thing. They are getting very cheeky now – taking their revenge on me for the slaughter you inflicted on them…. Tommy Rayner is being recalled from his indefinite leave to do a job which I think will rather suit him. He's got to conduct MPs and such people round the Malcolm Clubs. I can just imagine the s…t he'll shoot. Mitchell is away on leave, which makes things a bit easier. By the time he comes back I should be almost ready to go on mine – which suits me very well.

Best Wishes, Lefty

Another letter arrived from Barney Gilliland suggesting that they meet Tony Davis[11] at Oddenino's.... 'Getting your letter was grand. When I received it, I rang your home but unfortunately you had left.... I wrote to you from the camp and once again since returning to the Air Ministry.... I rang Mike's[12] home in Dublin and his mother told me the very sad news. That was for me the saddest of them all.'

Meeting Gilliland the next day, David heard of his escape from the POW camp.

After being shot down Gillie was put in an Italian POW camp, however as the Italians became more pro-Allied, he took advantage of this goodwill. Deciding that it was a perfect time to escape, he dressed in civilian clothes and walked into the nearest town where everyone was so friendly that he went to the hotel to have a drink. Sitting down he ordered some wine. Suddenly, in came a German officer who looked at him carefully and then said, 'Fancy meeting you Gillie!' Gilliland couldn't believe his bad luck. This Officer was a former Hitler Youth who had visited Northern Ireland as an eighteen year-old before the war and the only German he had ever met. 'We will have a drink after the war is over,' the Officer said, 'but now you are coming back to prison.'

David was posted to RAF Market Harborough, but by the middle of October he was still in uniform.

I'm feeling fed up with everything now. I have just heard from Trevor that Ted Holbech[13] was killed in a car crash. He and his brother were being driven by a friend and in a case of sheer bad driving the car came off the road and did two or three somersaults. Ted was thrown out and killed instantly, his brother was badly hurt but OK and the incredible thing is that the driver escaped without even a bruise or scratch. Trevor also said that Guy Brown[14] has died in hospital in Cairo but didn't know any further details.

Invited to London to receive his DFC, David set about the task of finding his parents a hotel room, which were at a premium in London. He eventually found a space at Brown's Hotel in Dover Street, although they regretfully wrote explaining that they could not guarantee a supply of bath-towels.

We went to Buckingham Palace to pick up my medal from the King. It was all very emotional and I desperately wished that Charles could have been there with us and received his at the same time.

In November, a disgruntled John Packwood wrote to David:

David took his parents to Buckingham Palace to see him receive his DFC from the King. (*Family Collection*)

Germany. Mitchell was rather annoyed when I got back but otherwise everything was the same as before. They've got a training chart out for each pilot – with all the stuff we did at OTU. The Squadron's supposed to do something like 240 hours a month all through the winter…. It doesn't look as though I shall be here much longer now, everyone here is certain Group 26 will be out by Christmas. I certainly won't be sorry…. Life is very dull, thank god I'm not here that often.
Best wishes, Lefty.

Fortunately, David did not have to wait until Christmas.

22 November 1945. My Last day in uniform! I took the train up to get my official release from the RAF. I have been looking forward to this day for so many years. But for now I feel as if I have lived my whole life already. I had hoped to go back to Cambridge to finish my studies but sadly Father needs me and I am afraid that I will probably have to forgo that luxury and take over the business before it all falls to pieces and will just have to learn the job as I go.

In December John Packwood was also demobbed.

West Beach, Whitstable, Kent. I had the most frightful trip across by sea of course. I very nearly didn't make it. I was due to leave by lorry at 9.30 on the 8th and round about that time I was hopelessly drunk. If it hadn't been for Bert Mann[15] and Dick Hill[16] I'd never have been able to reach the lorry. The journey was appalling – we finally reached Stapleford Tawney at 3 o'clock on Wednesday morning. They certainly moved then. Uxbridge must be the most efficient station the RAF possesses…. If only I had got a cloth cap I'd have looked a perfect bookmaker's tout. I've written to Oxford to ask the earliest date I can go back there – so far without any reply. If I can, I'll go back there for a while anyway. I'm in no great hurry at the present I'm pursuing a policy of masterly inactivity a well earned rest for the rigours of war! I've been looking forward to this for 6 years. As yet I find it hard to believe, it just seems like ordinary leave. No doubt realization will come with time….
Yours, Lefty.[17]

Looking Forward:
1945–2014

Due to his father's illness, David never returned to University. He took over the family Land Agency business. Although David never flew again, he received news from many friends and arranged several 35 Wing reunions. He sat at the controls of a Spitfire one last time, although its wheels remained firmly on the ground.

David met his wife Daphne, an ex-WAAF, while she was nursing her sister, who had broken her neck in a riding accident. They named their first son Charles, and he carried on the family tradition by becoming a Land Agent. His two daughters inherited David's love of horses and photography. Belinda became a keen rider and Sally-Anne a professional photographer. Their youngest son, Jeremy, was top cadet at Marlborough College and given a flying lesson in a Tiger Moth. While studying at Cambridge he flew with the University Air Squadron, then joined the RAF to fly Harriers.

David died in his eighties without ever learning of his brother Charles's fate.

Charles' body was never recovered.

David sat at the controls of a Spitfire for one last time at a No.16 Squadron reunion. *(Family Collection)*

Notes

Chapter 1: The Munich Crisis & Life as a Cambridge Undergraduate

1. At the Marine Aircraft Experimental Establishment the RAF High Speed Flight were testing several seaplanes before the 1927 Schneider Trophy race. The S5 Supermarine won the Trophy and R.J. Mitchell went on to design the iconic Spitfire – Flight Magazine + 'The Schneider Trophy Contest 50th Anniversary.' Edited by David Moldon.
2. Lawrence had been taken a prisoner in the First World War – 'Special Forces Commander Peter Wand-Tetley,' by Michael Scott.
3. Robert Rolt joined the RE in 1940, served in the Middle East and died in 2001. Henry Reginald Butcher joined the RE and was killed in Libya on 29/10/42.
4. Robert Richard Branford joined the Lincoln Regiment in 1939 and the Gurkhas in 1941. He became a Major in South-East Asia Command and died in August 1949 – Marlborough Register.
5. Marlborough College Register.
6. Britannia Historical Documents.
7. Moulton spent the summer working at the Sentinel Steam Waggon Works, Shrewsbury, which produced steam-powered lorries and trains. During the war he worked for the Bristol Aeroplane Company which made both Beaufighter and Blenheim aircraft in the Engine Research Department. Later Alex Moulton worked in the family rubber company as technical director, established a research department and designed the Moulton Bicycle and suspension system for the Mini. He died in 2012 age 92 – The Spaceframe Moultons' Tony Hadlan.
8. Archbishop Cosmo Lang played a role in forcing King Edward VIII to abdicate.
9. The Greatest Squadron of Them All – Ross, Blanche, Simpson + CWGC.
10. Wand-Tetley MC spent fourteen months behind enemy lines. When a rescue submarine stuck on a sandbank, Wand-Tetley swam out and salvaged a jar of rum, before blowing it up. He served in Singapore and Java, and worked in the Colonial Administrative Service as a district officer in Nigeria. He also worked in Kenya, Tanzania and the Seychelles; he retired to Wiltshire and died in 2003 age 83 – 'Special Forces Commander,' Michael Scott + Telegraph Obituary 22/5/03.
11. Gilbert Monckton was the son of Viscount Monckton who was chief legal advisor to King Edward VIII during his Abdication.
12. John Willet Reid joined the IXth Lancers and fought at El Alamein and Italy. Leaving the Army in 1961, he farmed in Yorkshire. – Steven Reid + specialforcesroh.com.
13. Anthony Nutting studied Agriculture at Trinity, joined the Leicestershire Yeomanry in 1939, but after a steeplechase injury was invalided out in 1940. He worked at the British Embassy in Paris, then in the Madrid embassy organizing escape routes for Allied servicemen. After the war Nutting became an MP, wrote several books and was a consultant for the film 'Lawrence of Arabia.' He died age 79 – New York Times 26/02/99 + Independent Obituary 03/03/99.

Chapter 2: A Sapper on a Searchlight

1. No.23 and No.213 Squadrons were based at Wittering – 'Squadrons of the RAF,' James Halley.
2. U.S. Department of State, Publication 1983, Peace and War: United States Foreign Policy, 1931–1941.
3. Ronald James Casemore became a Flt/Lt in the Meteorological Branch – London Gazette
4. Neville Ussher's notes 1996 – Christopher Ussher.
5. Peter Cruden became a captain with No.2 Troop of No.6 Commando – Julia Cruden + 6commando.com + pegasusarchive.org

6. Neville Ussher's notes 1996 – Christopher Ussher.
7. Gilbert Monckton's Obituary – The Telegraph 01/7/06.
8. For his actions Monckton received the MC – Telegraph Obituary 01/7/06.
9. 'A Wartime Log,' by Andrew Craig Harvey.
10. For his actions Peter Storie-Pugh received the MC – Telegraph Obituary 30/12/11.
11. After several moves Neville Ussher arrived at Spanenberg Oflag IX and was repatriated in October 1943 – Neville Ussher's notes. 1996 – Christopher Ussher.
12. 'A Wartime Log,' by Andrew Craig Harvey.
13. 'Life's too Short to Cry,' by Tim Vigors.

Chapter 3: Officer Training Sandhurst & Army Officer Portsmouth
1. Neil Soutar became Intelligence Officer and Adjutant of the 2nd Battalion Northamptonshire Regiment serving in Madagascar, India, the Middle East, Sicily and Italy – 'Round Half the World in Eighty Months' by Neil Soutar.
2. Firbank won an MC during the Landings at Taranto, Italy with the 1st Airborne Division and took part in 'Operation Market Garden' – 'I Bought a Star' by Thomas Firbank + The Telegraph Obituary 30/01/01
3. The Blue Pool Lido – An open-air swimming pool in Camberley.
4. 'Life's Too Short to Cry,' by Tim Vigors.
5. Chota pegs – A small measure of spirit.
6. ITW RAF Paignton.
7. The Guards Colonel, three majors and two junior officers were killed, but 694 survivors were rescued by the escort ships HMS Wolverine and HMS Stork – 'History of the Irish Guards in the Second World War,' by Major DJL Fitzgerald + Service Histories of Royal Navy Warships in WWII by Lieutenant Commander Geoffrey B Mason, Naval-History.Net.
8. Douglas Frank Kitchener Edghill DFC worked for David's father until 1935. He flew with No.229 Squadron in Egypt and shot down seven aircraft. On 7/9/41 he crash-landed and fractured his spine and due to crippling injuries resigned his commission in 1942 and died in 1962.
9. 'I bought a Star,' by Thomas Firbank.
10. Brodie Knight gained the rank of Captain in the Welsh Guards. William Archibald Ottley Juxon Bell was posted to North Africa and Italy and became 'the most popular man in his regiment while in charge of the mules which brought up the daily rum ration' – Times Obituary 14/4/05. Robert Roy Etherton joined the Grenadier Guards and won the MC in January 1945. While fighting in a minefield under heavy anti-tank and artillery fire he walked 'on foot through the minefield to see what further support he could supply the Infantry' – London Gazette.
11. 'Biggin on the Bump,' by Bob Ogley.
12. 'Invasion 1940,' by Peter Fleming.
13. Lieutenant Colonel Firbank retired from the Army in 1948, worked for Perkins Diesel in Indonesia, China and Japan. Returning to Wales in 1984, he wrote articles on conservation and guides of Snowdonia. He died in 2001 age 90 – The Telegraph Obituary 30/01/01 + 'I bought a Star,' by Thomas Firbank.
14. Robert Edward Vane De Lautour joined the Grenadier Guards then transferred to Special Forces – 22nd Independent Parachute Company, The Pathfinders – 'Walking D-Day' By Paul Reed + www.canadaatwar.ca + Airborne Forces Museum + www.pegasusarchive.org.
15. 'Battle over Portsmouth' by Paul Jenkins.
16. Lieutenant Richard Ernest Arnold served with the Royal Field Artillery between 1918–1920. In 1941 he was a Pilot Officer in A&SD Branch – London Gazette.
17. Eluned Rosemary Gwenlfian Maria Gordon Brooke Boone.
18. James Byce Joll wrote several books, lectured at Oxford and LSE and died in 1994 – The New York Times + The Independent Obituary 18/7/94.
19. 'Battle over Portsmouth,' by Paul Jenkins + www.raf.mod.uk.

20. After a dogfight over Andover, Paul Baillon bailed out on October 27 when his No.609 Spitfire's oil tank was hit. This aircraft was excavated in 2013 by 'Operation Nightingale,' a Ministry of Defence project + 'Fighter Command Losses' by Norman Franks.
21. BBC News 15/11/40.
22. David Muffett's Obituary – Daily Telegraph 13/10/07 + The Worcester News
23. Peter Storie-Pugh's Obituary – Daily Mail 29/10/11.
24. John Richard Martin.
25. Around 50 bombs were dropped and four 250 Kg bombs fell on Cosham – 'Battle over Portsmouth' by Paul Jenkins.
26. Pilot Officer Hugo James Ross Barker was at Eton and Oxford and joined the RAFVR. On 25/11/40 his Oxford crashed when taking off at night and he was killed – Christ Church Oxford Records + The Times 28/11/40 + CWGC.

Chapter 4: The Blitz Portsmouth and Tyneham
1. A month later on 28/12/40 his elder brother Flight Lieutenant Mark Baillon was also killed when his No.42 Squadron Beaufort crashed while attacking a tanker near Trondheim – 'Coastal Command Losses 1939–41' by Ross McNeill + CWGC + (WR) Squadron Association + Petr Kacha -www.luftwaffe.cz/wick
2. Richard's brothers Andrew went to Malta with No.148 Squadron and Peter served with the RNVR – Peter George Osborn, 1914 -1999 Papers, Barr Smith Library, Adelaide University.
3. Provost Howard – BBC Broadcast + Church Times 07/11/07.
4. Peter Urban Doyne Vigors was at Marlborough with David and joined the RNVR in 1939.
5. Tim Vigors DFC Citation. In January 1941 Vigors was posted to Singapore as flight commander of 'A' flight No.243 Squadron – London Gazette 1/10/40 + 'Life's too Short to Cry,' by Tim Vigors.
6. In two raids lasting from around 6pm to 10pm and 12pm to 2am, over 150 German bombers dropped between 20,000 and 40,000 incendiary bombs. Over 2,000 fires were started, 171 people were killed and 430 injured – 'Portsmouth At War' by Andrew Whitmarsh (p68) + James Daly, dalyhistory.wordpress.com.
7. In 1943 all residents were ordered to leave for the duration of the war, but the Army kept the area for training and they never returned home.
8. Gerald Walter Robert Templer was in the Royal Irish Fusiliers in WWI then transferred to the Loyals. He won a DSO in Palestine, was an Intelligence Officer at the WO in 1938, with the BEF in 1939 and was commanding the 210th Independent Infantry Brigade in Dorset – King's College London, Liddell Hart Centre for Military Archives.
9. Although David wrote that this was a German invasion barge there is no further evidence to suggest it was.
10. Squadron Leader William Dudley Williams went as an instructor to No.59 OTU and commanded No.615 Squadron in Feni, India and left the RAF in 1945 – 'Aces High' Shores & Williams.
11. No.53 Operations Record Book -NRO + Charles Log Book
12. No.53 Operations Record Book -NRO
13. No.53 Operations Record Book -NRO + Charles Log Book

Chapter 5: RAF Initial Training Wing Cambridge
1. John Earp gained an MA at Ridley Hall Cambridge from 1944–56 – Ridley Hall News 2013-autumn term magazine.
2. 'Eyes Over the Enemy,' by Peter Conant.
3. Wing Commander Roy Pryce Elliott survived the war completing three tours and was with Bomber Command No.1 Group until 1952. He commanded Nottingham University Air Squadron, worked for an air-to-air refuelling company and at BOAC. Elliot died in 2002 age 84 – Elliott's Obituary Telegraph 13/12/01 + PPrune Members, Union Jack, Brian Abraham, Alain Charpentier + Log Book of W/Cdr Roy Elliott + Barry Johnson Milford Trawlers.

4. Lord Trenchard 'The Father of the RAF' gained his pilot's licence in 1912 after two and a half weeks and just one hour four minutes flying. He was General Officer Commanding the RFC and the RAF's first Chief of Air Staff. He founded the University Air Squadron and the Auxiliary Air Force – The Defence Academy of UK MoD + History Learning Site, Chris Trueman + 'Trenchard' by Andrew Boyle.
5. Ian Scott Duffus.
6. Robert Stanley Cranston.
7. Wartime documents used both Bf109 and Me109 designation. David always referred to them as Me109s.
8. p35 'Dual of Eagles,' by Peter Townsend.
9. 'The Crowded Hours,' The Story of SOS Cohen' by Anthony Richardson.
10. Headley Parish Archive + British Pathé News.
11. Thomas Guy Ridpath was killed 17/3/43 at Medenine Ridge, Tunisia and brother Michael Dudley Ridpath on 9/9/1943, while under attack from a tank near Salerno, Italy – Marlborough College Register + The Grenadier Guards Association, Jim MacDonald.
12. London Gazette.
13. Black Vanities was a Revue and the cast included Frances Day, Chesney Allen, and Bud Flanagan – Encyclopaedia of the Musical Theatre by Stanley Green + 'A Patriot after All 1939–1941' by George Orwell

Chapter 6: Elementary Flying Training School Sealand
1. No.4 Course pupils passed out on the 18th. 11 were posted to SFTSs in Canada and 31 in the UK – 19 EFTS ORB, (NRO)
2. 'First Impressions of an E.F.T.S,' by J.R.M – Wingspan Magazine.
3. Pilot Officer John Leonard Skinner was fated to be unlucky. On 01/8/42 his No.107 Squadron Boston was hit by flak and after ditching in sea thirty miles from Felixstowe he was rescued by a No.277 Squadron Walrus. On 23/01/43 after a raid on German rail targets his No.105 Squadron Mosquito was lost in the North Sea – 'Another Kind of Courage' by Norman Franks + CWGC + aviation-safety.network.
4. PBI = Poor Bloody Infantry
5. 'A Dash of Courage,' by Jeremy Greville-Heygate + No.53 Squadron ORB + Schiff 24's Kriegstagebuch (War Diary).
6. A Dash of Courage,' by Jeremy Greville-Heygate.
7. Second Lieutenant William Maurice Clark was killed when his Tiger Moth collided with a Spitfire – 19 EFTS ORB (NRO)
8. Jeremy Greville-Heygate + Public Records Office NRO + Naval Historical Branch MoD.
9. Wriothesley Leege Montaque Denny.
10. 'Life's too Short to Cry,' by Tim Vigors.
11. Edward Brian Bretherton Smith received the DFC for shooting down six enemy aircraft. Smith trained pilots until 1943 then served on the Air Staff during the Italian invasion. Commander of a parachute training school he regularly jumped with his dog. He left the RAF in 1946 and died in 2013 age 98 – Telegraph Obituary 16/10/13 + London Gazette.
12. *The Times* 10/7/41.
13. 19 EFTS ORB Sealand (NRO).
14. In June 42, Lawrence Edwin Arthur Holt-Kentwell MBE became an observer, then in 1942 he returned to Army Duties, serving in the medical services of the RASC in North Africa and Italy. Joining the Foreign Service after the war he worked in Cairo, the Colonial Service in Uganda, was director of social welfare in Hong Kong and became assistant director of social welfare in Cumbria and died in 2012 age 97 – King's College, Cambridge Annual Report Obituary 2013 + Oxford Mail Obituary 6/9/12.
15. George Stanley Pennington Robinson was unsuccessful in transferring and remained with the Loyals until the end of the war – London Gazette.
16. 19 EFTS ORB Sealand (NRO).

Chapter 7: SFTS RAF Tern Hill flying Masters

1. Count Franz Ferdinand Colloredo-Mansfeld DFC was born in Rome and lived in Vienna before moving to the USA. Posted to No.611 Squadron, he became C/O No.132 Squadron and shot down at least three enemy aircraft. On 11/01/44 he was killed when his Spitfire was shot down near St. Pol – 'Fighter Command Losses' Vol 3 by Norman Franks + CWIC + Dennis Burke + jossleclercq + Stephilius blog + www.vord.net + en.valka.cz.
2. 5FSTF Tern Hill ORB Apendix-1 -NRO
3. Adolf Galland's final tally of victories was 104. He survived the war and died in 1996 age 83 – Steve Brew – Andy Ingham – Josleclercq + 'Adolf Galland,' by David Baker.
4. 'Fighter Pilot – The First American Ace,' by William R Dunn.
5. On August 9, Douglas Bader bailed out over France, minus one of his metal legs. Eric Lock the most successful pilot during the Battle of Britain was last seen attacking soldiers near Pas-de-Calais – The Times Newspaper 13/8/41.
6. Walter Harding won the DFC with No.105 Squadron – oldhaltonians.co.uk.
7. 'Fokker D.XXI Aces of World War 2' By Kari Stenman + www.monument.apeldoorn-onderwijs.nl.
8. jossleclercq + Bertrand H + «aviateurs de la Liberté» + Jacques Ghémard www.francaislibres.net.
9. jossleclercq + POW questionnaire WO344/95/ -NRO.
10. Flight Lieutenant Richard Brian Lord.
11. SE = single engine.
12. Wray Eller and Dennis Evers.
13. No.5 FSTS ORB -NRO + Thomas Thorne.
14. 'Jan Plesman. A Flying Dutchman,' by Albert Plesman.
15. Cecil Douglas Lovett Turner – David's uncle with the Royal Indian Army Service Corps.
16. No.5 SFTS ORB -NRO
17. No.5 SFTS ORB -NRO
18. Peter Storie-Pugh Obituary – The Telegraph 3/12/11 + 'Colditz, the German Story,' by Reinhold Eggers + 'The Colditz Story,' by Pat R. Reid.
19. James Allan 'Jim' Mollison set a record time of eight days nineteen hours flying from Australia to England. Mollison served in the Air Transport Auxiliary.
20. AO = Army Officers.
21. Charles Barton.
22. George Hugh Emmett.
23. Ralph Denis Mark Evers DFC joined No.500 Squadron. On 6/10/42 while in North Africa his Baltimore crash-landed in the desert. He hid under its wing until rescued by South African AFVs. He died in 2007 age 94 – Henk Welting + 'Volume One of Bomber Losses in the Middle East and Mediterranean,' by David Gunby and Pelham Temple.
24. ITC = Infantry Training Centre.
25. Richard Allenby www.yorkshire-aircraft.co.uk. + 5 SFTS ORB – NRO
26. Arthur Toyne DFC flew patrols over Holland and Belgium, shot down two enemy aircraft and damaged a third – Flight Magazine 20/6/40.

Chapter 8: Flying Hurricanes at Childs Ercall

1. 'Hurricane,' By Leo McKinstry.
2. Pilot Officer Claude Foster.
3. The Hurricane undercarriage lever was on the right and as inexperienced pilots changed hands to retract the wheels the nose would often drop – 'A Soldier in the Cockpit,' by Ron Pottinger.
4. Peter Arnold Biggart became a Captain in the 113 Light Anti-Aircraft Regiment RA which took part in the Normandy landings, crossed France, Belgium and the River Rhine. Biggart was awarded the Belgium Chevalier of the Order of Leopold II with Palm and Croix de Guerre 1940 with Palm in 1945 – NRO + Durham Record Office + London Gazette.
5. Robert John Heugh Drummond was posted to No.152 Squadron and killed on 24/4/43 in Tunisia – CWGC

6. In 1952 Humphrey Lestocq Gilbert played Flight Lieutenant Batchy Salter in the film 'Angels One Five' and Flying Officer Kyte in the radio show 'Much Binding In The Marsh.' He had a varied TV career, grew a magnificent moustache and as a member of the Handlebar Club opened the Brighton branch of the RAF Association's Flying Services Club. He died in 1984 aged 65 – 609 Squadron ORB (NRO) + 609 (WR) Squadron Association + Sussex Daily News + 609wrsquadron.co.uk/Archives + IMDb.com, Inc

7. No.5 SFTS ORB (NRO).

8. No.5 SFTS ORB (NRO).

9. Eric Marrs was killed and Sergeant Jimmy Short became a PoW.

10. Lieutenant Colonel Joseph Geoffrey Einem Hickson was Staff Captain L of C Troops, British Troops in Palestine in July 1936. He worked as British Resident in West Germany 1945–1951 and retired from the army in 1947 – London Gazette + Imperial War Museum. After the war David Muffett worked in the Colonial Service in Nigeria. While there he arrested a tribal chief who had eaten the local tax collector. Muffett held a lifelong soft spot for fishermen and continued to be noisy. Once when a large snake was discovered at the officers' club everyone except Muffett exited the room; after a great deal of noise they found him throwing armchairs at it. He died in 2007 aged 88 – Telegraph Obituary 13/10/07 + Louise Zbozny (Muffett's daughter).

11. 5SFTS ORB (NRO).

12. Flight Sergeant Garware's Spitfire suffered engine failure on 22/12/43 and attempting to land in a field was seriously injured and died twenty-four hours later. It is possible that this Spitfire was an aircraft contributed by Indian funds – Jagan Pillarisetti + The Illustrated Weekly of India + Library of Congress + Wallace Shackleton, 58 Operational Training Unit Roll of Honour + CWGC.

13. 5SFTS ORB (NRO).

14. Richard Bentley Osborn was awarded the DFC in November 1941. His brother Peter gained a commission in the RNVR and was on the new destroyer, HMS Calpe. – London Gazette 18/11/41

Chapter 9: Lysanders Operational Training Unit Old Sarum

1. Andrew Francis Atterbury Osborn won the DFC on 25/2/41 flying with No.148 Squadron in Malta. After attacking Catania aerodrome he flew 140 miles before crashing into the sea near a ship and supported an injured crewmember until rescued – The Times 28/7/1943 + London Gazette.

2. In the summer of 1942 Craig-Harvey moved to Oflag VIB, Eichstatt Germany. John Peyton read law at Trinity Oxford, was commissioned into the Supplementary Reserve of 15/19 Hussars and captured in 1940. In 1946 worked for Walter Monckton in India. He was an MP in Margaret Thatcher's Shadow Cabinet – 'Without Benefit of Laundry' by John Peyton.

3. Douglas Sampson's Letter.

4. Wing Commander Eric Lawson Fuller served in The Royal Flying Corps in WW1. Then worked for a German oil company feeding back intelligence on the industrial Ruhr region. Fuller was posted to Bomber Command's Photo Intelligence Unit, then No3.Photo Recce Unit and Medmenham in 1941. In 1943 he was posted to the Allied Northwest African Photographic Recce Wing as Colonel Roosevelt's deputy. Mentioned in despatches he was awarded the American Legion of Merit – 'Operation Crossbow' by Allan Williams Michael.

5. Michael George Ridley Harvey and John George Campbell Jameson.

6. Tim Vigors' Obituary – The Telegraph 19/11/03 + 'Life's too Short to Cry,' by Tim Vigors.

7. 'Life's too Short to Cry,' by Tim Vigors + 'Bloody Shambles' by Shores, Cull & Izawa.

8. Wing Commander Tim Vigors commanded RAF Yelahanka, returning to England in 1945 and retiring from the RAF in 1946. Vigors set up a bloodstock agency, a private aircraft firm and a stud farm. He married four times and died in 2003 aged 82 – The Times + Independent + Telegraph Obituaries + www.awm.gov.au.

9. No.41 OTU ORB (NRO).

10. Vivienne Lee married Davidson-Griffiths in Liverpool on 23/1/43.

11. CWGC + 'Friesland Wartime History' by Willem de Jong.
12. No.13 OTU.
13. Elias Alexander Phillips was posted to No.149 Squadron and killed 08/06/42 – CWGC
14. 'Aviateurs de la Liberté,' Henri Lafont + jossleclercq

Chapter 10: RAF Weston Zoyland with No.16 Squadron
1. Fairey Battles were used for bombing in conjunction with the local army battle schools.
2. Alastair Mowat Maclay farmed at Castle Douglas, Kirkcudbrightshire, gained his flying licence at the Renfrew Flying Club. In a reserved occupation he was not accepted for pilot training until December 1940 on his fourth application – Old Llorettonians Roll of Honour.
3. Anthony Norman Davis.
4. In Dennys Scott's Regiment 137 died while in Japanese hands. Scott survived and wrote to David after the war, 'I spent 3½ most unpleasant years with the Japs as our hosts in Siam.' – Dennys Scott letter + Ron Taylor, www.far-eastern-heroes.org.uk.
5. 'The Hinge of Fate,' Winston Churchill.
6. No.53 Squadron were based at North Coates.
7. William Malins won the DFC on a recce in Belgium 6/08/40 when under heavy fire 'He descended to 50 feet to ascertain the nationality of the hostile troops.' – Hans Houterman – www.unithistories.com + London Gazette +'Coming into Land,' Memoirs of Bill Malins edited by Chris Newton p79. + Richard Allenby – www.yorkshire-aircraft.co.uk.
8. Douglas Sampson's letter.
9. Patrick Furse, son of Sir Ralph Furse (one of Churchill's private secretaries) read Classics at Balliol,' but the bohemian streak got the better of him and he threw his books out of the college window and set off to London to become an artist.' He joined the Rifle Brigade before becoming an ALO – *The Times* 17/9/05 + Guardian 1/9/05 Obituaries +Pat Furse letter.
10. 'Adjidaumo' Tail in Air, History of No.268 Squadron, by Colin Ford.
11. Ross McNeil + No.247 ORB – NRO + CWGC.
12. 'For Your Tomorrow' by E Marty + aucklandmuseum.com + Errol Martyn + Ian Macdonald + CWGC.
13. Peter Langloh Donkin flew with No.16 Squadron and was No.4 Squadron's C/O. On 13/4/44, as C/O of No.35 Wing he ditched off the Belgian coast and having been briefed on the invasion plans, great effort was put into finding him, he was rescued six days later – 'Fighter Command losses Vol. 3' by Norman F Franks + Michael Ryan www.rafjever.org.
14. Edward Wigg later joined the SOE – NRA + The Most Secret List of SOE Agents by Eliah Meyer.
15. 'We Landed by Moonlight,' by Hugh Verity.
16. Peter Vaughan-Fowler was awarded the DFC and Bar, the DSO, AFC, CVO, Croix de Guerre and Palm and Chevalier of the Legion d'Honneur. Part of an aviation dynasty, his father Ivor Guy Vaughan-Fowler flew in WW1 and won the Air Force Cross in 1918. Peter's brother Denis George Vaughan-Fowler with No.41 Squadron was killed in a night flying accident on 07/08/31 – 'We Landed by Moonlight,' by Hugh Verity + Flight Magazine Archives + Commonwealth War Graves Commission + Independent Obituary 4/6/94 + ww2awards.
17. Flight Lieutenant Dr John Edward Sharpley.
18. Richard Allenby + No.4 Squadron diary – NRO – rafjever.org.
19. 'Incident at Imber,' Denis C Bateman. After the Battle Magazine Issue 49 + 'Fighter Command Losses Vol 2' by N Franks.
20. London Gazette 2/12/1918 p14215 + CWGC.
21. Douglas Sampson letter.
22. CWGC + 'Fighter Command Losses' Vol 2 by Norman Franks.
23. Douglas Sampson's letter.
24. Colonel Roy Stanley – Operation Crossbow,' BBC programme first aired 15/5/11.
25. Anthony Patrick Mahon worked at Bletchley Park from 1941 to 1945 and was Head of Hut 8 in 1945 when he wrote 'The History of Hut Eight,' which was not released until 1996 – Roll of Honour Bletchley Park – bletchleypark.org.uk + Graham Ellsbury + NRO.

26. At this time the job of FDO was not open to WRNS – Navigating and Direction Officers' Association + Tony Drury – Royal Navy Research archive Org.

27. Edward O'Farrell was shot down and a POW at Stalag Luft 3 – Ross McNeill RAF Commands Air Force POW Index.

28. J.J. Davies Interview.

29. J.J. Davies Interview.

30. 'History of No.16 Squadron' written 1969 at Laarbruch by Flt/Lt J.A.A. Dobbie.

31. John Conrad Devey.

32. Ronald Arthur Duce was seriously wounded at Dunkirk and transferred to the RAF at the same time as David – St Laurence Church Upminster Memorial Plaque + find a grave .com + Henk Welting.

33. Bowler hat – slang for sack. Pilots could be awarded a bowler hat if they didn't measure up to requirements. On 18/4/42 George Hugh Cavendish Emmett relinquished his commission due to ill-health – The London Gazette

34. Viscount Acheson C/O of No.613 Auxiliary Air Force worked with an Army Co-operation Squadron at RAF Twinwood Farm – 'The Squadrons of the Royal Air Force,' by James J. Halle + Michael Bowyer & John D.R. Rawlings 'Squadron Codes' 1937–56.

35. Every effort was made to provide the training crews with at least an experienced pilot but forty-nine aircraft out of the 208 provided by No.91 Group would take-off with pupil pilots.' The exact number of aircraft that bombed Cologne is uncertain. 'The Official History says 898 aircraft bombed but Bomber Command's Night Bombing Sheets indicate that 868 aircraft bombed the main target with 15 aircraft bombing other targets.' – 'The Thousand Bomber Raids' – www.raf.mod.uk – Crown copyright 13/6/13.

Chapter 11: In the Orchard Weston Zoyland

1. 'Men of the RAF,' by Sir William Rothenstein.

2. Govert Steen was posthumously awarded a second Dutch Flying Cross – STIWOT – www.ww2awards.com.

3. Peter Stansfeld interview.

4. No.2 Squadron pilot Flying Officer Graham Callaghan Brickwood, shot down at low level also survived with his Mustang dismantled in similar fashion.

5. Jimmy Taylor 16 Squadron Newsbrief 26 + Douglas Sampson letter + Peter Stansfeld interview.

6. History of No.16 Squadron March 1969 by Flt/Lt J.A.A. Dobbie.

7. History of No.16 Squadron March 1969 by Flt/Lt J.A.A. Dobbie.

8. Meyer was head of Millfield School.

9. Later No.16 Squadron pilot Alan Louden Pearsall, a pre-war first class Australian cricketer played for the United Services against Sussex.

10. During WW1 Major General Colin Arthur Jardine was wounded three times, mentioned in despatches four times and awarded the M.C. In 1941 he was Deputy Governor of Gibraltar – Charles Mosley, Burke's Peerage and Baronetage, 107th edition.

11. Figures by Major General Thompson – BBC History website + Battle over Dieppe by Petr Kacha -www.Luftwaffe.cz.

12. Daily Express 27/7/42.

13. 'Warfare Today,' Oldham's Press edited by Admiral Sir Reginald Bacon.

14. Charles Walter Bewick Hack was posted to No.54 Squadron in Australia shortly after this meeting. He emigrated to Australia in 1954 and worked at Pagewood Film Studios on films and documentaries. Hack was President of the Spitfire Association and Life Vice President of the RAAFA and died aged 88 in 2008 – Robert Hamilton, Spitfire Association.

15. 'Focke-Wulfs Fw190 Aces of the Western Front,' by John Weal + Pembrey Airport Ltd.

16. History of No.16 Squadron March 1969 by Flt/Lt J.A.A. Dobbie.

17. Gilliland was nicknamed Gillie or Barney – Douglas Sampson Letter.

18. Douglas Sampson Letter.

19. www.raf.mod.uk/history + 'Past Tense: Charlie's Story' By Charlie Hobb.

Chapter 12: On Operations Middle Wallop and Exeter

1. On 18/9/44 William John Griffiths' No.307 Squadron Mosquito was hit by Flying Officer Stanisław Madej and Gąsecki's aircraft; both were killed, however Flight Lieutenant Griffiths and Flight Lieutenant Lane survived. Griffiths left the RAF in 1947 – CWGC + ANS #72680 aviation-safety.net

2. Peter William Jarrett's Wellington was hit by flak on its way to Nuremberg; on crashing, their bombs exploded killing all the crew – *The Times* 22/10/42 + Polish Squadrons Remembered + aviation safety .network.

3. ATS = Auxiliary Territorial Service.

4. History of No.16 Squadron written at Laarbruch March 1969 by Flt/Lt J.A.A. Dobbie.

5. 'Spit and Sawdust' by George Hassall Nelson-Edwards.

6. Eric Chegwin.

7. Stanley James Wrinch gained his aviator's certificate at Ipswich Aero Club on 4/7/39 – Flight Magazine archive. On 16/7/42 a No.105 Mosquito flown by Paul Addinselli with observer John William Guy Paget attacked the shipyard at Wilhelmshaven. They were shot down by anti-aircraft fire and taken POWs – ANS #70927 aviation-safety.net + de Havilland production list.

8. Film C. 2027/I Anerk: Nr.112 Supplemental Claims from Films & Lists: O.K.L. Fighter Claims Reich & Western Front 1942 – Tony Wood.

9. 'Czechs in RAF Squadrons' by Zdenek Hurt.

10. www.navalhistory.net.

11. Commissioned in 1936 Squadron Leader Currie worked with Army Co-op with No. 208 in Egypt and wrote 'Operations in Western Desert and Crete 1941.' He took over 16 Squadron from Squadron Leader Pallot – 16 ORB + Combat Report NR AIR/50/8 + Tony Wood's Combat Claims & Casualties Lists + Jim Perry.

12. London Gazette 18/9/42.

13. No.460 Squadron flying the Avro Lancaster.

14. On the night of 27/28th 1942 Andrew Osborn's No.75 Squadron Wellington crashed at Melsungen killing all crew members – 'Royal Air Force Bomber Command Losses 1942' by W.R Chorley.

15. ALO for No.16 Squadron. Captain James Hamish Stothard won a Gold medal in 1934 and Silver in 1937 at 800 metres in the World Student Games held in Budapest and Paris respectively – gbrathletics.com + Athletics weekly.

16. Richard Allenby – yorkshire-aircraft.co.uk

Chapter 13: Andover, Ford and Exercise Spartan

1. The official accident form stated,'Engine failure due to oil coming in the oil cooler…, pilot should have landed immediately he noticed signs of engine trouble.' Coincidentally this Mustang (AG541) arrived at Hawarden around the same time as David and remained there until struck off charge in Sept 1944 – Richard Allenby – www.yorkshire-aircraft.co.uk.

2. After spending fourteen months as a POW, Osborn was evacuated home. On 28/7/42 Leutnant Wolfgang Kuthe shot down a No.75 Squadron Wellington and the surviving crew members were taken to a beer garden where they met Kuthe. He was killed flying an air test at Leeuwarden airport on 14/4/43 –'Luftwaffe Night Fighter Combat Claims, 1939–1945' +'The Last Landing of 'C' Charlie,' by Richard Osborn + www.aircrew remembrance society.com. John Foreman, Johannes Matthews Melvin Brownless. Archive Report:Allied Forces 1939–1945.

3. Drogue – A canvas windsock attached to a long cable.

4. Although accuracy rate may not seem high, ace Luftwaffe fighter pilot Erich Alfred Hartmann only claimed about twenty-four of fifty rounds hit a drogue, an average rate of forty-eight per cent – 'Fighter Aces of the Luftwaffe in World War WWII' Philip Kaplan.

5. V1186 crashed into sea off Worthing on 24/10/43. It was recovered but was not repairable – Cierva Autogiro AP506 is displayed at the Helicopter Museum, Weston-super-Mare and AP507 at the Science Museum in London. In April 1945 Pullin left the RAF medically unfit – Colin Ford + Ross McNeill + Henk Welting + Peter W Moss Air Britain Impressment Logs Kari

Lumppio + German Official evaluation report Beuteauswertung No 6 Mustang 1 + #52615 Air Safety Network + Marijn Ooms and Mr Master www.wingstovictory.nl.

6. The elder daughter of Sir Kenneth and Lady Gibson – *The Times* 30/1/43.

7. 'Test Pilot,' by Neville Duke.

8. The History of No.16 Squadron written at Laarbruch 1969 by Flt/Lt J.A.A. Dobbie.

9. Posted to No.234 Squadron, Potter helped cover the Normandy invasion beaches and was awarded the Croix de Guerre – History of No.16 Squadron written at Laarbruch 1969 by Flt/Lt J.A.A. Dobbie + Court Martial Records NRO Air18/11 + Dennis Burke + Steve Brooking.

10. Ron Parnell interview.

11. RAF Manston Spitfire & Hurricane Memorial Trust www.spifirememorial.org.uk.

12. Eric Chegwin returned to Army 8/4/43 – J.J. Davies Interview + London Gazette

13. A History of IV (Army Co-operation Squadron) – raf.mod.uk.

14. The 'Allied' Southland Army consisted of The First Canadian Army and RAF 'Z' Mobile Composite Group, their recce squadrons were No.16, 26, 170, 289, 400 and 414 Squadrons. The 'Axis' Eastland Army consisted of Eastern Command with the RAF 'X' Mobile Composite Group playing the Luftwaffe, their recce squadrons were No. 2, 4, 169, 268 and 613 Squadrons – Report No.94 GHQ Exercise 'Spartan' NRO + A History of IV (Army Co-operation Squadron) – raf.mod.uk.

15. Laurence Irving was grandson of Sir Henry Irving. His literary background later found an outlet in the 35 Wing's News Sheet – 'Great Interruption' by Laurence Irving.

16. In May 1942, photographing the docks at Cherbourg, Muspratt was spotted by a Fw190 but escaped after a thirty mile chase 'with the despairing German pilot firing bursts at him from 600 yards.' Muspratt became a test pilot and died on in 2009 age 91 – Muspratt Obituary *The Times* 3/4/09.

17. George William Patrick Grant.

18. Flying a No.24 Squadron Hudson from Sydenham on 17/7/42 Flight Lieutenant Brian Stanley Bannister lost control in cloud, his wing broke off and he crashed near St Asaph, Wales. The air accident report thought that lightning caused of loss of control which led to the wing's structural failure – CWGC + Alan Clark + Col Bruggy.

19. Report No.94 GHQ Exercise 'Spartan' (NRO).

20. RAF Little Rissington.

21. Douglas Sampson's letter.

22. No.16 Squadron ORB (NRO).

23. Exercise 'Spartan' files – AR16/55 (NRO).

24. Carlos Guerreiro + www.conscript-heroes.com + Dennis Burke + Catholic Herald 19/3/43.

25. 'Operation Torch' the Allied invasion of French North Africa

26. Flemings – A Georgian hotel built in the 1730's just off Piccadilly.

27. London Burning. 1940. History-bbc-Radio.

28. On the 23/03/45 Captain Ronald Hugh Monteith of the Grenadier Guards was killed in an accident between scout car and tank transporter – Jim MacDonald, 'Grenadier Guards Officer Casualties WWII' The Grenadier Guard Association.

29. After D-Day Pete Tickner flew No.181 Squadron Typhoons in Normandy, Belgium and Holland – Sandy Sproule.

30. London Gazette 20/4/42.

31. No.53 Squadron was recalled to Britain in December 1942 and after a two and a half year tour Squadron Leader Hilditch was posted as an OTU Instructor – 'United in Effort,' by Jock Manson + The U-boat War in the Caribbean,' by Gaylord Kelshal.

32. 'The Last Voyage of the S.S.Caribou,' by Henry K. Gibbons, 2006 + 'Guardian of the Gulf: Sydney, Cape Breton, and the Atlantic Wars,' by Brian Douglas Tennyson and Roger Sarty.

33. William Wendelken's Log Book – John Wendelken + Mark Wendelken.

34. On 5/12/43 Squadron Leader Morrin was posted to No.122 Squadron but killed on Operations on 8/5/44. 'Fighter Command Losses Vol 3' by Norman Franks + CWGC.

35. In July 1944 Basil Gibson Carroll was in Normandy when the airfield was attacked. Fire spread to a fuel dump and two Typhoons; one was quickly put out but the other, loaded with

cannon shells and rockets burned furiously. As its rockets were pointing towards a dispersal area, Carroll and Flight Lieutenant Wilfred Turner crawled under the wings and removed the rockets. They both won the George Medal – Flight Magazine 16/11/44.

36. Dam possibly at Lac de Gerledan west of Mûr-de-Bretagne.
37. 'Second To None. The History of No II (AC) Squadron' by Hans Onderwater + 'ADJIDAUMO Tail in Air' by Colin Ford + CWGC.
38. Douglas Sampson's letter.
39. Col Bruggy + Colin Ford.
40. 'The Squadrons of the Royal Air Force,' by James J Halley.
41. Douglas Sampson letter.

Chapter 14: No.34 Photo Recce Wing
1. RAF Hartford Bridge was later renamed RAF Blackbushe.
2. Hugh Rigby joined the TA before the war and posted to 2nd Battalion, The Oxfordshire and Buckinghamshire Light Infantry. Due to poor eyesight he worked as ADC to General Tollemache, then while training recruits a faulty grenade exploded in his hand, killing several men. Once recovered, he was posted ALO to No.268 Squadron – Robin Rigby, www.34wing.co.uk.
3. No.16 ORB –NRO.
4. '34 Wing an Unofficial Account' by Hugh Rigby and Michael Spender.
5. No.16 ORB –NRO.
6. No.16 ORB –NRO.
7. Douglas Sampson letter.
8. No.16 ORB –NRO.+ Peter Mason + Andy Ingham.
9. '34 Wing an Unofficial Account,' by Hugh Rigby and Michael Spender.
10. No.16 ORB –NRO.
11. No.16 ORB –NRO.
12. No.16 ORB –NRO.
13. Herbert Huppertz was shot down south of Caen two days after D-Day with a final tally of seventy-eight – Petr Kacha www.luftwaffe.cz/huppertz.html.
14. On 25/07/43 Edward Francis John Charles was on escort duty for a bombing raid on a factory in Amsterdam. In the dogfight, Charles claimed one FW190 and one Me109 damaged. His No.611 Spitfire V was shot down sixteen miles off Ijmuiden and he was picked up two hours later by a No. 278 Squadron ASR Walrus – 'Another Kind of Courage' Norman Franks + Fighter Command Losses Vol 2 Norman Franks.
15. Another kind of Courage,' by Norman Franks.
16. Exeter ORB – NRO.
17. Exeter ORB – NRO.
18. 'Another kind of Courage,' by Norman Franks.
19. Exeter ORB – NRO.
20. 'The History of No.16 Squadron' written Laarbruch 1969 by Flt/Lt J.A.A. Dobbie.
21. CWGC + Dennis Burke + David Gunby.
22. Lieutenant Commander Woods was exonerated of any blame – 'Some Afterthoughts on a Submarine Disaster' by S.G. Rainsford May 1956 NRO ADM/298/499 + 'The Admiralty regrets…' by C.E.T. Warren and James Benson 1948.
23. Later while serving on HMS Worcester, Woods received the DSC. On the staff of The Commander in Chief Mediterranean, Woods was killed in a road accident in Marseilles on 23/5/46 – The Admiralty Regrets…' by C.E.T. Warren and James Benson 1948 + The Times List of Casualties 31/5/46.
24. BNAF = British North Africa Forces.
25. Major Eric Glynn Evans was killed on 26/04/1943 while fighting with the 146th (The Pembroke Yeomanry) Field Regiment during the Tunisian Campaign – Ceredigion County War Memorial + CWGC.

26. Hugh Malcolm was awarded the VC and RAF Clubs were renamed in his memory – London Gazette 27/4/43 + raf.mod.uk/RAF Odiham news article + Victoria Cross.org.uk.
27. After completing his thirty-third operation Wray Eller DFC was posted to the Tactical Bomber Force HQ for Ops room duties – London Gazette 21/5/43 + H R Honeker 18 Squadron News Letter Issue 5. Nov 05 + ww2today.com /4th-december-1942.
28. Denis Clark was killed on 25/08/44 over Normandy and buried at Les Hogues Cemetery – CWIG + Fallen Heroes of Normandy.org.

Chapter 15: Flying Instructor at Hawarden and Poulton

1. After the war Squadron Leader Peter Duncan Morris was sent on loan to the Pakistani Air Force in charge of an air observation post – 'Coming into Land' Bill Malins.
2. Captain Hugh Barber was mentioned in despatches in 1942 with 7th Battalion The Wiltshire R. He became Master of C2 House Marlborough College and ran the M.C. Cadet Force – 68/ Gen/7276 -NRO + Marlborough College Register.
3. After the war Nelson-Edwards ran several pubs and restaurants and the Leander Club Henley before retiring to Cyprus. He died in 1994 – Spit and Sawdust' George Hassall Nelson-Edwards + Pamela Nelson's Obituary – The Telegraph 12/03/01.
4. Ralph 'China' Young won the DFC in October 1943 and the DSO in March 1944 as Acting Wing Commander, No.7 Squadron – London Gazette.
5. Roland Harold Dibnah posted to No.91 Squadron completed three tours and transferred to RACF in 1945. He died in 1990 – The Canadian Fighter Pilot & Air Gunner Museum.
6. The Me109 was repainted with RAF markings and flown by the RAF's Enemy Aircraft Flight Unit – No VI (AC) Squadron Web Site + RAF Rochford member, The Aviation Forum .key publishing ltd + www.rafjever.org/4squadhistory
7. It is possible that George's relative was John Stuart Hindmarsh, a noted racing driver who joined the RAF and flew with No.16 and 4 Squadrons. He was killed on 6/09/38 while testing a production flight Hurricane – Flight Magazine 15/09/1938 + Oxford Dictionary of National Biography.
8. George Hindmarsh Interview.
9. Robert Hudson Henderson Ireland was killed in Burma on 20/4/45 when his No.11 Squadron aircraft blew up while landing with a bomb on board – Kings Canterbury Roll of Honour + CWGC.
10. No.41 OTU ORB –NRO.
11. Ron Parnell Interview.
12. Homer Lynn Wolf was posted to No.430 Squadron flying tactical recces photographing German movements as the Allies tried to capture Caen. On 29/07/44, with No.430 Squadron Wolf was lost twenty-five miles from Caen – '430 Squadron' W/Cdr F H Hitchins + CWGC.
13. Squadron Leader Fletcher.
14. A black = an official rebuke.
15. John Parker Lucas.
16. Captain MacAlistair was at Hawarden observing instructing methods.
17. No.223 Squadron operated from Malta, Sicily and Italy.
18. In 1949 George Brian Walford commanded an RAF Antarctica Flight for a Norwegian-Swedish-British expedition to Queen Maud Land Antarctica. Walford took two Auster 6 aircraft equipped with both floats and skis. Their task was to aid navigation through pack ice, to find a landing place for the expedition, to undertake reconnaissance flights and to support a winter camp on Queen Maud Land – The Times Obituary + shortfinals.wordpress.com/2014/01/21/the-auster.
19. In 1940 with No.53 Squadron, Eric Plumtree DFC attacked ships and an army camp before three Me109s attacked and injured all crew members. C/O of No.169 Squadron, he retired as Air-Vice Marshal in 1977 – Glasgow Herald 16/1/60 + London Gazette 12/11/40 + 'History of Mosborough' by David English.
20. During training for D-Day, a photo of Robert Edward Vane de Lautour synchronizing watches appeared on the cover of Picture Post. On 20 June leading an attack near Le Mesnil he was

injured and died of his wounds. – Airborne Assault Museum, 'Walking D-Day' By Paul Reed + www.canada at war.ca + Airborne Forces Museum + CWGC + www.pegasus archive.org + wingwatch.blogspot.ch + Neil Barber.

21. Peter Cruden returned to the commandos later in the year. Troop Commander of No.2 Troop, No.6 Commando, he fought across the Rhine and into Germany. After the war became a tea planter in Assam and in 1976 was Lord Cowdray's Polo Manager – www.6commando.com + Pegasus Archive Mark Hickman + NA record WO 218/68 + Julia Cruden.
22. Douglas Sampson's letter.
23. Daily Mail Article June 1944.
24. Jimmy Taylor – 'Operation Crossbow' BBC 15/5/11.
25. 'Fighter Command Losses' by N Franks + CWGC.
26. 'Great Interruption' by Laurence Irving.
27. On 13/11/41 Gilliland had been severely injured in a mid-air collision while attempting a 'Prince of Wales's Feathers' manoeuvre in a Lysander – Jimmy Taylor No.16 Squadron Newsbrief Sept 03.
28. 'Great Interruption' by Laurence Irving.
29. No.4 Squadron ORB (NRO) + www.raf.mod.uk + www.rafjever.org/4squadhistory.htm.
30. Jimmy Taylor – 16 Squadron Newsbrief 24 + CWGC.
31. Desmond Alan Clifton-Mogg DFC joined the RAF, trained in USA in 1941 and was posted to No.168 Squadron in March 1942. By the end of the war he had flown 874 combat hours. He died in 2007 aged 92 – Association Bretonne du Souvenir Aerien 1939–1945. www.absa3945.com/
32. George Hindmarsh interview.

Chapter 16: Typhoon Training Bognor and Ops with No.168 Squadron Holland
1. Flight Lieutenant Harry Hardy's lecture at Royal Canadian Legion. YouTube .nightlite pictures. com.
2. 'Typhoon Pilot' by Desmond Scott.
3. 'Pilot's Notes for Typhoon Marks IA and IB; Sabre II or IIA engine' Air Ministry + 'The Typhoon and Tempest Story' Chris Thomas and Christopher Shores.
4. 'Typhoon Attack,' Norman Franks.
5. Bastow was devastated to hear that the day before Northern Holland was liberated, Mr Klooster was shot by the Gestapo. He ended the war instructing navigation at a Fighter OTU, returned to Canada and became CO of No.10 Wing, Royal Canadian Air Cadets. Promoted to Wing Commander and appointed Honorary Aide-de-Camp to the Governor General he retired from the Air Cadet in 1962 – Bastow's debriefing notes NRO + Gerry Bastow letter + Tony Bastow July 2004 + www.visitnewfoundland.ca + www.airforce.ca + Newfoundland's Grand Banks Site.
6. In 1938 2nd Lieutenant Edward Kenneth Barnes served with 4th Battalion The Loyal Regiment and transferred to the RAF in July 1940. Flying with No.239 Squadron he shot down an Fw190 in the Dieppe raid and won the Cross de Guerre. Barnes was at Hawarden before being posted to No.168 Squadron – RAF Commands Archive, Jubilee aircrew list Steve49.
7. On 1/9/44, Jan Plesman's Spitfire, hit by flak dived into the ground from 3,000ft – 'Jan Plesman. A Flying Dutchman,' by Albert Plesman.
8. Vasco Ortigao Gilbert.
9. On 1710/44 No.16 pilots Douglas Sampson, Paul Douglas Petrie and Eric Martin were awarded the DFC. Towards the end of the war, Sampson flew Hurricanes for the Air Despatch Letter Service from Eisenhower's HQ near Northolt and Montgomery at 21st Army Group in Europe. Eric Martin flew with the RAF until 15/8/52. He was killed while practising a Battle of Britain display; his Harvard collided with another – London Gazette 4th Supplement 13/10/44. PPRuNe Members Forum + Chris Pointon, raf commands forum
10. Tony Greenly.
11. Squadron Leader William Thomas Klersy DFC + Bar returned to No.401 Squadron in January. He destroyed or damaged ninety-eight enemy vehicles, eight trains and fourteen aircraft

before crashing into a hill on 22/5/45 – Hugh Halliday + Canadian Museum of Civilization Corporation + Joe Fukuto www.acesofww2.com + CWGC.

12. Figures from 'The Battle of the Airfields' by Norman Franks.
13. 'My Autobiography' by Harry Hardy.
14. Roger Michael Stevens was at Hawarden in June 1944.
15. Flight Lieutenant Harry Hardy's lecture at Royal Canadian Legion – YouTube .nightlite pictures.com.
16. Lieutenant Commander Thomas 'Tommy' Wade Harrington won both the DSC and Bar. After the war he joined staff of Air Warfare at Old Sarum, was chief instructor of Lossiemouth OTU, Air Commander of the Australian carrier 'Sydney' and Commander of RN Yeovilton. Retiring in 1958 he died in 1989 – Mark E. Horan,12oclockhigh forum + British Naval lists + Fleet Air Arm Archive + 'Personal Perspectives,' by Timothy C Dowling + Flight Global Magazine + Telegraph Obituary.
17. Hardy's lecture at Royal Canadian Legion – YouTube .nightlite pictures.com.
18. No.35 Recce Wing News Sheet.
19. John Packwood's letter.
20. On 7/9/43 Australian pilot Roderick Maton Mackenzie's No.168 Mustang was shot down north of Paris. Given a ramshackle bike he cycled 950 miles to Spain. After lecturing about his escape he rejoined No.168 Squadron in March 1944 – www.awm.gov.au/collection + RAF Commands Forum + vrajm + jossleclercq + Colin Ford + Steve Brooking + Col Bruggy + Lorraine + 'Empire Airmen Strike Back,' by Peter Ilbery.
21. No.168 Squadron ORB –NRO..
22. 'First Light' by Geoffrey Wellum.
23. 'Typhoon and Tempest Story' Thomas and Shores + '2nd Tactical Air Force, Vol 2,' Thomas and Shores
24. 'RAF Fighter Command Losses 1944–1945' by N R Franks + 168 Squadron ORB -NRO.

Chapter 17: No.2 Squadron 35 Recce Wing Gilze-Rijen

1. 'Air Recce' by HQ First Canadian Air Force.
2. Calcar is now spelt Kalcar
3. 'Spitfire. A Test Pilot's Story,' by Jeffrey Quill.
4. 35 Wing + No.2 + No.4 Squadron ORBs -NRO + 'Battle of the Airfields' and 'Fighter Command Losses' by Norman Franks.
5. Peter Stansfeld Interview.
6. 'Coming into Land,' by Bill Malins.
7. Dave Mercer – No.268 Squadron.
8. Stubbs was killed the next day so the combat report was submitted by Flight Lieutenant Charborneay the No.168 Intelligence Officer – NRO Personal Combat Report AIR50/70.
9. Squadron Leader LH Lambert – 'Typhoon Attack,' by Norman Franks.
10. Squadron Leader LH Lambert – 'Battle of the Airfields' by Norman L.R. Franks.
11. Derek Gordon Dickson was a POW in Stalag Luft I.
12. MT – Mechanized Transport.
13. 'The German Defence of The Siegfried Line' by Samuel W. Mitcham Jr.
14. Colin Dunford Wood had the distinction of flying the last Hurricane out of Burma before Japanese troops arrived. He returned to India, transferred to the Royal Army Service Corps and died in 1971 – Colin Dunford Wood's Letter + A Story of War' by James Dunford Wood.
15. Major Patrick John Dolignon Furse commanded No.140 ALO Section. After the war he married Elisabeth Ruth Wolpert who had worked for MI9 on the 'Pat Line.' Furse taught at the Central School of Arts and Crafts and died in 2005 aged 86 – *The Times* and Guardian Obituaries September 2005.
16. In 1941 Charles Dugdale Harris-St John DFC joined the RAF and was posted to No.140 Squadron. By December 1942 he had flown over 100 operations and in 1944 was C/O of No.4 Squadron, then Air ADC to Mountbatten in Asia – 8/12/92 LR Obituary, www.flickr.com + London Gazette + rafjever.org/4squadhistory

17. No.35 Wing News Sheet.
18. Principle dancer with the Royal Ballet, Helpman formed a successful partnership with Margot Fontaine.
19. Patrick Furse had met Fonteyn and letters written from 1940 to 1942 show that he was very close to her – 'The pain behind performance: Secret torment of Margot Fonteyn' The Independent 06/02/07 + The Telegraph article 'And as the Bombs fell they Danced on,' Sarah Crompton 05/02/07.
20. Flight Lieutenant Dennis Draper flew with No.73 Squadron. On 28/11/43, Oberleutant Stubbe landed his Me410 at Montecorvino airfield in error. Flight Lieutenant Noel George Quenet and Pilot Officer Dennis Draper, drove in front of him and captured it – Steve Brooking + Amrit + JohnE + Col Bruggy + 'The History of 73 Squadron,' by 'Don Minterne.
21. For his courage and determination Squadron Leader Stephenson received the DFC – London Gazette 20/3/45.
22. No.122 Wing, were at Volkel.
23. Cleve now spelt Kleve.
24. No.2 Squadron ORB -NRO + 'For Your Tomorrow,' by Errol Martyn.
25. No.35 Wing News Sheet.
26. No.35 Wing News Sheet.
27. For his part in this action he was awarded the DSO to add to his MC and Bar. Sir Basil Oscar Paul Eugster served with the Guards Division, BAOR 1945–1947. CO of both 1st and 3rd Battalion of the Irish Guards he worked at Joint Services Staff College, was Assistant Adjutant General at the War Office then posted to Cyprus and Hong Kong. In 1972 he was C-in-C UK's Land Forces and Aide-de-camp to the Queen. He died in 1984 age 74 – King's College London Liddell Hart Centre for Military Archives + Battalion War Diaries WO171/5148 TNA + DFC Recommendation + ww2guards.com.
28. On February 22nd a V1 landed 200 yards from the Operations Room at the end of the U/S runway. Between October 1944 and March 1945 over twenty V1 crashed near Gilze-Rijen – No.35 Recce Wing HQ ORB (NRO).
29. Woodbridge's report. No.35 Wing News sheet No.60 15/3/45.
30. 35 Wing ORB reported that a Doodle Bug was shot down by a Tempest and although no damage was caused, the resulting explosion had rocked the base. This pilot was probably Flight Lieutenant Jongbloed, who had shot down seven flying bombs over England the previous year – No.35 Wing HQ ORB(NRO) + '2nd Tactical Air Force Vol 3,' Shores and Thomas p4370 + Hawker Tempest page.
31. Elisabeth Jardine married Dr John Edward Sharpley on 4/5/46.
32. 35 Wing News Sheet.
33. 35 Wing News Sheet.

Chapter 18: 'Operation Varsity' Crossing the Rhine. Mill

1. 35 Recce Wing News Sheet.
2. 35 Recce Wing News Sheet.
3. 'Second to None' by Hans Onderwater.
4. Group Captain Andy Ford Anderson joined the Air Ministry, was CO of No.342 Squadron in the Middle East. Later working at Supreme HQ Allied Powers Europe and 61 Group Weston Sector. Retiring in 1957 he ran a hotel in Minehead and died in 2002 aged 92 – 'Second to None,' by Hans Onderwater + Telegraph Obituary 31/11/02.
5. 'Wings of Freedom,' by Norman Franks.
6. 35 Recce Wing News Sheet.
7. No.35 HQ ORB (NRO) + 35 Recce Wing News Sheet.
8. Figures from 'Bounce the Rhine' by Charles Whiting p112–115.
9. No.2 Squadron ORB (NRO).
10. On March 24, Allied air forces flew 8,000 aircraft and 1,300 glider sorties sighting fewer that 100 enemy aircraft in the air – 'Report by the Supreme Commander to the Combined Chiefs

of Staff on Operations in Europe of the Allied Expeditionary Forces' by Dwight D Eisenhower – HM Stationery Office 1946.

11. Isselburg – East of Emmerich.
12. 35 Recce Wing News Sheet.
13. PTC – Personnel transit camp.
14. 35 HQ ORB (NRO).
15. 35 Recce Wing News sheet.
16. After the war Peter Storie-Pugh, studied at the Royal Veterinary College in London, became a Fellow of Wolfson College and president of The Royal College of Veterinary Surgeons in 1977. He retired to France and died in 2011 age 91 – Telegraph Obituary 30/12/11

Chapter 19: Twente. The end of the War

1. No.2 Squadron ORB (NRO).
2. Air Chief Marshal Alexander McKay Sinclair Steedman DFC flew with 241 Squadron in Italy and Yugoslavia before being posted to No.2 Squadron – Kings College London Liddell Hart Centre for Military Archive + London Gazette.
3. This entry in David's Log Book is confusing as Kiwcke sur Mer is a misspelling. 35 Wing HQ ORB noted 'FIRGO last light sortie had a mystifying homing to B83?' Taking Gorinchem as the most southerly point David flew to, B83 Knocke Sur Mer was eighty miles SW, whereas Gilze-Rijen was just twenty miles south.
4. Before the war David's family friend, Captain Samuel Philip Symington MC flew a single-seater sports Comper Swift aircraft in the 1931 Kings Cup air race. Symington was captured in April 1940 fighting with The Leicestershire Regiment in Norway and photographed in the boxing ring at Oflag VIB in front of the POWs and German Officers – The Royal Leicester Regiment website + 'a fleeting peace.org' Terry D Mace + Australian War Memorial website + The London Gazette + 'The ABC. An Eichstatt address Book,' compiled by Colin D Yarrow + 'Without benefit of Laundry' by John Peyton + The New York Times.
5. Daily Mirror 8/5/45.
6. Daphne Whitehead's Letter – Daphne later became David's wife.
7. No.35 Wing ORB – NRO.
8. 'Normandy to Hanover.' A Brief Account of 84 Group,' Intelligence Main HQ 84 Group.
9. Reginald Charles William Togwell No.268 Squadron.
10. No.35 HQ ORB (NRO).
11. 35 Wing News Sheet.
12. After the war, Peter Critchley-Salmonson set up an aerial photography business 'Eagle Aero Photos' at White Waltham airfield. In 1947 his photographs of 'HMS Warspite,' which ran aground off Prussia Cove were published in the Daily Telegraph.

Chapter 20: Celle, Occupied Germany and Demob

1. After the war, Wing Commander William 'Bill' Malins DFC took charge of the German advanced aeronautical research centre at Volkenrode. Working with the RAF Directorate of Accident Prevention he travelled to RAF bases all over the world. After leaving the RAF he retired to the family farm and died in 2011 aged 95 – 'Coming into Land,' by Bill Malins + Colin Ford.
2. SMO = Senior medical officer.
3. A&SD Duties = Administrative and Special Duties.
4. Guy Richard Brown.
5. Trevor Mitchell joined the Colonial Service in Nigeria where among other things he bought a racehorse, taught his cook to make ice-cream, with a little help from Mrs Beeton, and built up three farms in Rhodesia. In the early 1970's he reluctantly moved his family back to England. He died in 1996 aged 86 – Trevor Mitchell's letters + RP Smith, Colin Ford, Peter Mitchell, Brendaria – Aviation Forum.

6. Anson Brian Howard returned home in July 46 for a gunnery course. Posted to Plymouth for three years he married at the Royal Citadel. After leaving the army he taught at Cheltenham College Junior School – www.hglambert.co.uk + A S Howard.
7. George Hindmarsh was demobbed in November 1945.
8. Donald Alfred James Draper studied as a Chartered Accountant became a partner in a London firm and Mayor of Lewisham.
9. John Packwood letter.
10. No.2 Squadron ORB (NRO).
11. Antony Norman Davis was posted to Palestine in June 1946. He was David's best man. Promoted to Air Commodore as the air attaché to Moscow in 1963 he was then O/C of the RAF Staff College. In 1971 a BBC programme about UFO's allegedly sighted over Banbury, Davis was interviewed as the MoD's official UFOs spokesman. He died in 1988 age 70 – David Clarke + BBC News 6/03/12.
12. Mike McGilligan.
13. Edward Ambrose Holbech DFC died on the 6/9/45. He and his brother Johnny were being driven home from a VJ Day party – Daily Telegraph Johnny Holbech Obituary 23/10/04.
14. Guy Richard Brown was awarded the DFC on 6/6/43. He flew over fifty sorties during the battle of Egypt and the capture of Tripoli. He died on 06/09/45 and was buried in Cairo – London Gazette + CWIG + Hugh A. Halliday + Resmoroh – RAF Commands Forum.
15. Group Captain Mann DFC joined the RAF in 1937 and served with 31 Squadron in the NW Frontier, India, then No.28 Squadron in Burma. Promoted to Squadron Leader he was C/O of 63 Squadron and 268 Squadron and CFI at RAF Valley. He died in 2010 age 90 – Isle of Wight Country press obituary 8/1/10
16. Alan Richard Hill No.2 Squadron.
17. John 'Lefty' Packwood returned to Oxford in April 1946 to study French and German. "I'm a ruddy schoolboy again … It's vastly different to before the war and not so pleasant. I think the chief trouble is that I've probably changed and the place hasn't." In 1951 he was working with The Combined Cadet Force at St. Lawrence College – Packwood's letter +London Gazette.

Roll of Honour

'Older men declare war. But it is youth that must fight and die.'

Herbert Hoover

Adcock, Kenneth Gordon. Hit a tree while low-flying. 18/09/42.

Aitchison, Harold Leslie John. Shot down, Flak, Abbeville. 12/07/43

Alexander, Gordon Redvers Mitchell. Collided with Hurricane, Totnes. 2/2/42.

Baillon, Paul Abbott. Shot down by a Bf 109 off the Isle of Wight. 28/11/40

Baker, Geoffrey Russell. Crashed off Portland Bill on return from his first op. 9/2/43

Bannister, Brian Stanley. Lightning caused loss of control, wing broke off. 17/7/42

Barnes, Norman. Shot dead on guard mounting parade. 15/02/41

Blundell-Hill, Christopher John. Shot down, Flak, Arnhem. 1/4/45

Booth, Ken Stanley. Collided with Hurricane at Totnes. 22/2/42

Boyce, Charles John Roger. Dominie aircraft crash on take-off. 11/4/42

Brown, Guy Richard. Ferrying abroad. Crashed Egypt. 06/09/45

Buck, Leonard Edward Gordon. Failed to pull out of training ground-attack. 17/2/42

Currie, Kirkwood Dundee. Shot down by Fw190 over Channel. 7/12/42

Day, Neville Lawrence Winkworth. Crash due to coolant leak on first flight in Hurricane. 29/4/41

De Lautour, Robert Edward Vane. Injuries sustained during post D-Day attack. 20/6/44

Dent Harry. Stirling shot down in first 1000 bomber raid over Cologne. 31/5/42

Drummond, Robert John Heugh. 152 Sqdn. In Tunisia. 24/4/43

D'Silva, George John Howard. Spun in from 800 feet during training. 29/9/41.

Duce, Ronald Arthur. Stalled while attempting to land at Snailwell. 17/5/42

Firman, John Evans. Shot down after attacking Essen. 09/06/42

Franklin, Cecil Ernest. Low flying, hit tree. 18/10/42

Garland, Patrick James. Landing accident at Gilze-Rijen 1/1/45

Garware, Ramo Digamber. Crashed in field attempting forced landing. 23/12/43.

Gibbons, Howard Plaistowe. Shot down by Me109 while taking off. 1/1/45

Gibbons, Ernest. Shot down by Fw190. 26/12/44

Gilbert, Vasco Ortigao. Failed to return from armed recce. 6/12/44

Hawkins, Christopher Alexander. Mistakenly shot down by Spitfire. 21/02/42

Herrick, Dennis. Shot down by German Anti-Submarine Ship 26/6/41

Holbech, Edward Ambrose. Killed in a car crash. 6/9/45

Huddart, William Grayson. Missing after a recce near Haltern 22/1/45

Hutton, John Peter. Missing over Bay of Biscay, ferrying Wellington. 9/9/43

Jarrett, Peter William. Failed to return after bombing Nuremberg. 13/10/41

Klersy William Thomas. Killed in a flying accident. 22/5/45.

Krakowski, Antoni. Killed in car crash. 23/8/45

Lee, Mark. Shot down in Holland. 9/12/41

MacDonald, Donald Kennedy. Shot down over sea in Battle of Britain. 28/8/40

Maclay, Alastair Mowart. Shot down by Fw190. 29/11/42

McGilligan, Michael Aidan. Crashed into ground in low cloud. 8/6/44

Maitland, Colin Edward. Shot down on Photo/Recce by flak guns near Doetinchem. 18/3/45

Malcolmson, George Keith. Crashed on emergency landing Woensdrecht. 17/1/45

Marrs, Eric Simcox. Shot down flying close escort for Hampdens. Brest. 24/07/41

Martin, Eric. Collision during practise Battle of Britain display. 15/8/52
Monteith, Ronald Hugh. Accident between scout car and tank transporter. 23/03/45
Morrin, Ian. Killed on operations over Germany. 8/4/44
Novak, Jaroslav Novak. Killed attacking enemy shipping Guernsey. 14/5/43
Osborn, Andrew Francis Atterbury. Wellington Crashed at Melsungen. 28/08/42
Pearsall, Alan Louden. Shot down off the coast of France. 8/3/44
Plesman, Jan. Dived into the ground while providing close air support duty for troops. 1/9/44.
Pickering, Peter Henry Albert. Crashed near Stafford while training. 28/08/41
Redfearn, George James. Japanese POW, died building Bangkok railway, 25/10/43
Ricard-Cordingley, Louis. Collided with Spitfire in training. 26/1/42
Ridpath, Thomas Guy. Killed on Medenine Ridge, Tunisia. 17/3/43
Ridpath, Michael Dudley. Killed in attack on tank near Salerno 9/9/43
Skinner, Leonard John. Missing during attack on rail targets Oldenburg. 23/1/43
Steen, Govert. Shot down on a sweep over Northern France 05/06/42
Stuart-Duncan, John Valentine. Crashed in crosswind landing, Weston Zoyland. 30/05/43
Stubbs, John Douglas. On take-off access panel flew up. A/C spun off and crashed. 02/01/45
Taylor, John Rosser Patrick. Shot down by Fw190. 29/11/42
Wolf, Homer Lynn. Lost on a recce near Vire. 29/7/44
Woods, Frederick Greville. Died in car accident, Marseilles 31/1/46

Service Record

Army

Sapper

400 Company 50th Northants Regiment.	13/8/39	31/5/40
Anti Aircraft (Searchlight) Battalion. Royal Engineers.		

Officer Training

Sandhurst Military College	31/5/40	21/9/40

Second Lieutenant – Infantry Officer
The Loyal North Lancashire Regiment

50th (H) Battalion – Clitheroe	27/09/40	30/09/40
10th Battalion – Portsdown School, Cosham	14/12/40	01/02/41
-Clarence Barracks, Portsmouth	30/09/40	14/12/40
– Tyneham Village Dorset	01/02/41	08/04/41

RAF Pilot Training

No.2 ITW Cambridge – *A flight No.1 Sqdn*	12/4/41	06/6/41
No.19 EFTS Sealand – *Course No 6*	18/6/41	30/7/41
No. 5 SFTS Tern Hill – *Course No 65*	7/8/41	19/11/41
No. 41 OTU Old Sarum – *Course No 44*	9/12/41	11/2/42

Pilot, No. 16 Squadron, Army Co-op Command

WESTON ZOYLAND	11/2/42	2/1/43
Night Flying -Colerne	17th Sept 42	23rd Sept 42
Fighter Affiliation – Middle Wallop	18th Oct 42	30th Oct 42
Operations – Exeter	20th Nov 42	8th Dec.42
ANDOVER	2/1/43	1/6/43
Air Firing – Weston Zoyland	23rd Jan 43	31st Jan 43
Exercise Spartan – Ford	26th Feb 43	13th March 43
Blind Approach Course – Thruxton	29th Mar 43	3rd April 43

Pilot No. 16 Squadron Fighter Command
2nd T.A.F. 34 Wing.10 Group

MIDDLE WALLOP	1/6/43	29/6/43
HARTFORD BRIDGE	29/6/43	3/11/43
Operation Holloway – Exeter	31st Aug 43	2nd Sept 43

Staff/Instructor Pilot
No. 9 GROUP No.41 O.T.U

HAWARDEN	4/11/43	5/9/44
No. 1 Tactical Exercise Unit		
Flight Commander 'B' Flight		
No. 1TEU 'E' Flight – Poulton		
Recce Instructor-Hawarden		
Officer Advanced Training School- **Cranwell**	17 July 44	7th August 44

Pool Pilot awaiting Overseas posting
No. 83 G.S.U (Group Service Unit

BOGNOR	5/9/44	24/9/44
THORNEY ISLAND	?/10/44	? /11/44
TANGMERE	?/11/44	30/11/44

Typhoon Pilot No.168 Squadron
148 Wing 83rd Group

EINDHOVEN Holland	1/12/44	28/12/44

Photo Recce pilot No. 2 Squadron
35 Recce Wing 84th Group

B77 GILZE-RIJEN Holland	28/12/44	
B 89 MILL Holland	9/3/45	
B106 TWENTE Holland	18/4/45	
B118 CELLE Germany	30/5/45	
B150 CELLE/HUSTEDT Germany	17/6/45	26/8/45
Air to Ground Firing WARMWELL England	7/7/45	29/7/45

Posting in UK while awaiting Demob

84 G.D.C.	26/8/45	10/9/45
H.Q. Fighter Command	10/9/45	11/9/45
Molesworth	11/9/45	23/9/45
Market Harborough	23/9/45	21/11/45

Record of Airfields Flown To

Andover
Aston down
Bisceter
Charmy Down
Cheddon Down
Childs Ercall
Chivenor
Codford
Colerne
Desford
Eastleigh
Ellstree
Exeter
Farnborough
Hartford Bridge
Hawarden
Hatfield
Heston

Ford
Harrowbeer
Ibsley
Madley
Market Harborough
Mount Farm
Middle Wallop
Neveravon
North Holt
Old Sarum
Odiham
Pembrey
Perranporth
Portreath
Poulton
Redhill
Roborough
Sawbridgeworth

Sealand
Shawbury
Shoreham
St Eval
Staverton
Tangmere
Tern Hill
Thorney Island
Thruxton
Turnhouse
Warmwell
Wescott
Weston Zoyland
White Waltham
Worthy Down
York
Zeal

Record of Aircraft Flown by David

Auster
Fairley Battle
Harvard
Lysander I, II, III
Hurricane (Merlin III and
Merlin 45 engines)
Magister
Martinet

Miles Master I and III
Mustang (I, IA, and III)
Spitfire Mrk I, V and XIV
(A&B).
Tiger Moth
Tomahawk P40
Typhoon 1B
Domine

Passenger in
Blenheim IV
Boston
Dakota
Oxford
Proctor
Whitley

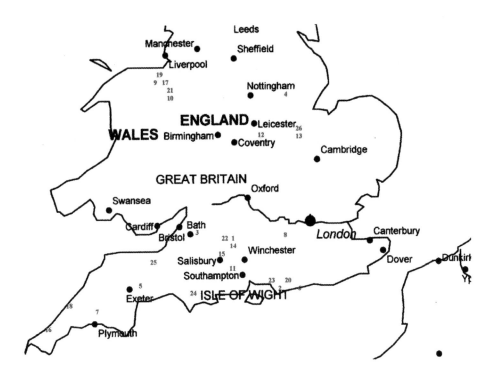

1. Andover
2. Bognor
3. Colerne
4. Cranwell
5. Exeter
6. Ford
7. Harrowbeer
8. Hartford Bridge.
9. Hawarden
10. High Ercall
11. Ibsley
12. Market Harborough
13. Molesworth
14. Middle Wallop
15. Old Sarum
16. Portreath
17. Poulton
18. St Eval
19. Sealand
20. Tangmere
21. Ternhill
22. Thruxton
23. Thorney Island
24. Warmwell
25. Weston Zoyland
26. Wittering

The main airfields that David flew to in England. *(SAGH)*

References and Bibliography

- The National Archives Kew (NRO).
- Marlborough College Register 1843–1952' (Ninth Edition.)
- The London Gazette.
- The Commonwealth War Graves Commission.
- The Imperial War Museum.
- The British Library.
- The RAF Museum Hendon.
- Action Stations' Books 1–9 (Patrick Stephens Ltd 1979–1983)
- 16 Squadron Newsletters.
- 35 Wing New Sheets.
- The History of No.16 Squadron by Flt/Lt J.A.A. Dobbie
- RAF Commands Forum

84 GROUP INTELLIGENCE. 84 GROUP 2nd TAF -*From Normandy to Hanover.* (July 1945)
AIR MINISTRY. – *Over to You. News Broadcasts by the RAF.* (HMSO 1943)
BABINGTON SMITH, Constance. – *Evidence in Camera.* (Chatto and Windus 1958)
BAKER, David. – *Adolf Galland: The Authorised Biography,* (Windrow & Greene Ltd 1997)
BISHOP, Edward. -*Hurricane.* (Air-Life 1986)
BOND, L.M.C. – *Tyneham* (Longmans (Dorchester) 1956)
BOWYER, Chas. – *Supermarine Spitfire* (Bison Books 1980)
BOWYER, Chas. – *Bristol Blenheim* (Ian Allen 1984)
BROOKES, A.J. – *Fighter Squadrons at War.* (Ian Allen 1980)
CHARLWOOD, Don. – *No Moon Tonight* (Goodall 1984)
CHORLEY W.R -*Royal Air Force Bomber Command Losses 1942* (Midland Publishing 1989)
COLSTON SHEPHERD, E. – *The Air Force of Today.* (Blackie & Son 1939)
CONANT, Peter. – *Eyes Above the Enemy.* (Blaisdon Publ & Bound Biographies 2002)
CONGDON, Philip. – *Behind The Hangar Doors* (Sonik Books 1985)
DANNE, Michael. – *Per Ardua Ad Astra.* (Fredrick Muller 1982)
DEIGHTON, Len. – *Goodbye Mickey Mouse.* (Grafton 1983)
DUNN, William R. – *Fighter Pilot -The First American Ace* (University Press of Kentucky 1982)
DUKE, Neville. -*Test Pilot* (Allan Wingate)
DUNMORE, Spencer. -*Bomb Run* (Pan 1971)
EGGERS, Reinhold. – *Colditz, the German Story* (New English Library Ltd; 1972)
EVERSON, Don. – *The Reluctant Messerschmitt* (Portcullis Press 1978)
EISENHOWER, Dwight D. – *'Report by the Supreme Commander to the Combined Chiefs of Staff on Operations in Europe of the Allied Expeditionary Forces'* (HM Stationary Office 1946)
FORD, Colin. – Adjidaumo "Tail in Air": *History of No.268 Squadron*
FIRBANK, Thomas. – *I bought a Star.* (John Jones Publishing 1999)
FITZGERALD, Major DJL. – *History of the Irish Guards in the Second World War* (Gale & Polden Ltd 1949)
FLACK, Jeremy. – *Spitfire A living Legend.* (Osprey 1985)
FLEMING, Peter. – *Invasion 1940* (Rupert Hart-Davis 1957)
FLYING OFFICER X. – *How Sleep the Brave and other stories* (Guild Books 1943)

FOREMAN. John. MATTHEWS, Johannes. -*Luftwaffe Night Fighter Combat Claims, 1939–1945* (Red Kite 2004)
FORRESTER, Larry. – *Fly For Your Life.* (Panther 1956)
FRANKS, Norman. L.R. – *Typhoon Attack* (Stackpole Military History 2010)
FRANKS, Norman. L.R. – *The Battle of the Airfields.* (Grubb Street 1994)
FRANKS, Norman. L.R. – *Another Kind Of Courage.* (Patrick Stevens 1994)
FRANKS, Norman. L.R. – *Wings of Freedom* (William Kimber 1980)
FRANKS, Norman. L.R. – *Fighter Command Losses Vols. 1–3,'* (Midland Publishing1997–2008)
FREEMAN, Roger. – *Mustang at War* (Ian Allen 974)
FREEMAN, Roger. -*The Fight for the Skies* (Arms and Armour Press 1998)
GUNBY & PELHAM. – *Bomber Losses in Middle East and Mediterranean* (Midland Publishing 2006)
GIBBONS, Henry K. – *The Last Voyage of the S.S.Caribou.* (www.visitnewfoundland.ca)
HADLAND, Tony. – *The Spaceframe Moultons* (Lit Verlag 2010)
HALLEY, James. – *Squadrons of the RAF.* (Air Britain 1980)
HAMILTON, Tim. – *The Life and Times of Pilot Officer Prune.* (HMSO. 1991)
HENSHAW, Alex. – *Sigh for a Merlin.* (Murray 1979)
HILLARY, Richard. – *The Last Enemy.* (MacMillan & Co 1961)
HOBBS, Charles. – *Past Tense… Charlie's Story.* (General Store Publishing House 1994)
HODGSON, David. – *Letters from a Bomber Pilot.* (Thames Methuen.1985)
IRVING, Laurence. – *Great Interruption* (Airlife 1983)
JENKINS, Paul. -*Battle over Portsmouth* (Middleton Press 1986)
KELSHAL, Gaylord – *The U-boat War in the Caribbean,* (Naval Institute Press 1994)
LADD, James D. – *By Land and Sea The Royal Marines 1919–1997* (Harper Collins 1998)
MCKINSTRY, Leo. – *Hurricane (John Murray 2011)*
MINISTRY OF INFORMATION. – *Roof Over Britain. AA Defences 1939–1942.* (Ministry of Information 1943)
NELSON-EDWARDS, George Hassall. – *Spit and Sawdust.* (Newton Books 1998)
NESBIT, Roy Conyers. – *Woe to the Unwary.* (William Kimber 1981)
MANSON, Jock. – *United in Effort* (Air-Britain Publication 1997)
MALINS, William. *edited by Chris Newton* – *Coming into Land* (Memoirs Books 2010)
MCNEILL, Ross. – *Coastal Command Losses Vol 1* (Midland 2003)
MILLINGTON, Geoffrey. – The *Unseen Eye* (Panther1968)
MITCHAM, Samuel W. Jr. – *The German Defence of The Siegfried Line* (Stackpole books 2009)
MOLDEN, David. editor -*The Schneider Trophy Contest 50*th *Anniversary* (Schneider 81 Agfa-Gevardt)
OGLEY, Bob. – *Biggin on the Bump,* (Froglet Publications 1990)
ONDERWATER, Hans. -*Second to None* (Airlife Publishing Ltd; 1992)
PAGET, Guy. – *Hints Subalterns, for use of* (Private Print 1943)
PASSMORE, Richard. – *Blenheim Boy.* (Thomas Harmsworth Pub 1981)
PEYTON, John. – *Without Benefit of Laundry.* (Bloomsbury 1997)
PLESMAN, Albert. -*'Jan Plesman' A Flying Dutchman* (Upfront Publishing Ltd. 2002)
POTTINGER, Ron. – *A Soldier in the Cockpit* (Stackpole Military History Series 2007)
QUILL Jeffrey. – *Spitfire. A Test Pilot's Story.* (John Murray Publishers Ltd 1983)
RAWLINGS, John. – *Coastal Support and Special Squadrons.* (Janes Publication 1982)
RICHEY, Paul. – *A Fighter Pilot* (Batsford 1941)
REID, Pat R. – *Colditz The Full Story* (Pan Books 2002)
RICHARDSON, Anthony. – *The Crowded Hours. The Story of SOS Cohen.* (Max Parrish 1953)
ROBERTSON & COLSTON & COOK. – *Squadrons of the RAF in War and Peace and other Units* (Flight 1937?)
ROSS, BLANCHE & SIMPSON. – *The Greatest Squadron of Them All* (Grub Street; 2003)
ROTHENSTEIN, Sir William. – *Men of the RAF.* (OUP 1942)
SCOTT, Desmond. – *Typhoon Pilot.* (Leo Cooper1982)
SCOTT, Michael. – *Special Forces Commander.* (Pen and Sword 2011)

SCOTT, Stuart. – *Battle-Axe Blenheims.* (Sutton Publishing 1996)
SHORES, CULL & IZAWA. – *Bloody Shambles* (Grubb Street1992)
SHORES, Christopher, – *Aces High Volume 1 & 2* (Grub Street; 1994)
SHORES, Christopher & THOMAS Chris. – 2nd *Tactical Air Force Vol 1–4* (Air War Classics Ian Allan 2004)
SMALLWOOD, Hugh. – *Spitfire in the Blue.* (Osprey Books. 1996)
SMITH, Frederick. – *633 Squadron.* (Corgi 1956)
SOUTAR. Neil. – *Round Half the World in Eighty Months* (Express Litho Service 1989)
THOMAS, Chris. – *Typhoon Wings of 2nd TAF* (Osprey 2010)
TOWNSEND. Peter. – *Time and Chance* (Collins 1978)
TOWNSEND. Peter. – *Duel of Eagles* (Weidenfeld and Nicolson 1970)
TUGWELL, Maurice. – *Airborne To Battle – A History Of Airborne Warfare 1918–1971* (William Kimber & Co Ltd.)
STENMAN, Kari. – *Fokker D.XXI Aces of World War 2* (Osprey 2013)
VERITY, Hugh. – *We Landed by Moonlight* (Ian Allan 1978)
VIGOR, Tim. - *Life's Too Short to Cry,* (Grubb Street. 2006)
WALBANK. FA editor. -*Wings of War.* (Batsford 1943)
WARREN & BENSON. – *The Admiralty regrets...* (George Harrap1948)
WEAL, John. – *Focke-Wulf Fw190 Aces of the Western Front* (Osprey 1996)
WELLUM, Geoffrey. – *First Light.* (Viking 2002)
WHITTLE, Ken. – *An Electrician Goes to War.* (Air Force Publishing Service 1994)
WHITMARSH, Andrew. -*Portsmouth at War.* (The History Press 2008)
WHITING, Charles. – *Bounce the Rhine* (Spellmount Ltd 2002)
WOODS, J.E.R. – *Detour. The Story of Oflag IVC* (Falcon Press 1946)

Index